Slash Pine:
Still Growing and Growing!

Proceedings of the Slash Pine Symposium

Jekyll Island, Georgia
April 23–25, 2002

Edited by

E.D. Dickens, J.P. Barnett, W.G. Hubbard, and E.J. Jokela

Hosted by

Florida and Georgia Divisions of the Southeastern Society of American Foresters
The University of Georgia, Warnell School of Forest Resources
University of Florida, School of Forest Resources and Conservation
U.S. Department of Agriculture Forest Service, Southern Regional Extension Forestry

Sponsored by

Florida and Georgia Divisions of the Southeastern Society of American Foresters
The University of Georgia, Warnell School of Forest Resources
University of Florida, School of Forest Resources and Conservation
The Florida Division of Forestry
The Georgia Forestry Commission
The Georgia Center of Continuing Education
U.S. Department of Agriculture Forest Service, Southern Regional Extension Forestry
U.S. Department of Agriculture Forest Service, State and Private Forestry, Southern Region

Preface

This general technical report on slash pine is printed 20 years after an earlier proceedings, "The Managed Slash Pine Ecosystem" was published. It was evident in 1983 that loblolly pine was becoming the species of choice where either species could be planted, especially in areas where fiber-volume production was a high priority. Since 1997–98, forest industry activities, pine pulpwood stumpage prices, timberland ownership patterns, and the economics of growing southern pines have dramatically changed in the Southeastern United States. Many scientists and land managers are rethinking species/site selection, cash outlays, and forest management intensities. The authors of this proceedings decided to share their new knowledge of slash pine.

Slash pine continues to be an important species of southern yellow pine on the southeastern Coastal Plain. While its native range is more limited than any other southern yellow pine, its value as raw material for wood products ranks third behind loblolly and shortleaf pine. Although slash pine may not produce as much wood volume or fiber on many of the sites where both loblolly and slash pine are found, it can produce more high-value, high-grade lumber than loblolly pine. Some of the papers in this proceedings either compare or include loblolly pine as a research subject, because these two species often are the only choice of pine species in the southeastern Coastal Plain.

The authors' intent is to give land managers an up-to-date guidebook on slash pine management. Although we have learned much in the last 20 years, there is still much we have to learn. The 1983 managed slash pine ecosystem proceedings has some very valuable information that remains current to this day. The reader should use his/her best judgment where conflicting opinions are presented; pine study findings may contradict one another due to several abiotic, biotic, management, and other factors.

The efforts of many people made the slash pine symposium possible. The following is a list of those who contributed to planning; conference program organization; making local arrangements; lining up sponsors and exhibits committees; and inviting symposium speakers, moderators, and reviewers.

Planning Committee: Jill Barbour, John Bridges, Chris Carey, Steve Chapman, David Dickens, Mark Frye, George Hernandez, John Holzaepfel, Bill Hubbard, Eric Jokela, Susan King, Charlie Marcus, Mike Mengak, Jarek Nowak, and Larry Thompson

Conference Chair: Bill Hubbard

Program Co-Chairs: David Dickens and Eric Jokela

Sponsors and Exhibits Committee: John Bridges, Steve Chapman, and David Dickens

Local Arrangements Committee: Chris Carey, Mark Frye, and Susan King

Contents

SLASH PINE: CHARACTERISTICS, HISTORY, STATUS, AND TRENDS

James P. Barnett and Raymond M. Sheffield[1]

Abstract—Slash pine is the premier tree species on many sites throughout the South. Its ease of establishment and early growth, however, has extended its range to many sites where its performance has been less than ideal. For that reason, the acreage and volume of slash pine are declining. Nonetheless, it will continue to be the favored species on many sites where it is the most appropriate and productive species. This paper reviews slash pine's important silvical characteristics, its history of use and management, and the status and trends of this important resource.

INTRODUCTION

Typical slash pine (*Pinus elliottii* Engelm. var. *elliottii*) is an excellent timber tree and one of the most important pine species in the Southern United States. Many prefer it for its fast growth and excellent utility for fiber, lumber, poles, and gum naval stores. The habitat and preferred sites within its natural range include poorly drained flatwoods and stream edges, as well as seasonally flooded areas such as bays and swamps.

The ease and success of planting slash pine have significantly increased in its range. Extensive planting and natural regeneration of open agricultural and forest land brought a sharp rise in slash pine acreage between 1952 and 1970 (Sheffield and others 1983). Much of the planting was on sites that did not favor slash pine, and where performance was less than optimal. As a result, land managers have planted either loblolly (*P. taeda* L.) or longleaf (*P. palustris* Mill.) after harvesting the slash pine. However, slash pine is an excellent species and should be favored on appropriate sites.

This paper reviews the important silvical characteristics of slash pine; provides a history of its development, use, and management; reviews its status in southern forest ecosystems; and explores trends in managed slash pine forests.

SILVICAL CHARACTERISTICS

Identifying Characteristics

The typical slash pine tree has a long, clear bole and a relatively short crown, which results from self-pruning. South Florida slash pine (*P. elliottii* var. *densa*) (Little and Dorman 1954) differs from the more northern variety in a number of ways, primarily because its seedlings go through a dwarf "grass stage" similar to longleaf pine. Its stem divides into large, spreading branches that form a flat-topped or rounded crown. Its uniqueness and limited range have encouraged neither research nor management of south Florida slash pine.

The needles and cones of the typical slash pine represent its primary identifying characteristics. Needles are 7 to 10 inches long in fascicles of two and three on the same tree. They are dark, glossy green, and tufted at the ends of tapering branches. They extend back some distance along the branch and persist until the end of the second season. Cones are 4 to 6 inches long, ovoid conic, and sessile (fig. 1). They usually remain on the tree until the second summer. Cones are reddish brown, lustrous, and armed with a sharp spine. The seeds are about one-fourth inch long, dark brown-black mottled, with thin, translucent wings about 1 inch long.

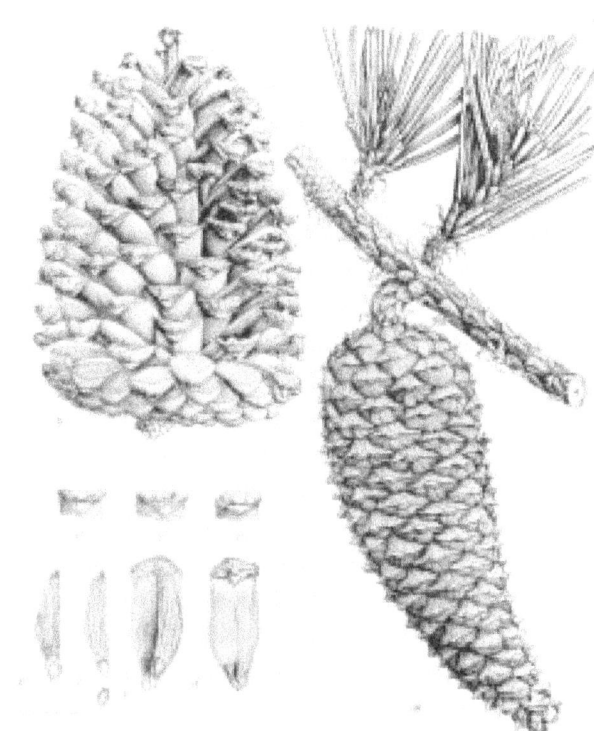

Figure 1—(A) mature, 2-year, closed cone (3 to 6 inches long); (B) mature cone open after shedding seed; (C) tips of cone scale showing variation in form of apophysis and stout prickle; (D) ventral side of cone scale with seed in place (left), and dorsal side (right); (E) and (F) seed and wing detached; (G) seed and wing intact (Mohr 1896).

[1] James P. Barnett, Chief Silviculturist; and Raymond M. Sheffield, Resource Analyst, U.S. Department of Agriculture Forest Service, Southern Research Station, Pineville, LA 71360 and Asheville, NC 28804, respectively.

Citation for proceedings: Dickens, E.D.; Barnett, J.P.; Hubbard, W.G.; Jokela, E.J., eds. 2004. Slash pine: still growing and growing! Proceedings of the slash pine symposium. Gen. Tech. Rep. SRS-76. Asheville, NC: U.S. Department of Agriculture, Forest Service, Southern Research Station. 148 p.

Phenology

Seeds mature in a 3-year period from when the strobili are initiated. The primordia of new strobili are detectable in late spring. These cone initials overwinter as buds the first year. When pollen is shed in late January or February of the second year, the male strobili are purple and 2 inches long. The female strobili appear on stalks in the upper crown and are about 1 inch long and red to purple at the time of pollination. Soon after pollination, the pollen tube stops growing and appears to remain in a quiescent state for the summer and winter. During the third growing season fertilization occurs—some 12 to 14 months after pollination. Cones enlarge and seeds mature during the third summer. Needles develop on new growth in spring and persist until the end of the second growing season.

Distribution

The natural range of slash pine is the most restricted of all major southern pines, extending from southern South Carolina to central Florida and westward to southeastern Louisiana (fig. 2). Although its natural range is relatively small, slash pine has been planted widely and its range extended into eastern Texas, southern North Carolina, and the sandhills between the Coastal Plain and the Piedmont through much of the Southeast (Fisher 1983).

Slash pine has been introduced into many countries for timber production. Large-scale introductions have occurred in Brazil, Chile, Argentina, Venezuela, China, South Africa, New Zealand, and Australia. In most of these countries, it is an adequate seed producer, and natural or artificial regeneration continues.

SOILS AND PHYSIOGRAPHY

Soils within the range of slash pine are mostly Spodosols, Ultisols, and Entisols. It is generally believed that prior to extensive fire suppression and planting programs, slash pine was restricted to ponds, pond margins, and Coastal Plain flatwoods where ample moisture provided some degree of protection for young trees that are often killed by fire (Gruschow 1952). Topography varies little throughout the southeastern Coastal Plain, but small changes in elevation often coincide with abrupt changes in soil and site conditions.

Although slash pine adapts to a wide variety of conditions, it grows best on deep, well-aerated soils that supply ample moisture during the growing season. Generally, growth and site index increase with depth to a restrictive layer or seasonally high water table, if these features occur within 20 to 30 inches of the soil surface. Where depth to a restrictive layer exceeds about 30 inches, site index declines with increasing depth to a reliable source of moisture, such as a stable water table or a soil horizon with large moisture-holding storage capacity. Soil properties useful in estimating site index of slash pine include depth to gray mottles, depth to a spodic horizon, depth to the least-permeable layer or to a fine-textured horizon, thickness of the A1 horizon, and texture of the least-permeable or finest textured horizon (Lohrey and Kossuth 1990, Shoulders and Parham 1983).

SILVICULTURAL CHARACTERISTICS

Slash pine is a subclimax species that without human intervention and in the absence of fire or other catastrophic event will proceed to a mixed hardwood forest. Some authors consider it intermediate in tolerance to shade, others consider it intolerant. It will reproduce naturally in small openings and invade poorly stocked longleaf pine stands, although competition from overstory and understory vegetation reduces growth and causes much mortality. The two varieties of slash pine differ in their patterns of growth. Typical slash pine makes excellent early height growth, but south Florida slash pine has a grasslike, almost stemless stage that lasts from 2 to 6 years. Moreover, south Florida slash pine lacks the straight axis or stem characteristic of the typical variety and often develops forked boles with large branches and an open, spreading, irregularly shaped crown (Little and Dorman 1954).

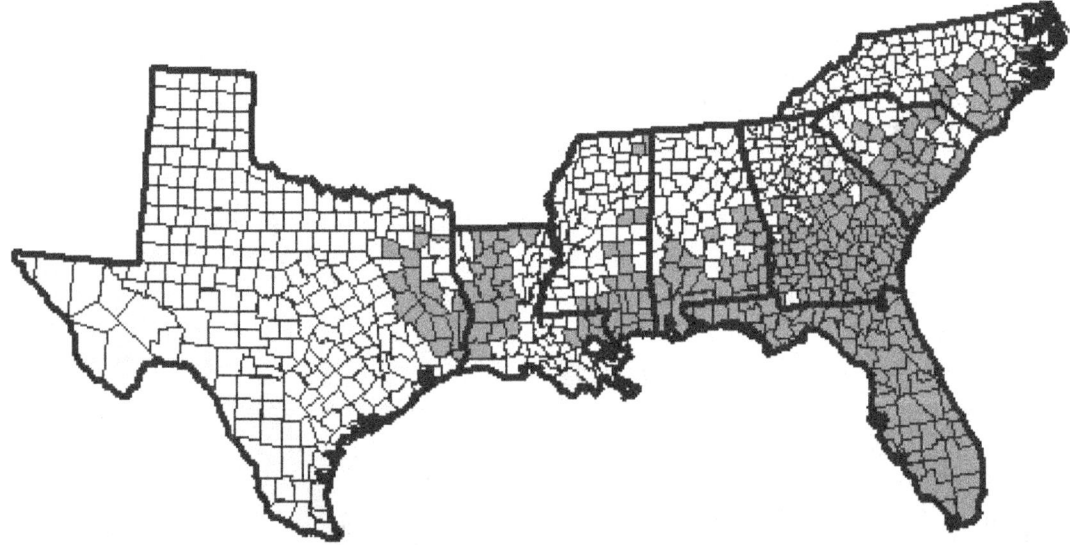

Figure 2—The current distribution of slash pine.

Typical slash pine is slow to express dominance in dense, even-aged stands. As a result, height growth is slower in very dense stands than in moderately or lightly stocked stands. Young stands respond promptly to thinning or release.

HISTORY
The development of steam-powered sawmills along the tidewater during the 1830s changed the entire complexion of timber use. Because the new mills required considerable timber to maintain continuous operations, they were built at river estuaries or along the banks of bayous. Slash pine stands were the most accessible and the first to be cut (Schultz 1983). However, it was not until post-Civil War times that more effective timber harvesting, transporting, and milling technologies were developed. It was about 1880 before more pines were cut for lumber than were being destroyed for the sake of clearing land (Vance 1935).

Naval Stores
In colonial times, the great wooden ships of domestic and international commerce needed large quantities of pitch and tar to seal cracks—and to protect operating lines from the deteriorating effects of moisture (Schultz 1983). By 1610, England was importing tree resin from the Colonies, and by 1700 South Carolina had made so-called naval stores its chief export (Schorger and Betts 1915). Production of this commodity from the South's piney woods became the State's first full-scale industry.

The primary method for producing naval stores was to tap standing slash and longleaf pine. For many years the "box" method was used (Fernow 1899), whereby deep holes were cut with a boxing ax in the tree's base and a container, or box, was attached to catch resin, "chipping" was wounding the tree surface or face with a hack tool—through the bark into the phloem. The tree's surface was chipped weekly to maintain resin flow, and boxes were emptied every 2 or 3 weeks to prevent resin loss. Because it produced more yield than longleaf, slash pine was preferred (Forbes 1930, Mattoon 1922).

Cutting deep cavities into trees for collecting gum caused significant damage to the trees. Cutting two or more boxes in larger trees nearly girdled them, causing mortality in a year or so. Through the untiring efforts of Dr. Charles Herty, the "boxing" method was largely replaced by the cup-and-gutter method around 1910. The new method yielded more and higher quality resin, killed fewer trees, and left the butt log in better condition for lumber (Croker 1979).

When U.S. Department of Agriculture Forest Service research stations were established in the South in 1921, the Southern Forest Experiment Station assigned Len Wyman to Stark, FL, to improve chipping technology for the naval stores industry. His work to reduce the size of the chipping face resulted in substantial labor savings, reduced tree mortality, and increased the length of time a tree could be worked. During World War II, research on naval stores production was emphasized, and it was determined that gum production could be stimulated by spraying the chipped area with sulfuric acid (McReynolds 1983).

Naval stores research continued into the 1980s with the development of paraquat-induced lightwood (Stubbs 1983). However, production of naval stores products dropped significantly as tree availability decreased, costs of labor-intensive work increased, and byproducts of the kraft pulping process met most of the need for turpentine and other products (McReynolds 1983).

The Influence of Railroad Logging
The first generation of logging in pine flatwoods was confined to coastal areas and the immediate vicinity of rivers and navigable streams. Therefore, much of the slash pine forest was selectively cut at least once by the late 1880s (Schutlz 1983). By the middle 1880s, high timber demands and expanding mill facilities required loggers to exploit new areas. Railroad logging was an answer to the problem of accessing forests away from rivers and streams. Wherever large pines grew, rail spurs were put in to systematically remove pine timber. Low-speed locomotives were used to pull cars loaded with timber over the temporary spurs. Steam skidders were mounted on flatcars, and wire cables could pull logs to the railcars from about 1,000 feet.

Logging and milling reached their peak in the coastal flatwoods between 1890 and 1914 (Schultz 1983). Once the logging boom arrived, it took a little more than two decades to clearcut and decimate the pure pine forests of the flatwoods. Most slash and mixed slash-longleaf pine forests were cutover in the early logging and rafting days between 1780 and 1860. Fifty to one hundred years later, these areas had again grown into pure stands of slash pine and also were logged over, as were virgin longleaf stands. The complete removal of old-growth pines provided conditions for slash pine to further dominate many sites formerly occupied by longleaf pine. Large areas of the cutover longleaf pine type in Alabama, Mississippi, Louisiana, and Texas were planted to slash pine, thus increasing the range and prominence of the species (Schultz 1983). Slash pine also was planted outside its range in Georgia, South Carolina, and North Carolina in cutover longleaf sites.

STATUS
The natural range of slash pine is more restricted than the range of other major southern pines (Critchfield and Little 1966), but extensive plantings of slash pine have greatly extended its range (fig. 2). We have not distinguished typical slash pine from the south Florida variety in these data, because the latter has very limited occurrence.

While the range of slash pine is small, the species is intensely managed. Sixty-nine percent of current slash pine stands are planted compared to 52 percent in 1980. The proportion of plantations to natural stands continues to rise with each new inventory.

Slash pine is the primary species on 10.4 million acres (table 1). The slash pine ecosystem is defined as stands where yellow pine makes up one-half or more of the stocking, and where slash is the predominant pine.

The most concentrated areas of slash pine are in Florida and Georgia. These two States contain about 79 percent of the slash pine ecosystem acreage.

Table 1—Area of timberland classed as a slash pine forest type, by State, 1980 and 2000

State	1980	2000
	- - - - - thousand acres - - - -	
Alabama	716	497
Florida	5,298	5,131
Georgia	4,683	3,026
Louisiana	609	631
Mississippi	671	610
North Carolina	91	156
South Carolina	499	136
Texas	212	188
Total	12,779	10,375

Nonindustrial private landowners hold 53 percent of slash pine stands, the largest proportion of ownership (table 2). Forest industries own 36 percent, while national forests and other public agencies control the remaining 11 percent.

The volume of slash pine growing-stock sized trees across the range totals 10.9 billon cubic feet (table 3). This inventory includes all slash pine growing stock, whether in stands classified as a slash pine type or in some other type. Growing-stock volume includes the solid wood content between a 1-foot stump and 4.0-inch top on only the central stem in

Table 2—Area of timberland classed as a slash pine forest type, by ownership class, 1980 and 2000

Ownership class	1980	2000
	- - - - - thousand acres - - - -	
National forest	522	493
Other public	569	684
Forest industry	4,649	3,719
Nonindustrial private	7,039	5,479
Total	12,779	10,375

Table 3—Volume of slash pine growing stock on timberland, by State, 1980 and 2000

State	1980	2000
	- - - - million cubic feet - - - -	
Alabama	747	868
Florida	3,772	4,305
Georgia	4,644	3,525
Louisiana	748	790
Mississippi	664	771
North Carolina	33	183
South Carolina	592	215
Texas	256	235
Total	11,457	10,891

trees 5.0 inches diameter at breast height (d.b.h.) and larger. The stated volumes exclude rough and rotten stems, stumps, tops, limbs, and trees < 5.0 inches d.b.h.

Seventy-two percent of the South's slash pine volume (7,830 million cubic feet) is located in Florida and Georgia. Alabama, Louisiana, and Mississippi account for 22 percent (2,429 million cubic feet) (table 3).

The diameter distribution of slash pine volume reflects the high proportion of slash pine in plantations and young natural stands (fig. 3). Volume peaks in the 8-inch diameter class and declines rapidly through the larger diameters. Fifty-nine percent of the slash pine volume is in the 6-, 8-, and 10-inch diameter classes.

The stand-age distribution shows that about 25 percent of slash pine stands are < 8 years old (fig. 4). This confirms the notion that the slash pine rotation age is 30 years or

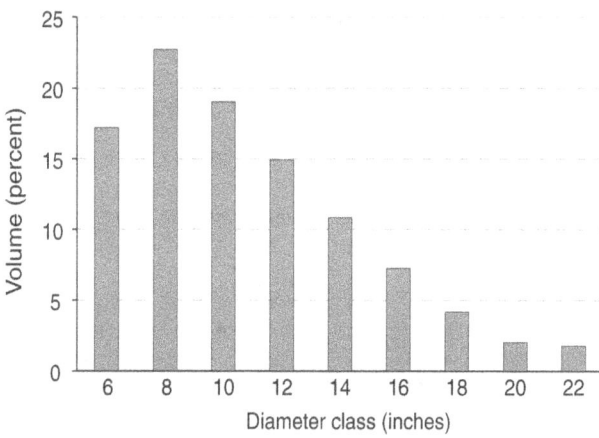

Figure 3—Slash pine growing stock by diameter class, 2000.

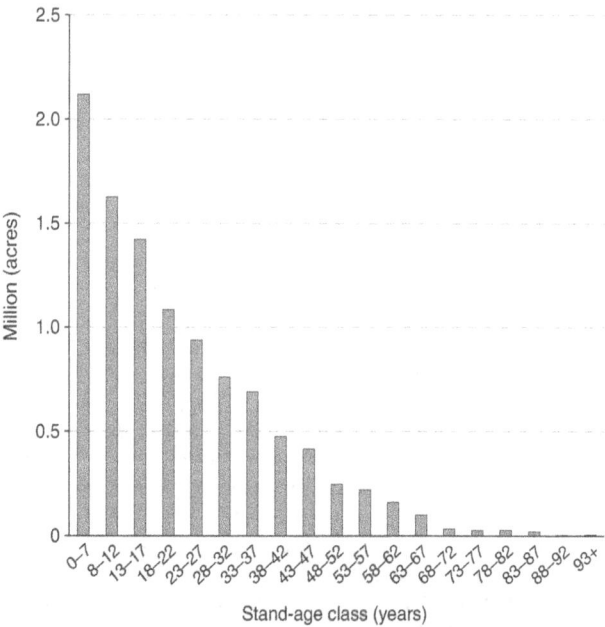

Figure 4—Stand-age distribution of slash pine, 2000.

younger, and that slash pine is intensively managed. Small-diameter trees make up a large proportion of the slash pine resource, primarily because forest industry has managed it for short rotations.

The current (2000) net annual growth of slash pine growing stock totals 871 million cubic feet (table 4). This is equivalent to a growth rate (growth as a percent of inventory) of 8.0 percent. Annual removals of slash pine growing stock total 927 million cubic feet, or 56 million cubic feet (about 6 percent) over annual growth. The most significant amount of removals over growth occurs in Florida, where it exceeded growth by 55 million cubic feet, or nearly 18 percent. Removal volumes include all slash pine trees removed from commercial forest land by human activities, regardless of whether the trees actually are used.

TRENDS
Sheffield and others (1983) published 1980 resource data in the proceedings of the 1981 managed slash pine ecosystem symposium (Stone 1983). These data, paired with year 2000 data in tables 1 through 4, provide a comparison of resource issues related to the slash pine ecosystem.

The fact that 69 percent of slash pine stands are planted indicates that the slash pine ecosystem is intensively managed. Most of the ecosystem is located in Georgia and Florida, and largely within areas adjoining the two States. However, over the last 20 years the area of timberland classified as slash pine has decreased from 12.8 to 10.4 million acres, or nearly 19 percent (table 1).

The loss of acreage in slash pine has occurred over most of its range. Data from the two States that show increases—Louisiana and North Carolina—may not represent current conditions, because forest survey data in those States have not been completely updated. Within Florida the acreage remains stable, whereas in Georgia there has been a 35-percent decrease over the last two decades.

Long-term trends indicate that slash pine acreage increased significantly during the 1950s and 1960s, with increases from about 8.4 to 10.4 million acres (Sheffield and others 1983). Those increases were related to the conversion of farmland to forests, reforestation of cutover forests, and planting out of the native range of slash pine. The trend leveled off in the 1970s and 1980s. Obviously, the trend now is one of decreasing acreage. This loss is at least partially a result of longleaf pine restoration efforts on many sites where slash pine had been planted, the loss of slash pine sites to urbanization, and the planting of loblolly pine on forest industry lands where slash was previously planted.

The greatest losses (about 20 percent) in slash pine timberland occurred on private ownership—both forest industry and nonindustrial private lands (table 2). Slash pine within the national forests decreased 5 percent, probably as a result of conversion to longleaf pine on forests outside the natural slash pine range. The only ownership showing an increase in slash pine timberland is the "other public" category.

Table 4—Net annual growth and removals of slash pine growing stock by State, 1980 and 2000

State	Net annual growth		Annual removals	
	1980	2000	1980	2000
	- - - - - - - - million cubic feet - - - - - - - -			
Alabama	48	60	35	55
Florida	383	309	262	364
Georgia	405	338	265	316
Louisiana	83	66	41	53
Mississippi	44	45	37	54
North Carolina	9	9	0	18
South Carolina	66	20	23	45
Texas	30	25	12	23
Total	1,068	871	675	927

The volume of slash pine growing stock in the entire ecosystem declined from 11.5 billion cubic feet in 1980 to 10.9 billion cubic feet in 2000 (table 3). It is particularly interesting to note the differing trends in Florida and Georgia. Although Florida's proportion of the growing stock increased 12 percent, from 3.8 to 4.3 billion cubic feet, there was a major decrease in Georgia. A 24-percent reduction in growing stock occurred in Georgia, with losses of 1.1 billion cubic feet. Texas and South Carolina were the only other States with losses of growing stock.

The year 2000 distribution of slash pine growing stock by diameter classes follows a pattern similar to that of 1980 (Sheffield and others 1983), although 59 percent of the current volume is in the 6-, 8-, and 10-inch classes compared to 64 percent in 1980 (fig. 3). In 2000, there was a smaller proportion in the 6-inch and a corresponding increase in the 14- through 22-inch diameter classes than there was in 1980. Stand-age data confirm the notion that older stands continue to be aggressively harvested, and that the average rotation age is 35 years or less (fig. 4). A relatively small proportion of stands are older than 40 years.

In contrast to the situation in 1980 when net annual growth exceeded annual removals, in year 2000 removals exceeded growth by about 6 percent (table 4). In Florida, removals far exceeded growth, although the acreage in slash pine remained relatively constant. This may be because where slash pine is intensively managed, there are large numbers of recently harvested stands that have been regenerated, but where trees have not reached a size that constitutes significant volume.

CONCLUSIONS
Slash pine is one of the most important pine species in the Southern United States, and its ecosystem produces a habitat that favors a wide range of biological diversity. It produces fast growing stands that are excellent for fiber, lumber, poles, and gum naval stores. It is adapted to short-rotation forestry, where ease of regeneration and fast early growth are important. Because of its favorable growth characteristics, the slash pine range has been widely extended.

Slash pine has performed less than ideally on many sites, particularly when rotation is longer than 35 years. However, on good sites within its natural range, it is the premier species.

Although it has been planted across the South from eastern Texas to eastern North Carolina, most slash pine volume occurs in southern Georgia and northern Florida. Even in Georgia, the volume of slash pine growing stock has declined. Many sites in the Southeast that are more adapted to longleaf pine were converted to slash pine decades ago because of the ease of regeneration and fast early growth. Recent interest in and financial support for converting such sites to longleaf pine have resulted in the reduction of slash pine acreage and volume.

Although the acreage and volume of growing stock have declined in recent years, slash pine remains the best-adapted and productive species for many sites within its range. On appropriate sites, slash pine is an excellent species that is well adapted for and should be favored in management.

LITERATURE CITED

Critchfield, W.B.; Little, E.L., Jr. 1966. Geographic distribution of the pines of the world. Misc. Publ. 991. Washington, DC: U.S. Department of Agriculture, Forest Service. 97 p.

Croker, T.C., Jr. 1979. The longleaf pine story. Journal of Forest History. 23: 32-43.

Fernow, B.E. 1899. Report upon the forestry investigations of the USDA, 1877–1898. Washington, DC: U.S. Department of Agriculture. 401 p.

Fisher, Richard F. 1983. Silvical characteristics of slash pine (*Pinus elliottii* Englem. var. *elliottii*). In: Stone, E.L., ed. The managed slash pine ecosystem: Proceedings of a symposium. Gainesville, FL: University of Florida, School of Forest Resources and Conservation: 48-55.

Forbes, R.D. 1930. Timber growing and logging and turpentining practices in the southern pine region. Tech. Bull. 204. Washington, DC: U.S. Department of Agriculture. 115 p.

Gruschow, G.F. 1952. Effect of winter burning on growth of slash pine in the flatwoods. Journal of Forestry. 50: 515-517.

Little, E.L., Jr.; Dorman, K.W. 1954. Slash pine (*Pinus elliottii*), including south Florida slash pine: nomenclature and description. Station Pap. 36. Asheville, NC: U.S. Department of Agriculture, Forest Service, Southeastern Forest Experiment Station. 82 p.

Lohrey, R.E.; Kossuth, S.V. 1990. *Pinus elliottii* Englem. Slash pine. In: Silvics of North America: conifers. Agric. Handb. 654. Washington, DC: U.S. Department of Agriculture: 338-347. Vol. 1.

Mattoon, W.R. 1922. Slash pine primer. USDA Farmer's Bull. 1256. Washington, DC: U.S. Department of Agriculture. 8 p.

McReynolds, Robert D. 1983. Gum naval stores production from slash pine. In: Stone, E.L., ed. The managed slash pine ecosystem: Proceedings of a symposium. Gainesville, FL: University of Florida, School of Forest Resources and Conservation: 375-384.

Mohr, C. 1896. The timber pines of the Southern United States. Bull. 13. Washington, DC: U.S. Department of Agriculture, Division of Forestry. 160 p.

Schorger, A.W.; Betts, H.S. 1915. The naval stores industry. Tech. Bull. 229. Washington, DC: U.S. Department of Agriculture. 58 p.

Schultz, Robert P. 1983. The original slash pine forest—an historical view. In: Stone, E.L., ed. The managed slash pine ecosystem: Proceedings of a symposium. Gainesville, FL: University of Florida, School of Forest Resources and Conservation: 24-47.

Sheffield, R.M.; Knight, H.A.; McClure, J.P. 1983. The slash pine resource. In: Stone, E.L., ed. The managed slash pine ecosystem: Proceedings of a symposium. Gainesville, FL: University of Florida, School of Forest Resources and Conservation: 4-23.

Shoulders, E.; Parham, G. 1983. Slash pine. In: Burns, R.M., tech. coord. Silvicultural systems for the major forest types in the United States. Agric. Handb. 445. Washington, DC: U.S. Department of Agriculture: 161-166.

Stone, E.L., ed. 1983. The managed slash pine ecosystem: proceedings of a symposium. Gainesville, FL: University of Florida, School of Forest Resources and Conservation. 434 p.

Stubbs, Jack. 1983. Paraquat-induced lightwood in southern pines. In: Stone, E.L., ed. The managed slash pine ecosystem: Proceedings of a symposium. Gainesville, FL: University of Florida, School of Forest Resources and Conservation: 385-393.

Vance, R.B. 1935. Human geography of the South. Chapel Hill, NC: University of North Carolina Press. 596 p.

SLASH PINE TREE IMPROVEMENT

Tim L. White and Tom D. Byram[1]

Abstract—Slash pine breeding programs in the southern USA began more than a half century ago and are conducted in two tree improvement cooperatives: Cooperative Forest Genetics Research Program, CFGRP, housed at the University of Florida in Gainesville, and Western Gulf Forest Tree Improvement Program, WGFTIP, centered at the Texas Forest Service, Texas A&M University, in College Station. These tree improvement cooperatives consist of private companies, state agencies and university personnel all working together to conduct selection, breeding, progeny testing and research to genetically improve slash pine. The CFGRP consists of 10 members improving slash pine in its native range. Six of the 14 members of the WGFTIP participate in the tree improvement program of slash pine as an exotic for the lower coastal plain areas of TX, LA and MS. Members of both cooperatives are: (1) In the second generation of breeding and testing; (2) Focusing on improvement of a few key traits, the most important of which are volume yield and resistance to fusiform rust; (3) Maintaining large breeding populations, consisting of several hundred selections, to sustain genetic diversity of the species; (4) Establishing operational plantations with expected genetic gains in total yield of more than 30 percent above plantations established with unimproved material; and (5) Making genetically-improved slash pine available to non-members and small private landowners through seed and seedling sales. Nearly 100 percent of all new plantations of slash pine are being planted with genetically-improved material, although the degree of improvement varies.

INTRODUCTION

Large-scale tree breeding programs (also called tree improvement programs) began in the 1950s. Zobel and Talbert (1984) cite 23 papers from 14 countries published in the 1950s that advocate or describe tree improvement programs. Today, there are breeding programs for nearly all commercially-important tree species and multiple programs sponsored by different organizations for some species in different regions or countries. Breeding of slash pine (*Pinus elliottii* Engelm.) also started in the 1950s.

Early on, slash pine was recognized as being second in importance to only loblolly pine as a target for tree improvement in the southern USA. This was despite the fact that it has the most restricted range of the four major species of southern pines (Dorman 1976). Slash pine is adapted to a variety of difficult sites in the southern most part of the commercial pine range and has been planted extensively. It is generally acknowledged to be more resistant to fire and tip moth than loblolly pine, and to be as well suited for naval stores production, as is longleaf pine. Its good stem form and wood quality traits make it extremely valuable for solid wood products as well as also being an excellent feedstock for pulp production.

Slash pine tree improvement in the southern USA is mainly conducted by the members of two regional cooperatives in which private industry, state agencies and university personnel all work together cooperatively. The purposes of this report are to: (1) Describe the nature and infrastructure of these two tree improvement cooperatives; (2) Summarize the first-generation tree improvement programs of both cooperatives, which have been completed; (3) Highlight key features of their on-going second-generation programs; and (4) Document the genetic gains and genetic diversity in the operational plantations currently being established by members of these two cooperatives.

TREE IMPROVEMENT COOPERATIVES OF SLASH PINE

Organization and Activities of Slash Pine Cooperatives

Slash pine breeding programs in the southern USA are conducted cooperatively through two regional tree improvement cooperatives: Cooperative Forest Genetics Research Program (CFGRP) housed at the University of Florida in Gainesville, FL and Western Gulf Forest Tree Improvement Program (WGFTIP) centered at the Texas Forest Service, Texas A&M University, in College Station, TX. These tree improvement cooperatives consist of private companies, state agencies and university personnel all working together to conduct selection, breeding, progeny testing and research to genetically improve slash pine. The CFGRP was initiated in the 1950s and has been conducting slash pine tree improvement continuously ever since. Tree improvement started at Texas A&M University in the early 1950s as a cooperative program between the Texas Forest Service and several organizations in East Texas. Soon after, there were several other independent programs operating in the area. WGFTIP was formally founded in 1969 when several of these former programs agreed to join forces and new members were added to the effort.

The CFGRP and WGFTIP have similar organizational structures and these structures have changed little since

---

[1] Tim L. White, Professor of Forest Genetics, School of Forest Resources and Conservation, University of Florida, Gainesville, FL 32611-0410; and Tom D. Byram, WGFTIP Geneticist, Texas Forest Service, and Assistant Professor, Forest Science Department, Texas A&M University, College Station, TX 77803-2585.

Citation for proceedings: Dickens, E.D.; Barnett, J.P.; Hubbard, W.G.; Jokela, E.J., eds. 2004. Slash pine: still growing and growing! Proceedings of the slash pine symposium. Gen. Tech. Rep. SRS-76. Asheville, NC: U.S. Department of Agriculture, Forest Service, Southern Research Station. 148 p.

the inception of the cooperatives. Each cooperative has a small staff (3 to 4 people centered at the University of Florida for the CFGRP and at the Texas Forest Service in College Station for the WGFTIP) which performs the following functions: (1) Provides scientific leadership in developing and implementing breeding strategies; (2) Conducts research and development in both basic forest genetics and applied tree improvement; (3) Provides technical support to cooperative members; and (4) Carries out data management and data analysis of all cooperative experiments and genetic tests. The latter function is especially important because both cooperatives have hundreds of field experiments with data collected every few years. With personnel changes and corporate mergers, a key function of the cooperative staff is to provide institutional memory about when, where and how to measure cooperative field tests.

The private companies and state agencies that are the members of the tree improvement cooperatives are active participants in every phase of cooperative activity. The members: (1) Set policy and direction of the cooperative through participation in advisory councils and executive committees that meet as often as needed, but at least annually; (2) Provide financial support to the cooperative in the form of annual dues and in-kind contributions; and, most importantly, (3) Conduct all field activities of the tree improvement programs using their personnel and their equipment on their timberlands (for example, selection, field testing and breeding). It is an understatement to say that the southern USA owes much to the foresight of the founding and continuing members of tree improvement cooperatives. The private companies compete in most every other aspect of their business, but decided long ago to cooperate in the long-term efforts to genetically improve southern pines for the betterment of the entire region.

Magnitude and Impact of Slash Pine Tree Improvement Efforts

The CFGRP consists of 10 members improving slash pine in its native range, principally in the lower coastal plain regions of GA, FL and AL. These members own or lease 2.7 million acres of slash pine plantations. They produce 50 million genetically-improved slash seedlings each year that are used to reforest 110,000 acres of their own timberlands. In addition to the seedlings produced for reforestation of their own timberlands, CFGRP members sell 70 million genetically-improved slash pine seedlings and 4,000 pounds of genetically improved seed each year to non-members.

Six of the 14 members of the WGFTIP (3 private companies and 3 state agencies) participate in the tree improvement program of slash pine as an exotic for the lower coastal plain areas of TX, LA and MS. These six WGFTIP members own or lease 0.7 million acres of slash pine plantations. They produce 6.5 million genetically-improved slash seedlings each year that are used to reforest 10,000 acres of their own timberlands. In addition to the seedlings produced for reforestation of their own timberlands, WGFTIP members sell 13.5 million genetically-improved slash pine seedlings and 1,500 pounds of genetically improved seed each year to non-members.

For members of both cooperatives, the relative importance of slash pine has diminished through the years as loblolly pine (*Pinus taeda* L.) has become more important, and both cooperatives also have tree improvement efforts for loblolly pine. Therefore, it is useful to estimate the total size of the plantation estate of slash pine being supported by the breeding efforts of the two cooperatives. One way to measure this is simply the sum of the slash pine plantations currently owned or leased by the members (2.7 and 0.7 million acres by the CFGRP and WGFTIP members, respectively). However, these figures suffer in two ways: (1) Current ownership reflects historical patterns of plantation establishment, not current or future trends (for example, members could be converting these plantations to loblolly pine as they reach harvest age); and (2) These ownership figures do not include slash pine plantations managed by non-members who purchase genetically-improved seed or seedlings from cooperative members. For example, small, non-industrial landowners who purchase genetically-improved seedlings directly benefit from the efforts of the two cooperatives.

Another way to estimate the current size of the slash pine plantation estate being supported by the breeding efforts of the cooperatives is to assume that annual reforestation rates and seed and seedling sales have reached equilibrium values that are not changing through the years. Then, if all of the seed and seedlings are being planted in the southern USA (we ignore the small fraction of seed being sold internationally), we can calculate the "regulated" plantation estate assuming a 20-yr rotation. For example, for the CFGRP, there are 50 million seedlings planted annually on member timberlands and 70 million seedlings sold to non-members. In addition, the 4,000 pounds of seed sold to non-members equates to another 32 million plantable seedlings (assuming 8,000 plantable seedlings per pound of seed). Therefore, total annual reforestation of genetically-improved seedlings of slash pine supported by CFGRP members is 152 million seedlings (50+70+32) which means approximately 215,000 acres of annually reforestation (assuming 700 trees planted per acre). Assuming a regulated forest with a 20-yr rotation, the total plantation estate of slash pine being supported by the CFGRP tree improvement cooperative is 4.3 million acres (215,000 * 20). Similarly for the WGFTIP, internal seedling use, seedling sales and seed sales sum to 32 million seedlings annually which supports a regulated plantation estate of slash pine of approximately 1 million acres.

To put these numbers in perspective, there were a total of 1.7 billion forest tree seedlings planted in the entire USA in 1999 and 1.2 billion of these were loblolly pine in the southern USA (http://www.afandpa.org/forestry/forestry.html). Slash pine reforestation with seedlings bred by the two cooperatives totals 180 million seedlings each year (150 and 30 for the CFGRP and WGFTIP, respectively) which is approximately 15 percent of the reforestation of loblolly pine and 10 percent of all tree seedlings planted nationwide. To our knowledge, these figures account for nearly all slash pine reforestation in the southern USA.

FIRST-GENERATION IMPROVEMENT OF SLASH PINE

Genetic improvement programs capitalize on the facts that there is tremendous genetic variation within most tree species and that family members resemble each other more closely than do unrelated individuals. One of the oldest and historically most successful schemes to take advantage of these facts is the method of genetic improvement referred to as recurrent selection (RS). Recurrent selection uses repeated cycles of breeding aimed at the gradual and cumulative improvement of a few traits in a population (Shelbourne 1969, Namkoong and others 1988 Chapter 3). The benefits of breeding accumulate in each cycle or generation as improvement builds upon advances made in prior generations.

The oldest form of RS is called simple recurrent selection in which each cycle of breeding involves: (1) Mass selection of individuals based solely on phenotypic appearance; and (2) Breeding of these phenotypically-superior individuals to produce the offspring available for selection in the subsequent generation. In this form, the selected and breeding populations are identical and there is no genetic testing or pedigree control. Simple recurrent selection was the method used more than 10,000 years ago by ancient farmers to improve their field crops (Briggs and Knowles 1967): seed from phenotypically-superior individuals was retained for next year's crop. Simple recurrent selection is what landowners practice when they leave the best trees to seed in the next generation.

Simple recurrent selection is rarely used in modern tree breeding programs, because it is less efficient at achieving genetic gains than forms of recurrent selection that incorporate genetic testing and pedigree control. The vast majority of conifer breeding programs employ recurrent selection for general combining ability (RS-GCA) (Shelbourne 1969, Namkoong and others 1988). In RS-GCA, genetic testing follows selection. This generally takes the form of progeny tests where the breeding values of parents are evaluated by tracking the performance of their offspring. Selections with high GCA values for any trait are those that produce top-performing offspring. To start the next cycle, parents with high GCAs and their offspring are selected for further breeding and testing, while poor-GCA selections are eliminated from the program. Genetic testing greatly increases the genetic gain above that possible from mass selection. This is especially true for traits with low heritabilities which, unfortunately, account for most economically-important traits of conifers.

This section documents the first-generation tree improvement programs of slash pine in the CFGRP and WGFTIP. These programs began in the 1950s and the CFGRP first-generation cycle was completed in the 1980s. The first-generation cycle for the WGFTIP is currently being completed. Both cooperatives employed similar breeding strategies involving: (1) Mass selection of outstanding trees from natural stands and plantations based solely on outward appearance; (2) Grafting a portion of those trees in clonal seed orchards to produce genetically-improved seed for operational reforestation, while establishing the remainder in scion banks for preservation and breeding;

(3) Establishment of progeny tests to rank the selections based on GCA; and (4) Breeding together of first-generation selections to create new combinations of genes and planting of these seedlings in tests to make second-generation selections. Details of the first-generation slash pine tree improvement programs are in tables 1 and 2 for the CFGRP and WGFTIP, respectively, and the highlights are summarized below.

Breeding Zones and Base Populations

Tree improvement programs are organized around geographic areas known as breeding zones. These are deployment areas where important economic traits are similar and in which the performance of the outplanted trees can be accurately predicted. Thus, the breeding zone is the geographical area for which an improved variety is being developed. Determining breeding zone boundaries is a critical decision in tree improvement programs, because each breeding zone requires a separate improvement program with its own distinct base, selected, breeding, and propagation populations. The tendency in conifer breeding programs is to develop large breeding zones to minimize costs associated with multiple programs and to breed improved varieties that have broad adaptability. This approach is suitable when genotype x environment interaction is not important for most traits across the edaphoclimatic region in the breeding zone and when conserving natural patterns of geographic variation is not a primary concern.

For slash pine in the southeastern USA (table 1), the CFGRP defined a single breeding zone consisting of the entire natural range of the species, approximately 10 million acres of timberlands (White and others 1986). A single program with its base, selected and breeding populations is being conducted for this zone. Similarly for slash pine in the Western Gulf, the WGFTIP defined a single breeding zone consisting of the flatwoods sites that stretch across the southernmost parts of the coastal plains in Mississippi, Louisiana, and Texas (table 2). Much of this area is outside the natural range of the species, but includes large areas in which slash pine has been planted as an exotic since the 1930s.

While there are many similarities between the two breeding zones of the CFGRP and WGFTIP, there are also some significant differences. In the southeastern USA slash pine is frequently found on well-drained sandy soils, while in the Western Gulf region it is favored for planting on poorly-drained, phosphorous-deficient silty clay soils. In the southeastern USA, there are areas where fusiform rust (*Cronartium fusiforme*) and its obligate alternative host, the red oaks, are present at only low levels. In these areas, growth rate is the most important economic trait. In the Western Gulf region, where slash pine has not coevolved with the endemic pathotypes and red oaks are plentiful, improving resistance to fusiform rust is the single most important goal of the tree improvement program.

The base population of a given cycle of improvement consists of all available trees that could be selected if desired (Zobel and Talbert 1984). It is the population of trees that will be improved upon through selection and breeding and

Table 1—First- and second-generation breeding programs for *Pinus elliottii* as conducted by the Cooperative Forest Genetics Research Program[a]

Category	First generation	Second generation
Breeding objectives	Increase volume yield, resistance to *Cronartium fusiforme* (rust) and stem straightness.	Increase volume yield, resistance to *Cronartium fusiforme* (rust), stem straightness and wood specific gravity.
Breeding unit	One large breeding unit encompassing the natural range of slash pine.	One large breeding unit encompassing the natural range of slash pine.
Base population	Ten million acres of predominantly natural stands encompassing the entire native range.	(1) Field tests containing 2,700 FS families and 200,000 trees available as forward selns; (2) 1,200 FG selns plus 1,250 FG infusions available as backward selns.
Selected population	1955–65: 1,200 intensive selns made by comparison tree method: volume, stem straightness, freedom from disease, crown form.	1987–88: 965 selns: (1) one-third are backwards selns of top first-generation parents; (2) one-third are forward selns; and (3) one-third are untested infusions not bred in FG.
Propagation population	1955–70: 2,500 acres of clonal SO established by CFGRP members. Each member's SO contained their 25 to 150 original selns. Bulk collections of wind-pollinated seed used for reforestation.	1990–95: 600 acres of clonal SO established by CFGRP members. Each SO contained the best 20 to 40 backward and forward selns from the selected population. Single-family collections of OP seed are used for reforestation.
Progeny testing	1965–80: 350 OP field tests (325,000 trees) to rank 1,200 selns. Seed collected from selns grafted in SOs.	No separate progeny testing to rank selns prior to breeding and testing described below.
Infusions	1970–85: 1,250 infusions: (1) 850 rust-free selns in highly-infected stands; (2) 125 selns from the southern part of the range; (3) 115 selns for high yield of oleo-resin; (4) 60 selns free of pitch canker fungus; and (5) 100 others.	1995: 85 infusions: (1) 70 selns obtained as top forward selns from USDA Forest Service field trials upon closure of USFA program; and (2) 15 new backward selns of top first-generation parents after reanalysis of data.
Breeding population	1970–85: 820 top selns (600 of 1,200 original selns plus 220 of 1,250 infusions) bred together in 6 parent disconnected diallels and factorials to create 2,700 FS families planted in 225 field tests containing 200,000 trees.	1995–2001: 1,050 selns in 24 BGs with 44 selns/BG. Complementary mating designs: (1) for ranking, polymix mating of 325 poorly-tested selns planted in 16 replicated tests containing 55,000 trees; and (2) for forward selection, breeding among all 1,050 selns use to create 1,500 FS families planted in unreplicated plots in 12 locations with 100,000 trees.

BG = breeding group; FG = first generation; CP = control-pollinated; FS = full-sib; OP = open-pollinated; seln = selection; SO = seed orchard.
[a] The generation intervals were: 1955 to 1985 for the first generation and 1987 to 2003 for the second generation.
Source: White and others (1986), White and others (1993).

hence is also called the foundation population. In first-generation conifer breeding programs, the base population is typically very large consisting of many thousands or millions of trees. In the case of the CFGRP, any tree growing in natural stands within the native range was, at least in concept, a potential candidate for selection and therefore inclusion in the program.

The WGFTIP base population drew on native stands of slash pine from southeastern MS and planted stands in MS, LA and TX. The intent was to capitalize on the beginnings of a land race that was created when slash pine was established as an exotic in the Western Gulf region.

However, as most of the WGFTIP first-generation selections originated from populations that were, at most, only one generation removed from the native range, both programs originally sampled the same genetic resource.

Selected Population

In the first generation, both the CFGRP and WGFTIP used a process called mass selection to select outstanding trees based on their phenotypic, outward appearance. For both cooperatives, first-generation selections were identified by comparing growth rates and other characteristics of candidate trees to five comparison trees chosen among the candidate's neighbors. The selection procedure emphasized

Table 2—First- and second-generation breeding programs for *Pinus elliottii* as conducted by the Western Gulf Forest Tree Improvement Cooperative

Category	First generation	Second generation
Breeding objectives	Increase resistance to *Cronartium fusiforme* (rust), volume yield, and stem straightness. Maintain regional averages for specific gravity.	Increase volume yield, resistance to *Cronartium fusiforme* (rust), stem straightness and wood specific gravity.
Breeding unit	One large breeding unit encompassing the flatwoods of MS, LA, and TX.	One large breeding unit encompassing the flatwoods of MS, LA, and TX.
Base population	Natural stands in MS and plantations in MS, LA, and TX where slash pine was planted as an exotic. Most of these plantations were of unknown origin, but came from seed collected in the native range.	(1) Field tests containing 712 FS families and 168,000 trees available as potential forward selns; (2) 500 FG selns.
Selected population	1955–83: 1,000 intensive selns made by comparison tree method: volume, stem straightness, freedom from disease, crown form. This was reduced to 500 selections based on performance at the Resistance Screening Center.	Target of 550 selns: (1) 90 will be backwards selns of top first-generation parents; (2) 460 will be forward selns; currently 166 second-generation selections have been identified. The remainder of the second–generation selns will be identified by 2010.
Propagation population	Six organizations currently manage 200 acres of first and 1.5 generation orchards. Bulk and family collections of wind-pollinated seed used for reforestation.	130 acres of advanced-generation SO established by WGFTIP members. Each SO contained the best 20 to 40 backward and forward selns chosen for disease resistance and volume growth. Bulk and family collections of OP seed are used for reforestation. Control-mass pollinated seed and rooted cuttings will also be used.
Progeny testing	120 progeny tests established to evaluate 367 parents in CP tests and 22 parents in OP tests. The last remaining first-generation progeny tests should be established in 2003.	Currently 3 polymix tests established to evaluate 37 second-generation parents. Eventually there will be approximately 550 parents evaluated in polymix tests.
Infusions	None	None

BG = breeding group; FG = first generation; CP = control-pollinated; FS = full-s b; OP = open-pollinated; Seln = selection; SO = seed orchard.

growth rate, wood specific gravity, stem straightness, and crown form. Selected trees were required to be free of fusiform rust, but otherwise no pressure was placed on improvement of this trait. Most selections were made in low hazard stands where rust was not prevalent; so, little advancement in rust resistance was made during the first round of selection.

From 1955 through 1965, the CFGRP made 1,200 selections in natural stands growing within the native slash pine range (table 1). These selections were widely distributed across many counties in FL, GA and AL with fewer from SC and MS. Most of the 1,000 first-generation slash pine selections by the WGFTIP were made in areas where slash pine was planted as an exotic in southern TX and LA. These selections originated from even aged plantations of unknown origin. Selection activity began in the mid 1950s by the Texas Forest Service and other organizations working independently. Selection continued from 1969

until 1983 as part of the WGFTIP cooperative. The bulk of the WGFTIP selections were made in the 1970s.

Propagation Populations: Clonal Seed Orchards
Cooperators soon realized that it was critical to capture value from these selections by establishing them in clonal seed orchards. A clonal seed orchard is a collection of selections grafted in one physical location and then managed to produce genetically-improved seed for operational reforestation. By establishing the selections in a single location, both male and female parents are selected and thus theoretical genetic gains are doubled compared to collecting seed from the selections growing in the original stands. The gains from these original first-generation clonal seed orchards reflect only the gains from mass selection. That is, the seed produced from these original orchards is genetically-improved only to the extent that the mass selection was successful in identifying genetically-superior trees.

Members of both the CFGRP and WGFTIP cooperatives used similar processes to establish their clonal seed orchards involving the following steps: (1) Selections were made in the base populations as described in the previous section; (2) Many branch tips (say 100 pieces), called scion material, were collected from each selection; (3) The scion pieces from each selection were grafted onto seedling rootstock to produce the plants for establishing the seed orchard; (4) All plants originating from a single selection have the same genotype as that selection, since all branches have the same genotype, and these plants are called a clone; (5) Each first-generation seed orchard established through this means contained 20 to 200 plants of each clone (that is, grafts from each selection) from a total of 20 to 150 different selections; (6) The grafted plants were established in the orchard location at relatively wide spacing (for example, 15 ft x 30 ft) compared to plantations to provide full sunlight to the crowns to promote flowering; (7) Each plant was identified by its clone number, and ramets of the same clone were maintained at a minimum distance from each other to reduce selfing; and (8) After planting, the orchard was managed intensively to produce mass quantities of open-pollinated seed, and this seed was used for operational forestation. Cultural management of clonal seed orchards is completely different than that of plantations and genetic tests due to the very different objective: seed production.

CFGRP members established nearly 2,500 acres of first-generation seed orchards between 1955 and 1970. These mainly contained each member's selections meaning there was little exchange of selections among cooperators. In the Western Gulf, some organizations were working independently prior to the formation of the WGFTIP cooperative, while others were working together from the very beginning. Early orchards emphasized a variety of different traits. The Texas Forest Service established its first slash pine orchard in 1957 selected for growth rate and form. Small orchards were later established that emphasized high wood density (1964) and known fiber properties (1966). The Louisiana Department of Agriculture and Forestry established one of their first slash pine orchards in 1967 with clones obtained from the USDA Forest Service that were selected for enhanced naval stores properties. Crown Zellerbach (now Weyerhaeuser Company) established their first slash pine orchard in 1964 with selections made off of their own land. Organizations establishing orchards in cooperation with the Texas Forest Service or after the cooperative was formed in 1969 shared many of the same clones. All of the later orchards were established with clones selected for growth and form.

All of these first-generation seed orchards were established solely on the basis of outward appearance of the trees that were selected and subsequently grafted. That is, there was no evidence from genetic tests that the selections were, in fact, genetically superior to other candidate trees that were not selected. As data from genetic tests began to become available (described in the next section), it turned out that, in fact, some of the selections were inferior and some were superior to average, unimproved trees for the few commercially-important traits being measured. As these data became available, cooperators

rapidly eliminated poor clones (that is, clones whose offspring had performed poorly in genetic tests) to upgrade the genetic quality of the orchard seed. This process is called roguing, and roguing poor clones from a seed orchard can increase expected genetic gains by 40-50 percent over the initial mean (Talbert and others 1985; Li and others 1999).

Through the process of roguing, expected gains of CFGRP first-generation seed orchards went from an average of 9 percent volume yield above unimproved material to 14 percent gain (table 3). These values are averages over more than 20 first-generation seed orchards owned by different CFGRP members and individual orchard gains vary markedly depending on the exact composition of selections originally grafted. As more and more data became available from genetic tests, CFGRP members began to exchange clones with other members so that all could have the very best tested clones. Members established, through grafting, new seed orchards containing these very best first-generation clones obtained from the pool of 1,200 selected by the entire cooperative. These so-called 1.5-generation orchards averaged 18 percent in volume yield and also contained selections with considerable rust resistance (table 3). While many clones were common to most 1.5-generation CFGRP seed orchards, some members put more emphasis on rust resistance and others on growth rate; so, expected gains and clonal composition did vary.

In the Western Gulf, fusiform rust was increasingly recognized as an important problem, and all orchard clones were tested for disease resistance at the USDA Forest Service's Resistance Screening Center between 1980 and 1983 (Anderson and others 1983; Anderson and Powers 1985). These greenhouse tests, employing artificial inoculation of progeny of the orchard clones, identified susceptible selections, and existing first-generation orchards were heavily rogued based on this criterion. All subsequent orchards were established with material selected for both growth and disease resistance. The WGFTIP now has 194 acres (76 ha) of first and 1.5 generation orchards improved for rust resistance, growth, and form managed by six organizations. Gain estimates cannot be compared across the cooperatives because data summarization procedures differ. The WGFTIP breeding values for volume include a survival factor to account for less mortality due to improved rust resistance. R50s, while similar in concept, are also difficult to compare because the fusiform rust populations and environmental conditions under which selections from the two programs were evaluated also differ. Current WGFTIP production orchards, which include heavily rogued first-generation orchards and advancing-front orchards with both backward and forward selections have an estimated breeding value for volume of 30 percent and an R50 of 32. The younger advancing-front orchards that are not yet into production have an average projected breeding value for volume of 38 percent and an R50 of 25.

Genetic Testing and Breeding
Genetic tests are central to all tree improvement programs and are established with pedigreed, well-labeled offspring or clonal plantlets, such as offspring from the first-generation selections planted in randomized, replicated tests

Table 3—Genetic gains from CFGRP slash pine seed orchards in volume and rust resistance[a]

Type of seed	Years seed planted	Volume gain	Rust resistance[b]
		percent	(R50)
Unimproved	<1960	0.0	50
1.0 Generation orchard unrogued	1965–1985	9.0	49
1.0 Generation orchard rogued	1975–1995	14.0	41
1.5 Generation orchard unrogued	1985–2005	18.0	35
Advanced-generation orchard	>2002	30	20

CFGRP = Cooperative Forest Genetics Research program.

[a] All gains are expressed relative to plantations established with unimproved material as it existed before domestication began in 1950. Volume gain is in percent above unimproved.

[b] Rust resistance is expressed in R50: the percentage of trees in a stand that would be infected with rust when 50 percent would be infected in an unimproved plantation (for example, R50 = 35 means that 35 percent of the trees would be rust-infected in plantations that would have had 50 percent infection if planted with unimproved material). All gain values are averages of 10 or more seed orchards of different members, and gains of the individual orchards vary markedly depending on clonal composition.

(McKinley 1983; Zobel and Talbert 1984, Chapter 8; van Buijtenen and Bridgwater 1986; White 1987; Bridgwater 1992). The tests are usually planted in field locations on forest sites, but may also occur in nurseries, greenhouses and growth rooms. The idea of these "common garden" tests is to grow genotypes in replicated environments so that genetic effects can be isolated from confounding environmental effects.

Tree improvement programs rely on genetic testing to: (1) Evaluate relative genetic quality of selections made in any cycle of selection (that is, progeny testing to rank the GCAs of first-generation selections based on the performance of their offspring); (2) Estimate genetic parameters such as heritabilities, genetic correlations, and genotype x environment interactions for key traits; (3) Provide a base population of new genotypes from which to make the next cycle of selection; and (4) Quantify or demonstrate genetic gains made by the program.

The third function of genetic tests mentioned above involves another activity, called breeding. Some or all of the individuals in the selected population are included in that cycle's breeding population and are intermated (cross bred) to regenerate genetic variability through recombination of alleles during sexual reproduction. Many different mating designs are used to intermate the members of the breeding population, and offspring from these intermatings are planted in genetic tests that form the next cycle's base population. This completes one cycle of the core activities of the breeding cycle (selection, breeding and testing), and

the next cycle begins with new selections being made from these genetic tests (that is, from the new base population).

The CFGRP and WGFTIP employed different strategies for genetic testing and breeding in their first-generation slash pine programs, emphasizing the myriad of alternative methodologies available to tree breeders. In the CFGRP, the progeny testing and breeding phases (functions 1 and 3 of genetic tests mentioned above) were separated in time by 10 or so years and employed a different set of parents. Shortly after the original 1,200 selections were made, it was recognized that it was impossible to rank these selections for their genetic quality, since they were selected in hundreds of different natural stands growing in 5 states. Therefore, CFGRP members mounted a large program of progeny testing with tests established from 1965-1980. Open-pollinated (OP) seed was collected from each of the grafted selections growing in seed orchards and kept labeled by the clone (that is, selection) that produced the seed. As seed from 20 to 100 selections became available, these were planted into randomized, replicated field tests located on members' timberlands throughout the slash pine native range. Altogether 350 separate field tests containing more than 325,000 OP progeny from the 1,200 selections were established (table 1). The performance of OP progeny was used to rank the 1,200 selections, mainly for volume growth and rust resistance (for example, a selection producing offspring that consistently grew well and were rust resistant in several replications on each of several field sites was judged as a top performer).

As soon as rankings became available from OP progeny tests (beginning in 1970 for the earliest OP tests), CFGRP members began to breed together top-ranking selections through control pollination. The idea was to increase genetic gain from the breeding efforts by eliminating poor-performing selections before breeding. The top 600 of the 1,200 original selections were combined 220 new infusions chosen as superior rust-free trees in high-hazard stands (see below) to create a breeding population of 820 parents (table 1) that were bred together to create 2,700 full-sib families that were established in 225 field tests containing 200,000 full-sib, pedigreed offspring. These tests were established from 1970 through 1985. The second generation of slash pine tree improvement began in 1987 (table 1) with selection of superior trees from top families in these selection tests.

In the WGFTIP, the plan initially adopted by the cooperative was to include each of the 1,000 first-generation selections in control-pollinated breeding where each selection would be in at least four crosses with other selections and each cross would be evaluated at three different locations for growth and form. By the late 1970s, it became apparent from analyzing the older test data that rust-related mortality was so significant that the best predictor of volume at age 15 was rust infection levels at age five. It also became apparent that parents selected only for good growth and form were frequently poor performers in the field when exposed to fusiform rust infection. This led to two changes in the WGFTIP breeding and progeny-testing programs. The first was a change in the evaluation criteria in progeny tests. The second was the adoption of a two-step screening procedure.

Rust-related mortality was the most significant factor causing changes in family ranks for volume production between ages five and 15. Therefore, the evaluation scheme was altered to use rust infection at age five as the indirect selection criterion for final volume. In order to have confidence that all families had been exposed to rust, only those tests in which the average rust infection of the test or that of the unimproved checklots exceeded 30 percent were used. At later ages (10 and 15 years), much of the rust-related mortality had already occurred, and both growth rate and infection levels were deemed to be important in determining final volume (Lowe and van Buijtenen 1991).

The second change in the first-generation progeny-testing program involved the adoption of a two-step screening procedure. This scheme combined greenhouse screening for disease resistance followed by breeding and testing of the most disease-resistant parents in field tests for growth and yield (Lowe and van Buijtenen 1989). All 1,000 first-generation selections were first crossed with a polymix of ten parents chosen because they lacked resistance in field tests. Rust-susceptible parents were chosen in order to ensure that any resistance apparent in the greenhouse tests would originate from the female parent under evaluation (Byram and Lowe 1987). The WGFTIP eliminated approximately half of its first generation breeding population on the basis of resistance screening at the USDA Forest Service Resistance Screening Center. The 500

remaining selections were divided into groups of six to nine parents that are being crossed in a modified half-diallel scheme in which each parent is included in four crosses. The current progeny test design consists of establishing each cross in three locations with each location containing 50 replications of single-tree plots. Growth and disease incidence are evaluated at five-year intervals. These tests are used both to rank parents and as a source for second-generation selections. To date, there have been 120 long-term first-generation progeny tests established to evaluate 389 parents. Twenty-two of these parents are only in open-pollinated tests, while 367 parents are evaluated in control-pollinated tests containing 712 full-sib families. WGFTIP anticipates that the last of the required first-generation progeny tests will be established in 2003.

Infusions

Some years after initial selections are made, many tree improvement programs add new selections into the breeding population that were not part of the original selected population. These infusions can be aimed specifically at improving a single trait or at generally broadening the genetic diversity existing in the program. The WGFTIP did not make any infusions in the first-generation slash pine program; however, the CFGRP doubled the size of the first-generation selected population by infusing 1,250 new selections obtained through several different opportunities (table 1): (1) 850 new selections were obtained to increase rust resistance in the program by selecting phenotypically-superior trees that were free of disease in natural stands that had 85 percent or more of the trees rust infected (Goddard and others 1975); (2) 125 new selections were made in central Florida in the counties near Orlando (the southern part of the natural range of the northern variety of slash pine) to broaden genetic diversity; (3) 115 new selections were made from diallels originally established by the USDA Forest Service as part of their program for naval stores production (that is, high yields of oleoresin); and (4) 60 selections were added to increase pitch canker resistance by selecting disease-free trees in natural stands heavily infected with the pitch canker fungus (*Fusarium circinatum* which was formerly *F. subglutinans*) (Rockwood and Blakeslee 1988).

ADVANCED-GENERATION BREEDING OF SLASH PINE

In both the CFGRP and WGFTIP, the goals of the advanced-generation breeding programs of slash pine include: (1) Achieving maximum short-term genetic gains in a few traits of high economic importance, mainly volume growth and rust resistance with less emphasis on stem form and wood specific gravity; (2) Maintaining sufficient genetic diversity in the breeding population to ensure near-optimal long-term genetic gains in the same or different traits as markets, products, technologies and environments change in the future; (3) Ensuring sufficient flexibility in program design to facilitate change in direction and incorporation of new technologies (such as biotechnologies); (4) Conserving genetic diversity in the species; and (5) Conducting all of these activities in a timely, cost-effective way that yields appropriate economic returns.

Because of the similar goals of the two cooperative programs, there are many similarities in second-generation breeding strategy and program implementation. There are also some differences. Details of the two second-generation programs are summarized in the following sections, but points of strong concurrence are: (1) Focus on improvement of two key traits, volume and rust resistance, with lesser emphasis on a few others; (2) Large selected and breeding populations designed to maintain sufficient levels of genetic diversity; (3) Use of overlapping generations in which excellent first-generation selections (called backward selections) are retained in the program and included in the selected population with forward selections of the top offspring from first-generation selections; (4) Reliance on a strategy aimed at improving the overall mean general combining ability (GCA) of the breeding population (which implies genetic testing to rank selections); (5) Subdivision of the breeding population into smaller sub-groups, called sublines or breeding groups, to manage inbreeding; (6) Use of complementary mating designs in which a polymix design is used for progeny testing and full-sib designs are employed to create a base population in which to make third-generation selections; (7) High quality field tests employing modern experimental designs in field sites that are intensively managed to minimize competition and maximize early expression of genetic differences in growth and rust resistance; and (8) Reliance on wind-pollinated seed orchards as the principle form of producing genetically-improved seed for operational reforestation.

Base Populations
The base population for the second generation consists of all possible selections from both the original first-generation selections that could be retained in the program (backward selections) and progeny from breeding of those selections growing in genetic tests. When the second-generation CFGRP program began in 1987 (table 1), the base population consisted of all of the following materials that could have been selected: (1) The original 1,200 first-generation selections; (2) 1,250 infusions that had been accumulated during implementation of the first-generation program and either had to be utilized or discarded; and (3) 200,000 progeny from 2,700 full-sib families growing in 225 field tests, all of which were available as potential forward selections. The base population for the WGFTIP second-generation program will include the approximately 500 first-generation parents and 168,000 progeny of those parents growing in first-generation genetic tests. Second-generation selections will be identified on the basis of rust resistance as progeny tests reach age 5 and these same tests will be screened again at age 10 on the basis of volume growth and rust resistance. The bulk of the tests will be screened during the next ten years.

For two reasons, the advanced-generation base populations for the two cooperatives will begin to diverge as the programs mature. First, each program started with a slightly different founder population, because different samples from the slash pine species were drawn for the first generation. Second, the populations will diverge as each program develops different land races as a result of testing in different environments and from selecting for slightly different traits to meet the specific requirements of their respective breeding zones. This will be a very slow process as many similarities exist in testing and selection criteria of the two programs and many generations of breeding and selection will be required to make large genetic differences in the two base populations. Therefore, opportunities for the two cooperatives to enrich each other's breeding programs through exchange of improved material will exist for the foreseeable future.

Selected Population
In 1987, the CFGRP initiated the second-generation slash pine program by predicting breeding values for volume and rust resistance of all trees in the base population (that is, of all backward and forward candidates for selection) using an analytical methodology called Best Linear Prediction (White and Hodge 1988). Next, using a growth and yield model (Nance and others 1983), economic weights for volume and rust resistance were estimated (Hodge and others 1989). Due to the imprecision of these estimated weights and the differences among CFGRP members in the relative importance of volume and rust, 3 indices were developed for each tree: I_B, I_G and I_R where the first index (B for both) weights volume and rust resistance according to their economic weights, I_G puts predominant weight on growth performance and I_R puts most emphasis on rust resistance. Generally, if any candidate (backward or forward) was excellent for any of the three indices, it was included in the second-generation selected population. This is similar to the multiple index selection strategy (Namkoong 1976) and aims to develop breeds for growth, rust and both within the CFGRP (Carson and others 1991).

To balance the objectives of maximizing genetic gain while maintaining adequate genetic diversity, the maximum number of relatives (full-sib, half-sib or parent-offspring) allowed in the CFGRP selected population was set at 7, and this number decreased with decreasing predicted genetic value. So, more second-generation selections were included from top families, in keeping with the principle of placing more emphasis on higher-ranking materials (Lindgren 1986). In addition, untested infusions were also included in the second-generation selected population, and many of these were infusions for rust resistance from the first generation (table 1) that had not been tested or utilized.

In summary, the CFGRP second-generation breeding population for slash pine was formed in 1987, and contained a total of 933 total selections with the following composition (White and others 1993): (1) 395 backward selections of the very best first-generation selections; (2) 318 top forward selections from the 225 field tests containing 200,000 trees from 2,700 full-sib families; and (3) 220 infusions from the first-generation. With a census number of N=933 total selections, there were 850 unrelated individuals that contributed genes to the selected population and the population had an inbreeding-effective population size of N_e=625 (which is lower than 933 due to relatedness, Falconer and Mackay 1996). The genetic gain for this genetically-diverse population is approximately 20 percent for volume and an R50=35 meaning 35 percent rust-infected trees in stands where unimproved material would have 50 percent of the trees infected. Subsequent to 1987, 30 or so new second-generation selections were added to bring the total to 965 and 85 new infusions were added to take advantage of special opportunities (table 1).

The WGFTIP program currently has 166 second-generation selections. It is anticipated that an additional 300 second-generation selections (forward selections) and approximately 90 proven first generation parents (backwards selections) will be added to this total. The WGFTIP second-generation population will then be approximately 550. Second-generation selections will be identified based on mid-parent values for rust resistance (age 5) and a combination of volume and rust resistance (ages 10 and older). Data summarization procedures for estimating these breeding values were reported by Lowe and van Buijtenen (1991).

Propagation Populations: Clonal Seed Orchards

In the second-generation, members of both the CFGRP and WGFTIP cooperatives are relying almost exclusively on open-pollinated clonal seed orchards to produce genetically-improved seed for reforestation. Control mass pollination (CMP), an alternative to seed orchards in which top parents are crossed together on an operational scale, is currently being used on a limited basis to capture additional genetic gain in the operational plantations by planting full-sib families (Bridgwater and others 1998), but plantations established through CMP account for less than 2 percent of current annual reforestation in the southern USA.[2] Operational planting of tested clones, produced either through tissue culture or rooted cuttings, is another alternative to seed orchards that is being explored by some companies. However, to date clonal forestry is still in the development stage. It is likely that operational deployment in the future will include all three of these options (open-pollinated seed orchards, CMP, and clonal forestry), but through 2010, the large majority of plantations will be established from seed orchard seed.

The designs and compositions of the clonal seed orchards vary between the 2 cooperatives and are described below; however, in both cooperatives a major change has occurred in how seed is collected and deployed from those orchards. In the 1970s and 1980s, most companies collected bulk seed from their orchards and, therefore, established operational plantations that were mixtures of many families. Currently, it is much more common to collect seed in one of two ways: (1) By groups of clones (for example, some organizations divide clones in the orchard into three groups, such as top growers, rust resistant and other, and collect seed according to this grouping); or (2) By clone (so if there are 20 clones in an orchard there are 20 bags of seed and each bag contains the OP family seed of a given mother-tree clone). Both options increase genetic gain in operational plantations in 2 ways. First, seed is not collected from less-desirable clones in an orchard, and second, seed is deployed to sites for which it is most suited (such as rust resistant material to high hazard sites). With the second

option, operational plantations are established with single OP families (that is, all trees in a plantation have a common female parent). Approximately half of all slash pine plantations are now established with single OP families and a given company might deploy from 2 to nearly 25 different families (see footnote 2).

In terms of the details of advanced-generation slash pine seed orchards, most CFGRP members established orchards shortly after 1987 when the second-generation selected population was formed. They employed a systematic design (Hodge and White 1993) in which 40 or so clones were grafted in the same order in each block of the orchard. Approximately half of the clones are backward, tested selections and half are forward, untested progeny. Thus, there can be parents and offspring in the same orchard. When data are available from second-generation genetic tests, the poorer clones can be rogued from orchard leaving a mix of unrelated forward and backward selections. CFGRP members currently manage about 600 acres of these second-generation clonal seed orchards, and the genetic gains are expected to be 30 percent for volume and R50=20 (table 3).

In the WGFTIP program, the second-generation clonal seed orchards are designed as advancing-front orchards where blocks are established on a periodic schedule that allows new material to be incorporated from the breeding program as it becomes available. Older blocks can also be removed from management as better material becomes available. In general, blocks for these advanced-generation orchards are established on a five-year cycle with the best 20 clones currently available. This strategy was adopted because different member's programs are at different stages and as a result, advances in the breeding program occur annually rather than in evenly-timed generational intervals. The WGFTIP cooperative currently has 140 ac (55 ha) of advanced-generation orchards under management.

Breeding and Progeny Testing

All advanced-generation breeding programs must cope with the fact that the number of relatives increases in closed populations through selection and breeding. This can have dire consequences in outbred species, such as pines, because matings among relatives frequently reduce family performance (called inbreeding depression) and confound the ability to accurately predict parental breeding values if families being tested suffer from different levels of inbreeding. The WGFTIP and CFGRP have adopted very similar strategies to deal with these problems. Namely, both breeding populations have been sib-divided into smaller subsets, called breeding groups or sublines, such that all relatives are assigned to and managed within the same breeding group (van Buijtenen 1976, Burdon and others 1977, van Buijtenen and Lowe 1979). This allows inbreeding to be concentrated in the breeding population by making only crosses within breeding groups to produce the next generation. At the same time, this ensures that unrelated individuals (from different breeding groups) will always be available to establish the propagation population. For example, the best selection from each breeding group could be grafted into a clonal seed orchard and

---

[2] McKeand, S.E.; Mullin, T.J.; Byram, T.D.; White, T.L. Deployment of genetically-improved loblolly and slash pine in the Southern U.S. Manuscript in preparation.

since all breeding groups are unrelated to each other, the seed from the seed orchard would be completed outcrossed.

Another important commonality between the 2 cooperatives is the use of complementary mating and field designs. These schemes use one set of crosses and field designs to rank parents and another set of crosses and field designs to produce the base population from which third-generation forward selections will be made. To rank parents, selections are being bred with a pollen mix and the polymix families are being planted in well-replicated field tests planted in single-tree plots. The second type of design makes control-pollinated crosses among the selections and the full-sib families are then planted in essentially unreplicated block plots of 50 to 100 trees per family. These full-sib families are ranked for their predicted performance based on the parental breeding values obtained from polymix tests. Selections for the next cycle of breeding will then be made from within the block plots.

In the CFGRP, the breeding population consisting of 1,050 selections (table 1) was divided into 24 breeding groups with each group containing approximately 44 selections. All selections were grafted into clone banks on members' timberlands in 1988 and 1989, and members began breeding as soon as the grafts began to flower. For the polymix breeding, the CFGRP decided not to re-test backward selections that already had been adequately tested in first-generation tests. In addition, many of the 220 infusions were not included in the polymix testing. The first series of polymix tests contained 138 PM families planted in 1998 on 8 sites with 20 replications per site. The second polymix series was planted in 2001 with 177 PM families on 8 sites with 20 replications. No other polymix testing is planned for the second generation meaning that 315 (138+177) of the 1,050 selections will be ranked in these tests. In the second part of the complementary designs, members have made 1,500 full-sib families using a flexible crossing design that makes more crosses among top selections within each breeding group and crosses the lowest ranking selections only once (White and others 1993). These crosses are being planted in selection blocks of 50 to 100 trees as crosses become available from 1995 through 2003. In total, more than 100,000 pedigreed trees will be available in these selection plots to begin making third-generation selections in 2003.

The WGFTIP advanced-generation breeding population has been divided into 35 breeding groups of approximately 18 to 25 individuals. The complementary mating scheme uses polymix seedlings planted at 3 locations, each with 50 single-tree plot replications, to rank parents. Block plots of control-pedigree crosses among members from the same breeding groups are also being established. Breeding and testing for the second generation is just beginning within the WGFTIP as first-generation testing was drawn out to allow screening at the RSC. Currently, there are 3 polymix tests established to evaluate 37 second-generation selections. Three of the six slash pine members are currently producing crosses for the control-pollinated selection population.

Genetic Gains and Genetic Diversity

Genetic diversity and gain are conflicting objectives for all tree improvement programs. In particular, it is impossible to make gains without reducing genetic diversity and genetic diversity decreases in all closed breeding populations during the course of many cycles of recurrent selection. In the current slash pine breeding population of both cooperatives, high levels of genetic diversity are being actively maintained by managing extremely large populations (500 to 1,000 selections) and by limiting the number of related selections. Since both programs are only in the second generation of breeding and both are improving only a few key traits, diversity levels have changed little in the breeding populations compared to the natural species. These breeding populations are large enough to sustain excellent genetic gains for many generations of breeding and contain sufficient levels of genetic diversity to provide considerable flexibility to changing climates, markets and technologies.

Genetic gain and diversity are also important in operational plantations. Most organizations want to maximize genetic gain in operational plantations and accomplish this by using only the best material available each generation. For example, a clonal seed orchard might contain the top 20 out of nearly 1,000 selections available in any generation, and the organization might chose to plant single OP families collected from that orchard. Most organizations are willing to take more risk in a plantation that exists for a single rotation compared with a breeding population that must sustain a program for many generations of improvement. Still, it is important to quantify the gains and risk associated with different options for operational deployment of genetically-improved material.

Genetic gains from different types of CFGRP seed orchards are shown in table 3. It is clear that steady gains have been made throughout the years as breeding technologies, data analysis methods and genetic testing have advanced. For the CFGRP, seed being planted from advanced-generation seed orchards is expected to have volume gains of 30 percent above unimproved material when planted on low hazard sites for fusiform rust. These yield gains will be enhanced on high hazard sites since the average orchard contains clones with mean R50=20 (so, seedlings from these orchards are expected to have 20 percent of the trees infected in stands that would be 50 percent infected were unimproved seedlings planted).

As mentioned earlier, many organizations are now planting single OP families on portions of their timberlands to capture maximum genetic gains. Further, some organizations are piloting or developing programs to deploy single full-sib families or single tested clones to increase genetic gains still further in operational plantations. Since each of these options decreases genetic diversity to increase genetic gain, it is important to analyze the implications of these alternatives: bulk mixtures of seed from seed orchards, single OP families from seed orchards, single full-sib family from unrelated parents and single, non-inbred clone. McKeand and others[2] recently approached this issue through a survey of all major organizations in the south to see if any plantation failures had been reported. First, 31 state and private companies returned the surveys (100 percent of all the members in the 3 tree improvement cooperatives in the southern USA) and these companies are directly or indirectly responsible for at least 90 percent of the annual reforestation southwide. None of these organizations had experienced in unexpected environmental or pest problems in plantations established with single OP families. The only problem mentioned was that of a family being deployed that had not been adequately tested for cold or drought tolerance, but this was extremely rare. Since clonal plantations have not been planted on a wide scale, experience is limited.

Unfortunately, there is never any perfect way to assess risk (for example, how much home, car and life insurance is enough?). Extremely diverse populations of American Chestnut and American Elm were decimated by introduced fungal pathogens while Chardonnay grapes, which have very little if any genetic diversity, have been grown worldwide for over 400 years. Still, it is clear both theoretically and empirically that single OP families retain the large portion of genetic diversity in the species (75 percent of the additive genetic variance and 100 percent of the dominance genetic variance) and have been used safely for many years. As organizations employ clonal forestry, genetic diversity of the deployment population will decrease. Deployment strategies will need to balance the need to maintain genetic diversity against the desire for maximizing genetic gain in determining the number of clones to plant and their arrangement across the landscape.

ACKNOWLEDGMENTS

The authors thank the members of the Cooperative Forest Genetics Research Program and the Western Gulf Forest Tree Improvement Program who have supported tree improvement of slash pine for a half century. This publication was approved by the Florida Agricultural Experiment Station as Journal Series No. R-10442.

LITERATURE CITED

Anderson, R.L.; Powers, H.R., Jr. 1985. The Resistance Screening Center - screening for disease as a service for tree improvement programs. In: Barrows-Broaddus, J. and Powers, Jr., H.R. eds. Rusts of Hard Pines IUFRO Working Party Conference: proceedings. University of Georgia. Athens, GA. 59-63.

Anderson, R.L.; Young, C.H.; Triplett, J.D. 1983. Resistance screening center procedures manual: a step-by-step guide used in operational screening of southern pines to fusiform rust. Forest Pest Management Report 83-1-18. U.S. Department of Agriculture, Forest Service. 55 p.

Bridgwater, F.E. 1992. Mating designs. In: L. Fins, S. T. Friedman, and J. V. Brotschol, eds. Handbook of Quantitative Forest Genetics. Boston, MA. Kluwer Academic Publishing. 69-95.

Bridgwater, F.E.; Bramlett, D.L.; Byram, T.D.; Lowe, W.J. 1998. Controlled mass pollination in loblolly pine to increase genetic gains. Forest Chronicles 74: 185-189.

Briggs, F.N.; Knowles, P. 1967. Introduction to plant breeding. Reinhold Publishing Corporation. 426 p.

Burdon, R.D.; Shelbourne, C.J.A.; Wilcox, M.D. 1977. Advanced selection strategies. In: Third World Conference on Forest Tree Breeding: proceedings. March 21-26. Canberra, Australia. 1133-1147.

Byram, T.D.; Lowe, W.J.; McKinley, C.R. 1987. Polymix crosses for rust resistance screening. In: 19th Southern Forest Tree Improvement Conference: proceedings. June 16-18. College Station, TX. 39-44.

Carson, M.J.; Burdon, R.D.; Carson, S.D. [and others]. 1990. Realizing genetic gains in production forests. In: 11th RWG1 (Forest Genetics) Meeting: proceedings. Coonawarra, SA. 170-173.

Dorman, K.W. 1976. The genetics and breeding of southern pines. Handbook No. 471. U.S. Department of Agriculture, Forest Service. Washington, DC. 407 p.

Falconer, D.S.; Mackay, T.F.C. 1996. Introduction to quantitative genetics. Essex, England. Longman Press. 464 p.

Goddard, R.E.; Schmidt, R.A.; Vande Linde, F. 1975. Effect of differential selection pressure on fusiform rust resistance in phenotypic selections of slash pine. Phytopathology 65: 336-338.

Hodge, G.R.; White, T.L. 1993. Advanced-generation wind-pollinated seed orchard design. New Forests 7: 213-236.

Hodge, G.R.; White, T.L.; De Souza, S.M.; Powell, G.L. 1989. Predicted genetic gains from one generation of slash pine tree improvement. Southern Journal of Applied Forestry 13: 51-56.

Li, B.; McKeand, S.E.; Weir, R.J. 1999. Tree improvement and sustainable forestry - impact of two cycles of loblolly pine breeding in the U.S.A. Forest Genetics 6: 229-234.

Lindgren, D. 1986. How should breeders respond to breeding values? In: IUFRO Conference on Breeding Theory, Progeny Testing and Seed Orchards: proceedings. October 13-17. Williamsburg, VA. 361-372.

Lowe, W.J.; van Buijtenen, J.P. 1989. Early testing procedures applied to tree improvement programs. In: 20th Southern Forest Tree Improvement Conference: proceedings. June 26-30. Charleston, SC. 250-258.

Lowe, W.J.; van Buijtenen, J.P. 1991. Progeny test data summarization procedures in the Western Gulf Tree Improvement Program. In: 21st Southern Forest Tree Improvement Conference: proceedings. June 17-20, Knoxville, TN. 303-310.

McKeand, S.E.; Mullin, T.J.; Byram, T.D.; White, T.L. 2003. Deployment of genetically-improved loblolly and slash pines in the Southern US. Journal of Forestry (In preparation).

McKinley, C.R. 1983. Objectives of progeny tests. In: Progeny Testing of Forest Trees. Southern Cooperative Series Bulletin 275. Texas A & M University, College Station, TX. 2-13.

Namkoong, G. 1976. A multiple-index selection strategy. Silvae Genetica 25: 199-201.

Namkoong, G.; Kang, H.C.; Brouard, J.S. 1988. Tree breeding: principles and strategies. New York, NY. Springer-Verlag Publishing. 180 p.

Nance, W.L.; Froelich, R.C.; Dell, T.R.; Shoulders, E. 1983. A growth and yield model for unthinned slash pine plantations infected with fusiform rust. In: 2nd Biennial Southern Silviculture Research Conference. November 4-6. Atlanta, GA. 275-282.

Rockwood, D.L.; Blakeslee, G.M. 1988. Genetic strategies for reducing pitch canker incidence in slash pine. Southern Journal of Applied Forestry. 12: 28-32.

Shelbourne, C.J.A. 1969. Tree breeding methods. Forest Research Institute Technical Paper 55. New Zealand Forest Service. Wellington, NZ. 4 p.

Talbert, J.T.; Weir, R.J.; Arnold, R.D. 1985. Costs and benefits of a mature first generation loblolly pine tree improvement program. Journal of Forestry. 83: 162-165.

van Bu jtenen, J.P. 1976. Mating designs. In: IUFRO Joint Meeting on Advanced Generation Breeding: proceedings. June 14-18. Bordeaux, France. 11-27.

van Bu jtenen, J.P.; Bridgwater, F. 1986. Mating and genetic test designs. In: Advanced Generation Breeding of Forest Trees. Southern Cooperative Series Bulletin 309. Louisiana Agricultural Experiment Station. Baton Rouge, LA. 5-10.

van Bu jtenen, J.P.; Lowe, J. 1979. The use of breeding groups in advanced generation breeding. In: 15th Southern Forest Tree Improvement Conference: proceedings. June 19-21. Mississippi State, MS. 59-65.

White, T.; Flinchum, M.; Rockwood, D. [and others]. 1986. 28th progress report, Cooperative Forest Genetics Research Program. University of Florida. Gainesville, FL. 35 p.

White, T.L. 1987. A conceptual framework for tree improvement programs. New Forests 4: 325-342.

White, T.L.; Hodge, G.R. 1988. Best linear prediction of breeding values in a forest tree improvement program. Theoretical Applied Genetics 76: 719-727.

White, T.L.; Hodge, G.R.; Powell, G.L. 1993. Advanced-generation breeding strategy for slash pine in the Southeastern United States. Silvae Genetica 42: 359-371.

Zobel, B.J.; Ta bert, J. 1984. Applied forest tree improvement. New York, NY. John Wiley and Sons. 505 p.

SLASH PINE ESTABLISHMENT:
WHAT HAS CHANGED—1981-2002?

Marshall Jacobson[1]

Abstract—Practices for the establishment of slash pine in 1981 are compared to current practices in that portion of slash pine range located in Georgia and Florida. About 80 percent of slash pine timberland is concentrated in these two states. Establishment and management of slash is most intensively practiced in south Georgia and Florida.

INTRODUCTION

Major changes have occurred since the last Slash Pine Symposium held in 1981, including changes in industry, new silviculture options, long-term research data, and new opportunities for landowners to profit from products such as pine straw. Forest industry consolidation has had a major impact on the companies that have historically planted slash pine in Georgia and Florida, where about 80 percent of the slash pine timberland is located (Barnett and Sheffield, 2004). At least ten companies actively planted slash pine in 1981. Due to consolidation and changes in management strategies, only three to four companies actively plant slash pine in 2002. Slash pine remains popular with non-industrial private landowners.

SLASH PINE PLANTING SITES

Slash pine is largely native to south Georgia and north Florida, but was planted extensively in central Georgia and many other areas outside its original range in 1981. A number of companies planted slash pine on 90 to 100 percent of their reforestation area. In 2002, slash pine is planted mostly within its original range, and much less is planted in central Georgia and other areas outside the natural range. Forest industry now regenerates using a higher proportion of loblolly than slash, even within the primary natural range of slash pine (Shiver and others 2000). This shift of industry to loblolly pine on typical slash pine sites may be related to the almost universal use of bedding and other intensive management practices on these sites. Outcalt (1984) has shown that loblolly pine can perform as well or better than slash pine when grown on poorly and very poorly drained sites that are bedded.

SLASH PINE STANDS HAVE CHANGED

Existing slash pine stands were a mix of plantations and natural stands in 1981, and rotation ages were commonly over 30 years. Today, most slash stands are plantation originated, and rotation ages on industrial land are often close to 20 years. Small private landowners are more likely to use longer rotations in order to obtain additional returns from selling poles or pilings or harvesting pine straw. These facts are particularly relevant to establishment because the residual cleanup and subsequent site preparation and planting are affected by the conditions just after harvest, being generally, easier following plantations.

EXPECTATIONS FROM ESTABLISHMENT TECHNOLOGY

For forest industry, which needs a future supply of wood, expectations for results from establishment practices have changed a great deal. Whether we plant slash pine or loblolly pine, the expectations have changed. In 1981, we had what we believed were adequate nursery and planting practices, and genetically improved trees were becoming available in large quantities. However, our expectations, and often our financial justifications were based primarily on survival. In fact, a large amount of time and effort went into monitoring and collecting data to track our survival performance. In 2002, in the north Florida and south Georgia area, we nearly take survival for granted, and we have added early growth as a major expectation. With improved establishment techniques, it is common to have slash pine seedlings reach 2 to 3 feet in average height in the first year (Vardaman 1989). This has become an expected result from our establishment technology.

SEEDLING PRODUCTION

In 1981, seedlings were produced from a mix of seed orchard seed and seed collected from natural stands. Today, all seedlings are grown from seeds collected from seed orchards, and many companies maintain orchard seed identity through establishment by family. Nursery seedbed densities have also changed. In the early 1980s, nurseries usually grew crops at 28 to 32 seedlings per square foot, but now 20 to 24 per square foot spacings are more typical. This change is due to research that shows better survival and early growth results from producing larger seedlings in the nursery (South 1993).

PLANTING TECHNOLOGY

Planting techniques have changed little since the early 1980s, and a three-point hitch planter attached to a farm tractor remains the normal technique on the flat land typical of the slash pine range. Numbers of seedlings planted per acre, however, continue to undergo change. In 1981, you could find planting densities from 400 to well over 1000 trees per acre, occasionally reaching 1200 to

[1] Marshall Jacobson, Manager, Forest Productivity, Plum Creek Timber Company, Watkinsville, GA 30677.

Citation for proceedings: Dickens, E.D.; Barnett, J.P.; Hubbard, W.G.; Jokela, E.J., eds. 2004. Slash pine: still growing and growing! Proceedings of the slash pine symposium. Gen. Tech. Rep. SRS-76. Asheville, NC: U.S. Department of Agriculture, Forest Service, Southern Research Station. 148 p.

1300. In 2002, we find a range of 450 to 850 stems per acre covering most of the slash pine planting prescriptions by forest industry. Other landowners, who have different product objectives, may plant at a closer spacing with the goal of obtaining early thinning and having a longer rotation (Bailey 1986).

SITE PREPARATION TECHNOLOGY

Equipment
The type of site preparation equipment and the number of options have changed significantly since the early 1980s. During the 1980s, industry in particular, was still cutting a large amount of natural stands, and this involved a high degree of land clearing with large tracked equipment. Some of this activity still exists, but in the North Florida and Coastal Georgia region preparation is predominantly done with rubber-tired equipment, some of which is designed specifically for the site preparation activity. Due to these changes, site preparation has become somewhat less expensive, and more acres can be done in a given amount of time.

Harvesting
Harvesting is very relevant to the establishment phase for two reasons: we now cut mostly plantations, and utilization has become much more efficient. In 1981, harvesting of older stands, mostly of natural origin, left large amounts of debris, both pine and hardwood, on the ground and standing resulting in high cleanup and site preparation costs. In 2002, we are harvesting many more plantations that are predominantly pine with small hardwood component. Trees that were once left standing are harvested, often leaving a very clean site to begin site preparation.

Bedding Practices
Bedding has become a nearly universal treatment on most coastal slash pine plantations in the Georgia and Florida coastal flatwoods, and is often used in middle coastal plain sites. In 1981, there were still a lot of plantations that were simply burned and planted, and many that were disked. Bedding raised the seedling root system above the high water table on many poorly drained sites, and may reduce woody-plant competition.

Silvicultural Herbicides
Twenty years ago, virtually all site preparation was done by mechanical methods, which included a burn to reduce debris remaining from the harvest. Herbicides for site preparation were largely still in the research phase. Management in 2002 includes a larger mix of chemical and mechanical site preparation as well as less use of fire. Herbaceous weed control after planting is a very common treatment, and in many cases, an industrial company may treat all of its regenerated property to reduce competing herbs and grasses during the first year, and sometimes the second year. This will increase the likelihood of obtaining the early height growth that is now expected with slash pine (Shiver and others 1990).

Establishment Fertilization
Fertilizing slash pine at establishment in 1981 was restricted to a few wet clay soils in the flatwoods. Fertilization was predominantly with phosphorus utilizing ground rock phosphate or triple super phosphate. Since 1981, the fertilization of young stands has expanded a great deal. Sandy spodosols as well as wet ultisols are now commonly fertilized (Shiver and others 1990). The predominant treatment is now diammonium phosphate, and it is most often combined with herbaceous weed control.

Use of Fire
Fire was a universal practice in 1981, being used both at establishment and for prescribed fire during the rotation. During the 1980s, concerns about smoke management and safety has greatly reduced the use of fire. There is also an increasing forestry-suburban interface in the slash pine range (Butry and others 2002). These changes result in a very small use of fire in reforestation of slash pine in 2002. With good mechanical, and often, chemical site preparation, excellent plantations can be established with no fire. Fire remains an important treatment in management strategies used for natural regeneration, or where non-pine objective may be important.

WHY DID WE CHANGE?
When looked at collectively, one could make the argument that everything has changed in slash pine regeneration. Better research information, increased focus on environmental protection, and a focus on productivity have driven change in this 20-year time span.

Research at University of Georgia, University of Florida, and Auburn University have provided long-term information to prove beyond any doubt that we can increase per acre yields, and do it within a disciplined economic environment.

Increased requirements for environmental protection are in place in 2002. Water quality protection, in particular, is a much larger program in 2002. BMP updates and audits are common, and compliance is very high in the South.

There is a much stronger focus on productivity in 2002, and our regeneration practices are prescribed as a part of a silviculture regime that should double or triple the per acre yields that the South has seen historically.

CONCLUSIONS
Through the combined use of operational experience, research from our universities, and an increased focus on environmental issues, foresters have changed nearly every aspect of slash pine regeneration in the past 20 years. Slash pine remains an important commercial species in the south, but is planted on fewer acres today than in 1981. Planting today is largely within the natural range of the species in Georgia and Florida.

LITERATURE CITED

Bailey, R.L. 1986. Rotation age and establishment density for planted slash and loblolly pines. Southern Jour. Applied Forestry 10: 162-168.

Barnett, J.P.; Sheffield, R.M. 2004. Slash pine: characteristics, history, status, and trends. In: Dickens, E.D.; Barnett, J.P.; Hubbard, W.G.; Jokela, E.J., eds. Slash pine: still growing and growing! Proceedings of the slash pine symposium. Gen. Tech. Rep. SRS-76. Asheville, NC: U.S. Department of Agriculture, Forest Service, Southern Research Station: 1-6.

Butry, David T.; Pye, John M.; Prestemon, Jeffrey P. 2002. Prescr bed fire in the interface: separating the people from the trees. Outcalt, K.W., ed. Proceedings of the eleventh biennial southern research conference. Gen. Tech. Rep. SRS-48. Asheville, NC: U.S. Department of Agriculture, Forest Service, Southern Research Station: 132-136.

Outcalt, K.W. 1984. Influence of bed height on the growth of slash and loblolly pine on a Leon fine sand in northeast Florida. Southern Jour. Applied Forestry 8: 29-31.

Shiver, Barry D.; Rheney, John W.; Hitch, Kenneth L. 2000. Loblolly pine outperforms slash pine in southeastern Georgia and northern Florida. Southern Jour. Applied Forestry 24: 31-36.

Shiver, Barry D.; Rheney, John W.; Oppenheimer, Michael J. 1990. Site-preparation methods and early cultural treatments affect growth of flatwoods slash pine plantations. Southern Jour. Applied Forestry 14: 183-188.

South, D.B. 1993. Rationale for growing southern pine seedlings at low seedbed densities. New Forests 7: 63-92.

Vardaman, J.M. 1989. How to make money growing trees. New York, NY: John Wiley & Sons Publishing. 296 p.

COMPETITION CONTROL IN SLASH PINE (*PINUS ELLIOTTII* ENGELM.) PLANTATIONS

J.L. Yeiser and A.W. Ezell[1]

Abstract—Harvesting intensity impacts the composition of the post-harvest recolonizing community and thereby influences the method and quality of post-harvest site preparation and resultant slash pine (*Pinus elliottii* Engelm.) response. Knowledge of the composition of the competitor community, growth state of the competition, and the efficacy and duration of the treatment contributes to appropriate treatment selection. A variety of chemical or mechanical treatments are available for pre-plant, post-plant or midrotation slash pine competitor control. Slash pine responds to weed control, bedding, and fertilization with significant increases in basal area, and total and merchantable volume per acre on many spodosols and nonspodosols. These treatments are the standard for contemporary slash pine plantation management. Control of arborescent, woody shrub, and herbaceous species is a vital part of increased slash pine plantation productivity.

INTRODUCTION

The South leads the United States in production forestry, but on a global scale, growth rates and yields of southern pines are moderate. To meet the challenge of foreign competition in markets, southern forests must be managed more efficiently and productively. Research indicates intensive and cost-effective management can potentially increase growth 50 to 70 percent (Pienaar and Rheney 1996) or more (Stanturf and others 2003) when compared to current conventional plantation management. Vegetation management, specifically chemical site preparation, plus woody shrub and herbaceous weed control, has an important role in increased plantation productivity.

Within the South, slash pine (*Pinus elliottii* Engelm.) is a major contributor to overall fiber production with more than 1.5 million seedlings planted annually (McKeand and others 2003). Slash pine plantation establishment commonly includes either or both mechanical and chemical site preparation. Post preparation sites are typically planted with genetically improved seedlings, fertilized, and treated for herbaceous weeds.

Slash pine responds to competition control (Swindel and others 1988; Shiver and others 1990). Cognoscience of species composition of the competitor community, growth state of the competition, the efficacy of the treatment, and duration of treatment effect contributes to wise treatment selection and justification.

HARVESTING CONSIDERATIONS

The best competition control often begins with utilization of both the crop and weed species on any given harvesting site. Thus, harvesting intensity, subsequent site preparation alternatives, revegetating plant community, and resultant slash pine seedling performance are all related. Increasing harvesting intensity can impact the method of post-harvest preparation, the quality of post-harvest treatments, and seedling response. However, harvesting intensity does not reduce the need for good site preparation if aggressive species occupy the site (Miller and Zhijuan 1994). For example, hard-to-control competitors such as gallberry (*Ilex glabra* (L) Gran), sawpalmetto (*Serenoa repens* (Bartram) Small), vacciumium (*Vaccimium* spp.), waxmyrtle (*Myrica cerifera* L), fetterbursh (*Lyonia lucida* (Lam) K.Koch) staggerbush ((*Lyonia ferruginea* (Walter) Nutall), sweetbay (*Magnolia virginiana* L.), and titi (*Cyrilla racemiflora* L.) commonly occupy poorly drained slash pine sites and will not be controlled by harvesting activities. An appropriate site preparation method addresses these competitors, else they will persist into the rotation, complicate midrotation control, and reduce pine growth. The importance of selecting the appropriate site preparation treatment cannot be overstated. The growth gain associated with site preparation can be detected 20 years later (Shiver and Harrison 2000).

HERBICIDE TREATMENTS

When applied prior to planting, Arsenal® AC, Chopper® EC, Tordon® K, Garlon® 4, Accord® concentrate, Accord® SP, Tordon® 101M, Escort® XP and Velpar® L may be used for the control of labeled grasses, broadleaf weeds, vines and brambles, and woody brush or trees on forest sites (BASF 2000, 2001; Dow AgroSciences 1999, 2001a-b, 2003; DuPont 2003a, 2003c). Slash pine seedlings may exhibit damage symptoms if planted too soon after certain chemical site preparation treatments. Minimum intervals between treatment and planting include: one month after Garlon® 4 at less than 4 quarts per acre, two months after Garlon® 4 at 4 to 8 quarts per acre (Dow AgroSciences 2001a), and six months after Tordon® K or Tordon® 101M (Dow AgroSciences 1999, 2003). If a Velpar® L treatment is to be followed with a second mechanical, chemical, or burning treatment, the second treatment should be delayed until competitors exhibit two complete defoliations (DuPont 2003c). Efficacy of specific herbicide stand-alone and tank mixtures are presented in Minogue 1985, Shiver and others 1991, and Minogue and Zutter 1986.

[1] J.L. Yeiser, Professor, Arthur Temple College of Forestry, Stephen F. Austin State University, Nacogdoches, TX 75962; and A.W. Ezell, Professor, Department of Forest Resources, Mississippi State University, Mississippi State, MS 39762-9681.

Citation for proceedings: Dickens, E.D.; Barnett, J.P.; Hubbard, W.G.; Jokela, E.J., eds. 2004. Slash pine: still growing and growing! Proceedings of the slash pine symposium. Gen. Tech. Rep. SRS-76. Asheville, NC: U.S. Department of Agriculture, Forest Service, Southern Research Station. 148 p.

REVEGETATION

Following site preparation, lower Coastal Plain flatwood sites rapidly revegetate (Conde and others 1983a, 1983b, 1986; Miller and Zhijuan 1994). Relationships between pre- and post-preparation communities have been noted (Schultz and Wilhite 1974; Conde and others 1983a, 1983b, 1986; Miller and Zhijuan 1994). First, with minimum preparation, the most abundant pre-preparation species may also be the most abundant post-preparation species (Conde and others 1986). Second, woody shrubs and herbaceous species differ in their response to site preparation treatments. Mechanical bedding disturbs roots and slows the re-establishment of woody shrubs (Schultz 1976, Conde and others 1986). Treatments with increased root disturbance provide slow recovery of woody shrubs and decrease the resultant density of the shrubs (Schultz 1976; Conde and others 1983a, 1983b, 1986; Miller and Zhijuan 1994). Thus, shrub recovery following a double bed operation is slower than following a single bed (Lauer and Zutter 2001). In each example, herbs proliferate in the absence of woody shrubs (Schultz 1976, Conde and others 1986, Miller and Zhijuan 1994, Lauer and Zutter 2001). Third, post-mechanical recolonizing herb communities may shift from grass towards forbs and blackberry (Miller and Zhijuan 1994). Collectively, this information suggests that a pre-harvest woody shrub and herb inspection can be used as an indicator of the post-harvest competitor communities yet to develop. Accordingly, the manager can prescribe a preparation method, timing, and sequence for woody shrub and herb control based on the impact each has on subsequent slash pine growth.

PRE-PLANT VEGETATION CONTROL

Herbicide Treatments

Pre-plant herbicide applications are less restrictive than post-plant applications because they can accommodate a broader array of rates and products. With proper herbicide selection and application, pre-plant treatments can potentially provide broader control than post-plant treatments (Lauer and Zutter 2001). However, timing of pre-plant applications is critical for overall efficacy and the planting restrictions associated with some herbicides.

Pre-plant, fall-applied (Oct and Nov) herbicide treatments following early bedding improve control of woody shrubs over that of a double bed and provide some first-year herbaceous vegetation control (Lauer and Zutter 2001). Examples of herbicide treatments and per acre rates successfully used as pre-plant fall applications with 20 gallons per acre of total spray volumes are: Garlon® 4+Arsenal® AC+ Accord® concentrate+Timberland 90 (2qt+10oz+24oz+0.75 percent v/v), Garlon® 4+Arsenal® AC+Escort®+Kinetic (1qt+8 oz+2 oz+0.1 percent v/v), Garlon® 4+Arsenal® AC+ Timberland 90 (2qt+8 oz+0.96 percent v/v), Garlon® 4+ Chopper®+Escort® (2qt+24oz+1oz) (Lauer and Zutter 2001). The planting delay restrictions apply in this example (Dow AgroSciences 1999; 2001a,b; 2003; DuPont 2003a,c). The improved competition control from early bedding followed by pre-plant, fall-applied herbicide versus early bedding alone results in better pine growth (4.9 ft versus 4.0 ft after two growing seasons) (Lauer and Zutter 2001).

Pre-plant treatments may be a manager's last opportunity to focus on specific weed problems prior to the midrotation thinning. If not controlled early, difficult-to-control weeds may increase in the early stand, reduce growth, and increase the difficulty of midrotation control. To reduce total costs, managers should combine pre-plant treatments with herbaceous weed control. Managers may select between a band on beds and a broadcast application for the herbaceous control treatments.

Mechanical Treatments

Slash pine is commonly managed on poorly drained sites, thus, bedding is the most common mechanical treatment used. Bedding is either single pass or double pass and rarely conducted without the use of herbicides. Thus, what becomes critical is the proper selection of herbicides and application timing if the land manager is to optimize the benefit of the bedding operation. On single bedded sites, vegetation control can be enhanced with a pre-plant or post-plant herbaceous treatment. Post-plant Arsenal® AC+Oust® (4+2 ounces per acre) controls herbs and suppresses shrubs (Lauer and Zutter 2001). Escort® mixtures (correctly timed) are appropriate if bracken fern, woody vines, or blackberry are issues. Timing is critical for herbaceous treatments that are used also for the control or suppression of woody shrubs. Good herbicidal coverage of foliage prior to the first flush of growth is essential. May or June applications will likely provide poor control (Kline and others 1994).

Shrub cover is reduced more with a double bed than with a single bed treatment (Lauer and Zutter 2001). Controlled shrubs are rapidly replaced by herbs. Double bedding without post-plant herbaceous control may not result in enhanced seedling performance because the short-term impact of woody shrub and herbaceous vegetation on seedling growth is similar (Lauer and Glover 1998).

POST-PLANT VEGETATION CONTROL

Post-plant vegetation management takes the form of either herbaceous or woody release. Some treatments have the capacity to control herbaceous and woody competitors. Perhaps the best management strategy is to control the woody competition prior to planting and the herbaceous competition after planting. However, when one or both types of control are needed, release operations in slash pine increase growth. After five growing seasons, slash pine total height responses average 2.8, 5.4, and 6.7 feet due to first-year herbaceous control alone, shrub control alone, and both herbaceous and shrub control, respectively (Lauer and Glover 1998). Good first-year shrub control can eliminate the need for follow-up or annual shrub control treatments (Lauer and Glover 1998, Zutter and Miller 1998). Following initial control, woody shrubs do not respond to herbaceous weed control (Lauer and Glover 1998, Zutter and Miller 1998), remain suppressed for years (Zutter and Miller 1998), and do not rapidly recolonize from seed. Recolonization is of interest because woody vegetation has the potential to limit growth in midrotation stands (Pienaar and others 1983, Oppenheimer and others 1989). Therefore, managers should carefully select site preparation treatments for shrub control and long-term pine growth. Lack of shrub control at the onset of the rotation (1) means reduced early pine growth, (2) allows shrubs to increase throughout early stand development, (3) complicates midrotation control, and (4) contributes to reduced late rotation growth. Although Lauer and Glover (1998) reported that pine response to shrub control was large compared to herbaceous weed control, it does not reduce the significant contribution of herbaceous weed control to slash pine seedling performance (Lauer and Glover 1998).

Herbaceous species will typically proliferate on prepared sites, especially if the woody shrubs are controlled. Accordingly, managers commonly select a herbicide treatment for herb control. When used properly, herbaceous release significantly enhances slash pine growth. For example, in a recent study, Ezell and Yeiser (2003) tested a number of herbaceous release treatments and found that 13 oz. Oustar® per ac provided the best overall competition control and growth response over a two-year period on sites in Alabama and Louisiana. Some trees were as much as nine feet tall after two growing seasons. By comparison, Lauer and Zutter (2001) noted that broad-spectrum control of herbs could be difficult with Oustar®. Thus, the species composition on the site is extremely important in determining final results. Arsenal® AC, Oust® XP, Oustar®, Escort® XP, and Velpar® (L or DF) are all used successfully to control herbaceous competition in slash pine plantations (BASF 2000; DuPont 2002a-b, 2003a, c). Proper use of herbicides includes a thorough familiarity with herbicide labels. Herbicide labels should always be consulted for any restrictions to applications or site conditions. Examples of application restrictions include the lack of an approved label for applying Arsenal® AC+Oust® XP and Arsenal® AC+Escort® XP tank mixtures over the top of slash pine seedlings. Interestingly, individual products (Arsenal® AC, Oust® XP, and Escort® XP), and a pre-mix blend of Oust® XP and Escort® XP (Oust® Extra) are labeled for use in slash pine (BASF 2000; DuPont 2002a, 2003a; DuPont 2003b). Furthermore, site conditions, such as water, can limit applications of Oust® XP, Escort® XP, or Velpar®. For specific details on water restrictions, see product labels (DuPont 2002a, 2003a-c).

VEGETATION CONTROL AND FERTILIZATION
Slash pine seedlings respond to bedding, vegetation control and fertilization (Colbert and others 1990, Shiver and others 1990, Shiver and Harrison 2000). At age 8, complete vegetation control in the flatwoods of southeast Georgia and Florida provided the most consistent improvement in slash performance (Shiver and others 1990). Bedding and fertilization provided significant growth improvement regardless of soil group. At age 20, bedding provided a total height gain of 1.50 feet. Total vegetation control increased total height 5.35 feet and d.b.h 0.9 inches. Fertilization enhanced total height 5.11 feet and d.b.h 0.6 inches. Projections from this study show intensified silvicultural practices can boost volume over conventional practices by 128 percent with a rate of return of 12 percent (Yin and others 1998). Slash pine responses to vegetation control and fertilization are additive (Baker 1973, Swindel and others 1988) although synergistic responses have been reported (Tiarks and Haywood 1981). In the latter case, vegetation control (hoeing) and fertilization together increased total biomass 347 percent, 207 percent more than expected if the two treatments had been additive (Tiarks and Haywood 1981). Although response to phosphorus commonly follows soon after application, it may not significantly affect pine growth for many years (Tiarks 1983; Haywood 1995).

MIDROTATION OPTIONS
Midrotation competition control treatments in slash pine are increasing across the South. Research shows slash pine responds very well to competition control in stands 10 to 15 years old. Oppenheimer and others (1989) controlled the vegetation in 9 to 15 year old slash pine plantations for 10 years. In response, height, basal area, total volume, and merchantable volume all increased significantly. While this type of control may not be operationally feasible, the results demonstrate that the species will respond to midrotation treatments.

Shiver (1994) examined the response of a slash pine plantation 14 years after it had received a midrotation competition control treatment. The plantations were 10 to 12 years old at the time of treatment and were located on a range of drainage categories. Overall, the worst results were generated on the poorly drained sites. However, on the sites with adequate drainage, volume was increased by 0.25 cords per acre per year.

Zutter (1999) noted similar results on a well-drained site. He studied slash pine plantations four years after an age 12 treatment of hexazinone at a rate of 1.4 lbs active ingredient per acre. Basal area, average d.b.h., and volume all increased. In his study, merchantable volume increased 0.33 cords per acre per year after the treatment.

Overall, it appears that midrotation competition control can be a cost-effective treatment in slash pine plantations. Applications will generate best results on better-drained sites and on those where the pre-treatment level of competition is restricting pine growth.

LITERATURE CITED
Baker, J.B. 1973. Intensive cultural practices increase growth of juvenile slash pine in Florida sandhills. Forest Science 19: 197-202.

BASF. 2000. Arsenal applicators concentrate herbicide. BASF Corporation. Research Triangle Park, NC. 6 p.

BASF. 2001. Chopper herbicide. BASF Corporation. Research Triangle Park, NC 27709. 5 p.

Colbert, S.R.; Jokela, E.J.; Neary, D.G. 1990. Effects of annual fertilization and sustained weed control on dry matter partitioning, leaf area, and growth efficiency of juvenile loblolly and slash pine. Forest Science 36(4): 995-1014.

Conde, L.F.; Swindel, B.F.; Smith, J.E. 1983a. Plant species cover, frequency, and biomass: early responses to clearcutting, chopping, and bedding in *Pinus elliottii* flatwoods. Forest Ecology and Management 6: 307-317.

Conde, L.F.; Swindel, B.F.; Smith, J.E. 1983b. Plant species cover, frequency, and biomass: Early responses to clearcutting, chopping, and bedding in *Pinus elliottii* flatwoods. Forest Ecology and Management 6: 319-331.

Conde, L.F.; Swindel, B.F.; Smith, J.E. 1986. Five years of vegetation changes following conversion of pine flatwoods to *Pinus elliottii* plantations. Forest Ecology and Management 15: 295-300.

Dow AgroSciences. 1999. Tordon K specialty herbicide. Dow AgroSciences. Indianapolis, IN. 6 p.

Dow AgroSciences. 2001a. Accord Concentrate herbicide. Dow AgroSciences. Indianapolis, IN. 14 p.

Dow AgroSciences. 2001b. Forestry Garlon 4 specialty herbicide. Dow AgroSciences. Indianapolis, IN. 4 p.

Dow AgroSciences. 2003. Tordon 101 Mixture specialty herbicide. Dow AgroSciences. Indianapolis, IN. 7 p.

DuPont. 2002a. DuPont Oust XP herbicide. E.I. du Pont de Nemours and Company. Wilmington, DE. 11 p.

DuPont. 2002b. DuPont Oustar herbicide. E.I. du Pont de Nemours and Company. Wilmington, DE. 7 p.

DuPont. 2003a. DuPont Escort XP herbicide. E.I. du Pont de Nemours and Company. Wilmington, DE. 11 p.

DuPont. 2003b. DuPont Oust Extra herbicide. E.I. du Pont de Nemours and Company. Wilmington, DE. 11 p.

DuPont. 2003c. DuPont Velpar L herbicide. E.I. du Pont de Nemours and Company. Wilmington, DE. 19 p.

Ezell, A.W.; Yeiser, J.L. 2003. Preemergent vs. postemergent weed control applications in slash pine plantations: second year results. Proceedings Southern Weed Science Society 56: 124-125.

Haywood, J.D. 1995. Responses of young slash pine on poorly drained to somewhat poorly drained silt loam soils to site preparation and fertilization treatments. USDA Forest Service Southern Forest Experiment Station Research Note SO-379. 5 p.

Kline, W.N.; Troth, J.L.; Shiver, B.D. 1994. Maximizing pine yields in the southern flatwoods using Garlon herbicide. Down to Earth 49(2).

Lauer, D.K.; Glover, G.R. 1998. Early pine response to control of herbaceous and shrub vegetation in the flatwoods. Southern Journal of Applied Forestry 15(4): 201-208.

Lauer, D.K.; Zutter, B.R. 2001. Vegetation cover response and second-year loblolly and slash pine response following bedding and pre- and post-plant herbicide applications in Florida. Southern Journal of Applied Forestry 25(2): 75-83.

McKeand, S.; Mulliin, T.; Byram, T.; White, T. 2003. Deployment of genetically improved loblolly and slash pines. Southern Journal of Applied Forestry 101(3): 32-37.

Miller, J.H.; Zh juan, Qiu. 1994. Pine growth and plant community response to chemical vs. mechanical site preparation for establishing loblolly and slash pine. In: Edwards, M.B., Ed. Proceedings of the eighth biennial southern silvicultural research conference; 1994 November 1-4; Auburn, AL. General Technical Report SRS-1, Ashville, NC; USDA Forest Service, Southern Forest Experiment Station: 537-548.

Minogue, P.J. 1985. Second-year results of 1983 flatwoods site preparation herbicide screening trials. Auburn University Silvicultural Herbicide Cooperative Research Note 85-13, Auburn University, AL. 35 p.

Minogue, P.J.; Zutter, B.R. 1986. Second-year results of herbicide screening trials for forest site preparation in the flatwoods. Proceedings Southern Weed Science Society 39: 219.

Oppenheimer, M.J.; Shiver, B.D.; Rheney, J.W. 1989. Ten-year growth response of midrotation slash pine plantations to control of competing vegetation. Canadian Journal Forest Research 19: 329-334.

Pienaar, L.V.; Rheney, J.W. 1996. Potential productivity of intensively managed pine plantations. A Report to the Georgia Consortium for Technological Competitiveness in Pup and Paper Fiber Supply. 41 p.

Pienaar, L.V.; Rheney, J.W.; Shiver, B.D. 1983. Response to control of competing vegetation in site-prepared slash pine plantations. Southern Journal of Applied Forestry 7(1): 38-45.

Schultz, R.O.; Wilhite, L.P. 1974. Changes in a flatwoods site following intensive preparation. Forest Science 20(3): 230-237.

Schultz, R.P. 1976. Environmental change after site preparation and slash pine planting on a flatwoods site. USDA Forest Service Research Paper SE-156. 20 p.

Shiver, B.D. 1994. Response and economics of midrotation competition control in southern pine plantations. Proceedings Southern Weed Science Society 47: 85-92.

Shiver, B.D.; Harrison, W.M. 2000. Slash pine site preparation study: age 20 results. Plantation Management Research Cooperative Technical Report 2000-4. pp 17.

Shiver, B.D.; Knowe, S.A.; Edwards, M.B.; Kline, W.N. 1991. Comparison of herbicide treatments for controlling common Coastal Plain flatwoods species. Southern Journal of Applied Forestry 15(4): 187-193.

Shiver, B.D.; Rheney, J.W.; Oppenheimer, M.J. 1990. Site-preparation method and early cultural treatments affect growth of flatwoods slash pine plantations. Southern Journal of Applied Forestry 14(4): 183-188.

Stanturf, J.A.; Kellison, R.C.; Broerman, F.S.; Jones, S.B. 2003. Productivity of southern pine plantations: where are we and how did we get here? Journal of Forestry 101(3): 26-31.

Swindel, B.F.; Neary, D.G.; Comerford, N.B.; Blakeslee, G.M. 1988. Fertilization and competition control accelerate early southern pine growth on flatwoods. Southern Journal of Applied Forestry 12(2): 116-121.

Swindel, B.F.; Neary, D.G.; Comerford, N.B. [and others]. 1988. Fertilization and competition control accelerate early southern pine growth on flatwoods. Southern Journal of Applied Forestry 12(2): 116-121.

Tiarks, A.E. 1983. Effect of site preparation and fertilization on slash pine growing on a good site. In: Jones, Earle P., Jr., ed. Proceedings of the second biennial southern silvicultural research conference; 1982 November 4-5; Atlanta, GA. General Technical Report SE-24. Asheville, NC: USDA Forest Service, Southeastern Forest Experiment Station: 34-39.

Tiarks, A.E.; Haywood, J.D. 1981. Response of newly established slash pine to cultivation and fertilization. USDA Forest Service Southern Forest Experiment Station Research Note RN-272. 4 p.

Yin, R.; Pienaar, L.V.; Aronow, M.E. 1998. The productivity and profitability of fiber farming. Journal Forestry 11(11): 13-18.

Zutter, B.R. 1999. Response of a midrotation slash pine stand to hexazinone. In: Haywood, James D. ed. Proceedings of the tenth biennial southern silvicultural research conference; 1999 February 16-18; Shreveport, LA. General Technical Report SRS-30. Asheville, NC: USDA Forest Service, Southern Research Station: 446-448.

Zutter, B.R.; Miller, J.H. 1998. Eleventh-year response of loblolly pine and competing vegetation to woody and herbaceous plant control on a Georgia flatwoods site. Southern Journal of Applied Forestry 22(2): 88-95.

NUTRIENT MANAGEMENT OF SOUTHERN PINES

Eric J. Jokela[1]

Abstract—Fertilization of slash (*Pinus elliottii* Engelm.) and loblolly pine (*P. taeda* L.) stands has increased dramatically over the last two decades. As a cost effective silvicultural tool, fertilization has been successfully applied for increasing forestland productivity. Effective operational use of fertilizers relies on a variety of diagnostic systems to identify site nutrient status and potential responsiveness of candidate stands. General principles of forest nutrition, including guides for implementing fertilization prescriptions, are discussed.

INTRODUCTION

In the southeastern United States the dominant plantation species are slash (*Pinus elliottii* Engelm.) and loblolly pine (*P. taeda* L.), occupying approximately 13 and 30 million acres, respectively (Sheffield and Knight 1982; Sheffield and others 1983). The productivity of these even-aged, single-species plantations can be influenced by a wide spectrum of processes, including soil nutrient supply, genetics, and pest dynamics (fig. 1). Early site occupancy and the development of a large and functioning leaf area represent important strategies for enhancing pine productivity, and fertilization is one of the most cost-effective silvicultural treatments that forest landowners can apply to increase growth rates and financial returns. As many forest soils throughout the South tend to be infertile, fertilizers are commonly applied to southern pine stands at-time-of-planting and at mid-rotation (6 to 15 yr) to enhance and sustain rapid tree growth. Recent statistics suggest that the area of southern pine stands receiving fertilizer additions in 2001 was about 1.3 million acres, down slightly from an annual peak of 1.5 million acres in 1999 (NCSFNC 2002). Levels of financial return associated with fertilizer applications depend on the magnitude and duration of growth

responses, costs associated with the fertilizer investment, and product values. It is safe to say that the potential productivity of most sites in the South is not being realized, and that nutrient limitations are largely responsible.

Effective operational use of fertilizers requires diagnostic systems, used individually or in combination, which accurately identify site nutrient status, needs, and potential responsiveness. Soil classification, visual criteria, foliage and soil testing, and growth and yield models can all aid decision making. Each of the methods has operational advantages and limitations because of differences in reliability, costs, and technical skills required for application (see Pritchett and Comerford 1981; Jokela and others 1991a; Amateis and others 2000). Understanding stand development dynamics and interactions among silvicultural treatments can also aid interpretations and the evaluation of treatment efficacy (Albaugh and others 1998; Jokela and Martin 2000). This paper addresses issues of soil fertility, growth-limiting nutrients, and fertilizer recommendations for slash and loblolly pine. Although many of the principles discussed in this paper are applicable across the South for these species, emphasis will be placed on lower Coastal Plain sites of Florida and Georgia where both slash and loblolly pine are commonly planted.

PRINCIPAL DIAGNOSTIC TOOLS

Soil Groups

As a diagnostic tool, soil descriptions are commonly used for characterizing and classifying sites as potential candidates for forest fertilization. Soil groupings, based on easily recognizable features, are used to identify sites where available nutrient supplies are low, or where other site factors (for example, moisture availability) influence growth. CRIFF soil groups (A-H), defined using soil drainage, texture and depth of the subsurface soil layers (Fisher and Garbett 1980; see also description in Fox 2004; Jokela and Long 2000) have found application in guiding operational fertilization efforts in the South. Average stand responses to fertilizers differ significantly among soil groups and, in some cases, knowing the soil type (for example, CRIFF A) is adequate for making fertilization decisions and estimating

Processes Controlling/Limiting Stand Productivity

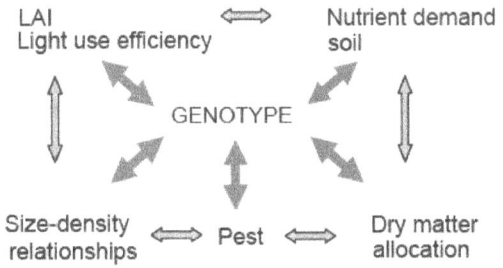

Figure 1—Processes and interactions that affect the productivity of southern pine stands.

[1] Eric J. Jokela, Professor of Silviculture and Forest Nutrition, School of Forest Resources and Conservation, University of Florida, Gainesville, FL 32611.

Citation for proceedings: Dickens, E.D.; Barnett, J.P.; Hubbard, W.G.; Jokela, E.J., eds. 2004. Slash pine: still growing and growing! Proceedings of the slash pine symposium. Gen. Tech. Rep. SRS-76. Asheville, NC: U.S. Department of Agriculture, Forest Service, Southern Research Station. 148 p.

response. In other cases, responses may vary significantly within a soil group, indicating that current groupings over-simplify important factors influencing response, and that additional information is necessary to increase prediction accuracy. Soil maps have been prepared for many industrial lands and they have been broadly integrated and applied to aid management decisions on a variety of issues such as management intensity, fertilization rates, species selection, site preparation, site quality (productivity classes), and disease hazard ratings.

Foliar and Soil Testing

Chemical analyses of soils and foliage have been widely used to evaluate the potential response of sites to fertilizer treatments. These techniques are based on the assumption that a stand will respond to an added nutrient when foliar or soil concentrations fall below established critical levels. The reliability of these techniques increase as the similarity between the candidate stands and reference stands used to derive the relationships increase. Although critical foliage nutrient concentrations have been published for southern pines (table 1), they are not known with any exactness, especially for elements other than N and P. Hence, they are used principally as qualitative guides. Variation in nutrient levels due to foliage age, sampling position within the crown, sampling date and analytical procedures can complicate interpretations, particularly when values are near the critical levels. Standardized sampling (for example, dormant season, upper third of the crown, fully elongated current-year needles) and analysis procedures are, therefore, essential for successful use of either foliar or soil analysis. The critical level concept further assumes that other elements are not limiting. Experience has revealed that multiple nutrient deficiencies can exist on some sites (see discussion below), and that evaluating the balance of nutrients can improve diagnostic capabilities (Comerford and Fisher 1984; Adams and Allen 1985).

Visual Symptoms and Fertilizer Field Trials

The inherent appeal of using visual symptoms for guiding fertilizer prescriptions reside in the potential simplicity of making quick field diagnoses without the need for laboratory determinations. Foliar discoloration (chlorosis, necrosis), needle twisting, irregular branching patterns (e.g., lack of apical dominance (fig. 2), premature needle fall, and dieback of young shoots are among the variety of symptoms used to describe nutrient deficiencies in conifers (Stone 1968). However, as multiple nutrient deficiencies (for example, N, P, K, micronutrients) are possible in southern pine stands, foliar analyses are often used in conjunction with visual symptoms and soil groups to confirm initial interpretations. To be reliable, visual criteria must be calibrated with stand response data.

Over the last decade, interpretations of what is considered "normal growth" among land managers have also changed dramatically. Prior to the implementation of intensive silvicultural growing systems, that include improved seedling quality, proper planting techniques, superior genotypes, site preparation, competition control and fertilization treatments, expectations were that 3-yr-old trees would average

Figure 2—Copper deficiency in young loblolly pine growing on a sandy Spodosol in north central Florida. Note: deficiency is expressed in lack of apical dominance of the terminal and leading lateral shoots.

Table 1—Foliar nutrient guidelines (minimum) for southern pines

Nutrient	Slash pine	Loblolly pine
	- - - - - - - - - percent - - - - - - - - -	
N	1.0	1.2
P	0.09	0.12
K	0.25 – 0.30	0.30
Ca	0.08 – 0.12	0.15
Mg	0.06	0.08
S	0.08	0.10
	- - - - - - parts per million - - - - - -	
B	4 – 8	4 – 8
Zn	10 – 20	10 – 20
Cu	1.5 – 3	2 – 3
Mn	20 – 40	20 – 40
Fe	15 – 35	20 – 40

Source: Allen (1987); Pritchett and Comerford (1983); Wells and others (1973).

about five ft tall. Currently, when using a variety of the treatment combinations listed above, it is not uncommon to have stands average 10 to 12 ft tall during the same time period. These well-established plantations also tend to be quite uniform in height and character across the site.

Experimental field trials have undoubtedly been the most reliable approach for estimating fertilizer responses. The fertilizer rate-growth response relationships commonly used today were largely developed through regional experiments established by cooperative forest research programs involving forest industry and southern universities (for example, University of Florida, North Carolina State University). In addition, operational monitoring plots have been used by many companies to corroborate suspected nutrient deficiencies and to estimate growth responses on a variety of soil types. These "in-house" plots, that include replicated fertilized and non-fertilized treatments (strips), are monitored over time, and their results are incorporated into geospatially based maps.

Response Models

A variety of models (primarily for mid-rotation aged stands) have been developed for slash and loblolly pine that relate tree and stand level responses (for example, dominant height, basal area, stand volume) to fertilization. Predictor variables have included site index, soil drainage class, fertilizer treatment, stand age, number of surviving trees and dominant height at time of treatment (Bailey and others 1989; Martin and others 1999; Amateis and others 2000). Response models, based on site and stand conditions, predict average growth responses for broad site types and can be useful for identifying potentially responsive stands, and selecting appropriate fertilizer treatments. Independent field testing and calibration by users is still required, however, as empirical models may not accurately account for changes in future conditions.

Process-based computer simulation models are also becoming available to aid site-specific fertilizer decisions by forest managers. The SSAND (Soil Supply and Nutrient Demand) model, for example, was recently developed at the University of Florida to diagnose nutrient limitations and determine fertilization regimes necessary to achieve preset stand production goals (Adegbidi and others 2002). With this type of model, the user determines a desired level of productivity. Simulations of soil nutrient supply, based on input variables, are compared with the stand nutrient demand estimates. If stand nutrient demand exceeds soil supply, fertilization regimes can be tested to determine the most efficient treatment for meeting production goals and plant nutrient demands.

RATES OF FERTILIZER APPLICATION

Fertilizer recommendations for southern pine stands have not been determined as precisely as those for agronomic crops. Rapidly growing southern pine stands place high nutrient demands on the soil, especially during the early stages of canopy development. Yet, few estimates of uptake exist for such stands, but these data are critical for quantifying plant nutrient demands and developing fertilizer prescriptions based on soil nutrient supply. Recently, Adegbidi and others (2003) reported that rapidly growing

(aboveground biomass ~16 tons per ac) 4-yr-old loblolly pine stands (CRIFF C soils) had accumulated about 175 lbs N per ac and 20 lbs P per ac, with the crown (foliage, branches) being the dominant pools (52 to 59 percent) for these elements. About 23 percent of the N and 29 percent of the P was accumulated in roots. Cation (K, Ca, Mg) accumulations were also highest in the aboveground components (~50 percent). Approximately 77 lbs per ac K, 65 lbs per ac Ca, and 25 lbs per ac Mg had accumulated in the total tree biomass by age 4 yr. In contrast, Colbert (1988) reported that aboveground nutrient accumulations were considerably lower for extensively managed, slow-growing (aboveground biomass ~ 1 ton per ac) loblolly pine stands on similar soils. For example, aboveground accumulations of N, P K, Ca, and Mg at age 4 yr averaged about 9, 1, 3.5, 3, and 2 lbs per ac, respectively. These results clearly indicate that rapidly growing stands place correspondingly higher levels of demand on soil nutrient pools and, in comparison to extensively managed stands, will require more frequent fertilizer additions to sustain high levels of production. Frequent removal of pine straw from the site may also necessitate the need for more frequent additions of fertilizers (Morris and others 1992).

When developing fertilizer prescriptions, practitioners must be aware that past management practices will influence both the timing and rates of future fertilizer treatments. In addition, trees are generally inefficient in terms of fertilizer recovery. For example, Fisher and Binkley (2000) suggested that less than 25 percent of the fertilizers applied to forest stands are taken up by trees, with about 25 percent being immobilized in soil microbes and organic matter, and an equally large but variable pool being lost through volatilization and leaching. Removal of understory vegetation may improve nutrient retention by the trees and additional research is required to determine if low application rates or repeated applications substantially improve fertilizer recovery by trees.

Described below are fertilizer recommendations commonly used across a variety of soil types in the Coastal Plain of Florida and Georgia. Treatment rates are presented for both young and established (after crown closure) stands and it is assumed that the stands have received effective understory competition control treatments at establishment. As with any silvicultural treatment, local conditions may cause results to deviate from those reported here. Therefore, the recommendations listed below should be used as general guides only. For example, as additional nutrient ramping studies are completed with southern pines, the sequence and amount of fertilizers required to sustain desired growth rates may change. Also, variable timber markets will directly affect the economic viability of different treatment regimes.

Phosphorus plus N, and P alone, are the nutrient elements that tend to be the most widely applied to southern pine stands. Application of N alone is not generally recommended in young stands because it often stimulates competing vegetation. In some cases, K and other macronutrients may also limit growth once N and P demands have been met (table 2). The fertilizer rate prescription ratio for southern pines is approximated as 100:10:35 (N,P,K). Similarly, examples of micronutrient deficiencies have been documented

Table 2—Recommended fertilizer application rates (elemental – pounds per acre) for loblolly and slash pine when diagnosed as limiting for growth

Species	Stand phase	N	P	K	Ca, Mg, S, B, Cu, Mn, Fe[a]
Loblolly	At planting	40 – 50	25 – 50	50 – 80	As needed based on foliar analysis (table 1) or other diagnostics
	Canopy closure	175 – 200	25 – 50	50 – 80	As above
Slash	At planting	40 – 50	25 – 50	50 – 80	As above
	Canopy closure	150 – 200	25 – 50	50 – 80	As above

[a] Approximate application rates based on stand needs: 25 to 40 pounds Ca per acre, 25 pounds Mg per acre, 25 to 40 pounds S per acre, 0.5 to 1 pound B per acre, 3 to 5 pounds Cu per acre, 3 to 5 pounds Mn per acre, and 10 to 15 pounds Fe per acre.

Source: Allen (1987), Jokela and others (1991), South and others (2003).

(for example, B, Cu, Mn, Zn) in southern pine stands, and are often induced when intensive silvicultural practices accelerate early stand growth. It should be noted that recommended fertilizer application rates for micronutrients are not known with any exactness and care should be taken to avoid possible toxicities in southern pine stands. For example, elemental application rates of B should not exceed about 1 lb per ac.

CRIFF A AND B SOILS
(Very Poorly to Somewhat Poorly Drained - Bays and Wet Savannas)
These soils are typically found in nearly level depressions, stream terraces, and broad wet flats. Excessive soil moisture and lack of available P commonly limit pine growth. Without adequate P nutrition, the pines often are no more than 40-45 feet in height after 25 years, and the stand leaf area is very sparse and consists of short, yellowish needles.

Young Stands
Fertilization with P or a combination of P and N is recommended at planting and growth responses can be dramatic on these soils. Yield differences of 2-3 fold have been documented following fertilization. For example, a 25-yr-old slash pine stand growing in the Panhandle of Florida produced about 4500 ft³ per ac of wood with fertilization (50 lbs per ac P) compared to 2040 ft³ per ac without fertilizer additions (Jokela and others 1989). Delaying fertilizer applications on such sites will cause significant growth losses.

If these sites have never had a history of fertilizer applications, approximately 40 to 50 lbs per ac of elemental P and 40-50 lbs per ac of elemental N are recommended rates. The superphosphates are the principal P fertilizers used when only P is required (triple superphosphate (0-44-0) and normal superphosphate (0-20-0). If a combination of N and P is desired, diammonium phosphate - (DAP) (18-46-0) represents an excellent fertilizer choice. An application rate of 250 lbs per ac DAP would, for example, provide an elemental equivalent of 45 lbs per ac N and 50 lbs per ac P. If stands growing on these soils received P applications late in the previous rotation, then 125-150 lbs per ac DAP would be applied at establishment.

When used in conjunction with N + P fertilization, herbaceous weed control treatments can augment pine growth responses on these soils. Results recently showed that volume growth of 8-yr-old loblolly pine stands growing on A group soils averaged 713 ft³ per ac when no fertilizer or weed control treatments were applied (Jokela and others 2000). In contrast, volume was doubled (1430 ft³ per ac) when herbaceous weed control was combined with 250 lbs per ac DAP. Volume growth for the fertilizer and herbaceous weed control treatments, when applied alone at planting, averaged 1202 ft³ per ac and 803 ft³ per ac, respectively. It is clear that on these soils weed control alone did not elicit much growth response, presumably because of the overarching limitations due to P deficiency.

Established Stands
Fertilizer requirements for older stands are based on the same principles as young stands. However, it is often more difficult to predict the need for fertilizers in older stands because deep root penetration may allow absorption of nutrients from subsoil horizons, even though surface horizons are low in available nutrients. Surface layers of organic debris (for example, pine needles) also serve as a nutrient reservoir, and can release nutrients for the pines as the material slowly decomposes (Polglase and others 1992). Deficiencies of N and P are most pronounced following crown closure. Decomposition processes generally slow down and nutrient availability decreases because they are immobilized in the stem, bark, branches, roots and foliage of the pines and understory plants.

Fertilization with combinations of N and P are recommended for closed canopy stands. The combined elemental treatment gives larger and more consistent responses than either element applied alone. Application rates of approximately 150 - 200 lbs per ac elemental N and 25 lbs per ac elemental P at about age 10 on A group soils and about 6-8 years on the sandier textured B group soils will usually result in growth responses averaging 50 ft³ per ac per yr or more. Fertilizer responses normally last for about 6 - 8 years. Although N application rates above 200 lbs per ac (with P) can result in higher levels of growth response, they are not generally economically justifiable on most soils. Common fertilizer sources would include DAP, superphosphates, and urea.

Evidence from six fertilizer trials suggested that land managers have flexibility in applying fertilizers either as a single or split mid-rotation fertilizer treatments without impacting the biological magnitudes of response or longevity (Jokela and Stearns-Smith 1993). For example, if 200 lbs per ac N and 25 lbs per ac P was the recommended treatment, it could be applied at age 10 years as a single combined treatment (DAP + urea). Alternatively, 125 lbs per ac DAP (equivalent to 22.5 lbs per ac N + 25 lbs per ac P) could be applied at age 10 years with a follow-up urea treatment (178 lbs N per ac; 395 lbs per ac urea) within 2 years. The split N treatment has the potential to provide economic benefits because a significant portion of the capital costs of fertilizer can be postponed for up to 2 years, and thereby reduce the total carrying costs over the investment period. It should be noted that mid-rotation fertilizer applications that include urea are generally recommended for all soils between January and May to avoid volatilization losses of N. In addition, if the stand is being managed for sawtimber, a second mid-rotation fertilizer application (150-200 lbs per ac N + 25 lbs per ac P) would typically be prescribed the year after thinning to sustain acceptable growth rates until rotation age is achieved. The actual age for the thinning treatment will vary among sites, but commonly occurs when merchantable height of the stand is > 40 ft.

CRIFF C AND D SOILS
(Very Poorly to Moderately Well Drained - Flatwoods Spodosols)
The Flatwoods represent one of the most extensive groups of forest soils in the Coastal Plain. The somewhat poorly to moderately well drained C and D group soils (Spodosols) developed in coarse textured sediments (acidic, sand to loamy sand texture) low in native fertility. Nitrogen and P fertilizer additions commonly elicit significant growth response in both slash and loblolly pine stands.

Young Stands
Fertilizer and herbaceous weed control treatments applied alone or in combination at time of planting can significantly increase pine growth on C and D group soils. These soils tend to be deficient in both N and P, although levels of K and micronutrients (B, Mn, Cu and Zn) are also in marginal supply. Broadcast applications of approximately 200 to 250 lbs per ac DAP (40 to 50 lbs per ac elemental N and 40 to 50 lbs per ac elemental P) represents the most common treatment for these soils if the sites have not previously received fertilizer additions. Pre-plant chemical site preparation or herbaceous weed control treatments applied in the spring of the first growing season can also enhance the probability and magnitude of growth responses derived from fertilizer applications. Loblolly pine, because of higher nutrient demands, has generally been more responsive than slash pine to fertilizer and weed control treatment on these soils. For example, 8th year volume response of loblolly pine on C and D group soils averaged 32 percent when 45 lbs per ac N + 50 lbs per ac P was applied at planting (Jokela and others 2000). Growth responses to the combination treatment of fertilizer + herbaceous weed control averaged 52 percent. Slash pine treatment responses were generally smaller in magnitude and averaged 10 percent for the combined treatment.

With the application of more intensive management systems, foresters must recognize that rapid growth rates can result in induced deficiencies (dilution effects) of other elements (for example, micronutrients) on these sandy soils, and periodic monitoring is warranted to avoid subacute deficiencies (fig. 2). Subacute deficiencies of Mn, Cu, B, and Zn on CRIFF B, C and D group soils appear to be easily corrected from a single application of a needed micronutrient at time of planting, and it may suffice for the entire rotation. For example, slash pine responses to Mn additions averaged 32 ft[3] per ac per yr above the control over 16 years (Jokela and others 1991). If deficiencies of K and micronutrients are suspected, on the basis of soil or foliar tests, a mixed fertilizer such as 10-10-10 + micronutrients should be applied at rates of 500 to 600 lbs per ac rather than the DAP treatment. Custom blended fertilizers, that contain both macro- and micronutrients, are also an option.

Established Stands
Older southern pine stands (post crown closure) growing in the Flatwoods are commonly deficient in both N and P. Typically, these sites are fertilized at about age 6 years with 150 lbs N per ac and 25 lbs P per ac. Growth responses average approximately 55 ft[3] per ac per yr when both N and P are applied. Note that the application of N or P alone is not recommended on these soils because growth responses have been largest and most consistent to the combined N + P treatment. Fertilizer responses on these soils commonly persist for 6-8 years. A second mid-rotation application of N and P (200 N, 25 P per ac) may be applied at age 12-13 years to sustain growth through rotation (perhaps following the first thinning). The most common fertilizer sources used for this prescription are a combination of DAP and urea. Where K is deficient, it should be included in the fertilizer program at rates ranging from 50 to 80 lbs K per ac. Common K fertilizer sources would include KCl (muriate of potash), KSO_4 or a mixed fertilizer material. A foliar test should be used to confirm suspected deficiencies of these elements, including micronutrients.

CRIFF E AND F SOILS
(Moderately Well to Well Drained - Uplands)
These Coastal Plain soils are found in upland areas and range from relatively deep, moderately well-drained sands to well-drained loamy sands and sandy clays. Many of the existing stands planted on these soils were established on abandoned farmlands, which have been seriously eroded. Unless the site has been in recent agricultural production, these soil groups tend to be naturally deficient in N and P.

Young Stands
These upland soils often receive combinations of mechanical tillage and chemical site preparation treatments. With good initial weed control, pine stands would typically receive N and P fertilization (100-150 N per ac, 25 P per ac) at about age 5 years. In some cases, DAP (200 lbs per ac) applications are made at establishment and the efficacy of fertilizer additions are enhanced when combined with herbaceous weed control. For example, when compared to untreated plots, 8th year loblolly pine volume on E group soils averaged 33 percent more on plots receiving 45 lbs

per ac N + 50 lbs per ac P (DAP – 250 lbs per ac), and 53 percent more on plots that received the same fertilizer treatment + herbaceous weed control (Jokela and others 2000).

Established Stands
Nitrogen and P tend to be the most limiting nutrients for loblolly pine on upland sites, although K and micronutrient deficiencies may also exist. Foliar analysis is recommended to delineate deficient areas among older stands (post crown closure). Where a deficiency is indicated, elemental application rates of 200 lbs N per ac and 25 lbs P per ac are recommended, often at about age 12 to13 years (assuming earlier treatment at age 5 to 6 years). On responsive sites, especially those that have a well-developed, shallow, clayey subsoil, volume gains due to fertilization can range from 70 - 90 ft^3 per ac per yr and persist for 6 to 8 years. A second mid-rotation fertilizer treatment may be warranted on sites being thinned and managed for sawtimber production.

CRIFF G SOILS
(Excessively Drained - Sandhills)
Extensive areas of deep sands, with little soil profile development, occur in north Florida, Georgia and the Carolina Sandhills. These soils often formed on former sand dunes and beach ridges. Sand pine (Florida) and longleaf pine are commonly planted on these soils. Management practices that conserve organic matter are recommended for these soils. As water deficits and competition generally limit pine productivity, intensive management that includes fertilizer applications are not generally recommended for these soils.

CRIFF H SOILS
(Very Poorly Drained - Depressions)
Soils of the H group are typically found in isolated, very-poorly drained depressions throughout the savannas and flatwoods (for example, cypress ponds or strands, bottomlands along rivers). They contain high levels of organic matter in the surface horizon, with little or no sand or clay present. Excessive wetness and frequent flooding, due to landscape position, limit their potential for intensive pine plantation management and forest fertilization is rarely recommended.

APPLICATION METHODS
The method of application (in other words, banding vs. broadcast) does not appear to affect growth responses to fertilization. Factors such as equipment availability, costs, terrain, uniformity of spread, and timeliness of the operation should be considered when formulating a prescription. Banding involves selective fertilizer placement, usually 3-4 ft wide over the recently planted row of trees. By comparison, broadcast methods spread fertilizers in swaths across the entire stand. Tractor-mounted spreaders are suitable for easily traversed areas, whereas rubber-tired skidders equipped with fertilizer spreaders or aerial application systems (helicopter, fixed-wing) may be more effective on wet or rough sites. Regardless of the application method, uniformity and rate control are important. Unequal distribution of fertilizers may contribute to irregular growth patterns.

Therefore, care should be exercised in applying fertilizers, particularly when micronutrient additions are made because they are applied in only modest amounts across the site.

FERTILIZATION EFFECTS ON SITE AND STAND PROPERTIES
Fertilizer additions can result in both short and relatively long-term changes in site and stand properties. Several long-term experiments have been established and maintained throughout the South, and they have been invaluable in understanding the effects of intensive management on stand dynamics. Results from one such trial series established on a CRIFF C group soil (Spodosols) in north central Florida will be used to illustrate these effects for both slash and loblolly pine. At this location, rotation-long nutrient management (macro- and micronutrient additions) was practiced, along with understory competition control (Jokela and Martin 2000). In general, growth responses to the various nutrient amelioration treatments were immediate, obvious and directly related to the intensity of management inputs (fig. 3). Stemwood growth responses were driven by large increases (2x) in LAI. Without nutrient additions or competition control, slash pine generally outperformed loblolly pine. The opposite was true, however, under an intensive management regime.

Fertilizer induced growth responses were associated with temporary increases in site quality and accelerated patterns of stand development. For example, when measured at age 18 years, site index varied from 58 to 82 for loblolly pine and from 72 to 84 for slash pine for the control (C; bedded and planted) and combination fertilizer plus weed control (FW) treatments, respectively. The levels of basal area supported on this unthinned site were also directly related to management intensity. The upper levels of basal area, hence stand density, accrued on the FW treatment was 193 ft^2 per ac for loblolly pine compared to 82 ft^2 per ac for the control (C) treatment. In contrast, basal area levels for slash pine were lower than loblolly pine on the FW treatment (168 ft^2 per ac), but comparatively higher on the C treatment (97 ft^2 per ac) (fig. 4). Culmination of stemwood mean annual increment for both species occurred at age 13 years for the FW treatment, but had not reached a maximum on the C treatment at age 18 yr. Hence, fertilization not only increased stand yields, but also shortened the rotation length and increased stand value. These effects were especially evident in the diameter distributions for each treatment (fig. 5). Fertilization significantly improved stand value by increasing the proportion of "grade" material produced. For example, the C treatment had 17 percent of the stems in 9-12 inch trees compared to 48 percent for the FW treatment. It should be noted that density control treatments, such as thinning, will be required sooner in fertilized stands to avoid reductions in diameter increment due to overstocking and selfthinning.

CONCLUSIONS
Large gains have been made in the South over the last two decades in identifying responsive sites for forest fertilization. Site classification is central to the wise use of fertilizers in forest stands. The development of cost-efficient, biologically sound fertilizer prescriptions will require integration of site, stand, and economic considerations. To aid site-specific

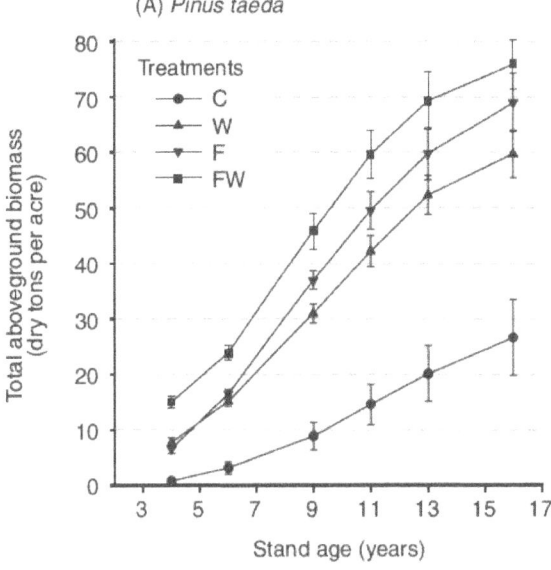

(A) *Pinus taeda*

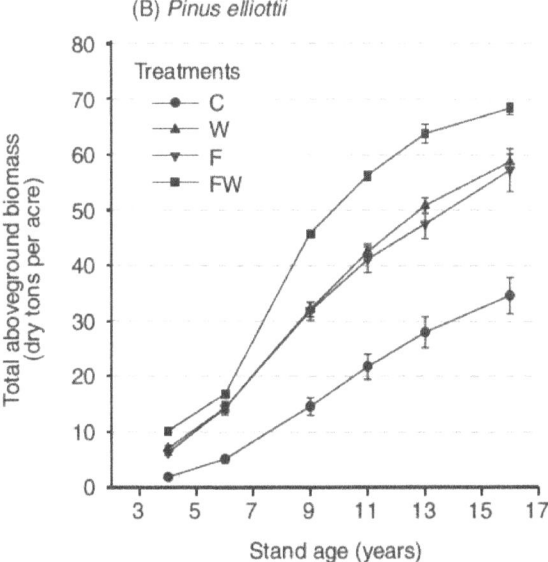

(B) *Pinus elliottii*

Figure 3—Standing aboveground biomass vs. stand age for control (C), weed control (W), fertilization (F) and combination (FW) treatments for loblolly and slash pine growing on Spodosols in north central Florida. Each point is the mean of three replicate plots, along with standard errors.

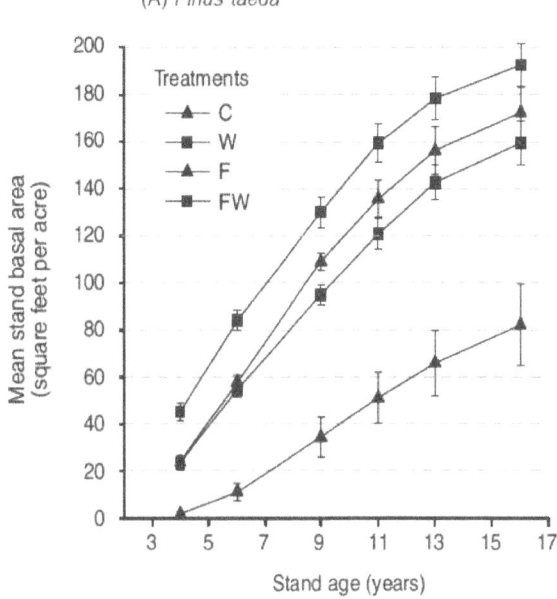

(A) *Pinus taeda*

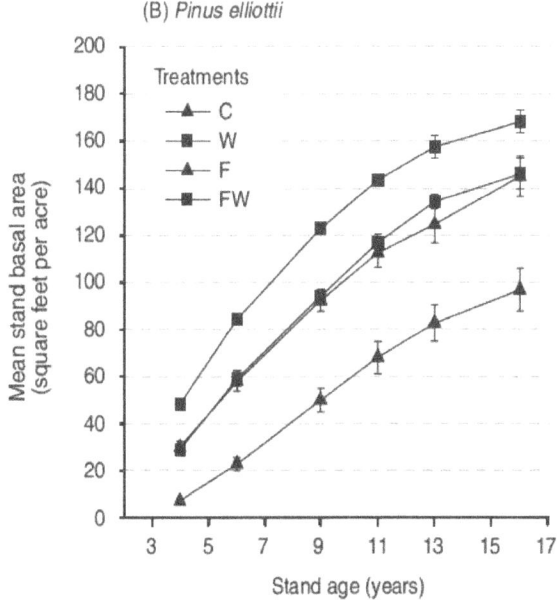

(B) *Pinus elliottii*

Figure 4—Basal area accretion vs. stand age for control (C), weed control (W), fertilization (F) and combination (FW) treatments for loblolly and slash pine growing on Spodosols in north central Florida. Each point is the mean of three replicate plots, along with standard errors.

fertilizer prescriptions in the future, additional technological advances will be required to improve the accuracy of diagnosing nutritional problems and accurately predicting stand responses. For example, a better understanding of soil nutrient supply (immobilization, retranslocation, mineralization) in relation to stand nutrient demand would aid both the timing and quantity of fertilizer applications necessary to sustain a desired level of growth. Intensive management and rapid growth rates may also induce (dilution) multiple nutrient limitations, especially during the early stages of stand development. As such, multiple element

fertilization may be necessary in southern pine stands, and additional research on nutrient balance, especially for elements other than N and P, will be required to support management applications. Finally, in order to achieve continued success in managing the nutrition of southern pine stands, foresters will require not only technical skill for developing prescriptions, but also appreciation of other environmental and silvicultural interactions with forest fertilization (for example, pest management, understory competition, wood properties, water quality).

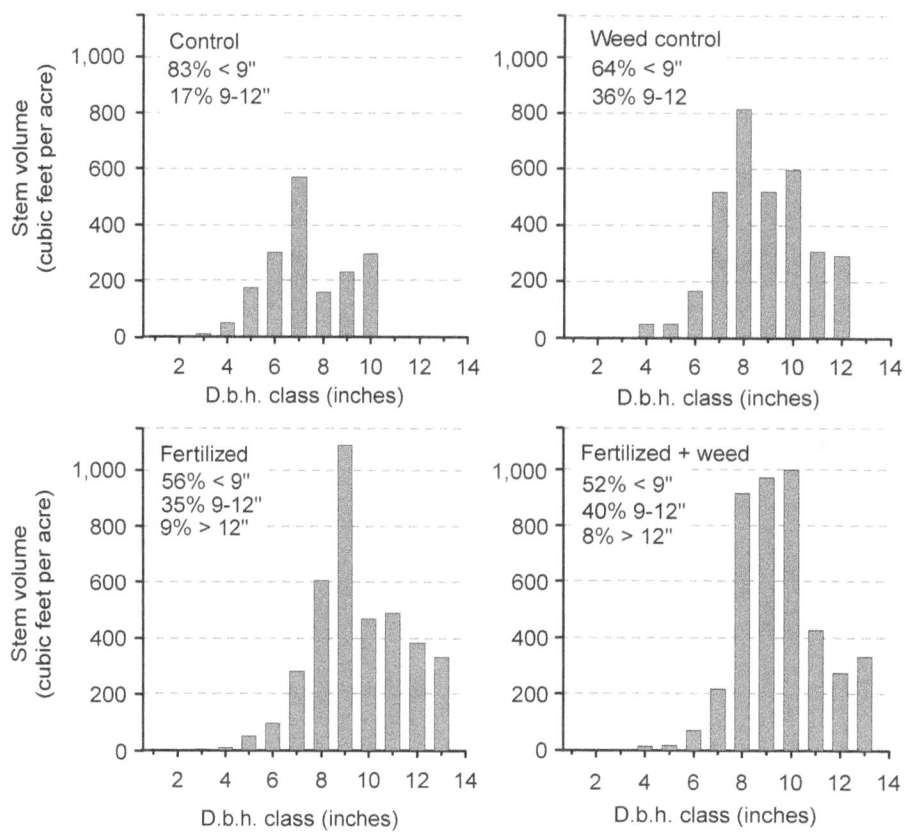

Figure 5—Effects of silvicultural treatments on the distr bution of stem volume by diameter class for 18-year-old loblolly pine growing on Spodosols in northcentral Florida. Trees < 9 inches were considered pulpwood; trees 9 to 12 inches were considered chip&saw; and trees > 12 inches were sawlogs.

LITERATURE CITED

Adams, M.B.; Allen, H.L. 1985. Nutrient proportions in foliage of semimature loblolly pine. Plant and Soil 86: 27-34.

Adegbidi, H.G.; Comerford, N.B.; Hua, L. [and others]. 2002. Determining nutrient requirements for intensively managed loblolly pine stands using the SSAND (soil supply and nutrient demand) model. In: Outcalt, K.W., ed. Proceedings of the eleventh biennial southern silvicultural research conference. Gen. Tech. Rep. SRS-48. Asheville, NC: U.S. Department of Agriculture, Forest Service, Southern Research Station: 26-30.

Adegbidi, H.G.; Jokela, E.J.; Comerford, N.B. 2003. Factors influencing growth efficiency patterns in an intensively managed loblolly pine chronosequence. [In preparation].

Albaugh, T.J.; Allen, H.L.; Dougherty, P.M. [and others]. 1998. Leaf area and above- and belowground growth responses of loblolly pine to nutrient and water additions. For. Sci. 44: 317-328.

Allen, H.L. 1987. Forest fertilizers: nutrient amendment, stand productivity, and environmental impact. J. For. 85: 37-46.

Amateis, R.L.; Liu, J.; Ducey, M.J.; Allen, H.L. 2000. Modeling response to midrotation nitrogen and phosphorus fertilization in loblolly pine plantations. South. J. Appl. For. 24: 207-212.

Bailey, R.L.; Burgan, T.M.; Jokela, E.J. 1989. Models to predict changes in stand structure and yields of fertilized mid-rotation-aged slash pine plantations. South. J. Appl. For. 13: 13-17.

Comerford, N.B.; Fisher, R.F. 1984. Using foliar analysis to classify nitrogen-responsive sites. Soil Sci. Soc. Am. J. 48: 910-913.

Fisher, R.F.; Binkley, D. 2000. Ecology and management of forest soils. John Wiley & Sons. New York. 489 p.

Fisher, R.F.; Garbett, W.S. 1980. Response of semimature slash and loblolly pine plantations to fertilization with nitrogen and phosphorus. Soil Sci. Soc. Am. J. 44: 850-854.

Fox, T.R. 2004. Species deployment strategies for the southern pines: site specific management practices for the flatwoods of Georgia and Florida. In: Dickens, E.D.; Barnett, J.P.; Hubbard, W.G.; Jokela, E.J., eds. Slash pine: still growing and growing! Proceedings of the Slash Pine Symposium. Gen. Tech. Rep. 76. Asheville, NC: U.S. Department of Agriculture, Forest Service, Southern Research Station: 50-55.

Jokela, E.J.; Allen, H.L.; McFee, W.W. 1991a. Fertilization of southern pines at establishment. IN Duryea, M. L.; Dougherty, P. M. eds. Forest Regeneration Manual. Kluwer Academic Publisher, Dordrecht, The Netherlands. 263-277.

Jokela, E.J.; Harding, R.B.; Nowak, C.A. 1989. Long-term effects of fertilization on stem form, growth relations, and yield estimates of slash pine. For. Sci. 35: 832-842.

Jokela, E.J.; Long, A.J. 2000. Using soils to guide fertilizer recommendations for southern pines. University of Florida, Institute of Food and Agricultural Sciences Extension Circular 1230. 11 p.

Jokela, E.J.; Martin, T.A. 2000. Effects of ontogeny and soil nutrient supply on production, allocation, and leaf area efficiency in loblolly and slash pine stands. Can. J. For. Res. 30: 1511-1524.

Jokela, E.J.; McFee, W.W.; Stone, E.L. 1991b. Micronutrient deficiency in slash pine: response and persistence of added manganese. Soil Sci. Soc. Am. J. 55: 492-496.

Jokela, E.J.; Stearns-Smith, S.C. 1993. Fertilization of established southern pine stands: effects of single and split nitrogen treatments. South. J. Appl. For. 17: 135-138.

Jokela, E.J.; Wilson, D.S.; Allen, J.E. 2000. Early growth responses of slash and loblolly pine following fertilization and herbaceous weed control treatments at establishment. South. J. Appl. For. 24: 23-30.

Martin, S.W.; Bailey, R.L.; Jokela, E.J. 1999. Growth and yield predictions for lower Coastal Plain slash pine plantations fertilized at mid-rotation. South. J. Appl. For. 23: 39-45.

Morris, L.A.; Jokela, E.J.; O'Connor, J.B. 1992. Silvicultural guidelines for pinestraw management in the Southeastern United States. Georgia Forest Res. Pap. No. 88. Georgia Foresty Commission. 11 p.

North Carolina State Forest Nutrition Cooperative. 2002. 31st annual report. Dept. of For., Coll. Nat. Resour., North Carolina State Univ., Raleigh. 21 p.

Polglase, P.J.; Comerford, N.B.; Jokela, E.J. 1992. Mineralization of nitrogen and phosphorus from soil organic matter in southern pine plantations. Soil Sci. Soc. Am. J. 56: 921-927.

Pritchett, W.L.; Comerford, N.B. 1981. Nutrition and fertilization of slash pine. In: Stone, E.L., ed. The managed slash pine ecosystem. 1981 June 9-11; Gainesville, FL: School of Forest. Resources and Conservation, Univ. of Florida: 69-90.

Pritchett, W.L.; Comerford, N.B. 1982. Long-term response of phosphorus fertilization on selected southern Coastal Plain soils. Soil Sci. Soc. Am. J. 46: 640-644.

Sheffield, R.M.; Knight, H.A. 1982. Loblolly pine resource: southeast region. In: Symp. on the loblolly pine ecosystem-east region; 1982 December 8-10; Raleigh, NC: School of Forest Resources, North Carolina State University: 7-24.

Sheffield, R.M.; Knight, H.A.; McClure, J.P. 1983. The slash pine resource. In: Stone, E.L., ed. The managed slash pine ecosystem. 1981 June 9-11; Gainesville, FL: School of Forest. Resources and Conservation, Univ. of Florida: 4-23.

South, D.B.; Carey, W.A.; Johnson, D.A. 2003. Copper deficiency in pine plantations in the Georgia Coastal Plain. In: Proceedings of the 12th Biennial Southern Silvi. Res. Conf., Biloxi, MS Feb 24-27, 2003.

Stone, E.L. 1968. Micronutrient nutrition of forest trees: a review. In: Forest fertilization – theory and practice. 1967 April 18-21; Gainesville, FL: Tennessee Valley Authority, Knoxville: 132-175.

Wells, C.G.; Crutchfield, D.M.; Berenyi, N.M.; Davey, C.B. 1973. Soil and foliar guidelines for phosphorus fertilization of loblolly pine. USDA Forest Serv., Southeast Forest Exp. Sta., Asheville, N.C. Res. Pap. SE-110.

PLANTING DENSITY IMPACTS ON SLASH PINE STAND GROWTH, YIELD, PRODUCT CLASS DISTRIBUTION, AND ECONOMICS

E. David Dickens and Rodney E. Will[1]

Abstract—The establishment phase is a very critical decision-making phase in the life of a pine plantation. Key choices in site preparation intensity and type, pre-plant competition control, species selection, seedling genetic quality and size, fertilization, and first year post plant herbaceous weed control have large and long lasting effects on wood yields, rotation length, and products grown. Within a level of forest management, planting density, spacing configuration, and subsequent survival rate can affect stand access, time of canopy closure, time to first pine straw harvest, age to first thinning, number of thinnings, and product class distributions over time. Initially, higher planting densities yield more volume. Eventually, without thinning, stand volumes converge between lower and higher initial stand densities. The more intensive the management and the higher the site productivity the sooner this convergence occurs. An attractive initial spacing for slash pine (*Pinus elliottii* Engelm. var. *elliottii*) may not be so attractive for loblolly pine (*Pinus taeda*, L.) or longleaf (*Pinus palustris*, Mill.). This is due to differences in self-pruning characteristics, branch base diameter, number of branches, branch angle, or potential survival differences by species on certain sites. This paper will discuss the impacts of planting density under different levels of site productivity and management on slash pine stand biology, yields, and economic returns using several long-term studies.

INTRODUCTION

Recent decreases in pine pulpwood demand and stumpage prices to near record lows (TMS 2002) in the southeastern U.S., along with increased demand and prices for pine straw (Doherty and others 2000), has made many forest and land managers re-evaluate initial planting densities. Some forest landowners and foresters are interested in delaying a thinning or forgoing thinning to rake pine straw for a longer period of time. Lower initial densities may help achieve those goals. Conversely, some forest product companies are currently investigating the potential benefits of high initial densities and intensive management for earlier first thinnings, smaller intervals between thinnings, and shorter rotations. The focus of this paper is to discuss the impacts of planting density on stand biology and yields as well as the economic ramifications for stands growing under different levels of site productivity and management.

Choosing a planting density for slash pine (*Pinus elliottii* var. *elliottii*, Engelm.) plantations has important economic and biological ramifications. In slash pine, and conifers in general, increasing planting density decreases tree diameter growth (Ware and Stahelin 1948, Worst 1964, Jones 1987). However, at high stand densities, (greater than 1200 trees per acre), tree height may be suppressed relative to stands planted at wider spacings, but to a lesser extent than is diameter growth (Rahman 1969, Jones 1987). In contrast to the growth of individual trees, total wood production per unit of land area increases as stand density increases because volume associated with the additional trees more than compensates for the decreases in the size of individuals. As stands age, however, convergence of wood production often occurs between different density stands because the growth rate of high density stands reaches a maximum and begins to decline earlier than lower density stands. In addition, greater density dependant mortality in the denser stands may hasten this convergence.

Site productivity, land use history (cut-over, old-field, or pasture), and management intensity have a large influence on how much wood is produced and the timing of growth convergence between different density stands. In general, the faster the growth rate the sooner this growth convergence between different density stands occurs. Some long-term slash pine spacing studies on former old-field sites (Bowling 1987, Jones 1987) have shown that resultant wood yields without thinning were similar by age 20- to 25-years for initial planting densities between 400 to 800 trees per acre (TPA). This rapid convergence of stem production between different density stands on old-field sites may be associated with rapid growth due to low initial hardwood competition, a residual fertilizer effect, and typically good soil tilth.

In contrast, convergence of wood production between different density stands takes longer on cut-over sites due to slower overall growth, but also due to a greater intensity of interspecific competition in the lower density stands. Sarigumba (1984) found that slash pine volume production on cut-over sites planted at 436 TPA was lower than wood volume production of stands planted at 605 TPA by age 25-years on sites of marginal productivity (MAI of 1.25 to 1.70 cords per ac per yr). These sites received low levels of site preparation and management. Borders and Bailey (1985) also found that wood yields on cut-over sites from lower planting densities (400 to 436 TPA) were lower (by 3 to 5 cords per acre) than higher planting densities (800 TPA) through age 25-years. Pienaar and others (1996)

[1] E. David Dickens, Associate Professor; and Rodney E. Will, Assistant Professor of Forest Productivity and Tree Physiology, Daniel B. Warnell School of Forest Resources, The University of Georgia, Statesboro, GA 30460, and Athens, GA 30602-2152, respectively.

Citation for proceedings: Dickens, E.D.; Barnett, J.P.; Hubbard, W.G.; Jokela, E.J., eds. 2004. Slash pine: still growing and growing! Proceedings of the slash pine symposium. Gen. Tech. Rep. SRS-76. Asheville, NC: U.S. Department of Agriculture, Forest Service, Southern Research Station. 148 p.

modeled slash pine planted at two densities on cut-over sites. They predicted that the wood volume production of 400 TPA stands (3300 and 3900 ft³ per acre) was lower than wood volume production from 800 TPA stands (3850 and 5075 ft³ per acre) through age 35-years on site index 60 and 70 feet (base age 25-years) sites, respectively.

When considering economic returns related to planting density, however, factors in addition to total wood production need to be considered; timing and intensity of thinning, tree size distribution and resultant product classes, cost of planting, cost of site preparation, potential for pine straw production, and ease of stand access. In two old-field site studies, for instance, planting at lower densities (400 and 436 TPA) resulted in larger diameter, more valuable wood and greater total economic return than the traditional 600 to 800 TPA planting densities under a no thin management regime by age 20- and 25-years (Bowling 1987, Jones 1987).

EFFECT OF PLANTING DENSITY OF INTENSIVELY MANAGED STANDS

Experimental studies have indicated that slash pine yield can be pushed to exceed 3 cords per acre per year with the application of complete control of interspecific competition and fertilization (Borders and Bailey 2001). The incorporation of intensive forest management may impact the relationship between stand density and stem growth, particularly if carrying capacity is altered. To address this question, the Plantation Management Research Cooperative (based at the Warnell School of Forest Resources, The University of Georgia) and its industrial cooperators installed a series of slash pine studies to examine the interaction between stand density and management intensity. Following six growing seasons, the more intensive forest management treatments (complete control of interspecific competition and multiple fertilization) significantly increased tree size. However, the effects of stand density were similar regardless of management intensity (fig. 1). Therefore, the effects of stand density appear to be consistent across a broad range of management intensities and environments.

Although the timing of when convergence in wood production occurs among different density stands is affected by site quality and management intensity, the nearly universal phenomenon of convergence in wood production raises the question as to what resource or biological mechanism limits stem growth as stand density increases. By identifying the limiting processes or resources, these limiting functions hopefully can be addressed through silvicultural inputs, genetic selection, or genetic manipulation. This question was addressed using the intensively managed (multiple fertilizer applications and complete control of interspecific competition) set of Plantation Management Research Cooperative studies discussed above. Given the intensive management and very fast growth rates, stand growth was becoming limited in the higher density stands very early during stand development. For instance, stem growth during the fourth growing season increased only about 3.5 times when planting density was increased five-fold from 300 to 1500 trees per acre (Burkes and others, in press).

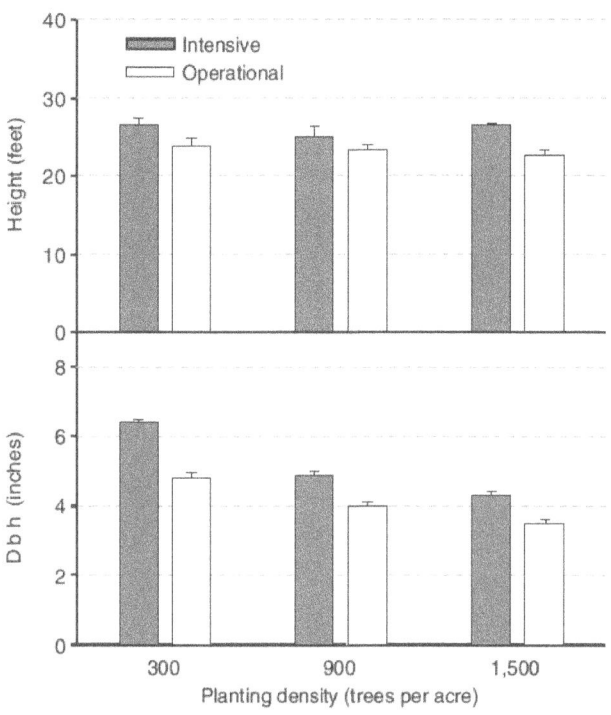

Figure 1—Effect of planting density on the height and diameter of slash pine stands following the sixth growing season. Intensive stands received multiple fertilization and complete interspecific competition control.

One possibility for the limitation of stem growth per unit of land area in the high density stands was that either the ability of foliage to gain carbon through photosynthesis decreased or the rate of carbon loss via respiration increased such that less photosynthate was available for stem growth. However, photosynthetic capacity and respiration rates were not affected by stand density (Will and others 2001). Another possibility was that the slowing of stem growth in higher density stands resulted from more photosynthate being partitioned to root or foliage and less to stem as the competition for above and below ground resources intensified. However, biomass partitioning to stem relative to other stand components did not decrease as stand density increased. Rather, growth efficiency (stem production per unit of leaf biomass) and the ratio between stem growth and standing fine root biomass increased as stand density increased (fig. 2) (Burkes and others, in press), indicating a greater fraction of fixed carbon was used for stem growth at higher stand densities.

What did appear to limit stem growth per unit land area was canopy size, which drives both radiation interception and photosynthetic surface area (fig. 3) (Will and others 2001). The initial greater stem growth rates in denser stands and later slowing of stem growth was well correlated to the development of leaf area. Therefore the limitation in stand growth as planting density increases appears related to a site's capacity to support leaf area which in turn is a function of nutrient and water availability. As a result, silvicultural activities should focus on increasing leaf area.

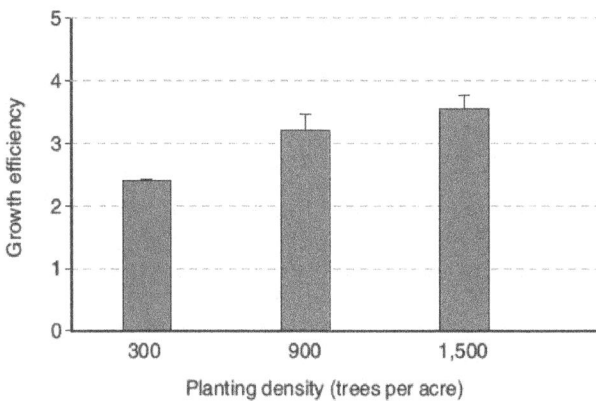

Figure 2—Growth efficiency (stem production per unit of leaf biomass) during the fourth growing season for slash pine stands planted in 1996 at different densities.

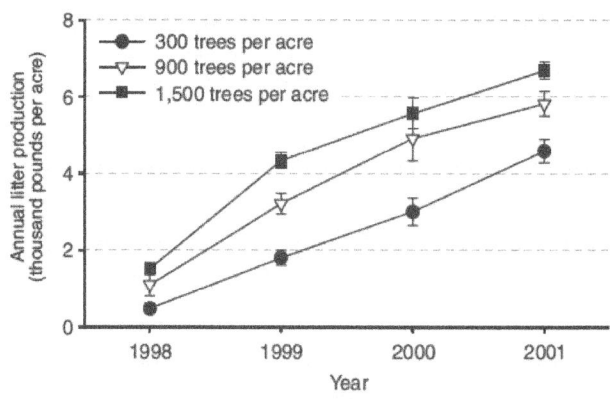

Figure 4—Annual litter production from intensively managed slash pine stands planted in 1996 at different densities. Litter was estimated using traps.

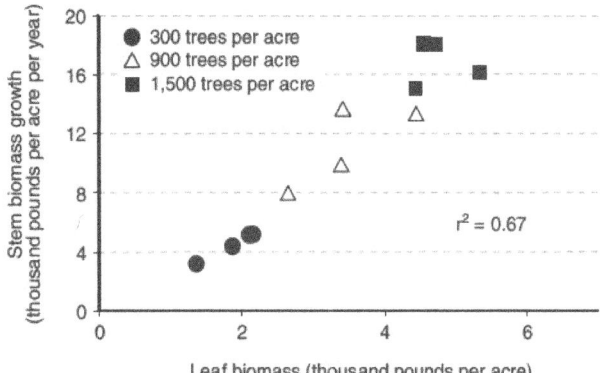

Figure 3—Relationship between leaf biomass and stem biomass growth during the fourth growing season for slash pine stands planted in 1996 at different densities. Leaf biomass was calculated using litter traps. Stem biomass growth was calculated using allometric equations.

Overall, increasing planting density has multiple benefits, including: accelerating early volume production, increasing the efficiency of stem production relative to other stand components, and early site occupancy. The declines in stand growth rate that occur at high stand densities as stand development progresses, combined with economics of stand establishment and product distribution (discussed below), can result in moderate stand densities as the best choice for planting. Higher initial stocking densities may be financially attractive if aggressive thinning regimes and other silvicultural practices can be employed.

POTENTIAL PINE STRAW PRODUCTION OF INTENSIVELY MANAGED STANDS
Of great interest to some growers of slash pine plantations is the production of pine straw. Intensive forest management, including fertilization and competition control, results in larger canopies and greater potential pine straw production. Intensive management also facilitates pine straw production by keeping the stand clean to maximize rakable area (Morris and others 1992, Dickens 1999, 2001). Overall,

intensive forest management results in very high potential pine straw production. Intensively managed stands planted at 1500 TPA produced 380 bales per acre during the sixth growing season (assuming 17.7 lbs per acre) (Morris and others 1992). In comparison, the stands containing 300 TPA (only one-fifth the number of trees) produced approximately 260 bales per acre during the sixth growing season (fig. 4). Canopy closure was realized at age 4-years in the 1500 TPA planting density, at 5-years for the 900 TPA density, and had not yet been reached through age 6-years for the 300 TPA stands. Early canopy closure at the higher initial densities provides forest landowners with pine straw raking income opportunities sooner than the lower initial planting densities. However, pine straw production per tree is greater in the lower density stands and given enough time, pine straw production will be fairly similar among stand densities. Time of first rake, bale per acre production, and number of years of raking are important factors if pine straw production is a high priority. In addition to total production, access between rows is an important consideration for pine straw raking operations and should be considered when choosing a planting density.

LONG-TERM EFFECTS OF PLANTING DENSITY FOR SITES WITH LOW TO MODERATE MANAGEMENT INTENSITY AND LOW TO MODERATE SITE PRODUCTIVITY
Several spacing studies were established in the 1950s and 1960s that provide an opportunity to examine the long-term impacts of planting density on stand growth. Since these stands were established in an era before intensive management, they reflect conditions that today would be considered low to moderate productivity.

Effects of Spacing on Low Productivity Sites — Brunswick Pulp and Paper Study
The Brunswick Pulp and Land Company slash pine spacing study was established in 1957 on four Flatwoods soil series on cut-over sites: the moderately well drained Orsino (Spodic Quartzipsamments), somewhat poorly drained Leon (Aeric Alaquods), poorly drained Mascotte (Ultic Alaquods), and poorly drained Pelham (Arenic Paleaquults). Four site

preparation levels were applied: burn (control), burn-scalp, burn-bed, and burn-harrow. Four spacings included 6x6 (1210 TPA), 6x12 (605 TPA), 10x10 (436 TPA), and 12x12 feet (302 TPA). The experimental design was split-plot randomized complete block with two replications for each of the four drainage classes. Only pre-plant site preparation was performed with no subsequent weed control, fertilization, or thinning during the 25-year study period.

Merchantable volume (3 inch top outside bark) mean annual increment ranged from 1.0 to 1.7 cords per acre per year (where 86 ft³ outside bark per cord) during the 25-year study period (Sarigumba 1984, Borders and Bailey 1985). Merchantable volume mean annual increment (MAI) culmination occurred between ages 20 and 25 on all soils but the Pelham. Generally the bed and harrow treatments and 6x6 and 6x12 spacing basal area and volume MAI culminated earlier across the soils than the control and scalp treatments and 10x10 and 12x12 feet spacing.

Age 25-years data from this study for the 6x12 and 10x10 feet spacings are summarized here, assuming that a mixed product class distribution of pulpwood and chip&saw and culmination of merchantable volume MAI are forest management goals. Data from the best site preparation treatment for each soil series were used at age 25-years to calculate stand parameters. These were the bed (Pelham soil) or harrow (Orsino, Leon, and Mascotte) site preparation treatments.

There was little difference in mean percent survival for the 6x12 and 10x10 feet spacing at age 25-years across the four soils. Survival ranged from 76 to 88 percent. Mean d.b.h. for the 10x10 feet spacing was significantly greater than the than the 6x12 spacing on the Leon (difference of 0.9 inch), Mascotte (difference of 0.6 inch), and Pelham (difference of 0.7 inch) soils (table 1). Diameter distributions from the 10x10 spacing produced more trees per acre of the larger diameter classes than the 6x12 spacing (fig. 5). Basal area for the 6x12 spacing was significantly greater than the 10x10 spacing on two of the four soils (table 1). Mean heights for the 6x12 spacing (60 feet) and 10x10 spacing (61 feet) were not significantly different across the four soils at age 25-years.

Merchantable volume (Bailey and others 1982, Borders and Bailey 1985) per acre followed the same pattern as basal area with the 6x12 feet spacing producing significantly greater volume by an average of 4.9 cords after 25-years than the 10x10 spacing. Merchantable volume MAI for the 6x12 spacing was greater than the 10x10 on the Orsino and Mascotte, but was not significantly different on the Leon and Pelham soils through age 25-years (table 1).

The 6x12 spacing produced significantly greater pulpwood volume (5 to 9 inch d.b.h class) than the 10x10 spacing by age 25-years on each soil series (table 1). The 10x10 spacing chip&saw volumes (≥ 9 inch d.b.h class) were not significantly greater than the 6x12 spacing on each individual soil (table 1), but was significantly greater when averaged across the four soils. Using stumpage prices of $20 per cord for pulpwood and $75 per cord for chip&saw

Table 1—Slash pine spacing effects on mean stand parameters at age 25-years on four Georgia flatwoods soils—the Brunswick Pulp and Land Company study

Stand parameter	Soil	Spacing (feet)	
		6 x 12	10 x 10
		inches	
D.b.h.[a]	Orsino	7.4a	7.6a
	Leon	6.6b	7.5a
	Mascotte	6.6b	7.2a
	Pelham	6.1b	6.8a
		square feet per acre	
Basal area	Orsino	142a	121b
	Leon	112a	107a
	Mascotte	131a	99b
	Pelham	107a	96a
		cords per acre per year	
Merchantable volume[b] MAI	Orsino	1.70a	1.38b
	Leon	1.34a	1.34a
	Mascotte	1.57a	1.19b
	Pelham	1.17a	1.10a
		cords per acre	
Pulpwood volume	Orsino	22.0a	12.9b
	Leon	16.1a	11.3b
	Mascotte	25.5a	12.2b
	Pelham	20.0a	12.8b
Chip&saw volume	Orsino	20.6a	21.5a
	Leon	17.3a	22.3a
	Mascotte	13.9a	17.5a
	Pelham	9.3a	14.8a
		dollars	
Value per acre	Orsino	1,985[c]	1,871
	Leon	1,620	1,899
	Mascotte	1,553	1,557
	Pelham	1,098	1,366

d.b.h. = diameter at breast height; MAI = merchantable volume mean annual increment.

[a] Within a stand parameter and soil treatment means followed by the same letter are not significantly different at the 5-percent alpha level using Duncan's Multiple Range Procedure test.

[b] 86 cubic feet outside bar per cord and 75 cubic feet inside bar per cord are assumed.

[c] Stumpage value based on $20 per cord for pulpwood and $75 per cord for chip&saw (TMS 2000) with a 15-percent defect for chip&saw assumption (PW = 5 to 9 and CNS ≥ 9 inch d.b.h. class).

(TMS 2000) the 10x10 spacing dollar per acre revenue was 7 percent greater (an average of $109 per acre) than the 6x12 spacing. This per acre value difference is minor and the financial picture may change if a fertilization and thinning regime were employed.

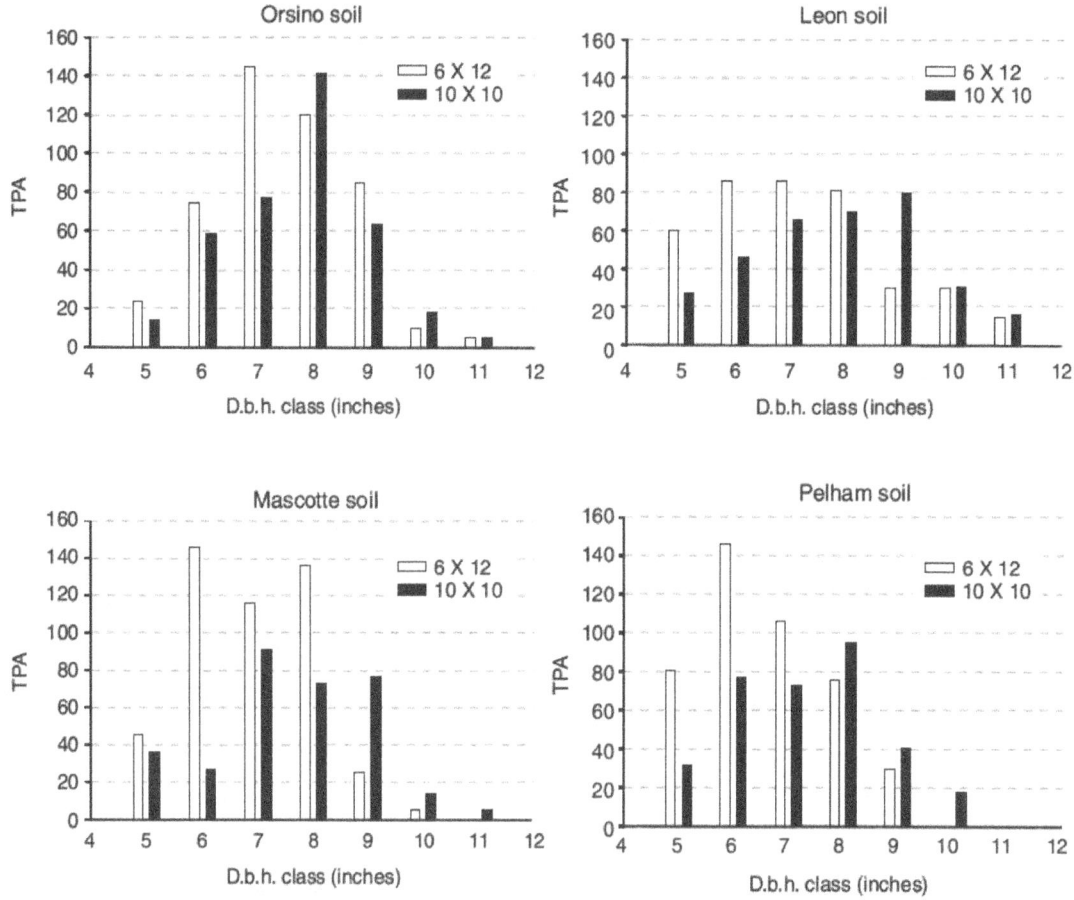

Figure 5—Slash pine diameter distributions by spacing at age 25-years on four Georgia cutover flatwoods soils: Orsino, Leon, Mascotte, and Pelham.

I. Effects of Spacing on Moderately Productive Sites — USFS Dooly County, GA Study

The United States Forest Service (USFS) slash pine spacing study in Dooly County, Georgia was initiated in 1952 on an old-field site. Nursery-grown 1-0 seedlings from the Georgia Forestry Commission nursery in Albany were planted in January 1952, with replanting in March and May 1952 to replace dead seedlings. The soil series represented were Lakeland (sandy Typic Quartipsamments) and Gilead (fine Aquic Halpudults) (Harms and Collins 1965, Jones 1987). Two replications of initial spacings included 6x6 (1,210 TPA), 6x8 (908 TPA), 5x10 (871 TPA), 8x8 (681 TPA), 6x12 (605 TPA), 10x10 (436 TPA), 7.5x15 (387 TPA), and 15x15 feet (194 TPA). The few invading volunteer pines, hardwood, and other woody vegetation were removed from the study area. No fertilizers were applied during the study.

Survival was excellent from study inception, averaging 97 percent by age 4-years (Harms and Collins 1965) and 93 percent at age 12-years. Bennett (1960) noted that by age 5-years, trees were significantly larger in the 10x10 feet and wider spacings than the denser spacings. In this case, Bennett postulated that age 5-years marked the beginning of intraspecific competition for growing space. Harms and Collins (1965) noted that 58 percent of the 6x6 spacing trees reached merchantability compared to 85 percent of

the 6x8 spacing by age 12 years old. In subsequent years, a sub-sample of total heights, d.b.h., survival, and live crown ratio were tallied at ages 15-, 20-, 25-, and 30-years (Jones 1987).

This is a brief summary comparing all spacings from age 15- to 30-years. Merchantable volume (4 inch top outside bark) mean annual increment culminated at age 20-years for all initial densities except the widest spacing (15x15 feet), which peaked at age 25 years old (Jones 1987). Merchantable volume MAI at age 20-years ranged from 1.8 cords per acre per year for the 6x6 spacing to 2.10 cords per acre per year for the 6x8 and 8x8 feet spacing. However, merchantable volumes at age 20-years were not significantly different among spacings except that the volume of the 15x15 feet spacing was significantly less than the other spacings (Jones 1987).

Examination of the intermediate spacings (5x10 (871 TPA at planting), 8x8 (681 TPA), 6x12 (605 TPA), and 10x10 (436 TPA), revealed that percent survival was not significantly different among the four spacings at age 20-, 25-, or 30-years (table 2). At age 15-years, the mean d.b.h. for the 10x10 spacing was significantly greater than the three denser spacings. The average d.b.h. of the 6x12 spacing and 8x8 spacing were not significantly different from one

Table 2—Mean stand parameters by spacing and age from the old-field slash pine spacing study in Dooly County, GA

	Age (years)							
Spacing	15	20	25	30	15	20	25	30
feet	- - - - - Arithmetic d.b.h. *(inches)*[a] - - - - -				- - Basal area *(square feet per acre)* - -			
10 x 10	7.3a	8.2a	9.0a	9.7a	111a	134a	141a	136a
6 x 12	6.4b	7.1b	7.9b	8.5b	118a	134a	140a	133a
8 x 8	6.2b	6.9bc	7.6bc	8.1bc	133a	151a	153a	143a
5 x 10	5.6c	6.2c	6.9c	7.5c	133a	147a	148a	134a
	- - - - - - - - - Percent survival - - - - - - - - -				Merchantable volume[b] *(cords per acre)*			
10 x 10	86a	83a	72a	60a	26.7a	40.5a	48.4a	50.0a
6 x 12	85a	77a	66a	55a	26.2a	37.0a	44.6a	46.6a
8 x 8	92a	84a	71a	58a	29.3a	41.8a	48.3a	48.6a
5 x 10	86a	78a	63a	48a	26.8a	38.2a	43.9a	44.2a
	Dominant, codominant total height *(feet)*				- - - - Live crown ratio *(percent)* - - - -			
10 x 10	48a	58a	66a	70a	44a	35a	27a	25a
6 x 12	46ab	55ab	62ab	67ab	42ab	31b	25b	24a
8 x 8	46ab	55ab	62ab	66ab	38bc	30b	23c	22a
5 x 10	45b	53b	60b	64b	36c	31b	24bc	23a

[a] Within an age and stand parameter treatment means followed by the same letter are not significantly different at the 5-percent alpha level using Duncan's Multiple Range Procedure test.
[b] 86 cubic feet outside bar per cord and 75 cubic feet inside bar per cord are assumed.

another, but were significantly greater than the average d.b.h. of the 5x10 spacing (table 2). This d.b.h. trend continued though age 30-years. Diameter distributions at ages 20- and 25-years (fig. 6) illustrate that the 10x10 spacing produced more chip&saw sized trees compared to the higher densities. Basal area per acre of the different spacings was not significantly different between 15- and 30-years and converged by age 30-years. Basal area per acre decreased for all four spacings by 5 to 13 feet² per acre between ages 25- and 30-years (table 2) due to increased mortality of the larger diameter trees. Eighteen

trees in the > 8 inch d.b.h. classes died between ages 20- and 25- compared to 66 trees between ages 25- and 30-years across the four spacings.

At age 15-years, mean live crown ratio (LCR) followed a similar pattern as d.b.h. among spacings with the greatest LCR's found in the wider spacings (table 2). However, by age 30-years, LCR of all spacings had decreased and was similar among spacings (table 2). An LCR of 33 percent is generally considered the threshold to maintain fast growth rates. The 5x10, 8x8 and 6x12 spacing trees should have

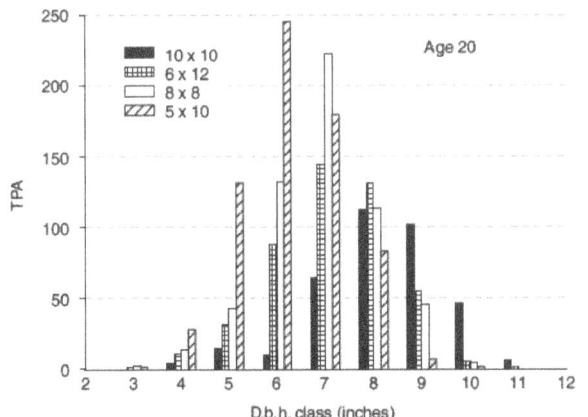 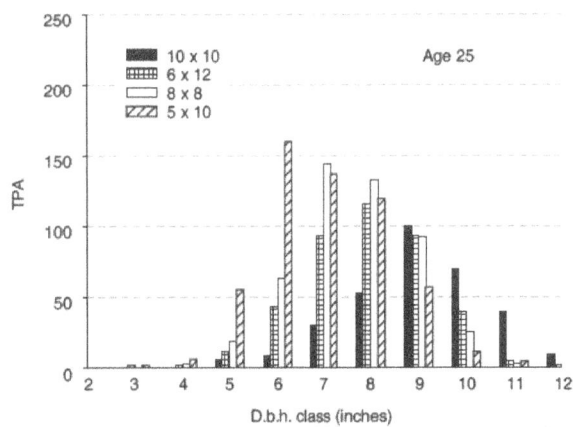

Figure 6—Diameter distributions by spacing and age on the old-field slash pine U.S. Department of Agriculture Forest Service spacing study in Dooly County, GA.

been thinned between age 15- and 20-, while the 10x10 spacing trees thinning could be delayed to maintain LCR greater than 33 percent (table 2) providing a wider thinning window. The mean total height for codominants and dominants was significantly lower in the highest density (5 x 10 feet spacing) compared to trees in the widest spacing (10x10) starting at age 15-years (table 2). This difference was maintained though age 30-years. There were no significant differences in merchantable volume per acre among the four intermediate spacings at age 15-, 20-, 25-, or 30-years (table 2).

II. Effects of Spacing on Moderately Productive Sites — International Paper Study

A slash pine spacing study was initiated by the International Paper Company in 1964. The study area is located in Decatur County, Georgia on an old-field site (Orangeburg soil series - fine-loamy Typic Kandiudults) (Bowling 1987). The study area had six replications of four spacings (400, 600, 800, and 1000 TPA in square configurations), with three of six replications thinned at age 15-years. The study was followed in five year intervals for 20-years (Bowling 1987). Bowling reported that by age 5-years intraspecific competition had not yet occurred as there were no significant differences in mean total height or d.b.h. across the four initial densities. Percent survival ranged from 95 to 98 percent by age 5-years. Basal area per acre was a direct function of surviving TPA (Bowling 1987).

Age 10-years mean d.b.h for the 400 TPA initial density was 0.6, 0.9, and 1.3 inches greater than the 600, 800, and 1000 TPA initial density, respectively, with these differences increasing with stand age (table 3). Basal area peaked in the 800 TPA plots at age 20-years (174 square ft^2 per acre) surpassing the 1000 TPA basal area. The basal area of the 400 TPA and 600 TPA plots were starting to converge with

those of the 800 and 1000 TPA plots between ages 15- and 20-years. At age 10-years, mean height increased with decreasing stand density by approximately one foot per two hundred TPA decrease in planting density (table 3). These differences remained fairly stable except for a relative decrease in height increment for the 1000 TPA plot trees at age 20-years. Merchantable volumes were within two cords per acre among the four planting densities by age 10- and 15-years (table 3). By age 20-years, merchantable volume was greatest in the 800 TPA plots (45 cords per acre). The 400 and 600 TPA densities had intermediate volumes (42 cords per acre), while the 1000 TPA had the lowest volume (38 cords per acre).

ECONOMICS OF PLANTING DENSITY UNDER VARIOUS LEVELS OF SITE PRODUCTIVITY

The lower 436 TPA planting density on the relatively low productivity cutover sites (Brunswick Pulp and Land Study) produced 4.9 cords per acre less volume than the 605 TPA planting density. However, the proportion of pulpwood (5 to 9 inch d.b.h. classes) and chip&saw (≥ 9 inch d.b.h. class less a 15 percent defect assumption) varied with density. An average 8.1 cords per acre less pulpwood, but an average 3.7 cords per acre more chip&saw volume were produced at the lower planting density (436 TPA) by age 25-years.

The lower densities (400 and 436 TPA) on the two old-field site study areas (IP and USFS) produced similar merchantable volumes as the higher, traditional planting densities (600 to 605 TPA) during the study periods. However, the lower planting densities (400 to 436 TPA) produced much greater volumes in the chip&saw class, 9 to 13 cords per acre for the IP and USFS studies using a 15 percent defect assumption. Value per acre for the lower planting densities (400 to 436 TPA) was greater than the higher planting

Table 3—Mean stand parameters by spacing and age from the International Paper old-field slash pine spacing study in Decatur County, GA

Planting density	Age (years)							
	5	10	15	20	5	10	15	20
TPA	------ D.b.h. *(inches)* -----				Basal area *(square feet per acre)*			
400	2.3	6.1	7.6	8.4	12	77	115	144
600	2.3	5.5	6.7	7.3	17	95	136	156
800	2.2	5.2	6.2	6.9	22	112	150	174
1,000	2.1	4.8	5.8	6.4	24	122	154	166
	- - - - Total height *(feet)* - - - -				- - - Merchantable volume[a][b] - - -			
400	12	34	53	63	—	10	27	42
600	12	33	51	62	—	10	28	42
800	12	32	51	61	—	9	28	45
1,000	12	31	50	58	—	8	26	38

TPA = trees per acre; d.b.h. = diameter at breast height.
[a] Cords per acre.
[b] Eighty-six cubic feet outside bark per cord and 75 cubic feet inside bark per cord are assumed.
Source: Bowling (1987).

Table 4—Product class distributions and value per acre[a] for the slash pine spacing studies

Study	Age	TPA	PW	CNS	Value
	years		*Cords per acre[b]*		*$ per acre*
BP&LC	25	605	20.9a	15.3a	1,564
		436	12.3b	19.0b	1,673
USFS	20	871	37.2a	0.74b	800
		681	37.5a	3.4b	1,002
		605	31.2a	4.9b	989
		436	21.6b	14.8a	1,540
	25	871	35.5a	6.2c	1,174
		681	33.2a	11.1bc	1,498
		605	26.3b	13.8b	1,558
		436	14.3c	26.9a	2,302
	30	871	28.2a	11.7c	1,439
		681	26.4a	16.7bc	1,776
		605	21.4b	21.4b	2,035
		436	11.1c	30.8a	2,535
IP	20	1,000	30	8	1,200
		800	31.5	13.5	1,643
		600	27	15	1,665
		400	17.5	24.5	2,188

TPA = initial planting density per acre; PW = pulpwood; CNS = chip&saw; BP&LC = Brunswick Pulp and Land Company; USFS = U.S. Department of Agriculture Forest Service; IP = International Paper Company.
[a] At $20 per cord pulpwood and $75 per cord chip&saw (TMS 2000) and a 15-percent chip&saw defect assumption.
[b] Within a study, age and product class treatment means followed by the same letter are not significantly different at the 5-percent alpha level using Duncan's Multiple Range Procedure test.

densities (600 or greater TPA) on the two old-field sites discussed here (table 4).

Value per acre increases associated with the lower planting densities ranged from $109 (7 percent gain) on the relatively low productivity cutover sites, $500 to $750 (25 to 92 percent gain) on the USFS old-field study area, and $500 to $900 per acre (31 to 75 percent gain) on the IP old-field site (table 4). Because there was a greater total volume production in the higher density stand on the cutover site and similar volumes on the old-field sites, the greater value of the lower density stands resulted from the large price disparity between pulpwood and chip&saw. Therefore, for all three long-term studies, the value per acre was higher at the lower planting density.

The best planting density can depend largely on future product prices as well as landowners needs and objectives. If the price disparity between pine pulpwood and chip&saw continues to be large, then the combination of maximizing wood volume production, product class distribution to favor higher valued products, and wood quality will be high priorities. Maximizing wood volume alone may not be as high a priority that is once was in the mid-1990s when pulpwood prices reached all time highs (TMS 1998).

DISCUSSION

Forest landowners, practicing foresters, and land managers should address the following when choosing a spacing for slash pine plantations: (1) rotation age, (2) products grown (pulpwood, chip&saw, sawtimber, poles, pine straw), (3) product prices, (4) thinning timing, number, and intensity, and (5) equipment access needs. In addition, the intensity of forest management also must be considered since growth within a planting density can be dramatically affected by activities such as site preparation, competition control, and fertilization.

Higher density plantings achieve canopy closure, site utilization, and pine straw production earlier than lower density plantings under the same level of management. An early first thinning (as early as age 8- to 10-years-old assuming the removed stems are merchantable) may be warranted to maintain stand vigor, diameter growth, and volume production in the intensively managed higher density stands. Generally stands are operationally thinned later, between ages 12- to 18-years or when average total tree height is at least 40 feet. The higher planting densities thinning window to optimize growth rates are narrower than for the lower planting densities. Higher planting densities also may be beneficial on cut-over sites with low site preparation and management inputs. The higher planting densities help crop trees occupy the site, whereas the lower planting densities may permit high interspecific competition until much later during stand development, reducing early stand volume production.

In contrast, for those forest landowners whose objective is delaying or forgoing a thinning, raking pine straw as long as possible, and growing mostly chip&saw and larger sized wood, lower planting densities may be the best choice. A disadvantage though is a time delay in canopy closure with lower planting densities, increasing the time to first pine straw revenue. The lower planting densities (400 and 436 TPA) produced the same or greater volume as the higher planting densities (600 to 800 TPA) by age 20-years and much more chip&saw volume on the two old-field sites (IP and USFS studies). Excellent pre- and early post-establishment competition control to maximize survival, growth, and site occupancy should be a high priority for lower density stands. In addition, stand access for ground equipment will often dictate row width and depends on equipment size and operator experience.

LITERATURE CITED

Bailey, R.L.; Pienaar, L.V.; Shiver, B.D; Rheney, J.W. 1982. Stand structure and yield of site prepared slash pine plantations. UGA College of Ag. Exp. Stn. Res. Bull. 291. 83 p.

Bennett, F.A. 1960. Spacing and early growth of planted slash pine. Journal of Forestry Vol. 58: 966-967.

Borders, B.E.; Bailey, R.L. 1985. Stand density effects in slash and loblolly pine plantations. PMRC res. Paper. 1985-1. 149 p.

Borders, B.E.; Bailey, R.L. 2001. Loblolly pine: pushing the limits of growth. South. J. Appl. For. 25: 69-74.

Bowling, D. 1987. Twenty year slash pine spacing study: what to optimize? In: Proceedings of the 4th Biennial So. Silvi. Res. Conf., Atlanta, GA. Nov 406, 1986. SRS GTR SE-42. pp. 300-304.

Burkes, E.C.; Will, R.E.; Barron, G.A. [and others]. [In press]. Biomass partitioning and growth efficiency of intensively managed *Pinus taeda* and *Pinus elliottii* stands of different planting densities. Forest Science.

Dickens, E.D. 1999. Effect of inorganic and organic fertilization on longleaf pine tree growth and pine straw production. In: Proceedings of the 10th Biennial So. Silvi. Res. Conf. Shreveport, LA, February 16-18, 1999. USDA Forest Service GTR SRS-30. Pp. 464-468.

Dickens, E.D. 2001. Fertilization options for longleaf pine stands on marginal soils with economic implications. In: Proceedings of the 31st Annual So. Forest Econ. Workshop. March 27-28, 2001. Pp. 67-72.

Doherty, B.A.; Teasley, R.J.; McKissick, J.C.; Givan, B. 2000. Nineteen ninety-nine farmgate value report. UGA CAES Center for Agribusiness and Econ. Dev., Center Staff Report No. 6. Athens, GA 160 p.

Harms, W.R.; Collins, A.B. 1965. Spacing and twelve-year growth of slash pine. Journal of Forestry. Vol. 63: 909-912.

Harms, W.R.; DeBell, D.S.; Whitsell, C.D. 1994. Stand and tree characteristics and stockability in *Pinus taeda* plantations in Hawaii and South Carolina. Canadian Journal of Forest Research. 24: 511-521.

Jones, E.P. 1987. Slash pine plantation study – age 30. Proceedings of the Fourth Biennial Southern Silviculture Conference. USDA Forest Service Gen. Tech. Rep. SE-42. pp. 45-49.

Mann, W.F.; Dell, T.R. 1971. Yields of 17-year-old loblolly pine planted on a cutover site at various spacings. USDA Forest Service Research Paper SO-70. 9 p.

May, J.T.; Rahman, S.; Worst, R.H. 1973. Effects of site preparation and spacing on planted slash pine. J. of For. 71: 333-335.

Morris, L.A.; Jokela, E.J.; O'Connor, J.B., Jr. 1992. Silvicultural guidelines for pine straw management in the southeastern United States. Georgia Forest Res. Paper. #88, Georgia Forestry Commission, Macon, GA. 11 p.

Rahman, S. 1969. Effects of site preparation and spacing on planted slash pine. MS Thesis. UGA. 41 p.

Ross, S.M.; McKee, W.H., Jr.; Mims, M. 1995. Loblolly and longeaf pine responses to litter raking, prescribe burning, and fertilization. In: Proceedings of the 8th Biennial So. Silvi. Res. Conf. Auburn, AL. Nov. 1-3, 1994. Pp. 220-224.

Sarigumba, T.I. 1984. Sustained response of planted slash pine to spacing and site preparation. In: Proceedings of the 3rd Biennial So. Silvi. Res. Conf. USDA Forest Service. So Exp. Stn. Gen. Tech. Rep. SO-34, pp. 79-84.

Sarigumba, T.I.; Anderson, G.A. 1979. Response of slash pine to different spacings and site preparation treatments. SJAF 3: 91-94.

TMS. 1998. Timber Mart South stumpage prices – 2nd qrtr for south GA 1998. Warnell School of Forest Resources. UGA, Athens, GA.

TMS. 2000. Timber Mart South stumpage prices – 2nd qrtr for south GA 2000. Warnell School of Forest Resources. UGA, Athens, GA.

Ware, L.M.; Stahelin, R. 1948. Growth of southern pine plantations at various spacings. Journal of Forestry. 46: 267-274.

Will, R.E.; Barron, G.A.; Burkes, E.C. [and others]. 2001. Relationship between intercepted radiation, net photosynthesis, respiration, and stem volume growth of *Pinus taeda* and *Pinus elliottii* stands of different densities. Forest Ecology and Management. 154: 155-163.

Worst, R.H. 1964. A study of effects of site preparation and spacing on planted slash pine in the Coastal Plain of southeast Georgia. Journal of Forestry 62: 556-560.

LOBLOLLY VERSUS SLASH PINE GROWTH AND YIELD COMPARISONS

Barry D. Shiver[1]

Abstract—Growth and yield of slash (*Pinus elliottii* Engelm.) and loblolly pine (*Pinus taeda* L.) were compared where both were grown on sites within the native range of slash pine. Comparisons were made using growth and yield models developed for each species, using published studies from the literature, and by evaluating means from studies where both species are being grown at a variety of densities and at different levels of management intensity. Results indicate that even on sites that are considered to be slash pine sites, loblolly produces as much or more wood than slash pine. When intensively managed, the gap between loblolly and slash pine increases. Though there are other good reasons to grow slash pine, and some of these are discussed, landowners and foresters should not choose slash pine because they believe it will produce more total or merchantable fiber than loblolly pine.

INTRODUCTION

Slash pine (*Pinus elliottii* Engelm.) has the smallest natural range of the four major southern pines. The range extends from Georgetown, SC south to Central Florida and west to Louisiana across the lower and middle coastal plains. Slash pine has been planted extensively outside it's native range as far north as Tennessee and as far west as east Texas. Loblolly pine (*Pinus taeda* L.) by comparison has the largest range of the southern pines. It's range extends from southern New Jersey south to central Florida and west to East Texas. It has proven to be a very adaptable species widely planted outside it's native range and even internationally. Loblolly is also very responsive to cultural practices such as fertilization and weed control.

Since the ranges of slash and loblolly overlap to a great extent and since they are both proven valuable commercial species, a major decision that must be made by foresters is which of the two to plant on a given site. There are many different factors that can possibly play a role in this decision, but one factor that is usually important is the differential volume or weight per acre yield for the species.

In an attempt to answer the species-site question, I looked at estimated expected yield values for slash and loblolly pine, published studies in the literature comparing yields of slash and loblolly pine on the same site, and data from Warnell School of Forest Resources Plantation Management Research Cooperative (PMRC) plots where loblolly and slash pine are being intensively managed on the same sites. The objective was to determine the current state of our knowledge of species preference by site based only on volume and weight yield. Other factors did not enter into the decision, though they should be considered along with yields in an attempt to best meet landowner objectives.

GROWTH AND YIELD MODELS

Growth and yield models provide estimated volumes or weights at different ages. Most of the models in the Southeast have been developed for plantations. In addition to age, the quality of the site, the number of trees per acre, and the basal area per acre are typical inputs to predict the yield. Growth and yield models are developed from plots established in operational plantations. On the plots, each tree is measured for diameter at breast height (D) and total height (H) and crown class is noted. The volume and/or weight of each tree is predicted using an equation that uses D and H as inputs. The volume and weight equation was developed from cutting down hundreds of trees, weighing them in sections, measuring their taper from butt to tip, and fitting an equation to these data. From the diameters and plot size, basal area per acre can be calculated. From the frequency of trees on the plot, trees per acre can be calculated. The heights of all dominant and codominant trees are averaged to obtain the average dominant height used to estimate site index. The volumes and/or weights are summed for the plot and expanded to an acre basis. The result is a dataset that has age, average dominant height, basal area per acre, trees per acre, and volume and weight per acre. If the plots are measured at more than one point in time, it is possible to not only model the expected yield at any age in the dataset, but also to model the development of the different model inputs such as dominant height, basal area per acre, and trees per acre over time. The difference in expected yield between two ages represents growth. Good growth and yield models have been developed for both slash and loblolly pine for the coastal plain region where the ranges of the two species overlap.

If we begin with individual trees, the weight models that have been developed indicate that for trees of the same size (same D and H), slash pine will have a higher weight than loblolly pine. For example, the PMRC weight equations for trees with D of 10 inches and H of 60 ft predict a weight of 865 lbs for slash pine compared to 817 lbs for loblolly pine. The reasons for this discrepancy are twofold. Slash pine has slightly less taper than loblolly pine (it is more cylindrical). For the tree size in our example, the expected diameter at 20 ft for slash pine is 8.4 in vs 8.3 in for loblolly. In addition, the specific gravity of slash pine is

[1] Barry Shiver, Professor of Timber Management and Silviculture, Warnell School of Forest Resources, University of Georgia, Athens, GA 30602.

Citation for proceedings: Dickens, E.D.; Barnett, J.P.; Hubbard, W.G.; Jokela, E.J., eds. 2004. Slash pine: still growing and growing! Proceedings of the slash pine symposium. Gen. Tech. Rep. SRS-76. Asheville, NC: U.S. Department of Agriculture, Forest Service, Southern Research Station. 148 p.

Table 1—Basal area (square feet per acre) for slash and loblolly pine as predicted by the Plantation Management Research Cooperative yield models given the same site index and trees per acre

Species	Age	Trees	Basal area
	years	*square feet per acre*	
Site index 60			
Slash	20	400	95.6
Loblolly	20	400	119.8
Site index 70			
Slash	20	400	124.6
Loblolly	20	400	140.7

slightly higher than for loblolly pine. Given this, if slash pine plantations grew at the same rate as loblolly plantations from planting, we would expect slash pine to have higher yields than loblolly. As we will see, however, the yield models indicate that the growth from planting is not equal.

Table 1 presents the expected basal area values for the two species if both the site index and the basal area values are held constant. For both site 60, about an average site index, and site 70, an above average site index, loblolly produces more basal area than slash pine. This indicates that diameter growth for loblolly, under the same competition as slash pine as measured by trees per acre, is higher than for slash pine.

Values for trees per acre in table 2 indicate that even when the two species have the same number of trees per acre after regeneration mortality (age 2), the mortality rate is higher on average for slash pine than for loblolly pine over the rest of the rotation. This trend, in combination with the higher d.b.h. growth for loblolly as evidenced in table 1 overcomes the slight advantage of slash pine from taper and specific gravity. As a result, the growth and yield models predict that loblolly pine has a distinct advantage

Table 2—Green weight (tons per acre) for slash and loblolly pine at age 25 as predicted by the Plantation Management Research Cooperative yield models given the same trees per acre at age 2 and the same site index

Species	Trees Age 2	Trees Age 25	Green weight
	- - - per acre - - -		*tons per acre*
Slash	500	320	121
Loblolly	500	352	151
Slash	600	383	130
Loblolly	600	400	154

to slash pine in expected yield when both species start at about the same density and are growing on the same site. The reasons for the higher mortality rate for slash pine are not clear, but there is at least some evidence to suggest that for the same rate of fusiform rust (*Cronartium fusiforme* Hedg. and Hunt) infection, the slash pine mortality rate is higher than it is for loblolly pine. The expected yields in table 2 indicate almost 20 percent more wood expected on the same site for loblolly pine than for slash pine on a site index 60 site.

These yield models do not have site specific information as inputs. There is no soil classification information involved. Many proponents of slash pine would say that there are definite slash sites and loblolly sites. To evaluate these claims, we first look to the literature and then to some specific studies that have evaluated the two species on a site by site basis. The attempt here is not to present a complete literature review of species comparison studies, but to present results from those that have included a range of different soil types in an attempt to identify "slash" sites and "loblolly" sites.

LITERATURE REVIEW

Cole (1975) reported nine year results of a study on which slash pine was planted at five locations and loblolly was planted at seven locations across South Carolina, Georgia, and north Florida. Across all sites, loblolly was more productive averaging 49 percent to 61 percent more volume per acre than slash. Slash was more productive at only one location, a poorly drained flatwoods site.

Shoulders (1975) reported 15 year results of a study established by the Southern Forest Experiment Station at 113 locations in Louisiana and Mississippi. Across all locations, loblolly survival was better by 10 percent and loblolly had lower fusiform rust infection and lower mortality of infected stems. Slash pine height growth was greater than or equal to loblolly height growth only on wet sites. Height growth was about equal on intermediate or dry sites. Using growth and yield models and the age 15 stand characteristics as inputs, volumes of loblolly pine were projected to surpass slash pine volumes at age 25 on all but the wet sites.

Haines and others (1981) reported seven year results of a species comparison study on nine sites across the South. Survival was much higher on average for loblolly than for slash pine. Slash pine height growth exceeded loblolly at only one location. Five of the nine sites were cutovers and four were old fields. Loblolly outgrew slash pine by 2 to 1 on the old field sites. On the cutover sites, the loblolly volume exceeded the slash pine volume by 57 percent. This study also contained a fertilizer treatment and loblolly had a higher response to this treatment. Slash pine was recommended only on spodosols with no argillic (fine textured loam or clay) horizon.

Shiver and others (2000) reported on a 14 year old PMRC species comparison study with 160 locations spread across eight soil groups. All sites were cutovers and there was no fertilization, no herbaceous weed control, no chemical site preparation, no release, and no thinning. All site preparation was mechanical site preparation and on the wetter soil

Table 3—Average values for stand characteristics of the Plantation Management Research Cooperative species comparison study at age 14 across all soil classes

Characteristic	Loblolly	Slash
Stems with *Cronartium* (percent)	20	18
Survival (percent)	71	66
Basal area (square feet per acre)	98	81
Trees per acre	516	479
Merchantable volume[a] (cubic feet per acre)	1,497	1,310
Merchantable green weight[b] (tons per acre)	45	35

[a] Volume of all trees > 4.5 inches d.b.h. to a 3-inch top diameter outside bark.
[b] Green weight of all trees > 4.5 inches d.b.h. to a 3-inch top diameter outside bark.

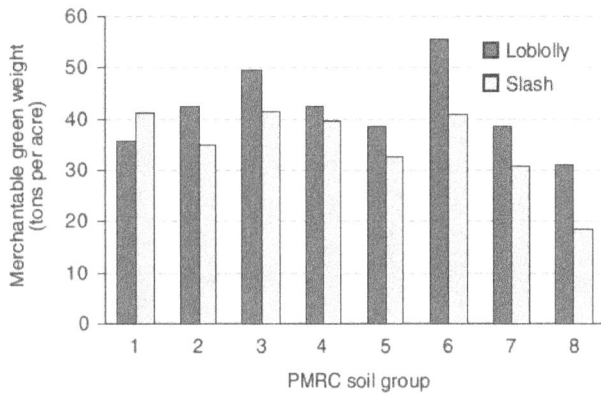

Figure 1—Average merchantable green weight (tons per acre) for trees > 4.5 inches d.b.h. to a 3.0-inch top (outside bark) by PMRC soil group for slash and loblolly pine.

groups most areas were bedded. Loblolly pine yields were as high or higher than slash pine yields on all soil groups. Table 3 values indicate that even though the average percentage of stems with fusiform rust is slightly higher for loblolly than for slash, the survival is higher for loblolly. The higher infection rate at age 14 for loblolly may be due to the infected slash stems dying. Once dead they are no longer included in the dataset as infected and the percent infection goes down. The basal area and volume averages follow the same trends as on the other studies cited.

The Shiver and others (2000) study soil groups are presented in table 4. The poorly drained and very poorly drained soils, especially those without an underlying argillic horizon, would be considered classic slash pine sites. The only soil group on which slash wood production is higher than loblolly is the very poorly to poorly drained soil with no underlying argillic, and that difference is not statistically significant (fig. 1). In other words there is so much variability from one site to another within that soil

group that the amount by which slash pine is larger is not different from zero. All other soil groups have loblolly equal to or greater than the slash volume, though many of them are also not significantly larger.

Another soil classification that is widely used in the slash pine native range is the Cooperative Research in Forest Fertilization (CRIFF) classification developed at the University of Florida. We regrouped our installations in the PMRC study into CRIFF groups as described in table 5. Of these, soil group D would be considered a slash pine site by conventional wisdom. Figure 2 indicates that loblolly produces more merchantable weight by age 14 across all CRIFF groups though the differences for B, C, and D soils are minimal.

An evaluation of the differences in species production over time indicates that the difference in total green weight from age 5 to age 14 is diverging (fig. 3). At age five the differences were minimal, but since age 5 loblolly has increased it's weight per acre advantage over slash pine at every measurement. This indicates that the differences in species over time do not diminish, but rather increase in favor of loblolly pine.

Table 4—Soil groups on the Plantation Management Research Cooperative species comparison study

Soil group	Drainage	Description
1	P, VP	Spodosol with argillic
2	P, VP	Spodosol, no argillic
3	P, VP	Nonspodosols
4	SP, MW	Spodosol with argillic
5	Sp, MW	Spodosol, no argillic
6	Sp, MW	Nonspodosols
7	W	Nonspodosols
8	SE, E	Nonspodosols

P = poorly drained; VP = very poorly drained; SP = somewhat poorly drained; MW = moderately well drained; W = well drained; SE = somewhat excessively drained; E = excessively drained.

Table 5—Soil group descriptions for the Cooperative Research in Forest Fertilization soil classification system

Soil group	Drainage	Description
A	P, VP, SP	Argillic < 20 inches
B	P, VP, SP	Argillic > 20 inches
C	P, VP, SP	Spodosol with argillic
D	P, VP, SP	Spodosol, no argillic
F	MW, W	Argillic > 20 inches
G	SE, E	None or deep argillic

P = poorly drained; VP = very poorly drained; SP = somewhat poorly drained; MW = moderately well drained; W = well drained SE = somewhat excessively drained; E = excessively drained.

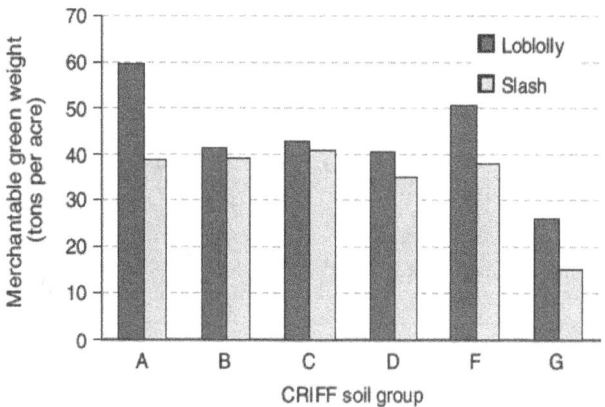

Figure 2—Average merchantable green weight (tons per acre) for trees > 4.5 inches d.b.h. to a 3.0-inch top (outside bark) by CRIFF soil group for slash and loblolly pine.

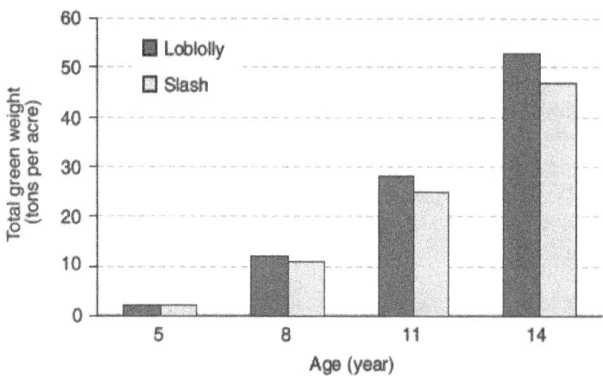

Figure 3—Average total green weight production by species over time and across all soil groups for the PMRC species comparison study.

INTENSIVE MANAGEMENT STUDIES

What about changes in management? In the last decade, pine has been planted on many acres in the CRP program. Those acres typically lack the hardwood component found on cutover sites and the ability of those sites to provide nitrogen and other nutrients to pines without fertilization is high. Concurrently, the level of management intensity has risen on cutover sites. Many cutover sites routinely now receive chemical site preparation to largely eradicate woody competition, at least early in the rotation. Many also receive herbaceous weed control in the first growing season and may receive fertilization at some point in the first few years.

The PMRC has an intensive culture density study in the coastal plain with both slash and loblolly present across a range of soil classes. The study is 6 years old. The species can be compared on plots that have planting densities of 300, 900, and 1500 trees per acre. There are two levels of culture. On the intensive level, all of the competing vegetation, both herbaceous and woody, is removed from the site and kept off as much as possible at all times. This requires a great deal of work for the first two or three years, but once crown closure is established the shade does the work of

keeping the plots clean. Plots were fertilized at planting with 500 pounds of 10-10-10 fertilizer per acre and have been fertilized since then at least every two years. On the operational culture plots, there was both chemical and mechanical site preparation, one year of banded weed control, and fertilization only at planting with five hundred pounds of 10-10-10 fertilizer per acre.

Figure 4 shows that there is an effect on height growth from both culture and species. Loblolly has the ability to respond to the added nutrients, moisture, etc. afforded by the intensive culture and it responds with greatly increased height growth. It is 5 to 7 ft. taller than loblolly growing in operational stands. Slash, by comparison, adds about 2 ft. to the average height it obtains with operational culture with all of

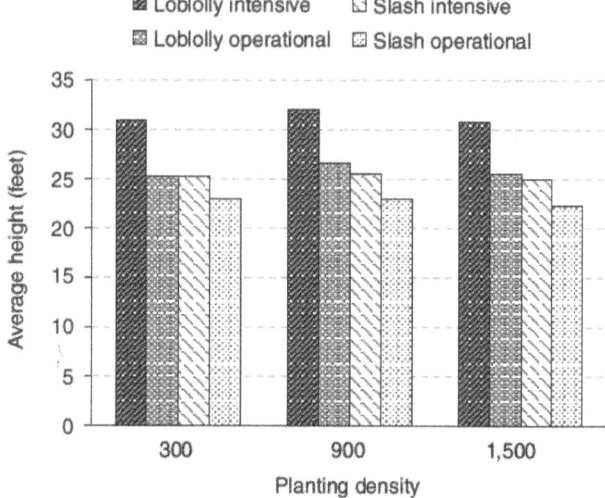

Figure 4—Average height by species, planting density, and management intensity for 6-year-old loblolly and slash pine on the PMRC culture/density trials.

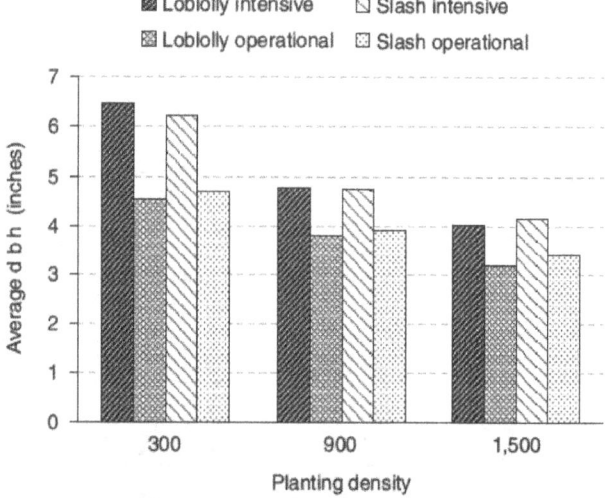

Figure 5—Average d.b.h. by species, planting density, and management intensity for 6-year-old loblolly and slash pine on the PMRC culture/density trials.

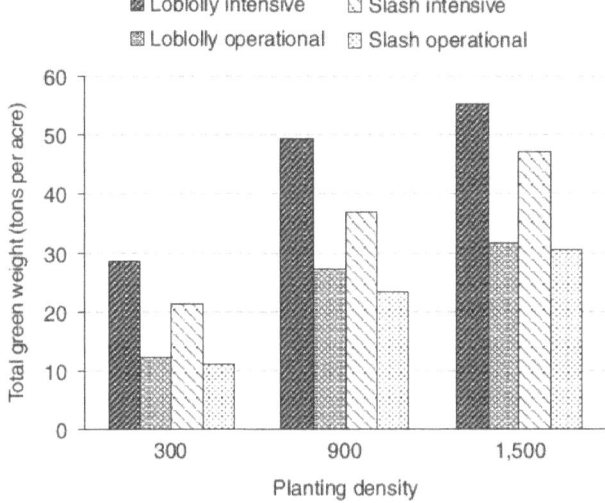

Figure 6—Average total green weight (tons per acre) by species, planting density, and management intensity for 6-year-old loblolly and slash pine on the PMRC culture/density trials.

the added benefits from intensive culture. In fact, the intensive slash pine height is about equal to the operational loblolly pine height. By comparison, the average d.b.h. values at age 6 are roughly equal for the two species across all densities when both receive the same culture (fig. 5). The total green weight at this young age shows the same pattern we have seen on the other studies discussed (fig. 6). On the operational culture plots, the loblolly has slightly more green weight per acre than the slash pine. On the more intensively managed plots, loblolly's ability to use more nutrients and moisture when they are provided results in a larger difference between species.

CONCLUSIONS

We have seen that on virtually all soil types evaluated in the native slash pine range loblolly produces more wood than slash pine. Does this mean that everyone who is planting slash pine is making a mistake? I would say no for several reasons. One is that the difference between the species is very small on what we would say are classic slash pine sites that will receive operational management. On CRIFF B, C, and D soil groups slash will produce on average about the same amount of wood as loblolly. Though this has not been verified with research data, some foresters

believe that there is less risk with slash pine on these sites. If management will be more intensive, then the decision swings more toward loblolly on any of these sites because of it's superior ability to take advantage of weed control and fertilization. Intensively managed slash pine sites can produce about 7 green tons per ac per yr whereas intensively managed loblolly stands can produce about 10-12 green tons per ac per yr.

Foresters and landowners may favor slash pine over loblolly for reasons other than wood yields. Slash pine would be the favored species for landowners who want to sell pinestraw for instance. Slash pine also prunes itself much better than loblolly, and for solid wood products the lumber grade will probably be higher for slash pine. This means that loblolly would have to produce more lumber quantity to stay even on value. Based on the differences in production on at least some of the soil types, loblolly may be able to produce enough more wood to still be favored. That will depend somewhat on the soil group and how the stand is to be managed. Slash pine is more resistant to southern pine beetle attack than loblolly and it is rarely bothered with pine tip moth which can decimate young loblolly stands. Planting both species across the landscape may afford an ownership with less risk and the opportunity to participate in different markets than going with either species alone. As with most decisions in life, the choice of species rarely rests with a comparison of only one characteristic. However, in terms of tons of wood produced, on most sites loblolly pine will produce more wood than slash pine. The decision to plant slash pine must then be made because of it's superiority by some other criterion.

LITERATURE CITED

Cole, D.E. 1975. Comparisons within and between populations of slash and loblolly pine. Georgia For. Res. Counc. Pap. No. 81. Macon, GA. 12 p.

Haines, L.W.; Gooding, J.; Wilhite, L. 1981. Site selection: slash pine versus the other species. In: The managed slash pine ecosystem. Sponsored by Institute of Food and Agric. Sci., Univ. of Florida, Gainesville, FL. 47 p.

Shiver, B.D.; Rheney, J.W.; Hitch, K.L. 2000. Loblolly pine outperforms slash pine in southeastern Georgia and northern Florida. South. J. Appl. For. 24(1): 1-6.

Shoulders, E. 1976. Site characteristics influence relative performance of loblolly and slash pine. USDA For. Serv. Res. Pap. SO-115, 16 p.

SPECIES DEPLOYMENT STRATEGIES FOR THE SOUTHERN PINES: SITE SPECIFIC MANAGEMENT PRACTICES FOR THE FLATWOODS OF GEORGIA AND FLORIDA

Thomas R. Fox[1]

Abstract—Four species of southern pine are commonly planted in the Coastal Plain of Georgia and Florida: slash pine (*Pinus elliottii*), loblolly pine (*P. taeda*), longleaf pine (*P. palustris*), or sand pine (*P. clausa*). These species vary greatly in their site requirements and growth rates. Appropriate deployment decisions must be made in order to insure adequate survival, growth and yield of plantations. Species deployment options based on the silvical characteristics of the four species and soil properties in the Flatwoods are discussed. A species deployment decision key is presented that provides site specific recommendations for in the planting southern pines in the Flatwoods based on the CRIFF soil group classification system.

INTRODUCTION

Implementing site-specific silvicultural prescriptions is the key to optimizing stand growth and financial returns in pine plantations in the South. Selecting the appropriate species of pine to plant on each site is perhaps the most difficult decisions facing foresters during the regeneration process in the Coastal Plain of Georgia and Florida. It is also the most important decision, because the ultimate success or failure of a plantation usually depends on this decision, which is irrevocable.

The Coastal Plain of Georgia and Florida is characterized by generally level topography with soils derived from relatively recent marine sediments (Huddlestun 1988, Randazzo and Jones1997). This region is generally referred to as the Flatwoods. Soils in the Flatwoods vary from excessively well-drained sands to very poorly drained clays. These soil differences frequently occur over very short distances, with drastically different soils existing adjacent to one another on the landscape. Minor changes in elevation of only a few feet, have major impacts on soil drainage class, site quality and tree growth. Disease hazard, including fusiform rust, and annosus root rot, also varies widely across the region (Anderson and Mistretta 1982). These factors contribute to the diverse mosaic of site types in the region. Planting the same species on all sites across the Flatwoods is almost certainly going to produce poorly growing plantations or even failures on many sites. Unfortunately, this approach was employed by numerous organizations throughout the South for many years. The legacy of this "one size fits all" approach is evident in the number of poorly growing "off site" plantations that still exist across the region.

The complexity of the species deployment decision in the Flatwoods is greater than in other regions of the South because four different species of southern pine are viable alternatives. Slash pine (*Pinus elliottii*), loblolly pine (*P. taeda*), longleaf pine (*P. palustris*), or sand pine (*P. clausa*) may be the best species for a particular site. In other regions, there are usually only two alternative pine species suitable for planting, and in many cases only one.

The species deployment decision is also influenced by changes in growth rate and disease resistance resulting from tree improvement efforts. This is particularly true for slash and loblolly pine. As gains from tree improvement become available in genetically improved seedlings, the deployment options for a given species change. For example, significant gains in fusiform resistance in slash pine have been made through tree breeding , which now permits successful deployment of slash pine to sites with higher fusiform rust hazard (Hodge and others 1993). As advanced generations of improved species produced through control pollination, rooted cuttings and somatic embryogenesis become available, the deployment decision will likely shift from a species decision to a specific family or clone decision. In this scenario, an individual family or clone of a given species may be best for a given site while a different family or clone of the same species is not suitable.

THE CRIFF SOIL CLASSIFICATION SYSTEM

Soil properties determine site quality and thus strongly influence the species deployment decision. Forest soils in the Flatwoods of Georgia and Florida are classified taxonomically into six major soil orders including Alfisols, Entisols, Histosols, Inceptisols, Spodosols, and Ultisols. A large number of individual soil series are identified and mapped by the USDA Natural Resource Conservation Service, based on the physical and chemical properties of the various soil horizons present. Unfortunately, the general soil maps that are prepared based on established soil series are often not well suited for forestry applications because soil properties important for silvicultural decisions are not recognized. Consequently, forest site quality often varies greatly within one soil series while different soil series may have similar site qualities. It is often difficult to

[1] Thomas R. Fox, Associate Professor of Silviculture and Forest Soils, Department of Forestry, Virginia Polytechnic Institute and State University, Blacksburg, VA 24061.

Citation for proceedings: Dickens, E.D.; Barnett, J.P.; Hubbard, W.G.; Jokela, E.J., eds. 2004. Slash pine: still growing and growing! Proceedings of the slash pine symposium. Gen. Tech. Rep. SRS-76. Asheville, NC: U.S. Department of Agriculture, Forest Service, Southern Research Station. 148 p.

accurately interpret existing soil maps and use the information to assist with silvicultural decisions without special training in forest soils or considerable experience in the area. Compounding the problem, published soil maps are not available for large areas in the Flatwoods where row crop agriculture is a minor land use. To overcome these limitations, many industrial forest products companies mapped soils on their own land to provide foresters the tools needed to make site-specific silvicultural decisions. However, these maps are proprietary and not usually available to the general public.

The Cooperative Research in Forest Fertilization (CRIFF) program at the University of Florida, recognized the need for a simplified soil classification system that could be used to improve silvicultural decisions. They developed a classification system that divides soils in the Flatwoods into 8 broad classes based on soil drainage class, soil texture and depth to the B horizon (Fisher and Garbett 1980). These CRIFF soil groups are useful tools in making site-specific silvicultural decisions, including species deployment.

The properties of the eight CRIFF soil groups are presented schematically in figure 1. The CRIFF A and B groups soils are found in wet, mineral flats. They are very poorly to somewhat poorly drained and contain a fine textured B horizon (clayey subsoil). In the CRIFF A group, the clayey subsoil occurs within 20 inches of the surface while in the CRIFF B group it is deeper than 20 inches. CRIFF A group soils are locally referred to as "gumbo clays". The CRIFF C and D group soils are very poorly to moderately well drained soils of the Flatwoods that contain a spodic horizon, which is a reddish brown to black subsurface horizon containing organic matter, iron and aluminum. This subsurface horizon is often referred to locally as a "hardpan". The surface soil in CRIFF C and D group soils are sandy textured. The distinguishing feature separating CRIFF C and D group soils is the presence of a clay horizon below the hardpan in the CRIFF C group soil. CRIFF E and F soils are moderately well drained to well drained soils that occur on uplands that contain a fine textured B horizon (clay subsoil). They are distinguished from one another by the depth to the clay subsoil. In the CRIFF E group soil, the clay subsoil is within

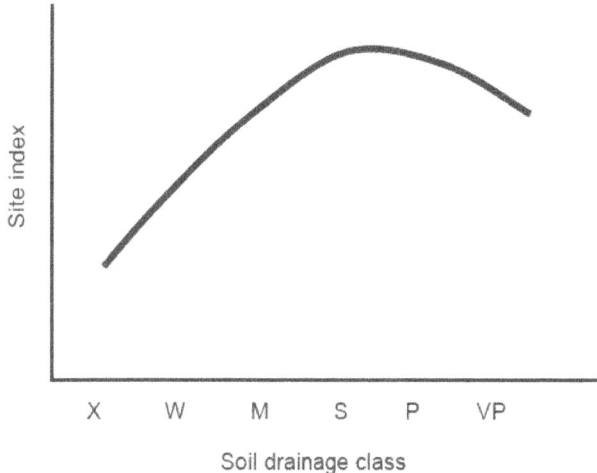

Figure 2—Relationship between soil drainage class and site index for slash pine on CRIFF soil groups in the flatwoods.

20 inches of the surface while in the CRIFF F group it is deeper than 20 inches. The CRIFF G group soils are well to excessively well drained sandy soils, with no subsurface horizons. These are the sandhill soils in the region. CRIFF H group soils are muck (organic) soils that are very poorly drained. They typically occur in hardwood swamps and cypress ponds and strands.

Results from soil-site comparisons conducted as part of large scale forest land classification programs in the Flatwoods indicate that site quality, as measured by site index, varies considerably within the CRIFF soil groups. Site quality is related to soil drainage class (fig. 2). The most productive soils tend to be somewhat poorly drained. Site index decreases slowly as soils get wetter and more rapidly as soils get drier.

SPECIES CHARACTERISTICS AFFECTING THE DEPLOYMENT DECISION

The silvical characteristics of a species determine its ability to survive, grow and compete on a particular site. The most important silvical characteristics of slash, loblolly, longleaf and sand pine affecting the deployment decision in the Flatwoods include tolerance to anaerobic soil conditions, drought tolerance, soil fertility requirements, relative growth rate throughout the life of the tree, and insect and disease resistance. The following discussion summarizes the important characteristics of each species that influences the deployment decision using CRIFF soil groups to classify sites.

Sand Pine

Sand pine is adapted to grow on excessively drained, infertile, deep sandy soils (Brendemuehl 1990). These soils are included in the CRIFF G group. Sand pine is susceptible to root rot diseases when it is planted on soils where fine textured horizons or a fluctuating water table occur within the rooting zone. Stands planted where these conditions exist within 10 feet of the soil surface almost always fail. Therefore, care must be exercised to insure that sand pine is planted only on the deepest, driest sandhill soils. Sites

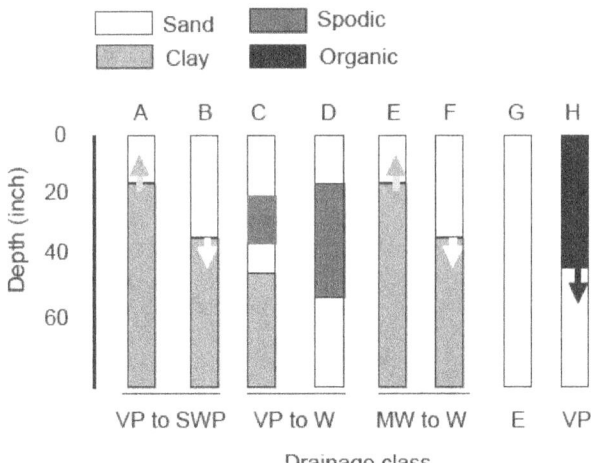

Figure 1—CRIFF soil groups.

suited for sand pine are often smaller areas within larger tracts. The presence of rosemary (Ceratiola ericoides) and lichen mats (Cladonia spp.) are useful indicators of sites suited for sand pine. In most cases, no other species of pine will produce merchantable stands on the sites best suited for sand pine. Although sand pine grows remarkably well on these sites, it is often difficult to sell sand pine stumpage, except during extremely wet periods. Therefore, sand pine stumpage must be marketed opportunistically.

Longleaf Pine

Longleaf pine naturally occurs on a wide variety of sites in the Flatwoods, from excessively drained, deep sandy soils to poorly drained clay flats (Boyer 1990). Longleaf pine will even occur on hummocks and other elevated micro topographic features in cypress ponds and muck swamps. Although it occurs on a wide variety of sites, the growth rate of longleaf pine is slower than that of slash and loblolly pine except on moderately well, well drained and excessively drained sandy soils with low site index (Wilhite 1976, Shoulders 1990). These sites include CRIFF G group soils and the moderately well and well drained CRIFF D group soils. Longleaf is also suited for the well drained to excessively well drained soils in the CRIFF F group where the clay is deeper than 5 feet. Longleaf is less susceptible to insect and diseases than the other pines. Most importantly, it is practically immune to fusiform rust, which is a serious problem on the dry sandy sites best suited to longleaf pine. Southern pine beetle is also seldom a serious problem in longleaf pine. Longleaf does not tolerate competition, whether from herbaceous vegetation or hardwoods (Boyer 1990). On sites with even moderate amounts of competing vegetation, longleaf pine will remain in the grass stage for extended periods. In the presence of competing hardwoods, growth and yield of longleaf pine stands will be drastically reduced. In the absence of competition, longleaf pine can grow fairly rapidly on relatively poor sites. It has excellent form and high stumpage value. Longleaf pine straw is an important product in many stands. The value of pine straw can exceed the timber value in some stands.

Slash Pine

Slash pine occurs on most soil types throughout the Flatwoods, with the exception of the driest sandhill soils (Lohrey and Kossuth 1990). Slash pine is often preferred in local markets because it tends to have good form and self prunes well (Koch 1972). Slash pine is less nutrient demanding than loblolly pine and grows well on the infertile, wet, sandy soils that naturally occur in the region. Slash pine is best suited to poorly drained to moderately well drained soils in the CRIFF B, C and D groups. Slash pine tends to be more plastic in its site requirements than loblolly pine in the Flatwoods. Consequently, the growth of slash pine is more consistent than loblolly across the soil and site differences that occur with minor topographic changes in this region. For example, slash grows better in the small, minor depressions that are common in this landscape where poorly and very poorly drained soils develop. It appears to tolerates flooding better than loblolly pine, although this may be an interaction with soil fertility because many of the very poorly drained soils that flood periodically tend to have low available phosphorus (Jokela 2004).

Susceptibility to fusiform rust is the most important factor limiting slash pine deployment. Although genetically improved slash pine are more rust resistant than non improved sources, fusiform rust infection rates are unacceptably high on high rust hazard sites, even with genetically improved families (Schmidt and others 1986). On well drained soils in the CRIFF D and G groups, where rust hazard is usually fairly high and site quality is poor, longleaf pine should be considered as an alternative to slash pine. Slash pine is more resistant than loblolly to tip moth and southern pine beetle attack. Anecdotal observations comparing slash and loblolly pine in operational plantations suggest that slash pine is less susceptible to nutrient deficiencies, and diseases such as needle cast. Slash pine is very susceptible to ice and snow damage. Rust and glaze hazards are the main factors limiting the slash pine deployment outside the Lower Coastal Plain of Georgia and Florida.

Loblolly Pine

Loblolly pine is native throughout the Flatwoods region; however, historically it was much less common than longleaf and slash pine in this region, occurring mostly on wetter sites along pond margins (Baker and Langdon 1990). Loblolly pine was probably most prevalent in stands growing on wet clay soils where calcareous deposits such as limestone and shell fragments were present in the rooting zone. These sites, often locally referred to as hammocks, typically supported stands containing mesic hardwoods and included a significant component of cabbage palm (Sabal palmetto). Loblolly pine has been widely planted on a variety of soils types in the Flatwoods in recent years.

Loblolly pine tends to be more nutrient demanding than slash or longleaf pine. On high fertility sites, or in stands that are intensively managed, loblolly grows very well. Loblolly grows best in the Flatwoods on CRIFF A group soils, provided that the severe phosphorus deficiencies commonly occurring on these soils are corrected through fertilization (Jokela and others 1991). Loblolly also appears well suited to the drier soils in the CRIFF E and F groups where an argillic horizon is present. These soils are more typical of the Upper Coastal Plain and Piedmont. However, most soils in the Flatwoods, including CRIFF B, C and D group soils, suffer from deficiencies of multiple nutrients, including nitrogen, phosphorus, and potassium. Growth of loblolly pine on these soils is generally poor unless balanced fertilizers are applied throughout the rotation. It may be necessary to fertilize as often as every three to five years to maintain acceptable growth rates in loblolly pine because these sandy soils do not retain nutrients (Ballard and Fiskell 1974). On moderately well drained and well drained CRIFF C and D group soils, loblolly pine tends to grow very poorly even when intensively managed. Several instances of sudden and complete mortality of young loblolly pine stands in intensively managed research plots have been observed on these soils. Loblolly pine should not be planted on these soils. Fortunately, these drier sites can be recognized relatively easily using gallberry (Ilex glabra) as an indicator species. Gallberry becomes much less common and grows less vigorously as drainage class changes from somewhat poorly drained to moderately well drained. It tends to disappear completely from the understory shrub community on well drained and drier sites in the Flatwoods.

Loblolly pine is much more resistant to fusiform rust than slash pine, which is especially important because rust hazard is usually high on CRIFF A, E and F soils where loblolly grows best. Loblolly is much more susceptible than slash and longleaf pine to southern pine beetle attack (Thatcher and others 1980). Southern pine beetle hazard is related to stand density, with increased susceptibility in loblolly pine stands with basal areas greater than 100 ft² per acre (Belanger and others 1993). Thinning dense loblolly stands and maintaining a mixture of loblolly and slash pine stands across the landscape in the Flatwoods are effective strategies for reducing southern pine beetle incidence (Belanger and others 1993)

GROWTH RATE OF SLASH VERSUS LOBLOLLY PINE

It is easy for most foresters to recognize the deep, droughty, sandy soils where longleaf pine or sand pines are best suited. In this regard, it is unfortunate that these dry, sandy sites usually occur on a fairly small percentage of the landscape in the Flatwoods. On most sites in the Flatwoods, foresters are faced with a more difficult species deployment decision regarding slash versus loblolly pine. The fundamental question that continues to perplex foresters faced with this decision in the Flatwoods is 'What is the relative growth rate of the two species?". Over the years, numerous studies have been published that compare the growth rate of the two species (Wakely 1954, Shoulders 1976, Wilhite 1976, Haines and Gooding 1981, Shiver and others 2000). The data from Shiver and others (2000) clearly demonstrates the effect of soil type on relative growth of slash and loblolly pine (fig. 3). On the CRIFF A group soils (poorly drained gumbo clays), loblolly pine grows much better than slash pine. Loblolly also grows better than slash pine on the upland well drained clay soils in the CRIFF F group. On the CRIFF B, C and D group soils, that represent the majority of sites in the Flatwoods, the growth of slash and loblolly pine are similar. This occurred in spite of somewhat lower overall survival of slash than loblolly pine on these soil groups due to higher rust related mortality in the slash pine (Shiver and others 2000).

At one time, site index was considered a fixed property determined by the interaction of climate and soil properties.

It is now recognized that site index is strongly affected by silvicultural inputs. For example, a stand growing on an infertile soil with an inherently low natural site index, may have a high "expressed" site index if an appropriate fertilization regime is employed. The expressed site index for a stand is still an important property because it significantly affects growth and yield in the stand. Results from Jokela and others (2000) illustrate the impact of management intensity on the relative growth of the two species and how that would likely change the expressed site index (table 1). On the CRIFF A and B group soils, which are inherently very productive once phosphorus deficiencies have been corrected, loblolly pine grew better than slash pine, regardless of treatment. However, it is clear that loblolly responded more than slash pine to weed control and fertilization on these soil types. Expressed site index will be much greater on CRIFF A groups following phosphorus fertilization. Volume growth through age 8 more than doubled from 713 ft³ per acre in the control to 1430 ft³ per acre in the weed control plus fertilization treatment with loblolly pine while growth increased much less in slash pine (499 ft³ per acre vs 645 ft³ per acre), respectively in the two treatments. However, slash pine grew as well or better than loblolly on the CRIFF C and D group soils. Again, both species positively responded to fertilization and weed control and these silvicultural practices will significantly alter expressed site index of the stand.

The above results illustrate how the relative growth rate of the two species, and thus expressed site index, varies depending on the soil type and the intensity of silviculture used to manage the stand (Jokela and others 2000, Shiver and others 2000). A general conclusion from these data is that on better quality sites or those sites that are more intensively managed, loblolly pine generally grows better than slash pine. On poorer quality sites, or those sites with less intensive management, slash pine grows better than loblolly pine. On intermediate sites or with moderate levels of silvicultural input, the growth of the two species will likely be similar. Graphical site index comparisons for several species have been developed in other parts of the United States (Dolittle 1958). Figure 4 illustrates the generalized relationship between the site index for slash pine and loblolly pine in the Flatwoods. The dashed one-to-one line

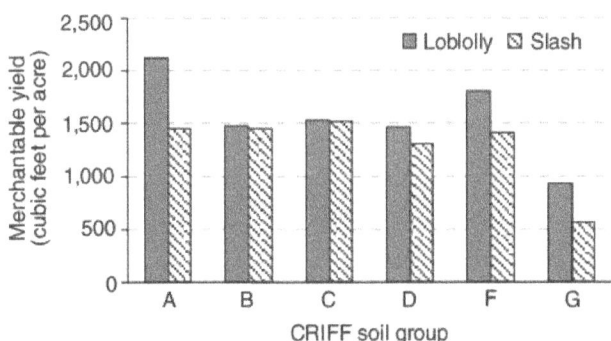

Figure 3—Merchantable volume production of loblolly and slash pine through 14 years on different CRIFF soil groups in the flatwoods of Georgia and Florida (Shiver and others 2000).

Table 1—Stand volume after eight growing seasons for slash and loblolly pine receiving fertilization and weed control at establishment

Treatment	CRIFF A and B soil		CRIFF C and D soil	
	Loblolly	Slash	Loblolly	Slash
	- - - - - - - cubic feet per acre - - - - - - -			
Control	713	499	452	733
Fertilization	1,202	605	598	761
Weed control	803	694	521	707
Fertilization plus weed control	1,430	645	688	805

CRIFF = cooperative research in forest fertilization.
Source: Jokela and others (2000).

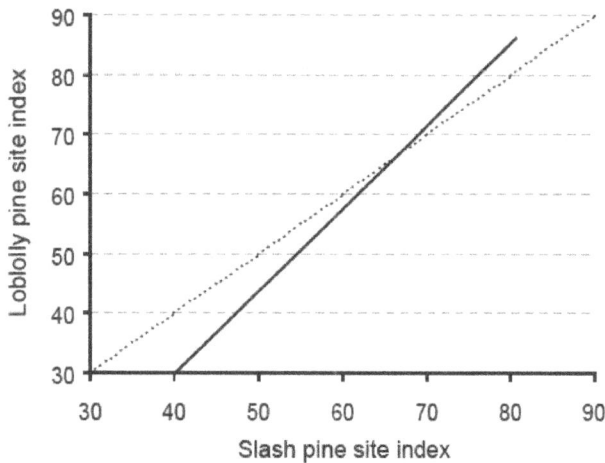

Figure 4—Relationship between slash pine and loblolly pine site index (solid line) on CRIFF soils in the Flatwoods. The dashed line represents the one-to-one relationship where site index of the two species are equal. Below a site index of 60, slash pine will grow better than loblolly pine. Between site index 60 and 70, growth of the two species is equivalent. Above a site index of 70, loblolly pine will grow better than slash pine.

represents points where the expressed site index of slash and loblolly pine would be equivalent. The solid line represents the author's view of the growth of the two species based on observations in research trials and operational

plantations throughout the Flatwoods. At low expressed site index ($SI_{25} < 60$), slash pine will generally grow better than loblolly pine. At intermediate site index values ($60 < SI_{25} < 70$), the growth of the two species will be about the same. At high expressed site index values ($SI_{25} > 70$), loblolly pine will grow better than slash pine.

SPECIES DEPLOYMENT DECISION KEY

A decision key for selecting the appropriate species to plant in the Flatwoods is presented in figure 5. The decision key consists of a series of questions that leads the user to a recommended species. The decision key is based on CRIFF soil groups, expressed site index (base age 25), depth to subsurface soil clay or spodic horizons, and fusiform rust hazard. The decision key is not intended to serve as a cookbook to be followed blindly. Rather, it provides a way to systematically consider these factors that affect the decision on which species to plant. Numerous factors can influence which species is best suited for a particular site including growth rate of previous stand, desire for species diversity across the landscape, local rust hazard, projected silvicultural practices, genetic quality of the seed lots available for planting, and local stumpage markets or mill requirements.

Several conventions and assumptions are used in the decision key that should be recognized. The key frequently requires the user to estimate site index. The key assumes that this is the expressed site index (base age 25) for slash pine. It used the relationship in figure 3 to determine which species will grow better, and thus be the preferred species.

Species deployment decision key for southern pines in the Coastal Plain of Georgia and Florida

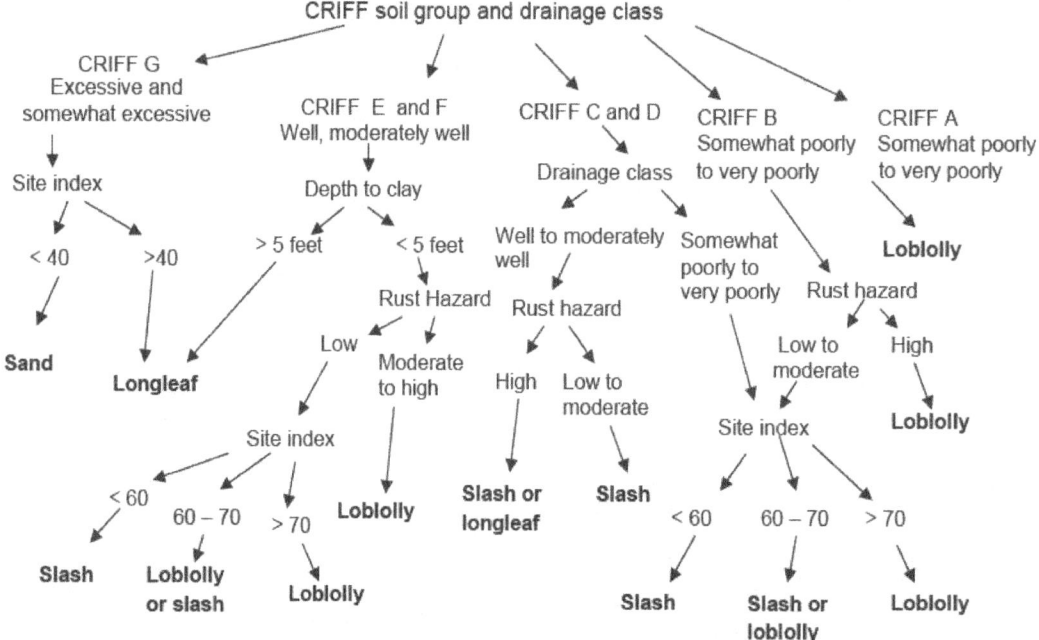

(Note: Soils in CRIFF Group H are generally not well suited for pine management.)

Figure 5—Species deployment decision key for southern pines in the Coastal Plain of Florida and Georgia.

Because expressed site index is so strongly affected by management intensity, it assumes that the silvicultural treatments, such as weed control and repeated fertilization, required to maintain that expressed site index will be maintained throughout the rotation. If future silvicultural inputs are uncertain, it would be wise to use a conservative value for the estimate of expressed site index.

The use of the key is illustrated in the following examples. On a CRIFF G group soils that is excessively well drained with an estimated slash pine site index of 45, longleaf pine would be the recommended species. On a site with a CRIFF C group soil that is somewhat poorly drained with an expressed site index of 60, slash pine would be the preferred species. On this same site, if more intensive silvicultural inputs were anticipated and the expressed site index were estimated to be 68, the growth of slash and loblolly would be roughly equal and either species would be acceptable. If very intensive silvicultural practices were applied and the expressed site index was expected to be higher than 70, loblolly pine would be the preferred species because at this level of productivity loblolly would produce greater stand volume than slash pine.

LITERATURE CITED

Anderson, R.L.; Mistretta, P.A. 1982. Management strategies for reducing losses caused by fusiform rust, annosus root rot, and littleleaf disease. Agricultural Handbook No. 597. U.S. Department of Agriculture, Forest Service. Cooperative State Research Service. 30 p.

Baker, J.B.; Langdon, O.G. 1990. *Pinus taeda* L.: loblolly pine. In: Silvics of North America: Volume 1. Conifers. Burns, Russell M.; Honkala, Barbara H., tech. cords. Agricultural Handbook No. 654. U.S. Department of Agriculture, Forest Service, Washington, DC. 675 p.

Ballard, R.; Fiskell, J.G.A. 1974. Phosphorus retention in Coastal Plain forest soils: I. relationship to soil properties. Soil Sci. Soc. Am. Proc. 38: 250-255.

Belanger, R.P.; Hedden, R.L.; Lorio, P.L., Jr. 1993. Management strategies to reduce losses from the southern pine beetle. South. J. Appl. For. 17(3): 150-154.

Boyer, W.D. 1990. *Pinus Palustris* Mill. longleaf pine. In: Silvics of North America: Volume 1. Conifers. Burns, Russell M.; Honkala, Barbara H., tech. cords. Agricultural Handbook No. 654. U.S. Department of Agriculture, Forest Service, Washington, DC. 675 p.

Brendemuehl, R.H. 1990. *Pinus clausa* (Chapm. ex Engelm.) Vasey ex Sarg. sand pine. In: Silvics of North America: Volume 1. Conifers. Burns, Russell M.; Honkala, Barbara H., tech. cords. Agricultural Handbook No. 654. U.S. Department of Agriculture, Forest Service, Washington, DC. 675 p.

Dolittle, W.T. 1958. Site index comparisons for several forest species in the Southern Appalachians. Soil Sci. Soc. Am. Proc. 22: 455-458.

Fisher, R.F.; Garbett, W.S. 1980. Response of semimature slash and loblolly pine plantations to fertilization with nitrogen and phosphorus. Soil Sci. Soc. Am. J. 44: 850-854.

Haines, L.W.; Gooding, J. 1981. Site selection: slash pine versus other species. In: Stone, E.L., ed. The managed slash pine ecosystem. 1981 June 9-11; Gainesville, FL.: School of Forest Resources and Conservation, University of Florida: 112-130.

Hodge, G.R.; White, T.L.; Schmidt, R.A.; Allen, J.E. 1993. Stability of rust infection ratios for resistant and susceptible slash and loblolly pine across rust hazard levels. South. J. Appl. For. 17(4): 188-192.

Huddlestun, P.F. 1988. A revision of the lithostratigraphic units of the Coastal Plain of Georgia. The Miocene through Holocene. Bull. 104. Dept. of Natural Resources, Environ. Protection Div., Georgia Geol. Surv. Atlanta, GA. 162 p.

Jokela, E.J. 2004. Nutrient management of southern pines. In: Dickens, E.D.; Barnett, J.P.; Hubbard, W.G.; Jokela, E.J., eds. Slash pine: still growing and growing! Proceedings of the slash pine symposium. Gen. Tech. Rep. SRS-76. Asheville, NC: U.S. Department of Agriculture, Forest Service, Southern Research Station: 27-35.

Jokela, E.J.; Allen, H.L.; McFee, W.W. 1991. Fertilization of southern pines at establishment. In: Duryea, M.L.; Dougherty, P.M. eds. Forest Regeneration Manual. Kluwer Academic Publishers, Dordrecht, The Netherlands. 263-280.

Jokela, E.J.; Wilson, D.S.; Allen, J.E. 2000. Early growth responses of slash and loblolly pine following fertilization and herbaceous weed control treatments at establishment. South. J. Appl. For. 24(1): 23-30.

Koch, P. 1972. Utilization of the southern pines. Vol. 1. The Raw Material. Agricultural Handbook No. 420. U.S. Department of Agriculture, Forest Service, Washington, DC. 734 p.

Lohrey, R.E.; Kossuth, S.V. 1990. *Pinus elliottii* Engelm. slash pine. In: Silvics of North America: Volume 1. Conifers. Burns, Russell M.; Honkala, Barbara H., tech. cords. Agricultural Handbook No. 654. U.S. Department of Agriculture, Forest Service, Washington, DC. 675 p.

Randazzo, A.F.; Jones, D.S., eds. 1997. The geology of Florida. The University of Florida Press. Gainesville, FL 327 p.

Schmidt, R.A.; Holley, R.C.; Klapproth, M.C.; Miller, T. 1986. Temporal and spatial patterns of fusiform rust epidemics in young plantations of resistant slash and loblolly pines. Plant Disease 70: 661-666.

Shiver, B.D.; Rheney, J.W.; Hitch, K.L. 2000. Loblolly pine outperforms slash pine in southeast Georgia and northern Florida. South. J. Appl. For. 24(1): 31-36.

Shoulders, E. 1976. Site characteristics influence the relative performance of loblolly and slash pine. Res. Pap. SO-115. U.S. Department of Agriculture, Forest Service, New Orleans, LA. 16 p.

Shoulders, E. 1990. Identifying longleaf pine sites. In Farrar, R.M. ed. Proceedings of the symposium on the management of longleaf pine. Gen. Tech. Rep. S0-75. U.S. Department of Agriculture, Forest Service. New Orleans, LA. 23-37.

Thatcher, R.C.; Searcy, J.L.; Coster, J.E.; Hertel, G.D., eds. 1980. The southern pine beetle. Science and Educational Admin. Tech. Bull. 1631. U.S. Department of Agriculture, Expanded Southern Pine Beetle Research Applications Program. 266 p.

Wakely, P.C. 1954. Planting the southern pines. Agricultural Monograph No. 18. U.S. Department of Agriculture, Forest Service. Washington, DC. 233 p.

Wilhite, L.P. 1976. Slash, loblolly, longleaf and Sonderegger pines 20 years after planting on Leon sand in northeastern Florida. Res. Pap. SE-153. U.S. Department of Agriculture, Forest Service. Asheville, NC. 8 p.

AN ECONOMIC COMPARISON OF SLASH AND LOBLOLLY PINE UNDER VARIOUS LEVELS OF MANAGEMENT IN THE LOWER ATLANTIC AND GULF COASTAL PLAIN

Coleman W. Dangerfield, Jr., E. David Dickens, and David J. Moorhead[1]

Abstract—Non-industrial private forest (NIPF) landowners have perceived reduced product market availability and increased price uncertainty since late 1997 in the southeastern United States. Lower Atlantic and Gulf Coastal Plain NIPF landowners seek management options utilizing two commonly available pine species; loblolly (*Pinus taeda* L.) and slash (*Pinus elliottii*, Engelm.) to enhance feasibility, profitability, and cash-flow of production forestry enterprises. At the same time, NIPF landowners desire heightened flexibility across time required to achieve marketable forest products. This study examines feasibility, profitability, and cash-flow of short-rotation management options affecting wood-flow for slash and loblolly pine plantations including thinning, fertilization, and pine straw harvests under alternative levels of stocking, productivity and product prices. Financial measures of profitability calculated include soil expectation value (SEV), annual equivalent value (AEV), and internal rate of return (IRR).

INTRODUCTION

Private non-industrial forest (NIPF) landowners in the Atlantic and Gulf Coastal Plain from South Carolina to Mississippi question whether to plant loblolly or slash pine on cut-over and old-field sites. They also question spending moderate to relatively large sums of money in intensive forest management under the current and anticipated stumpage prices and economic uncertainty. To address these questions, we used the Georgia Pine Plantation (GaPPs 4.20) growth and yield Model developed by Bailey and Zhao (1998). The data to develop the growth and yield models for loblolly and slash were constrained to data up to age 25-years. Therefore we used a 24-year rotation age that had a mixed product class distribution of pulpwood, chip&saw (C-N-S) and small sawtimber (ST). Generally culmination of merchantable volume mean annual increment occurs for both species on average to good sites and management in the early 20-years (Pienaar and others 1996). Older rotation ages are often financially attractive but will not be addressed in this paper.

METHODOLOGY
Common Assumptions

The rotation age was set at 24-years for loblolly and slash pine plantations. A discount rate of 8 percent was used to calculate soil expectation value (SEV), annual equivalent value (AEV), and internal rate of return (IRR). Fire protection cost was assumed to be $2 per ac. per yr., stand management at $2 per ac per yr and property taxes at $5 per ac per yr. Thus, the total annual costs for each year of the rotation was $9 per acre. This value cost goes in the transaction table as an annual cost during the rotation. The present value of this net, annual cost flow is $94.75 during the 24-year rotation. Results are reported in constant dollars, before taxes.

Site preparation and planting costs totaled $250 per acre. This cost could include a mechanical site prep treatment, burn and plant or a herbicide, burn, plant, and herbaceous weed control (Dubois and others 1999). Site preparation options and associated costs vary extensively by location, prior stand history, harvesting utilization, landowner objectives and monies available. The assumption used was that level of site preparation intensity was matched to level of competition control needed so that wood-flows were comparable within site productivity levels, after site preparation and planting.

South Georgia stumpage Prices, reported through Timber Mart-South® (TMS) for 4th quarter year 2000 average, used in this analysis for loblolly and slash were net of property taxes at harvest (2.5 percent) and net of marketing costs (8 percent). The low TMS prices for pulpwood and chip&saw were used for thinning prices and average TMS prices for pulpwood, CNS, and ST are used for the clearcut. Net converted prices are found in table 1. Product class specifications are: pulpwood at a d.b.h. of 4.5 to 9 inches to a 3 inch top; CNS at a d.b.h of 9 to 12 inches to 6 inch top; and, ST with a d.b.h greater than 12 inches to a 10 inch top (inside bark). Product class stumpage prices are listed in table 2.

A fertilizer and application cost of $100 per ac for slash and loblolly per application at age 6-years (slash) or 8-years (loblolly) and 15-years-old was assumed. Fertilization with 150 then 200 N + 40 P (as diammonium phosphate and urea) per acre was part of this scenario to maintain pine straw production rates (Dickens 1999), to enhance wood volume (NCSUFNC 1998), and change product class distribution (Peinaar and Rheney 1996, Dickens 2001). Fertilization timing at age 6-years-old was 2 years prior to the initiation of straw raking (just prior to canopy closure). The second application 7 to 9 years later was just after a

---

[1] Coleman W. Dangerfield Jr., Forest Economics Professor; E. David Dickens, Associate Professor; and David J. Moorhead, Silviculture Professor, Daniel B. Warnell School of Forest Resources, The University of Georgia, Athens, GA 30602-2152.

Citation for proceedings: Dickens, E.D.; Barnett, J.P.; Hubbard, W.G.; Jokela, E.J., eds. 2004. Slash pine: still growing and growing! Proceedings of the slash pine symposium. Gen. Tech. Rep. SRS-76. Asheville, NC: U.S. Department of Agriculture, Forest Service, Southern Research Station. 148 p.

Table 1—Fertilizer periodic, per acre cost levels expressed as present values and annual equivalent values as used in the profitability analysis of slash and loblolly scenarios

Species	Cost per acre	Age	Present value of a periodic cost	AEV of the periodic cost
		years	- - - - - - - cost per acre - - - - - - -	
Loblolly	100	8, 15	81.05	7.70
Slash	100	6, 15	94.54	8.98

AEV = annual equivalent values.

Table 2—Cash and net (net of property taxes and marketing costs) per cord stumpage prices used in the profitability analysis of slash and loblolly scenarios

Price level	Cash or net	Pulpwood	Chip&saw	Sawtimber
		- - - - - - - - - cost per cord - - - - - - - - - -		
Low	Cash	18.36	83.96	88.65
	Net	16.43	75.14	79.34
Medium	Cash	24.15	92.85	107.51
	Net	21.61	83.10	96.22

Source: TMS (2000).

thinning (thinning scenario) and after the response (wood and straw) to the first application has become negligible. The periodic fertilizer application costs are converted to present values (PV) in year one, then re-computed as annual equivalent values (AEV). These AEVs were then put in the transaction table as annual expense cash-flows.

The pine straw income assumptions included were as follows: $50 and $100 per ac per yr raking income for slash

scenarios, and $25 and $50 per ac per yr for loblolly has been noted in south (slash) and central (loblolly) Georgia between 1998 and 1999 (Doherty 2000). Pine straw raking starts in year 8 for slash and two years later (year 10) for loblolly due to less contractor demand. Periodic pine straw income was converted to present values (PV) in year one, then re-computed as annual equivalent values (AEV) at the discount rate of 8 percent. These AEVs were then put in the transaction table as annual income cash-flows (table 3).

Table 3—Pine straw periodic per acre income levels expressed as present values and annual equivalent values as used in the profitability analysis of slash and loblolly pine scenarios

Species/scenario	Periodic income per acre per year raked	Present value of periodic income	AEV of periodic income
	- - - - - - - - cost per acre - - - - - - - -		
Loblolly w/thin	25	81.41	7.73
	50	162.82	15.46
Loblolly w/o thin	25	95.47	9.07
	50	190.93	18.13
Slash w/thin	50	208.75	19.83
	100	417.50	39.65
Slash w/o thin	50	239.11	22.71
	100	478.21	45.42

AEV = annual equivalent values.

The thinning scenarios include no thinning or one thinning at 15-years-old. Total woodflow of scenario with thinning is approximately 95 percent of total woodflow of scenario without thinning for slash and loblolly without fertilization, and 100 percent with fertilization. Residual basal area, after thinning (5th row with selection from below) is set at 65 sq. ft per ac.

Species Specific Assumptions

The slash pine scenarios assumed 500 living trees per acre (TPA) at age 5-years-old and a mean annual increment of 2.09 cds per ac per yr at age 24-years-old without fertilization. The base slash scenario woodflow was 15 percent less than base loblolly woodflow (Shiver and others 1999) at age 24-years. The assumed fertilizer applications will conservatively increase merchantable volume by 0.4 cd per ac per yr during for nine years following treatment (Jokela and Stearns-Smith 1996).

The following are the nine slash pine scenarios: (a) no thinning, no pine straw income, and no fertilization costs, (b) thin (at age 15-years to 65 ft² per ac), no straw, no fertilization, (c) no thin, fertilize at age 6- and 15-years-old, no straw, (d and e) no thin, fertilize,(as c), and rake pine straw in years 8 - 14 & 17 - 23 at $50 or $100 per ac per yr, (f) thin, fertilize, no straw, (g and h) thin, fertilize, and rake straw (as d and e), and (i) thin, fertilize, and pine straw at $100 per ac in years 8 through 14.

The loblolly pine survival was assumed to be the same as slash (500 TPA at age 5-years-old). The mean annual increment for loblolly was assumed to be 2.35 cds per ac per yr through age 24-years-old without fertilization. The base loblolly woodflow is approximately 15 percent greater than the slash base woodflow (Shiver and others 2000) at age 24. The assumed fertilizer applications will conservatively increase merchantable volume by 0.5 cd per ac per yr for nine years (NCSUFNC 1998).

The following are the nine loblolly pine scenarios: (a) no thin, no pine straw income, and no fertilization costs, (b) thin (at age 15-years to 65 ft² per ac), no straw, no fertilization, (c) no thin, fertilize at age 8- and 15-years-old, no straw, (d and e) no thin, fertilize,(as c), and rake pine straw in years 10 through 14 and 17 through 23 at $25 or $50 per ac per yr (f) thin, fertilize, no straw (g and h) thin, fertilize, and rake straw (as d and e), and (i) thin, fertilize, rake pine straw at $50 per ac in years 10 through 14.

RESULTS

The 2.09 and 2.35 cd per ac per yr productivity levels at age 24-years-old for slash and loblolly, respectively, are very realistic on most cut-over sites with chemical site preparation and post-plant herbaceous weed control (Pienaar and Rheney 1996) and is very conservative on most old-field sites. The 0.4 (slash) and 0.5 (loblolly) cds per ac per yr increase in wood production is conservative compared to other published reports (Jokela and Stearns-Smith 1993, Martin and others 1999, NCSFNC 1999) with nitrogen plus phosphorus fertilization at ages 6 or 8 and 15-years. No increase in pine straw income per acre was assumed with fertilization. Fertilization studies (Blevins and others 1996,

Dickens 1999) illustrate that pine straw production can be increased by an average of 40 to 50 percent over unfertilized stands. Fertilization was included in the pine straw production scenarios to maintain straw production as nutrients are removed/displaced with each raking.

All scenarios for both species achieved an internal rate of return of 8 percent or better using the aforementioned assumptions. Generally, the levels of forest management are economically justifiable in these cases, even using low to medium 2000 stumpage prices (TMS 2000) for South Georgia.

Thinning loblolly and slash pine stands increased internal rate of return by 1½ percent (slash) to 2 percent (loblolly) over unthinned stands (without pine straw income, tables 4 and 5). Thinning also increased total cash flow by $450 (slash) to $730 per acre (loblolly) compared to the unthinned counterpart with no additional cost.

The addition of pine straw income for slash pine increased rate of returns from 8.17 and 8.24 percent to 12.24 and 18.13 percent in unthinned stands (table 4). In thinned slash pine stands, pine straw income increased rate of returns from 9.71 to 13.84 percent and 19.62 percent (table 5). Pine straw raking in the slash scenario prior to thinning only (age 8 through 14-years) at $100 per ac per yr produced a rate of return of 15.55 percent. Pine straw raking in Georgia and North Florida typically does not continue after a thinning, but often continues in South and North Carolina.

Pine straw income in the loblolly scenarios increased rate of returns from 8.91 and 8.96 percent in the unthinned scenario to 10.10 and 11.36 percent (table 5). In the thinned loblolly scenarios, pine straw income increased rate of returns from 10.79 to 11.80 and 12.89 percent. Pine straw raking in the loblolly scenario prior to thinning only (ages 10 through 14-years) at $50 per ac per yr produced a rate of return of 11.94 percent.

Fertilization with 150 N+40 P and 200 N + 40 P per acre at ages 6 or 8-years (approaching canopy closure) and 15-years-old, respectively in the unthinned slash and loblolly scenarios increased cash flows by approximately $700 per acre over the unfertilized scenario but at a cost of $200 per acre. The highest SEV, AEV, IRR, and cash flow came from the slash pine scenario with a thinning, fertilization, and pine straw at $100 per ac per yr realized both pre- and port-thinning. The unthinned, fertilized slash pine scenario with pine straw income at $100 per ac had the second highest SEV, AEV, IRR, and cash flow. The thinned, fertilized, and pine straw raked prior to thinning produced the third highest SEV, AEV, and IRR. When wood value only is considered, loblolly produced more wood, more wood value (a diameter driven function),a higher SEV, AEV, IRR and cash flow with the aforementioned assumptions. Recent studies (Shiver and others 1999) have shown that loblolly will grow more wood than slash on a number of soils where both species are grown. Loblolly's superior wood volume yields do not necessarily equate to higher per acre or per unit wood stumpage prices. Clark (2002) noted that slash pine yielded more number one

Table 4—A comparison of slash pine plantation management scenarios[a] under a 24-year rotation and their effect on economic variables

Fertilization	Thin	Pine straw	Pulpwood	MAI	SEV	AEV	IRR
	year 15	cost per acre	percent		cost per acre		percent
N	N	N	62	2.09	20	2	8.24
N	Y	N	44	2.01	153	12	9.72
Y	N	N	48	2.33	18	1	8.17
Y	N	50	48	2.33	365	29	12.24
Y	N	100	48	2.33	711	57	18.13
Y	Y	N	38	2.37	179	14	9.71
Y	Y	50	38	2.37	526	42	13.84
Y	Y	100	38	2.37	873	70	19.62
Y	Y	100[b]	38	2.37	641	51	15.55

MAI = mean annual increment of wood growth, cord equivalents per acre per year; SEV = soil expectation value, calculated from perpetual rotations; AEV = annual equivalent value, net present worth expressed as an annual annuity; IRR = internal rate of return of the investment scenario (percent).
[a] Uninflated, 8-percent discount rate, before taxes, Georgia pine plantation v 4.20, general Plantation Management Research Cooperative (PMRC) model with treatment.
[b] Age 8 to 15 years.

Table 5—A comparison of loblolly pine plantation management scenarios[a] under a 24-year rotation and their effect on economic variables for southeast Georgia

Fertilization	Thin	Pine straw	Pulpwood	MAI	SEV	AEV	IRR
	15 years	cost per acre	percent		cost per acre		percent
N	N	N	61	2.35	81	7	8.91
N	Y	N	38	2.32	300	24	11.07
Y	N	N	49	2.69	105	8	8.96
Y	N	25	49	2.69	219	18	10.10
Y	N	50	49	2.69	332	27	11.36
Y	Y	N	38	2.68	313	25	10.79
Y	Y	25	38	2.68	410	33	11.80
Y	Y	50	38	2.68	506	40	12.89
Y	Y	50[b]	38	2.68	423	34	11.94

MAI = mean annual increment of wood growth, cord equivalents per acre per year; SEV = soil expectation value, calculated from perpetual rotations; AEV = annual equivalent value, net present worth expressed as an annual annuity; IRR = internal rate of return of the investment scenario (percent).
[a] Uninflated, 8-percent discount rate, before taxes, Georgia pine plantation v 4.20, general Plantation Management Research Cooperative (PMRC) model with treatment.
[b] Age 10 to 15 years.

lumber, had a slightly greater (4 to 11 percent greater) density, and 4 percent less moisture content than loblolly pine in growing in the same stand.

Non-industrial private forest landowners do have some attractive forest management options with both slash and loblolly pine even when using low to medium stumpage prices. Until pine straw contractor preferences and pricing change, where both slash and loblolly pine are grown, slash pine is preferred where pine straw can be raked for the higher per acre price.

LITERATURE CITED

Bailey, R.L.; Zhao, B. 1998. GaPPS 4.20 model. Warnell School of Forest Resources- UGA, Athens, GA.

Blevins, D.; Allen, H.L.; Co bert, S.; Gardner, W. 1996. Nutrition management for longleaf pinestraw - woodland owner notes. NC Coop. Ext Serv. Paper.

Clark A., III; Daniels, R.F. 2002. Wood quality of slash pine and its effect on lumber, paper, and other products. Presentation at the Slash Pine Symposium. Jekyll Island, GA. April 23-25, 2002.

Dickens, E.D. 1999. The effect of inorganic and organic fertilization on longleaf tree growth and pine straw production. In: Proceedings of the 10th Biennial So. Silvi. Res. Conf., Shreveport, LA, Feb 16-18, 1999. pp. 464-468.

Dickens, E.D. 2001. The effect of one-time biosolids application in an old-field loblolly pine plantation on diameter distr butions, volume per acre, and value per acre. In: Proceedings of the 11th Biennial So. Silvi. Res. Conf., Knoxville, TN. March 19-22, 2001. pp.

Doherty, B.A.; Teasley, R.J.; McKissick, J.C.; Givan, B. 2000. Nineteen ninety-nine farmgate value report. UGA CAES Center for Agribusiness and Econ. Dev., Center Staff Report No. 6. Athens, GA. 160 p.

Dubois, M.R.; McNabb, K.; Straka, T.K. 1999. Costs and cost trends for forestry practices in the South. Forest Landowner Magazine. March/April 1998. pp. 3-8.

Jokela, E.J.; Stearns-Smith, S.C. 1993. Fertilization of established southern pine stands: effects of single and split nitrogen treatments. SJAF 17(3): 135-138.

Martin, S.W.; Bailey, R.L.; Jokela, E.J. 1999. Growth and yield predictions for lower Coastal Plain slash pine plantations fertilized at mid-rotation. SJAF 23(1): 39-45.

Morris, L.A.; Jokela, E.J.; O'Connor, J.B., Jr. 1992. Silvicultural guidelines for pinestraw management in the SE US. GA Forest Res. Paper #88. GFC, Macon, GA. 11 p.

NCSFNC. 1998. North Carolina State University Forest Nutrition Coop - 26th annual report. School of Forest Resources, NCSU, Raleigh, NC. 23 p.

Pienaar, L.V.; Rheney, J.W. 1996. Potential productivity of intensively managed pine plantations - final report. The GA Consortium for Tech. Competitiveness in Pulp and Paper. 41 p.

Peinaar, L.V.; Shiver, B.D.; Rheney, J.W. 1996. Yield prediction for mechanically site-prepared slash pine plantations in the southeastern Coastal Plain. PMRC Tech. Rep. 1996-3. 57 p.

Shiver, B.D.; Rheney, J.W.; Hitch, K.L. 1999. Loblolly pine outperforms slash pine in southeast Georgia and northern Florida. SJAF 24(1) pp. 31-36.

TMS. 2000. Timber Mart South stumpage prices - 2nd quarter south Georgia 2000.

WOOD QUALITY OF SLASH PINE AND ITS EFFECT ON LUMBER, PAPER, AND OTHER PRODUCTS

Alexander Clark III and Richard F. Daniels[1]

Abstract—The majority of timber harvested in the South, the woodbasket for the United States, is southern pine. Slash pine (*Pinus elliottii* Engelm.) is one of the more important pine species harvested. Its wood has high specific gravity, long tracheids, low microfibril angle, high alpha cellulose, and medium lignin content. The high specific gravity and branching habit of slash pine make it an excellent species for manufacturing dimension lumber. When planted at wide spacings, slash pine will produce a higher proportion of No. 1 and better lumber than loblolly pine (*P. taeda* L.) because of its natural pruning and smaller diameter branching habit. The tracheid characteristics of slash pine make it an excellent species for linerboard and sack paper production.

INTRODUCTION

The South is the woodbasket for the United States, producing 58 percent of the timber harvested in the United States and 16 percent of the World's timber harvest (Wear and Greis 2002). Most timber harvested in the South is southern pine, and slash pine (*Pinus elliottii* Engelm.) is one of the more important pine species. Its wood properties make it a desired species for manufacturing structural lumber, structural plywood, poles, pilings, posts, pulp, and paper products. This paper discusses those properties and considers why they are so important in lumber and paper production.

WOOD PROPERTIES

Slash pine wood consists principally of closely packed tracheid cells that run vertically up the stem, and parenchyma tissue or rays that extend horizontally from the pith toward the bark. Tracheids make up more than 90 percent of southern pine wood volume (Koch 1972) and, thus, the properties of the tracheids determine the properties of the wood. Tracheids are like long straws with tapered ends, and whose cell walls surround an air space or cell lumen. Cell walls have two major constituents—cellulose and lignin.

Because the specific gravity (SG) of cellulose is almost identical to that of lignin, the SG of cell wall substance is considered to be constant for all wood species. Thus, wood SG is an excellent and simple measure, independent of species, of a wood's total cell wall substance (Megraw 1985) and a moderate-to-high SG is universally accepted as a desirable wood quality trait. The cell wall of a mature tracheid consists of a primary wall or middle lamella, composed largely of lignin, and a secondary wall that has three layers: (1) the S_1 (outer), (2) S_2 (middle), and (3) S_3 (inner) (Koch 1972). The S_2, or secondary layer, makes up the bulk of the tracheid wall. Cave (1976) showed that the middle lamella and S_1 and S_3 layers remain essentially fixed, while variation in volume of the S_2 layer is solely responsible for change in tracheid wall thickness. The secondary wall layer consists of helically arranged cellulose microfibrils oriented in the long axis of the tracheid. The orientation of the microfibrils relative to the long axis of the tracheid is known as the microfibril angle (MFA). The MFA is an important property in determining the stiffness and dimensional stability of solid wood products.

When assessing wood properties of a species for end use, it is important to consider SG, tracheid length, MFA, alpha cellulose content, and lignin content. Each plays an important role in determining the suitability of a species for a specific end use (table 1). Slash pine mature wood has SG, tracheid length, MFA, alpha cellulose, and lignin contents that make it highly desirable for solid wood products, such as structural lumber and veneer. It also has wood properties that make it desirable for paperboard production, such as kraft paper and sack paper. Slash pine mature wood is less suitable for production of fine papers because of its long tracheids with thick walls and corresponding high SG.

The weighted stem SG of slash pine wood, when averaged across the species' geographical range, is 0.53, compared to 0.47 for loblolly pine (*P. taeda* L.) (Wahlgren and others 1975). The difference in SG between species is due to both genetic and environmental factors. The weighted stem SG of pine is determined by the amount of thick-walled, high

Table 1—Slash pine wood properties and desired wood properties for southern pine wood products

Species and product	Specific gravity	Wood properties			
		Tracheid length	MFA	Alpha cellulose	Lignin contents
Slash pine	High	Long	Low	High	Medium
Solid wood	High	Long	Low	High	Medium
Paperboard	High	Long	Low	High	Low
Fine paper	High	Short	Low	High	Low

MFA = microfibril angle.

[1] Alexander Clark III, Research Wood Scientist, U.S. Department of Agriculture Forest Service, Southern Research Station, Athens, GA 30602–2044; and Richard F. Daniels, Professor, University of Georgia, Warnell School of Forest Resources, Athens, GA 30602.

Citation for proceedings: Dickens, E.D.; Barnett, J.P.; Hubbard, W.G.; Jokela, E.J., eds. 2004. Slash pine: still growing and growing! Proceedings of the slash pine symposium. Gen. Tech. Rep. SRS-76. Asheville, NC: U.S. Department of Agriculture, Forest Service, Southern Research Station. 148 p.

SG latewood tracheids produced each growing season. The natural range of loblolly pine is large and extends from Virginia to Texas and north to Tennessee and Arkansas, whereas the range of slash pine is smaller and extends only from the lower Coastal Plain of southeastern South Carolina to the eastern Gulf Coastal Plain of Louisiana. The SG of southern pines decreases from the Atlantic or gulf coast inland because the inland trees have less summer precipitation and a shorter growing season for latewood production (Clark and Daniels 2004). Thus, the SG of slash pine when averaged across its range is 11 percent higher than that of loblolly when averaged across its range. However, differences between the species are not as great when the species are growing in the same geographic region.

To minimize the effect of environmental factors or geographic location on SG, we sampled slash and loblolly pines planted in a study established by the Plantation Management Research Cooperative (PMRC) administered by the University of Georgia. That study's objective was to compare the growth of slash and loblolly pine when the two species are growing together at 141 locations in south Georgia and north Florida (Shiver and others 1996). Results of the PMRC study at age 14 show that loblolly pine produced more volume per acre, had better survival because of less *Cronartium* infection, and displayed less ice damage compared to slash pine. We felled three trees of each species in each of six stands at age 21. The diameter of the largest live or dead branch in each 8-foot section was recorded, and cross-section disks were harvested from along the stem for wood and bark SG, and moisture content determination. Preliminary results show that when the two species are growing together, the slash pine's weighted stem average SG was 4 percent higher than that of loblolly, and its SG average was 0.51 compared to 0.49 for loblolly. Thus, it appears that approximately 4 percent of the reported difference in species average SG is probably related to genetic or species differences and 8 percent is related to environmental factors.

When pine tree-length logs are purchased at a mill yard they are bought and sold on a weight basis, and a weight-scaling factor is used to convert the weight of a truckload of logs to cubic feet of wood. The weight-scaling factor is the weight of wood and bark per cubic foot of wood. Based on disks collected from the two species where they were growing together, we found that the slash contained 4 percent more dry wood because of its higher SG, 12 percent less water, and 3 percent more bark than the loblolly trees (table 2). The average weight-scaling factor for slash was 72.5 pounds per cubic foot compared to 70.4 pounds per cubic foot for loblolly when the two species were growing in the same stands. Although loblolly has a higher wood moisture content than slash pine, the weight-scaling factor for slash pine is higher because it has a higher SG and, thus, contains more oven-dry wood per cubic foot and more bark per cubic foot than loblolly.

Table 2—Average wood and bark properties for planted 21-year-old slash pine compared to loblolly pine when the species are growing in the same stand

Property	Slash pine	Loblolly pine
Wood specific gravity	0.51a	0.49b
Wood oven-dry weight per cubic foot (pounds)	31.9a	30.5b
Wood green weight per cubic foot (pounds)	63.0a	63.7a
Wood moisture content (percent)	97a	108b
Bark content (percent)	13.3a	9.8b

Within a property, values with a different letter are statistically different at the 0.05 level.

LUMBER GRADE YIELD

When visually grading southern pine structural lumber, one of the most important defects to evaluate is diameter of knots in relation to width of a board. In a No. 1 grade 2 by 4, the largest centerline knot allowed under southern pine dimension grading rules (Southern Pine Inspection Board 1994) is 1.5 inches width, and the largest centerline knot allowed in a No. 2 grade 2 by 4, is 2.0 inches. When growing in fully stocked stands, slash pine generally has smaller diameter branches and is a better natural pruner than loblolly pine, and, thus, it produces a greater proportion of higher grade lumber.

The diameter of the largest branch in each 8-foot saw-log stem section was plotted over stem height for 21-year-old slash and loblolly pine trees growing in the same stand planted at the same spacing (fig. 1). On average, the loblolly trees had larger diameter knots than the slash trees. Based on average maximum knot size, No. 1 or better 2 by

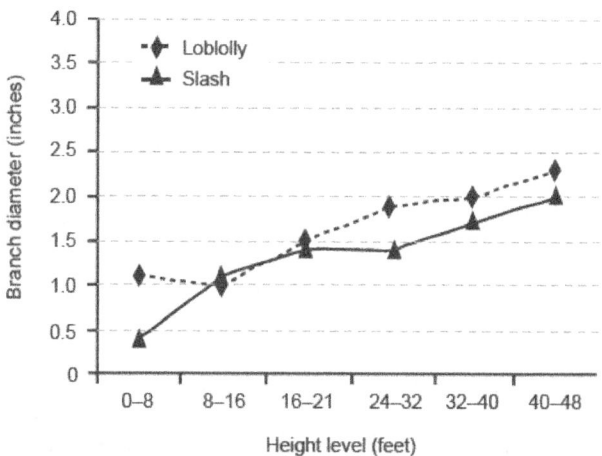

Figure 1—Average maximum branch diameter by 8-foot intervals up the stem of slash pine compared to loblolly pine when both species are growing in the same 21-year-old stand.

4 lumber could be manufactured from the butt 16-foot saw log of both species. The second 16-foot slash pine saw log could also produce all No. 1 and better 2 by 4 lumber; however, the second loblolly log would produce some No. 2 grade 2 by 4 lumber because of the knots > 1.5 inches in diameter. The third 16-foot slash log could produce all No. 2 and better 2 by 4 lumber; however, in the loblolly trees a portion of the 2 by 4 lumber from the third log would have to be trimmed back to remove knots larger than 2.0 inches to make No. 2 grade 2 by 4 lumber. Thus, the slash trees generally produced a higher proportion of No. 1 and better lumber.

The branching habit and natural pruning of slash pine also affect lumber yield, as illustrated in the lumber grade yield of a first thinning in a 17-year slash and 14-year loblolly pine stand.[2] The loblolly pine was planted at 600 trees per acre (TPA) in 1983 in a planting density plus competition control study on the University of Georgia, B.F. Grant Memorial Forest in the Piedmont of Georgia (Pienaar and Shiver 1993). In 1997, when the loblolly plantation was 14 years old, the study plots were marked for thinning. The slash pine trees came from the site-preparation and soil-type study planted in 1979 at 545 TPA by the PMRC in the lower Coastal Plain (Shiver and others 1994). The study was established at 20 sites ranging from Savannah, GA, to Apalachicola, FL.

In 1997, when the plantation was 17 years old, four trees from each of eight locations were marked for thinning from the site-preparation plus competition control study plots. The 32 loblolly and 32 slash trees were processed into 2- by 4-inch and 2- by 6- inch lumber at the same chipping sawmill on the same day. The lumber produced from each log was followed through the mill, kiln dried, planned, and graded using Southern Pine Inspection Bureau (Southern Pine Inspection Bureau 1994) lumber grades. When a board did not make a No. 2 or better, the reason for the downgrade was recorded.

Ninety-seven percent of the lumber produced from the 17-year slash pine was No. 2 or better compared to only 80 percent for the 14-year loblolly pine. The slash pine produced a significantly higher proportion of No. 1 and better, a lower proportion of No. 2, and a significantly lower proportion of No. 3 and No. 4 lumber compared to that of the loblolly pine (table 3). Three percent of the slash pine lumber and 3 percent of the loblolly lumber was downgraded below a No. 2 because of manufacturing defects (wane and skip). The proportion downgraded below a No. 2 because of drying defects (bow, twist, or crook) was 4 percent for loblolly compared to 2 percent for slash. Lumber that contains < 15 percent latewood is classified as exceptionally light weight and cannot be included in No. 2 nondense or higher grades of stress-rated lumber (Southern Pine

Table 3—Average proportion of dimension lumber produced by grade for 17-year slash pine planted at 545 TPA in the lower Coastal Plain compared to 14-year loblolly pine planted at 600 TPA in the Piedmont

Lumber grade	Slash pine	Loblolly pine
	- - - - - - - - *percent* - - - - - - - -	
No. 1 and better	53	21
No. 2	44	59
Nos. 3 and 4	3	20

TPA = trees per acre.

Inspection Bureau 1994). Less than 1 percent of the slash pine lumber was downgraded because of insufficient latewood compared to 5 percent of the loblolly lumber. A significantly larger proportion of loblolly lumber was downgraded because of drying defects or insufficient latewood, because the loblolly trees were growing in the Piedmont and contained twice as much juvenile wood as the slash pine growing in the lower Coastal Plain (Faust and others 1999). The Piedmont loblolly pine produced juvenile wood with thin-walled tracheids, wide MFA, and a small proportion of thick-walled latewood tracheids for 9 to 10 years compared to the lower Coastal Plain slash, which produced juvenile wood for only 5 to 6 years. The difference in time until mature wood production is probably more related to physiographic region than to species. Clark and Daniels (2003) showed that loblolly pine grown in the Coastal Plain also transitioned to mature wood production in the 5- to 6-year range. Less than 0.5 percent of the slash pine lumber was downgraded below a No. 2 because of knot size, compared to 7 percent of the loblolly lumber. A significantly higher proportion of the loblolly lumber was downgraded, because the average loblolly log had more knots (24 knots vs. 17 knots for slash pine), and the maximum diameter knot was significantly larger for the loblolly (1.7 inches compared to 1.3 inches).

When loblolly pine is planted at wide spacings, the trees produce large diameter branches that result in a high proportion of No. 3 and worse lumber and a low proportion of No. 1 and better (Clark and others 1994). A simulated final harvest of loblolly pine at age 38 showed stands planted at 6 by 6 feet and thinned to ≤ 100 square feet basal area (BA) at age 18 produced ≥ 60 percent No. 2 and better lumber compared to ≤ 42 percent No. 2 and better lumber from stands planted 12 by 12 feet and thinned to the same BA. In contrast, when slash pine is planted at wide spacings and harvested at age 40, the trees produced 90 to 95 percent No. 2 and better lumber (fig. 2). When initial spacing is increased from 8 by 8 feet to 10 by 10 or 15 by 15 feet, the proportion of No. 2, No. 1, and dense grade lumber remains relatively constant because of slash pine's characteristic small diameter branches and early natural pruning.

[2] Clark, A., III; Shiver, B.D.; Pienaar, L.V. 2004. Effect of initial spacing and competition control on lumber grade yield of young fast-growing southern pine. 20 p. Unpublished report. On file with: A. Clark, III, U.S. Department of Agriculture Forest Service, Southern Research Station, 320 Green Street, Athens, GA 30602.

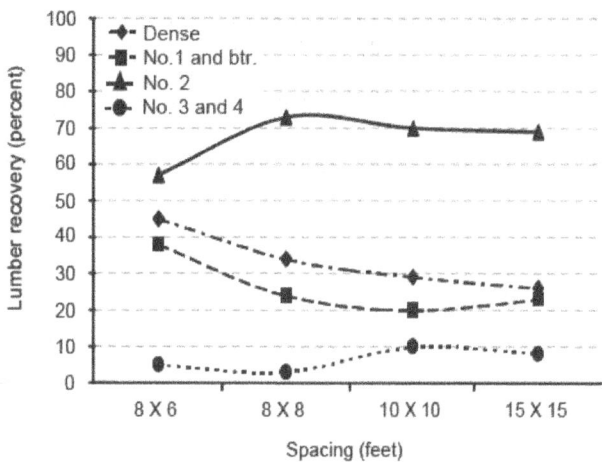

Figure 2—Effect of initial spacing on dimension lumber grade recovery for 40-year-old unthinned slash pine.

PULP AND PAPER YIELDS

Slash pine is not only an excellent species for structural lumber production, it is also good for linerboard and sack paper manufacturing. Wood for paper production can come from the whole stem, saw-log residues, or topwood above the saw-log stem. The 17-year-old slash pine trees harvested for lumber-yield analysis from the PMRC site-preparation and soil-type study were subsampled for pulp and paper analysis (Courchene and others 2000). Cross-section disks were cut at the butt, the top of each saw log, and from the 6-, 4-, and 3-inch diameter outside bark top. The chipping saw chips (CSC) were collected when the saw logs were sawn into lumber. The disks were chipped to provide pulp chips representing the whole tree and tops, and the CSC represented sawmill residue. The weighted whole stem SG averaged 0.52, saw-log stem SG averaged 0.53, and the topwood SG averaged 0.45. The SG of topwood was significantly lower because of the large proportion of thin-walled juvenile wood tracheids present. The packed bulk density, a measure of the weight of chips that can be packed into

unit area for digesting, was highest for the whole stem (175 kg/m³) and CSC (189 kg/m³), and significantly lower for the topwood chips (157 kg/m³).

One-half of the chips from each wood source were pulped in a batch digester to a kappa no. 90 for linerboard production, and the other half was pulped to a kappa no. 60 for sack paper production. Because slash pine is a high SG southern pine species, it has a high yield when pulped. Pulp yields for the kappa no. 90 cooks averaged 54 percent for the whole stem and CSC, compared to only 51 percent for the topwood chips. The pulp yields for the kappa no. 60 averaged only 47 percent for topwood compared to 50 percent for the whole stem and CSC. The weighted average tracheid lengths for the CSC, composed primarily of mature wood, averaged 4.1 mm for the kappa no. 90 and 3.9 mm for the kappa no. 60. The average length of tracheids in the topwood, composed primarily of juvenile wood, was significantly shorter averaging 3.3 mm for the kappa no. 90 and 3.5 mm for the kappa no. 60.

To test paper properties, hand sheets were made from the sack paper and linerboard pulps. The topwood chips produced linerboard that was higher in short span compression, burst strength, tensile strength, and specific modulus compared to the linerboard made from the whole stem or CSC (table 4). The topwood hand sheets were higher in strength properties because of the higher percentage of thinner walled juvenile tracheids in topwood. The thin-walled tracheids collapsed around each other and, thus, increased bonding and corresponding higher burst, tensile, and compression strength.

The sack paper hand sheets made from the topwood chips were higher in sheet density, short span compression, burst, tensile strength, and specific modulus, but significantly lower in tear resistance than the sheets made from the whole stem or CSC (table 5). The sack paper hand sheets were significantly lower in tear resistance because of the significantly shorter tracheids in the topwood compared to that of the whole stem or CSC.

Table 4—Average properties of linerboard hand sheets manufactured from whole stem chips, chipping saw chips, and topwood chips produced from 17-year-old slash pine growing in the lower Coastal Plain

Chip source	Sheet density	Short-span compressive test	Burst index	Tensile index	Specific modulus
	kg/m³	N m/g	kPa m²/g	N m/g	N m/g
Whole stem chips	715	26.7	5.20	54.2	5550
Chipping saw chips	645	27.2	5.13	49.6	5260
Topwood chips	717	30.02	5.53	72.5	7010

kg/m³ = kilograms per cubic meter; N m/g = Newtonmeters per gram;
kPa m²/g = kilopascals square meters per gram.

Table 5—Average properties of sack paper hand sheets manufactured from whole stem chips, chipping saw chips, and topwood chips produced from 17-year-old slash pine growing in the Lower Coastal Plain

Chip source	Sheet density	Tear index	Burst index	Tensile index	Specific modulus
	Kg/m^3	$mN\ m^2/g$	$kPa\ m^2/g$	$N\ m/g$	$N\ m/g$
Whole stem chips	630	19.9	5.80	73.7	6690
Chipping saw chips	618	20.0	6.03	68.3	6320
Topwood chips	670	17.6	7.03	88.5	7570

Kg/m^3 = kilograms per cubic meter; $mN\ m^2/g$ = milliNewtons square per gram; $kPa\ m^2/g$ = kilopascals square meters per gram; $N\ m/g$ = Newtonmeters per gram.

SUMMARY

Slash pine wood SG is higher, wood moisture content is lower, and bark content higher than that of loblolly pine. Thus the weight-scaling factor, weight of wood, and bark per cubic foot of wood is higher for slash pine than loblolly pine. The high SG and branching habit of slash pine make it an excellent species for manufacturing dimension lumber. Because of the small diameter branches and early natural pruning, slash pine produces more No. 1 and better dimension lumber and less No. 3 and No. 4 lumber than loblolly pine. When planted at wide spacings, slash pine will produce a higher proportion of No. 1 and better lumber than loblolly pine because of its natural pruning and smaller diameter branching habit. The tracheid characteristics of slash pine make it an excellent species for linerboard and sack paper production. The lower SG, thin-walled tracheids of topwood chips produce linerboard with higher strength properties than those of whole stem or CSC. However, the whole stem and CSC produced sack paper with higher tear resistance than topwood chips because of the longer tracheids.

LITERATURE CITED

Cave, I.D. 1976. Modeling the structure of the plant cell wall. Wood Science Technology. 2: 268-278.

Clark, A.; Daniels, R.F. 2004. Modeling the effect of physiographic region on wood properties of planted loblolly pine in the Southern United States. In: Nepveu, G., ed. Proceedings, connection between forest resources and wood quality, modeling approaches and simulation software. IUFRO WP S5.01.04. Nancy, France: LERFoB/2004 INRA-ENGREF: 54-60.

Clark, A., III; Saucier, J.R.; Baldwin, V.C.; Bower, D.R. 1994. Effect of initial spacing and thinning on lumber grade, yield and strength of loblolly pine. Forest Products Journal. 44. (11/12): 14-20.

Courchene, C.E.; Clark, A., III; Belli, M.L. [and others]. 2000. Effect of intensive silvicultural treatments on kraft pulp quality of loblolly and slash pine. In: Proceedings, 2000 TAPPI pulping/process & product quality conference. Boston: TAPPI Press: 210-219.

Faust, T.D.; Clark, A., III; Courchene, C.E. [and others]. 1999. Effects of intensive forest management practices on wood properties and pulp yield of young, fast growing southern pine. In: 1999 Proceedings, TAPPI international environmental conference. Atlanta: TAPPI Press: 501-512.

Koch, P. 1972. Utilization of the southern pines. The raw material. Agric. Handb. 420. Washington, DC: U.S. Department of Agriculture, Forest Service. 734 p. Vol. I.

Megraw, R.A. 1985. Wood quality factors in loblolly pine. Atlanta: TAPPI Press. 88 p.

Pienaar, L.V.; Shiver, B.D. 1993. Early results from an old-field loblolly pine spacing study in the Georgia Piedmont with competition control. Southern Journal of Applied Forestry. 17(4): 193-196.

Shiver, B.D.; Pienaar, L.V.; Hitch, K.L.; Rheney, J.W. 1994. Slash pine site preparation study results at age 14. PMRC Tech. Rep. 1994-2. Athens, GA: University of Georgia, Warnell School of Forest Resources. 32 p.

Shiver, B.D.; Rheney, J.W.; Hitch, K.L.; Shackelford, L. 1996. 14 year results of the PMRC species comparison study. PMRC Tech. Rep. 1996-4. Athens, GA: University of Georgia, Warnell School of Forest Resources. 15 p.

Southern Pine Inspection Bureau. 1994. Standard grading rules for southern lumber. Pensacola, FL: Southern Pine Inspection Board. 133 p.

Wahlgren, H.E.; Schumann, D.R.; Bendtsen, B.A. [and others]. 1975. Properties of major southern pines: part I–wood density survey; part II–structural properties and specific gravity. Res. Pap. FPL 176–177. Madison, WI: U.S. Department of Agriculture, Forest Service, Forest Products Laboratory. 76 p.

Wear, D.N.; Greis, J.G. 2002. Southern forest resource assessment: summary of findings. Journal of Forestry. 100(7): 6-14.

PRESCRIBED FIRE AND SLASH PINE

A.J. Long, A. Behm, L. Cassidy, J. DiMartino, D. Doran, D. Freeman, J. Helmers, K. Keefe, A. Miller, S. Ranasinghe, C. Randall, M. Rasser, A. Ruth, D. Shipley, and A. Van Loan[1]

Abstract—Fire has been a significant ecosystem process in the Southeast for thousands of years. It kept slash pine in the wetter parts of the flatwoods pine forests historically. Today, when slash pine covers a much larger landscape, fire still plays an integral role in its management. Wildfire has had some extreme moments in slash pine plantations where understory shrubs were dense from a lack of prescribed fire or other treatment. However, prescribed fire has also been an important tool for regenerating natural and plantation slash pine as well as for restoring longleaf pine in place of slash. Prescribed fire is also used in slash pine systems for reducing fuel accumulations, improving wildlife and range habitat, and enhancing accessibility. Fire will continue to be an essential, and sometimes critical, element in the slash pine system. Wildfires in the wildland-urban interface and smoke management are significant public issues and influence opportunities for prescribed burning. Future application of prescribed fire will be dependent on policies and issues related to public acceptance, health and safety. Landowner and public education will be critical components of future fire management programs. Since the last Slash Pine Symposium, research, objectives for fire management, and the wildland fire environment have changed substantially. This paper will build on the excellent baseline provided by Wade (1983) at that Symposium. We will repeat some of the important principles outlined in earlier work, but our focus is on new information and challenges in the last two decades.

HISTORICAL PERSPECTIVES

Role of Fire in Natural Slash Pine Ecosystems

Wildland fires have been a prominent force shaping the ecosystems of the southeastern United States for thousands of years. Evidence suggests that Native Americans set fires for centuries before the arrival of European settlers (Robbins and Myers 1992). Even before humans began using fire as a tool in North America, the climate and vegetation of the southeastern United States supported frequent wildfires ignited by lightning during the growing season (Frost 1998). The climate in the Southeast is characterized by long, hot growing seasons with thunderstorms, annual cycles of wet and dry seasons, and periodic extended droughts (Wade and others 2000). After thousands of years of exposure to frequent fires, plant communities evolved mechanisms to survive fire, and in some cases, they developed a dependence on fire for their maintenance.

In pine flatwoods forests of the southeastern Coastal Plain, fire frequency, which is related to site hydrology, influences the natural distribution of slash pine (*Pinus elliottii*), longleaf pine (*Pinus palustris*) and many other species. The two pines often occur together on the landscape with slash pine occupying wetter sites. Slash pine develops naturally in poorly drained, low elevation areas that frequently flood during major rain events (Abrahamson and Hartnett 1990, Lohrey and Kossuth 1990), while longleaf pine occurs on better-drained sites (Monk 1968). Due to moist site conditions and fewer fine (grass) fuels, natural slash pine communities burn less frequently and completely than the drier, surrounding longleaf pine communities (Christensen 1981). Historically, probable fire return intervals in slash pine were 6 to 10 years, while longleaf pine burned every 2 to 4 years

(Landers 1991). South Florida slash pine (*P. elliottii* var. *densa*) inhabits sites with similar conditions and fire frequencies (every 3 to 7 years) as longleaf pine.

Longer fire return intervals on typical moist slash pine sites are important for slash pine regeneration because seedlings are not fire resistant during their first four years of growth. Their fire resistance increases once they reach a height of 10 to 15 feet (Lohrey and Kossuth 1990), with 10- to 12-year-old slash pine capable of surviving many surface fires (Wright and Bailey 1982). Historically, the susceptibility of young slash pine seedlings to fire precluded their encroachment into adjacent longleaf pine stands where shorter fire return intervals were common. South Florida slash pine seedlings are more resistant to fire than the typical variety; they have thicker bark and enter a grass stage similar to longleaf pine (Ketcham and Bethune 1963, Abrahamson 1984). As slash pine matures, it is able to survive moderately intense fires. The species characteristically has thick bark with platy layers that overlap to provide substantial insulation from fire (Landers 1991). In addition, slash pine has the capacity to recover from 70 to 100 percent crown scorch (de Ronde 1982, Wade 1983).

Different fire frequencies in pine flatwoods ecosystems lead to differences in understory vegetation, fuel loading and fire intensities. Fires in typical slash pine stands are more intense than in longleaf pine or South Florida slash pine due to the presence of highly flammable shrubs such as palmetto (*Serenoa repens*) and gallberry (*Ilex glabra*), greater vertical structure, and heavy needle drape (Hough and Albini 1978). However, crown fires are rare in natural slash pine stands because trees self-prune the lower

[1] A.J. Long, Associate Professor, School of Forest Resources and Conservation, University of Florida, Gainesville, FL 32611-0410; Behm, Cassidy, DiMartino, Doran, Freeman, Helmers, Keefe, Miller, Ranasinghe, Randall, Rasser, Ruth, Shipley, and Van Loan, Graduate Students, University of Florida, Gainesville, FL 32611-0410.

Citation for proceedings: Dickens, E.D.; Barnett, J.P.; Hubbard, W.G.; Jokela, E.J., eds. 2004. Slash pine: still growing and growing! Proceedings of the slash pine symposium. Gen. Tech. Rep. SRS-76. Asheville, NC: U.S. Department of Agriculture, Forest Service, Southern Research Station. 148 p.

branches, frequent fires prevent heavy fuel buildup, and stands are open (Hough and Albini 1978, Abrahamson 1984). Other natural disturbances, such as hurricanes and pest outbreaks, can also affect fire behavior and severity by changing the fuel structure and loads. The shorter fire return intervals in longleaf pine maintain an understory of grasses and forbs that burn with low intensities (Abrahamson and Hartnett 1990). South Florida slash pine has an understory composed of various species of subtropical hardwoods, shrubs, and palms in addition to grasses (Abrahamson and Hartnett 1990, Landers 1991).

In the absence of fire, slash pine ecosystems may develop along one of several successional pathways, depending on site conditions (Abrahamson and Hartnett 1990). On wetter sites, plant succession moves toward cypress or hardwood swamps, cabbage palm hammocks (Edmisten 1963), or bayheads (Monk 1968, Peroni and Abrahamson 1986). Better drained sites may develop into mesic southern mixed hardwoods.

Human Management and Consequences

Presettlement—Human occupation of the southeastern United States began approximately 12,000 years ago. The environment they encountered was probably vastly different from the one with which we are familiar, with indications that the area was then a semi-arid savannah. Climate changes since then included a period approximately 7,000 years ago that was much wetter than the present (Brown 1994).

As was the case elsewhere in the pre-Columbian Americas, one of the first uses of fire was to promote growth of favored food plant species over less desirable plants (Lentz 2000). Anthropological records suggest that fire may have been used for maize production and swidden (slash and burn) farming around 1,200 years ago. Fire was also used in hunting to flush out game, primarily deer. These two activities were often done jointly: when an area needed to be cleared for fields, fires would be lit in a circle, and the game would be hunted as it was driven out of the enclosed area by the fire (Brown 1994). Fire was also used to attract game to areas with new succulent grass and forbs, to improve accessibility, and possibly in warfare (Wade 1983).

Studies in the Mississippi River Valley suggest that most large fires were not anthropogenic. Fires set by people tended to be localized. Hunting fires as well as those set to alter vegetation, while frequent, were typically less than 3 miles wide (Fritz 2000). Another human effect on fire regimes might have been through the collection of dead wood for domestic fuel, resulting in lower fire intensities (Fritz 2000).

Early 1900s vs late 1900s—wildfire vs prescribed burning—Like the Native Americans, the earliest European settlers were more interested in farming than in forestry (Wade 1983). In the South, the local custom was to burn in forests every winter, to remove litter and dead grass and to make new spring grass available for cattle grazing. Fire was also used to: protect fences, farm buildings, and turpentine orchards from high intensity wildfires; control insects and pests; and to maintain an open landscape for hunting. Between the late 1800s and early 1900s the indiscriminate use of fire after timber harvesting often resulted in high intensity burns and damage to residual timber and human settlements. As a result, federal and state policies in the early 1900s focused on protecting forests from all fires.

During this period of blanket fire suppression, the benefits of 'controlled' fire were noted by various authors (for example, Demmon 1935, Stoddard 1931) and by professional foresters such as Austin Cary and H.H. Chapman. Apparent contradictions in the effects and benefits, coupled with some disastrous wildfires in the 1940s, contributed to the recognition of a need for balance between the use and suppression of fire. The need for balance between suppression and use was highlighted in the longleaf-slash pine ecosystem, where fire suppression allowed slash pine to expand into the drier areas historically dominated by longleaf pine. By the mid 1940s prescribed fire was acknowledged as a necessary tool for managing vegetative fuels and ecosystems.

ENVIRONMENTAL EFFECTS OF FIRE

Vegetation Communities

Effect of fire on species composition—With the suppression of fires and expansion of plantations, slash pine now occupies a greater range and variety of sites than it did naturally. In most of these areas, fire is a very important ecological factor that determines forest structure and species composition. In typical flatwoods, the primary understory species include: gallberry, saw palmetto, wax myrtle (*Myrica cerifera*), *Vaccinium* spp, fetterbush (*Lyonia lucida*) and persimmon (*Diospyros virginiana*). In wetter areas species such as red maple (*Acer rubrum*), sweetgum (*Liquidambar styraciflua*), black gum (*Nyssa sylvatica*), water oak (*Quercus nigra*) and laurel oak (*Q. laurifolia*) gradually dominate the midstory.

Periodic fires prevent the less fire adapted hardwood species from invading and maintain an understory comprised of grasses, especially wiregrass (*Aristida stricta*) and bluestem (*Andropogon* spp.), forbs and a few shrubs that are well adapted to such disturbances. Prescribed burns can maintain the grass and forb understory if frequent enough to reduce existing shrub species. Depending on site characteristics, prescribed fire applied in different seasons affects the understory in different ways. Kush and others (2000) found that winter burns resulted in a greater increase in overall species diversity than summer or spring burns. On the other hand, experience on the Apalachicola Ranger District in Florida indicates that growing season burns (compared to dormant season) have substantially increased the flowering and spread of wiregrass and a number of threatened and endangered species, reduced the frequency and size of saw palmetto, gallberry and hardwoods, and pushed titi species (*Cliftonia monophylla, Cyrilla racemiflora, and Cyrilla parvifolia*) back into their natural wet habitats (Ferguson 1998). These changes in vegetation communities have had the added benefit of reducing wildfire intensity, which improves firefighter safety and reduces suppression costs.

Effect of fire on slash pine growth, damage and mortality—A fine line separates the positive and negative effects of prescribed fire on growth and yield. Fuel reduction has two primary advantages with respect to growth: it reduces the ability of wildfire to cause damage or mortality; and it reduces understory plant competition for nutrients and water.

Negative effects on growth occur when moisture conditions are low and temperatures are high enough to result in crown scorch or needle consumption. Trees respond by using stored resources to replace the needles at the expense of annual growth. For example, a January prescribed burn under 25-year old planted slash pine resulted in up to 100 percent crown scorch, but no tree mortality. Subsequent evaluation of diameter growth indicated that total crown scorch resulted in a 60 percent growth loss over the next two years (Johansen and Wade 1987). Even slightly scorched (< 10 percent of needles) trees showed a growth loss of 15 percent during the same period. Following a prescribed burn in a nine-year-old slash pine plantation, Johansen (1975) found similar growth losses on trees with a high percentage of needle scorch. However, trees with only small percentages of needle scorch (< 15 percent) actually grew better than unburned check trees.

In addition to growth loss, defoliation in the late summer or fall is generally after the last growth flush and may preclude the ability of the tree to survive until the following spring. Weise and others (1990) observed 40 percent mortality in slash pine and 93 percent in loblolly pine (*P. taeda*) when all the needles of four-year-old trees were manually removed in October. In contrast, all trees survived after complete needle removal in January, April or July.

Prescribed fire and exotic species—Fire is a common mode of disturbance in the Southeast that can promote the spread of invasive exotic species. Cogongrass (*Imperata cylindrica*) is a good example. It is aggressive, well adapted to varying site conditions, and has invaded natural forests and agricultural lands. Prescribed fire generally burns off cogongrass shoots, but the effect is short lived unless combined with an herbicide treatment, as it resprouts vigorously from rhizomes (Bryson and Carter 1993). In addition, volatiles in the foliage and accumulated thatch raise fire intensity, often killing the overstory trees. Cogongrass thrives in open sunlight and one method for controlling it is to promote shading by other desirable plants. Unfortunately, frequent prescribed fire may eliminate shade-providing undergrowth, thus enabling the proliferation of cogongrass.

Japanese climbing fern *(Ophioglossum japonicum)* and old world climbing fern *(Lygodium scandens)* occur in slash pine systems in the Coastal Plain and south Florida, respectively. Both create ladder fuels into tree canopies that can be problems for prescribed burning or wildfire. Both can also be killed back, but not eliminated, by fire. *Melaleuca quinquenervia* is another aggressive non-native species that invades South Florida slash pine stands following a fire.

Animals
General populations—Many animals and insects native to the Southeast depend, at least partly, upon pine forest ecosystems for their habitat needs. Some species benefit from frequent fires; others need very little fire; and many species require a mix of fire regimes to meet their food, breeding and cover habitat requirements. Certain species, such as red-cockaded woodpecker (*Picoides borealis*), bobwhite quail (*Colinus virginianus*), and gopher tortoise (*Gopherus polyphemus*), will decline or disappear completely from areas where fire is excluded, forest canopies close, and dense, brushy understories develop (USFWS 2000). Conversely, species which prefer a dense or brushy habitat structure increase in abundance where fire has been absent (Breininger and Smith 1992). In general, fire tends to increase species richness and abundance by creating habitat heterogeneity and increased forage.

Food availability—Fire affects animals through changes in food quantity and quality. Fire stimulates the regrowth of plant shoots that are available to browsing animals. After fire, many plant species are more palatable and of higher nutrient quality than in unburned areas (Carlson and others 1993). The type and quantity of food also varies with the season in which fire occurs. Kush and others (2000) found that dormant season burns in longleaf pine forests resulted in more legume production than unburned controls, while growing season fires tended to increase grass biomass. In both cases, fires resulted in additional forage. The benefits of fire to birds and small animals are three-fold: enhanced foraging access, increased insect abundance, and higher nutritional value of insects (Landers 1987, USFWS 2000).

Fire can also negatively impact animals by changing food availability. Florida black bears (*Ursus americanus floridanus*) depend upon acorns as a food source in the fall. Growing-season fire can topkill or eliminate oaks and reduce acorn production for several years (Maehr and others 2001).

Habitat structure—Animals react in different ways to fire-altered groundcover, woody understory and canopy cover. Bobwhite quail require patches of brushy habitat as nesting and brooding cover. However, coverage of dense undergrowth beyond a minimum threshold leads to excessive predation rates (Brennan 1991). As understory fills in with woody shrubs and trees, quail and red-cockaded woodpeckers leave and the area becomes suitable for a different suite of bird species (Breininger and Smith 1992). Fire which opens the area and reestablishes plants to an earlier successional stage favors recolonization by open habitat bird species (Fitzgerald and Tanner 1992). Growing season burns, in particular, tend to reduce total numbers of hardwood stems and are more likely to topkill brushy vegetation than will dormant season burns (Haywood and others 2001). A varied burn regime in relation to size of burns, season of burn, and fire return interval creates a mosaic of successional stages which tend to favor the greatest diversity of animal species.

Threatened and endangered species—Red-cockaded woodpeckers nest in cavities or artificial boxes in living longleaf and slash pine trees (USFWS 2000). They inhabit open, park-like forests with little or no understory vegetation. Frequent, growing season fire maintains these habitat characteristics (Loeb and others 1992).

Another endangered species which benefits from fire in pine ecosystems is the Florida panther (*Felix concolor coryi*) (USFWS 1995). Panthers are attracted to burned pinelands up to one year after fire because of increased prey browsing in the burned areas (Dees and others 2001). In contrast, panthers tend to seek areas of dense vegetative growth for denning sites. Dense areas are those that have not burned in several years or patches of vegetation that tend not to burn due to hydrology or fuel breaks. Fire-maintained slash pine forests comprise the bulk of panther habitat in south Florida.

Florida black bears also prefer to locate denning sites in densely vegetated areas in wetlands and pine forests, but they forage for soft mast in a variety of burned habitats (Maehr and others 2001, Schaefer and Sargent 1990). Current burning recommendations avoid winter burning to prevent cub mortality and favor a growing-season fire return interval of five to seven years to allow oaks to produce acorn crops at least once before being burned again. Saw palmetto fruit production is considered the single most important food component of Florida black bear diets and growing-season burns every four to nine years should promote optimum palmetto berry production.

Slash pine forests also support threatened and endangered amphibians and reptiles. The flatwoods salamander (*Ambystoma cingulatum*) breeds in ephemeral ponds, but adults and sub-adults spend much of their lives in open longleaf and slash pine forests (Means and others 1996). They benefit from frequent fires which maintain an open understory and diverse herbaceous groundcover.

Soils, Nutrients and Microorganisms
The soils of the Lower Coastal Plain and flatwoods vary considerably in pH and nutrient content. They are, however, characteristically poorly drained soils composed of lightly textured sands resulting in acidic conditions with low cation exchange capacity, low organic matter, and low clay content (Abrahamson and Hartnett 1990).

Fire can affect many soil characteristics including organic matter (litter and humus), water repellency, nutrient dynamics, and soil moisture. Burning the forest floor obviously results in a depletion of litter organic matter (Bell and Binkley 1989, McKee 1987). However, the loss of forest floor biomass does not necessarily translate to a loss of soil organic matter. In McKee's (1987) prescribed fire study in Alabama, Florida and South Carolina, organic matter in the top 3 inches of mineral soil increased between 0.4 percent and 2.6 percent, most likely due to transport of fine particulate matter from the ash into the soil. Nonetheless, caution must be exercised to protect soil organic matter, especially on deep sandy soils.

After fire, water repellency is typically found as a discrete layer of variable thickness and spatial continuity on, or a few inches below, the soil (DeBano 2000). When fire burns, hydrophobic substances are vaporized and may move downward along temperature gradients until they condense.

The effects of fire on soil nutrient dynamics can be described in generalities, but they also vary depending on fuel loads,

fire severity and how much of the duff and other surface organic matter remains after the fire. In general, fire affects the following nutrient-related processes:

- Nutrients stored in plants and the forest floor are transferred from living tissue, litter and duff to soil and air;
- Nutrients change from organic to inorganic forms;
- Volatilized nutrients are lost to the atmosphere in smoke;
- Precipitation may erode or leach ash and nutrient-rich surface soil;
- N-fixing systems (microbes and plants) are altered;
- The decomposition process of litter and soil organic matter is modified;
- Nutrient availability more than 2 inches below the soil surface changes little, except with severe fires.

Specific increases associated with fire include: soil pH; cations of K, Ca and Mg; and volatilization of N, K, P, Ca and Mg. Specific decreases include: total nitrogen; P and S anions lost as particulates or volatiles; and cation exchange capacity. Nitrogen effects are especially important, but variable. Most of the N is tied up in organic forms; some of that is contained in burned fuels and is converted to inorganic ammonia or nitrate products during a fire. The result is often a short-term increase in inorganic N (either as it is leached into the soil or generated by new microbial activity). Both inorganic forms (NO_3, NH_4) are used by plants or other organisms as the ecosystem changes after a fire, but they generally return to pre-burn levels within one or two years after a fire.

Several recent studies with southern pines help to demonstrate the variety of these nutrient responses. Following prescribed fire under loblolly pine, Bell and Binkley (1989) found that significant losses of forest litter (and therefore forest litter nitrogen) led to a higher rate of nitrogen immobilization by microbial populations than in the unburned soils. The resulting decrease in available nitrogen in the soil contrasts with Boyer and Miller's study (1994) in which low intensity biennial winter burns in longleaf pine did not significantly affect the total nitrogen or available phosphorous levels within the soil when compared with similar stands that had not been burned in 22 to 24 years. A comparable study of Coastal Plain soils similarly demonstrated that there were no statistically significant differences in the amount of total nitrogen and available phosphorous in the mineral soil after burning (McKee 1982).

Fire may also influence water retention in the soil profile through changes in surface and/or soil organic matter. Boyer and Miller (1994) found that the moisture holding capacity of soils exposed to biennial winter fires was 27 percent less in the surface soil (0 to 2 inches) and 18 percent less in the subsurface soil (6 to 8 inches) than in unburned soils.

Effects of Fire on Water and Air Quality
Water quality—Fire effects on water quality are highly dependent on soil, weather, topography and fire characteristics. In general, fire has not produced appreciable impacts

on water quality in terms of soil and nutrient influx in the Atlantic and Gulf Coastal Plains, perhaps because of the relatively flat terrain (Richter and others 1982, Douglas and Van Lear 1983).

However, fire does have the potential to impact water quality both chemically and physically. Chemical changes occur when soil particles, particulate matter, and soluble compounds enter water bodies after a fire and are directly related to the effects of fire on vegetation and ground cover, especially in riparian zones. Physical effects of fire on water quality include temperature, flow rates, and timing of peak flows. Stream temperatures can change when vegetative cover that shades the water is reduced by fire (LaFayette 1995, Pyne and others 1996). Reduction of vegetative ground cover throughout a burned area increases potential runoff by decreasing rainfall interception, evapo-transpiration, and infiltration (LaFayette 1995). Peak flow often occurs earlier following a rain event because of the increased runoff.

These hydrological effects have been observed in monitored watersheds after severe fire events (Helvey and others 1974). Most prescribed burning in the Southeast is far less severe, and if these hydrological effects are detectable, they are temporary as new vegetation establishes pre-fire hydrology within a few years.

Other fire management practices can also impact water quality. Fire line construction and site preparation following a fire increase opportunities for erosion, sedimentation and altered hydrological flow. Similarly, constructing fire lines around the perimeters of cypress domes embedded in slash pine plantations may alter the direction of sheet flow into and out of the wetlands. Nonpoint-source pollution is minimized in pine flatwoods silviculture with Best Management Practices that minimize disturbance near streams, protect riparian zones, and restrict prescribed burning on steep slopes adjacent to streams (Riekerk 1985). When different units within the same watershed are scheduled for prescribed burning they should be separated spatially and temporally in order to minimize potential impacts (LaFayette 1995).

Air quality—Air quality concerns are directed primarily to human health and safety issues. Air-borne particulate matter is regulated at the state and federal level by the Clean Air Act and the Environmental Protection Agency (EPA), and managed locally through State Implementation Plans. In many cases, wildland fires can contribute significantly to total particulate matter production. Particulate matter released per acre from prescribed fires is significantly less than wildfires (Peterson and Ward 1990, Core 1995).

Smoke has the potential to affect the public more than any other aspect of burning through its impacts on air quality, health and safety at distances far removed from the fire. In the last ten years, special attention has focused on the health effects of particulate matter less than 2.5 microns in size. The high proportion of elderly people who have moved to the South increases the potential for respiratory complications from the inhalation of smoke particulate matter. Yet

some smoke is necessary if the benefits from burning are to be realized, and this message must be shared with the public (Monroe 1999).

For a land manager, air quality is addressed in terms of smoke management. Smoke production and dispersion depend on weather, fuel, and burning technique (Johansen and Phernetton 1982). Emissions can be reduced by proper burning techniques and prompt mop-up. For example, backing fires typically produce much less smoke than heading fires due to more complete fuel consumption by a slow moving flame front. Dispersion conditions should move smoke away from smoke sensitive areas such as roadways, airports, schools and hospitals. Slightly unstable atmospheric conditions are also helpful.

Roadway accidents that result from smoke-impaired visibility are of great concern. Many smoke-related accidents occur at night or during early morning hours (Mobley 1991) when smoke or smoke/fog mixtures stay close to the ground. Windrow and pile burning is especially dangerous due to the residual smoke from long smoldering fires in compact fuels which often have high moisture contents. Large burns and aerial burns can also present smoke hazard situations due to residual smoke where complete mop-up is not feasible.

MANAGING FIRE IN NATURAL SLASH PINE SYSTEMS

Uses in Natural Stands and Public Land Management

Natural stands of slash pine occur on both public and privately owned land, often as a result of reseeding of cutover lands in the early 1900s. Although natural stands were originally limited to the mesic areas lying between well-drained upland and poorly drained lowland habitats, they cover much larger flatwoods areas today and even occur in upland areas that have remained unburned for at least 10 years. Depending on landowner objectives, managing those stands may focus either on retaining slash pine as a dominant species in the overstory or replacing it with longleaf pine.

Promoting slash pine regeneration—Slash pine seed production is frequent and abundant. The seeds germinate in conditions of bare mineral soil, sparse canopy cover and high light levels, which are typical after a fire (Lohrey and Kossuth 1990). However, regeneration under natural slash pine will usually only be successful with fire intervals of 8 to 10 years after seedling establishment. Maintaining that interval allows shrubs and hardwoods to become well established. If desired future conditions for the stand include an open understory, fire management under natural stands will probably have to include a long fire-free interval to establish a new seedling crop, followed by a series of shorter intervals to control shrubs and promote grass and forbs.

Prescriptions for burning to achieve regeneration standards should be based on the seasonal effects of fire, on local experience, and on state and regional guidelines (such as Wade and Lunsford 1989). A few important guidelines point out the types of information that should be considered for burning under natural slash pine stands:

- Burns are more detrimental to plant material that is physiologically active at the time of the fire rather than dormant

- Moisture content of needles is lowest in spring (Robbins and Myers 1990)

- Winter burns generally result in less root kills — both hardwood and pine

- Defoliation in autumn is detrimental to slash pine (Robbins and Myers 1990)

- Spring and summer fires may leave trees susceptible to insect attack; winter and autumn burns can give trees more time to recover before peak insect activity.

Hazard reduction—Accumulation of litter and development of a thick vegetative understory creates conditions that can lead to intense wildfires during droughts or lightning storm seasons. Large quantities of litter and flammable vegetation may build up rapidly in Coastal Plain pine forests and can reach serious threat levels within 5 to 6 years after a disturbance (Wade and Lunsford 1989). Although some plantation owners may have reservations about using fire in managed stands, fire is a practical way to reduce hazardous fuel buildup in natural stands and plantations.

Hazard reduction was cited as the greatest resource benefit of prescribed burning in the South from 1985 to 1994 by federal, state, and private forest managers and 72 percent of the total area prescribed burned was for this reason (Haines and others 2001). The amount of burning conducted for this purpose has increased in the last ten years, and survey respondents expect it to continue increasing. The increase reflects a shift in public land management goals away from post-harvest slash reduction toward managing at an ecosystem level to accommodate the habitats of fire-dependant and/or threatened and endangered species.

However, the survey results described by Haines and others (2001) also listed "excessive fuel loading" as a barrier to using fire as a management tool. A standard practice for burning dense shrub understories is to conduct a winter burn before switching to growing season burns in order to reduce fuel loads during favorable conditions (Robbins and Myers 1990) and to minimize pine damage (Crow and Shilling 1980). If possible, stands might be ignited aerially when they are burned for the first time, with close spacing of ignition spots to deplete fuels before fires can reach unmanageable levels. Subsequent burns can be smaller, with the end result being a patchy distribution of burned areas that reduce fuel continuity in future fires (Wade and Lunsford 1989).

Aesthetics and access—Access and appearance are also increasingly important considerations in forest management. Recreation users vary from hunters and bike riders to canoeists and wildlife observers. All have their particular perceptions about how the forest should look, and those ideas usually do not include burned landscapes. Precautions can be taken when burning to reduce the visual impacts of fires, such as burning under conditions that will minimize scorch in areas of high visibility interest. In addition, areas can be burned in patches to leave some unburned areas and create visual diversity (Wade and Lunsford 1989).

Ecosystem management and restoration—Restoration of longleaf pine to areas it once occupied is probably the most widespread ecosystem restoration concern in southern forests today. Although many private lands are contributing to this effort, public lands are particularly focused on the goal of restoring longleaf pine. For example, one U.S. Forest Service goal is to restore between 10,000 and 15,000 acres of longleaf pine which now contain offsite slash pine on National Forests in Florida (USFS 1999). Prescribed fire is a key tool in the management plans for longleaf restoration. According to the interim report on restoring longleaf pine at Eglin Air Force Base: "As a general rule, apply fire to longleaf pine and associated communities when you can, where you can, and as frequently as you can" (Provenchar and others 2001). The U.S. Forest Service has established the goal of burning National Forests in Florida on a variable 3-year cycle with half of the fires conducted during the growing season.

Vegetation control methods other than fire have been used to prevent hardwood encroachment and maintain pine savanna. Among these are herbicides, chain saw felling and girdling, and mechanical clearing. Each provides certain benefits in terms of duration of shrub control or flexibility for when they can be conducted. However, in most situations fire is the most economical management prescription. In a study conducted at Eglin Air Force Base in the Florida panhandle, prescribed burns with ground ignition cost approximately $9 per acre and aerial ignition as little as $4 per acre. By comparison, herbicide applications cost about $90 per acre and chainsaw felling/girdling $60 per acre (Provencher and others 2001). Each of the methods (including fire) has various risks or undesirable effects that need to be weighed in planning restoration activities.

Wildlife management—Wildlife populations generally benefit from habitat improvements caused by fire (Main and Tanner 1999). Most wildlife management practices focus on particular species of interest whether the property is publicly or privately owned. Prescribed fire is used to reduce woody vegetation and increase both herbaceous biomass and species diversity in southern pine forests (Moore and others 1982b).

Bobwhite quail, white-tailed deer (*Odocoileus virginicus*), and wild turkey (*Meleagris gallopavo*) are important game species in slash and other southern pines. Bobwhite quail benefit from frequent fires (every 1 to 3 years) that keep midstory vegetation low and increase the quantity and variety of seeds available for foraging (Evans 1989, Block and others 1995). However, burning should also leave unburned thickets for nesting and protective cover. Prescribed fires for quail management should avoid the March through September breeding and nesting season (Wade 1983), although quail will renest within the same season (Moser and Palmer 1997).

Wild turkeys require a mosaic of habitat types. Turkeys need open habitats for seed and insect foraging and brood rearing. They benefit from management practices that include frequent burning (every 2 to 4 years) to reduce midstory vegetation. However, they also use thicker vegetation for nesting from March to June.

White-tailed deer also benefit from periodic fires in both natural and planted slash pine. They prefer the lush new growth of grasses, herbaceous plants, berries, woody species and vines that follows burning (Hurst 1989). Fire improves the nutritive quality of deer browse for up to eleven months after a fire (Carlson and others 1993). Prescribed fires in the winter are best to promote shrub and hardwood resprouting, usually at a 2 to 3 year interval (Hurst 1989).

Management for non-game wildlife species is also important in slash pine forests. Forest management practices that improve the habitat of the red-cockaded woodpecker also benefit the Bachman's sparrow (*Aimophila aestivalis*). Both species prefer open old-growth pines with open midstories and dense herbaceous vegetation (Plentovich and others 1998). Frequent prescribed fires in the growing season are necessary to maintain these habitat qualities.

Bald eagles utilize the southern pine ecosystem for nesting and roosting in mature trees in open forests. Forest management practices that benefit eagle habitat include thinning younger pines (Chester and others 1990) either mechanically or with careful use of prescribed fire. Emphasis should be placed on minimizing fire damage to mature trees.

Many species of neotropical migratory birds stop in southern pinelands on their journeys north and south each year (Dickson and others 1995). They require a variety of different habitats (Block and others 1995). Using prescribed fire to manage for a heterogeneous blend of different habitat types will benefit these neotropical migrants.

MANAGING FIRE IN SLASH PINE PLANTATIONS

Effects of Plantations on Fire Regimes
The extensive conversion from acres dominated by longleaf pine to domination by slash pine has had a concurrent impact on landscape level fire potential including likelihood of occurrence, intensity, severity, and area burned. One of the factors that has favored regeneration of slash and loblolly pine over longleaf pine is the need for frequent, specifically timed prescribed fire for successful longleaf pine establishment (Hedman and others 2000, Boyette 1996). While recognized as beneficial for management and wildfire prevention in slash and loblolly pine stands, prescribed fire is applied much less frequently than might be recommended due to a combination of factors:

- Sensitivity of young slash pine to fire-induced mortality or damage;

- Accumulation of ground fuels and vegetation;

- Complexity of applying prescribed fire given urbanization, smoke considerations, training, and available burn days;

- Risk of losses in wood volume production.

Slash pine management and fuels—Fire exclusion from plantations allows a dense shrub or hardwood midstory to develop which shades out native grass and herbaceous groundcover species (particularly wiregrass). These ground cover species could comprise a significant component of the fine fuels on such sites (Clewell 1989). Standard site preparation techniques, such as chopping, root raking, and bedding, can also significantly alter native groundcover species (Shultz and Wilhite 1974, Moore and others 1982a, Swindel and others 1983). Wiregrass is of particular importance because of its apparent influence on fire spread and effects (Clewell 1989). Wiregrass seed production is also directly dependent upon occurrence of lightning season fire (Clewell 1989). Therefore, the standard dormant season fire regime utilized in most managed slash pine systems, while effective for fuel reduction, does not contribute significantly to the maintenance of the critical wiregrass fine fuel component.

Hedman and others (2000) attempted to specifically address the question of the impact of longleaf, slash, and loblolly pine plantations on native groundcover species. Findings included: longleaf stands had significantly more herbaceous species and cover than slash or loblolly sites; loblolly sites had significantly greater overstory and midstory density; and longleaf and slash pine stands were otherwise similar in species richness and stand structure. A significant and logical observation was that land-use history, particularly transition from agriculture to forestry, had the most significant impact on groundcover structure and composition with former agricultural field sites supporting lower species diversity than cutover sites.

Traditional silvicultural recommendations for slash pine management have centered on even-aged management, intensive site preparation and commercial thinning of dense stands. Stands treated with intensive site preparation techniques may be burnable by ages 10- to 15-years-old if understories are mainly grasses and herbs. Plantations with excessive shrubby fuel accumulations generally require low intensity winter burns, or preclude safe application of fire.

Fire behavior—The Florida Fire Behavior training course recognizes the complexities and influences of pine management on wildfire behavior through designation of "Dense Pine" as a major fuel group with four size classes: young trees up to 10 feet tall, saplings 10 to 20 feet tall (stem d.b.h. 3 to 5 inches), pulpwood (at least 20 feet tall, stem d.b.h 5 to 9 inches), and poles (d.b.h. 9 inches or greater). Typical fire behavior in the sapling class includes "crowning even under moderate weather conditions". Behavior in the pulpwood class is described as being the "most intensive" and releasing the "greatest amount of energy when the crown becomes involved", leaving standard control measures highly ineffective and presenting hazardous firefighting conditions (Parry and others, date unknown). This fire behavior can result from a high density of pines, hardwood trees, shrubs, palmetto, climbing vines and other fuels typical of unburned slash pine flatwoods forests and plantations. The palmetto-gallberry shrub community characteristic of many slash pine plantations is listed as a second major fuel type in Florida.

In contrast, complete canopy closure and/or intensive vegetation control may result in low intensity fire due to reduction of herbaceous groundcover (Means 1997) and midstory species. Periodic dormant season prescribed fires can also maintain woody shrubs at a lower height and fuel hazard than would occur in the absence of fire.

Herbicide use—The increasing use of herbicides for vegetation management and restoration also offers an opportunity to alter fire regimes. For example, chemically-treated shrubs will leave standing dead fuels for one to three years, but as the dead shrubs break down, grass and herbs increase and become the dominant understory fuel. The extent of these fuel conversions will depend on plant communities and specific herbicides. As application of prescribed fire becomes more challenging, it is likely that fuel reductions with herbicides will continue to increase.

Primary Objectives for Prescribed Fire in Plantations

The primary reasons for application of fire in managed slash pine stands include: fuel/hazard reduction, site preparation, and control of understory hardwoods and shrubs which compete for resources and limit access by forest managers (Williams 1985). Additional objectives may include pest management in certain situations, range improvement where cattle grazing and pine trees are managed together, and preparation of old field plantations for pine straw collection. The following discussion elaborates on several of these objectives that were not covered previously in the Managing Fire in Natural Slash Pine Systems section.

Hazard reduction—Wildfires are a significant hazard in almost all natural ecosystems in the South, endangering homes, people, and timber investments. In Florida in 1998, over 500,000 acres burned in wildfires in a matter of weeks, with losses totaling over $1 billion. Many of these fires burned through pine plantations which had dense understory vegetation.

Prescribed burning is an effective and efficient technique to reduce the quantity of dead debris and fine fuels (Hunt and Simpson 1985). Prescribed burning before stand establishment can reduce the risk of wildfire when slash pine stands are young and at the greatest mortal risk from wildfires. A study in Australia demonstrated that the use of low intensity prescribed burning every three years reduced fine fuels and had no effect on the diameter or growth of slash pine in southeast Queensland (Hunt and Simpson 1985).

The effect of invasive exotic grasses such as cogongrass and silk reed (*Neyraudia reynaudiana*) can also influence fire behavior. In South Florida slash pine savannas these grasses increase fine fuel loads and litter and change fire behavior by increasing the fire intensity 1 to 2 m above the ground (Platt and Gottschalk 2001). Prescribed burning will have to be combined with other treatment methods to help keep these new fuel load additions in check.

Site preparation—Reforestation objectives were the second most common reason for prescribed fire on state and private forests in the South (Haines and others 2001).

Mechanical treatments, herbicides, and burning all have advantages and problems related to site preparation objectives of reducing competition, exposing mineral soil, and keeping young pine seedling roots above standing water. In recent years the liability associated with prescribed burning, smoke regulations, and public perception has considerably curbed the use of burning in commercial site preparation prescriptions. However, burning is still an economical alternative for site preparation.

Pines are best planted on mineral soil. Successive summer fires before planting can be used to expose mineral soil and temporarily reduce the amount of hardwood and herbaceous competition. For example, Harrington and others (1998) found that the abundance of vines and hardwoods after a site preparation treatment of herbicides plus burning was approximately half of the abundance in untreated areas.

Pest management—Prescribed fire can be used to curb the hazards of certain diseases and insects, but should not be applied if a stand is already stressed by drought, disease or other conditions. Prescribed fire before and after thinning reduces the infection of annosum root rot (*Heterobasidion annosum*) by destroying the litter associated with this fungus (Froelich and others 1978). Fungal sporophores are normally produced in the litter at the base of infected trees and serve as a spore source for fresh stumps after thinning. Froelich and others (1978) noted that a fungal competitor of root rot also increased in the soil after burning and may have helped reduce the infection of root rot.

Fire will control the spread of bark beetles from infested trees that are cut and piled, but it is unclear if prescribed burning has any other effects on southern pine beetles in slash pine plantations unless it is to stress trees and increase their susceptibility during times of high beetle populations. Some other pests that are controlled by regular prescribed burning are the ticks and chiggers that await forest workers and recreationists.

Range improvement—Fire objectives for range management are two fold: prescribed burning may be used to improve range resources; at the same time, livestock grazing can keep fuel loads low enough for protection from wildfires. Regular burning (two to four year intervals) improves forage quality and quantity for livestock. Forage utilization is greatest the year following burning with new shrub, herb, and grass sprouts that capture the quick flush of nutrients into the soil after a fire and are often more nutritious and palatable than older plants. Common slash pine planting densities (600 to 800 trees per acre) usually shade out herbaceous plants necessary for grazing by the tenth year after planting. Only if stands are thinned early and kept fairly open by frequent burning can forage be maintained (Grelen 1978).

Although grazing in plantations is not as common as in the past, increasing interests in silvopasture will probably lead to more prescribed burning to accommodate land-use combinations of cattle and pine plantations (Nowak and Long 2004). Fire is widely used in southern Florida slash pine prairies to support large grazing operations in those areas with low pine densities.

Pine straw management—Pine straw has become an important product from many old field plantations. By raking and selling the straw, landowners receive a financial return through the midyears of the timber rotation. Raking can begin between ages six to eight, but is most productive around age 15. Prescribed fire does not play a role in the management of pine stands during the years of pine straw collection. However, prescribed burns before raking begins can consume shrubs, grasses, and debris that make baling difficult.

IMPORTANT CONSIDERATIONS AND ISSUES FOR PRESCRIBED BURNING

The ability of natural resource managers to take advantage of prescribed burning as a land management tool is an undeniable benefit. To maintain that benefit, a number of special considerations need to be addressed prior to prescribed burning. Some of the most important issues are described in this section.

Best Management Practices

Best Management Practices are guidelines that are designed to protect water quality, riparian zones and related resources during forestry activities. These guidelines assist forest managers in defining sensitive areas and in the proper use of various practices or operations, including prescribed burning.

Best Management Practices regarding prescribed fire primarily address the construction and maintenance of firelines: utilize natural boundaries or roads as much as possible; construct lines with the minimum acceptable plow depth; do not run lines directly into waterways; follow contours; and avoid streamside management zones. Prescribed burning is also generally restricted on slopes greater than 18 to 20 percent adjacent to waterways. Many of the states in the Southeast have similar BMPs, although specifications vary with differences in topography and soils.

Evaluation

Evaluation of a prescribed fire is as important as the planning stages. The primary purpose of the evaluation process is to determine if the burn met the objectives set by the managers and to serve as a learning tool for future burns (Wade and others 1989). The experience gained through monitoring and evaluation will improve planning and predictions for future burns. The evaluation process should consider air quality and smoke management, soil and root damage, needle scorch, and the overall impact of the burn on vegetation and wildlife.

Smoke Management and Liability Concerns

Prescribed burn plans incorporate weather conditions and fuel loads that will generally result in less smoke than wildfires. A variety of forecasts are now available through the National Weather Service and state forestry offices and should be used to avoid the unfortunate "wind changes" that moved smoke to unplanned areas in the past. Nevertheless, the number of smoke-related lawsuits against landowners has increased (Brenner and Wade 1992). Smoke management laws and the risk of liability were rated in the top four barriers to prescribed burning in the recent survey of foresters in the South (Haines and others 2001).

Burning permits are required by law in most states and their issuance is dictated, to some degree, by State Implementation Plans. Many states have also followed Florida's lead in developing statutes or rules that provide liability protection for burners who have been certified through a prescribed fire training program. Despite these legal supports for prescribed burning, a major concern for many practitioners is still the possibility of civil or criminal lawsuits, in spite of the fact that negligence must be proven before property owners can be found responsible for damage or injury from the fire (Siegel 1984). State laws are increasingly declaring that the standard for liability in prescribed burning cases will be based on simple (carelessness) or gross (willful and wanton) negligence rather than strict liability. According to Stanton (1995), "In strict or unlimited liability situations, a defendant may be morally blameless and the act fully unintentional; nevertheless, the defendant is legally at fault and will be required to satisfy any judgments created." When the situation is not within the strict or unlimited liability guidelines the court has to determine if the defendant was indeed negligent, and if so to what extent. Given the litigious nature of the general public, landowners and resource managers should be knowledgeable about legal requirements and liability issues before becoming involved in prescribed burning practices (Eshee 1995).

Just as with poorly placed smoke, prescribed fires that escape the intended boundaries can be devastating. Incidents of escape can happen even with perfect planning and execution of a prescribed burn. Burn plans are not complete without a contingency plan for how to respond and who to contact in case of an escape.

Public Perceptions about Prescribed Burning

The biggest challenge facing land management practices, such as prescribed fire, is often public perception and actions that emanate from those perceptions. Land managers and decision-makers need to understand how citizens perceive fire to build support for their programs (Lichtman 1998). Despite an often negative perception of fire, the public's tolerance and knowledge of prescribed fire have increased over the past several decades, especially when the participants were provided with educational materials (including various media sources) on prescribed burning and wildfires (Loomis and others 2001).

One survey of Florida residents assessed their awareness and attitudes dealing with fire. The results indicated that "There is a somewhat schizophrenic perspective on fire in Florida" (Monroe and others 1999). The general public knows the benefits of prescribed burning; they believe tolerance of smoke should be higher; and they understand prescribed burning versus wildfire. However, they also supported stricter burning regulations. Maybe some of the confusion in the respondents' preferences arises from misconceptions of terminology. For example, the survey also showed that only 40 percent of the respondents defined the term "prescribed fire" correctly (Monroe and others 1999). Educational programs will play a key role in clarifying such misunderstandings.

Wildland-Urban Interface and Prescribed Burning

The increasing popularity of homes in natural settings has resulted in an expanding wildland-urban interface. Yet many people living next to wildlands are unaware of the risks of fire to their homes, they value the ambience of their surroundings, and they expect emergency services to take responsibility for fire threats (Feary and Neuenschwander 1998). Issues arising at the wildland/urban interface are related to both the risk from dangerous wildfires and the use of prescribed burns to minimize those risks.

Fragmented forest landscapes have increased opportunities for wildland fires to cross paths with human development. Some of the most acute problems occur in residential areas in, or adjacent to, slash pine plantations. Many property owners in the wildland-urban interface have preconceived notions about fire and tend to oppose prescribed fires. They may view prescribed fire as a threat to public health and safety concerns, a source of liability, evidence of lack of landowner management savvy, or a threat to community development (Macie 2001). Their perceptions and attitudes may limit the use of prescribed fire as an interface management tool.

The role of public education in addressing fire at the wildland/urban interface is crucial to limiting the impacts on people's lives. Education has become a valuable tool for increasing public understanding of the role of fire in nature and the opportunities to use prescribed burning (Monroe and others 1999). Education can change knowledge and attitudes about prescribed fire (Loomis and others 2001), and introduces homeowners to practices that will reduce the risk of fire to their property, homes, and lives. A diverse set of educational materials are now available or being developed for landowners.

Just as landowners need to be persuaded to take responsibility for making their homes firesafe, developers need to accommodate wildfires in their plans. Subdivision infrastructure should be able to limit wildfires and provide for evacuation and control operations when fires do occur. Buffer zones, firewise structures, multiple access routes and water resources for fire fighting are crucial, as are open communications among neighbors, resource managers, and community/business members (Monroe and Marynoski 1999). FireWise workshops are becoming a valuable mechanism for encouraging that communication and planning.

ADVANCES IN FIRE CONTROL AND MANAGEMENT

Fire Behavior Modeling

Classifying fuel and weather characteristics according to spatial and temporal scales facilitates our ability to understand and predict fire behavior. Fuel classification and fire modeling have been evolving at a rapid pace. In the last 20 years, developments in computers, software and fuel classification systems have greatly increased the number of tools used to quantitatively assess fire behavior and plan fire control operations.

Fire behavior prediction models are used to provide real-time support for suppression tactics, safety, and prescribed fire planning. The Windows® based wildland fire prediction tool Behave was developed by the USDA Forest Service, Rocky Mountain Research Station and Systems for Environmental Management. Predictions are developed from user inputs on fuel, weather, topography, and fire characteristics. Fire behavior estimates include: surface fire spread, fireline intensity, spotting, flame length, scorch, tree mortality, and probability of ignition (Andrews 1986). Several versions of this software are now available from different vendors. Other fire forecasting models and fire information resources, ranging from pollutant emissions applications to emergency incident tools for Geographic Information Systems (GIS), are described at www.fire.org.

Fuel Loads

Accurate information about woody fuel size classes and fuel loads are needed to run BehavePlus and smoke dispersion models. The U.S. Forest Service and National Wildfire Coordinating Group have recently published photo series for estimating fuel loads in the Southeast (Ottmar and Vihnanek 2000, Scholl and Waldrop 1999). These photo series focus primarily on longleaf and loblolly pine and can be used to quickly estimate fuel load characteristics in a variety of stand conditions. Fuel loads are also being assessed on a much larger scale through the use of satellite imagery, GIS and ground truthing. The resulting state and regional models will be an important tool in planning fire mitigation and control operations in the future.

Fire Weather

Weather forecasting and fire modeling have a direct influence on prescribed fire planning. For example, the Florida Division of Forestry manages an online resource (http://flame.fl-dof.com) that houses current fire weather information used to forecast weather and predict fire danger levels. Daily readings of temperature, relative humidity, surface winds, mixing height, transport winds, dispersion index, Keetch-Byram Drought Index (KBDI), Haines index, low visibility risk index, and fire weather indices are available. The Division of Forestry also updates a "spot forecasting system" that produces hourly estimates of temperature, relative humidity, and wind speed and direction 20 ft above the vegetative surface for a landowner's specific location. These outputs are an efficient way of obtaining requirements for the BehavePlus modules and other fire prediction software.

CONCLUSION

Wildfire is a significant public issue for natural resource management and it will be even more so in the future, especially where it becomes a serious threat near the wildland-urban interface or in slash pine plantations. However, prescribed fire will also remain as an important and strategic tool for both plantation and natural stand management; but its application will be dependent on policies and issues related to public acceptance, health and safety. Landowner and public education will be critical components of future fire management programs.

LITERATURE CITED

Abrahamson, W.G. 1984. Species responses to fire on the Florida Lake Wales Ridge. American Journal Botany. 71(1): 35-43.

Abrahamson, W.G.; Hartnett, D.C. 1990. Pine flatwoods and dry prairies. In: Myers, R.L.; Ewel, J.J., eds. Ecosystems of Florida. Univ. of Central Florida Press, Orlando, FL: 103-149.

Andrews, P.L. 1986. BEHAVE: fire behavior prediction and fuel modeling system-BURN subsystem, part 1. Gen. Tech. Rep. INT-194. Ogden, UT: U.S. Department of Agriculture, Forest Service, Intermountain Research Station. 130 p.

Bell, R.L.; Binkley, D. 1989. Soil nitrogen mineralization and immobilization in response to periodic prescribed fire in loblolly pine plantations. Canadian Journal of Forest Research. 19: 816-820.

Block, W.H.; Finch, D.M.; Brennan, L.A. 1995. Single species versus multiple-species approaches for management. In: Martin, T.E.; Finch, D.M. eds. Ecology and management of neotropical migratory birds: A synthesis and review of critical issues. New York, NY: Oxford University Press. 489 p.

Boyer, W.D.; Miller, J.H. 1994. Effect of burning and brush treatments on nutrient and soil physical properties in young longleaf pine stands. Forest Ecology and Management. 70: 311-318.

Boyette, W.G. 1996. Executive summary, results of 1995 survey of longleaf pine restoration efforts in the South (parts I, II, III). Raleigh, NC: North Carolina Division of Forest Resources. 51 p.

Breininger, D.R.; Smith, R.B. 1992. Relationships between fire and bird density in coastal scrub and slash pine flatwoods in Florida. American Midland Naturalist. 127: 233-240.

Brennan, L.A. 1991. How can we reverse the northern bobwhite population decline? Wildlife Society Bulletin. 19: 544-555.

Brenner, J.; Wade, D.D. 1992. Florida's 1990 prescribed burning act: protection for responsible burners. Journal of Forestry. 90(5): 27-30.

Brown, R.C. 1994. Florida's first people. Sarasota, FL: Pineapple Press. 262 p.

Bryson, C.T.; Carter, R. 1993. Cogongrass, *Imperata cylindrica*, in the United States. Weed Technology. 7(4): 1005-1009.

Carlson, P.C.; Tanner, G.W.; Wood, J.M.; Humphrey, S.R. 1993. Fire in key deer habitat improves browse, prevents succession and preserves endemic herbs. Journal of Wildlife Management. 57(4): 914-928.

Chester, D.N.; Stauffer, D.F.; Smith, T.J. [and others]. 1990. Habitat use by nonbreeding bald eagles in North Carolina. Journal of Wildlife Management. 54(2): 223-234.

Christensen, N.L. 1981. Fire regimes in southeastern ecosystems. In: Mooney, H.A.; Bonnighsen, T.M.; Christensen, N.L.; Lotan, J.E.; Reiners, W.A. tech. coords. Fire regimes and ecosystem properties conference: proceedings; 1978 December 11-15; Honolulu, HI. Gen. Tech. Rep. WO-26. Washington DC: U.S. Department of Agriculture, Forest Service: 112-136.

Clewell, A.F. 1989. Natural history of wiregrass (*Aristida stricta* Michx., Graminae). Natural Areas Journal. 9(4): 223-233.

Core, J.E. 1995. Air quality regulations: treatment of emissions from wildfires vs. prescribed fires. In: Bryan, D.C. ed. Environmental regulation & prescribed fire: Legal and social challenges, conference proceedings; 1995 March 14-17; Tampa, FL. Tallahassee, FL: Center for Professional Development, Florida State University: 53-62.

Crow, A.B.; Shilling, C.L. 1980. Use of prescribed burning to enhance southern pine timber production. Southern Journal of Applied Forestry. 4(1): 15-18.

De Ronde, C. 1982. The resistance of *Pinus* species to fire damage. South African Forestry Journal. 122: 22-27.

DeBano, L.F. 2000. The role of fire and soil heating on water repellency in wildland environments: a review. Journal of Hydrology. 231-232: 195-206.

Dees, C.S.; Clark, J.D.; Van Manen, F.T. 2001. Florida panther habitat use in response to prescribed fire. Journal of Wildlife Management. 65(1): 141-147.

Demmon, E.L. 1935. Silvicultural aspects of the forest-fire problem. Journal of Forestry. 33: 323-331.

Dickson, J.G.; Thompson, F.R., III; Conner, R.N.; Franzreb, K.E. 1995. Silviculture in central and southeastern oak-pine forests. In: Martin, T.E.; Finch, D.M. eds. Ecology and management of neotropical migratory birds: A synthesis and review of critical issues. New York, NY: Oxford University Press. 489 p.

Douglas, J.E.; Van Lear, D.H. 1983. Prescribed burning and water quality of ephemeral streams in the Piedmont of South Carolina. Forest Science. 29: 181-189.

Edmisten, J.E. 1963. The ecology of the Florida pine flatwoods. Ph.D. Thesis; Gainesville, FL: University of Florida.

Eshee, W.D., Jr. 1995. Legal implications of using prescribed fire. In: Bryan, D.C. ed. Environmental regulation & prescribed fire: Legal and social challenges, conference proceedings; 1995 March 14-17; Tampa, FL. Tallahassee, FL: Center for Professional Development, Florida State University: 126-130.

Evans, R. 1989. Managing for quail in southern woodlands. Forest Farmer. 48(8): 12-14.

Feary, K.M.; Neuenschwander, L.F. 1998. Predicting fire behavior in the wildland urban interface. In: Pruden, T.L.; Brennan, L.A. eds. Fire in ecosystem management: Shifting the paradigm from suppression to prescription: proceedings, 20th Tall Timbers fire ecology conference; 1996 May 7-10; Boise, ID. Tallahassee FL: Tall Timbers Research Station: 44-48.

Ferguson, J. 1998. Prescribed fire on the Apalachicola Ranger District: the shift from dormant season to growing season and effects on wildfire suppression. In: Pruden, T.L.; Brennan, L.A. eds. Fire in ecosystem management: Shifting the paradigm from suppression to prescription: proceedings, 20th Tall Timbers fire ecology conference; 1996 May 7-10; Boise, ID. Tallahassee FL: Tall Timbers Research Station: 120-126.

Fitzgerald, S.M.; Tanner, G.W. 1992. Avian community response to fire and mechanical controls in south Florida. Journal Range Management. 45: 396-400.

Fritz, G.J. 2000. Native farming systems and ecosystems in the Mississippi River Valley. In: Lentz, D.L. (ed.) Imperfect balance: Landscape transformations in the Precolumbian Americas. New York, NY: Columbia University Press. 788 p.

Froelich, R.C.; Hodges, C.S.; Sackett, S.S. 1978. Prescribed burning reduces the severity of annosus root rot in the South. Forest Science. 24(1): 93-100.

Frost, C.C. 1998. Presettlement fire frequency regimes of the United States: a first approximation. In: Moser, W.K.; Moser, C.F. eds. Fire and forest ecology: Innovative silviculture and vegetation management: proceedings, 21st Tall Timbers fire ecology conference; 1998 April 14-16; Tallahassee, FL. Tallahassee FL: Tall Timbers Research Station: 70-81.

Grelen, H.E. 1978. Forest grazing in the South. Journal of Range Management. 31(4): 244-250.

Haines, T.K.; Busby, R.L.; Cleaves, D.A. 2001. Prescribed burning in the South: trends, purpose and barriers. Southern Journal of Applied Forestry. 25(4): 149-153.

Harrington, T.B.; Minogue, P.J.; Lauer, D.K.; Ezell, A.W. 1998. Two-year development of southern pine seedlings and associated vegetation following spray-and-burn site preparation with imazapyr alone or in mixture with other herbicides. New Forests. 15: 89-106.

Haywood, J.D.; Harris, F.L.; Grelen, H.E.; Pearson, H.A. 2001. Vegetative responses to 37 years of seasonal burning on a Louisiana longleaf pine site. Southern Journal of Applied Forestry. 25(3): 122-130.

Hedman, C.W.; Grace, S.L.; King, S.E. 2000. Vegetation composition and structure of southern Coastal Plain pine forests: an ecological comparison. Forest Ecology and Management. 134: 233-247.

Helvey, J.D.; Tiedemann, A.R.; Fowler, W.B. 1974. Some climatic and hydrologic effects of wildfire in Washington State. In: Pacific Northwest: proceedings, 15th Tall Timbers fire ecology conference; 1974; Portland, OR. Tallahassee FL: Tall Timbers Research Station: 201-222.

Hough, W.A.; Albini, F.A. 1978. Predicting fire behavior in palmetto-gallberry fuel complexes. U.S. Department of Agriculture, Forest Service SRS Res. Pap. SE-174. Asheville, NC. 44 p.

Hunt, S.M.; Simpson, J.A. 1985. Effects of low intensity prescribed fire on the growth and nutrition of a slash pine plantation. Australian Forest Research. 15: 67-77.

Hurst, G.A. 1989. Deer management in the southern pine forest. Forest Farmer. 48(8): 10-11.

Johansen, R.W. 1975. Prescribed burning may enhance growth of young slash pine. Journal of Forestry. 73: 148-149.

Johansen, R.W.; Phernetton, R.A. 1982. Smoke management on the Okefenokee national wildlife refuge. Southern Journal of Applied Forestry. 6: 200-205.

Johansen, R.W.; Wade, D.D. 1987. Effects of crown scorch on survival and diameter growth of slash pines. Southern Journal of Applied Forestry. 11: 180-184.

Ketcham, D.E.; Bethune, J.E. 1963. Fire resistance of south Florida slash pine. Journal of Forestry. 61: 529-530.

Kush, J.S.; Meldahl, R.S.; Boyer, W.D. 2000. Understory plant community response to season of burn in natural longleaf pine forests. In: Moser, W.K.; Moser, C.F. eds. Fire and forest ecology: Innovative silviculture and vegetation management: proceedings, 21st Tall Timbers fire ecology conference; 1998 April 14-16; Tallahassee, FL. Tallahassee FL: Tall Timbers Research Station: 32-39.

LaFayette, R.A. 1995. Overview of clean water act requirements. In: Bryan, D. C. ed. Environmental regulation & prescribed fire: Legal and social challenges, conference proceedings; 1995 March 14-17; Tampa, FL. Tallahassee, FL: Center for Professional Development, Florida State University: 89-98.

Landers, J.L. 1987. Prescribed burning for managing wildlife in southeastern pine forests. In: Dickson, J.G.; Maughan, E.O. eds. Managing southern forests for wildlife and fish. Gen. Tech. Rep. SO-65. Asheville, NC: U. S. Department of Agriculture, Forest Service, Southern Forest Experiment Station:19-27.

Landers, J.L. 1991. Disturbance influences on pine traits in the Southeastern United States. In: Hermann, S.M. ed. High-intensity fire in wildlands: Management challenges and options: proceedings, 17th Tall Timbers fire ecology conference; Tallahassee FL: Tall Timbers Research Station: 61-98.

Lentz, D.L. 2000. Anthropocentric food webs in the Precolumbian Americas. In Lentz, D.L. ed. Imperfect balance: Landscape transformations in the Precolumbian Americas. New York, NY: Columbia University Press. 788 p.

Lichtman, P. 1998. The politics of wildfire: lessons from Yellowstone. Journal of Forestry. 96(5): 4-9.

Loeb, S.C.; Pepper, W.D.; Doyle, A.T. 1992. Habitat characteristics of active and abandoned red-cockaded woodpecker colonies. Southern Journal of Applied Forestry. 16: 120-125.

Lohrey, R.E.; Kossuth, S.V. 1990. *Pinus elliottii* Engelm. slash pine. In: Burns, R.M.; Honkala, B.H. tech. coords. Silvics of North America: volume 1, Conifers. Agric. Handbook 654. Washington, DC: U.S. Department of Agriculture: 338-347.

Loomis, J.B.; Bair, L.S.; Gonzalez-Caban, A. 2001. Prescribed fire and public support: knowledge gained, attitudes changed in Florida. Journal of Forestry 99(11): 18-22.

Macie, E. 2001. Managing forests in the wildland-urban interface. Florida Forests. Fall: 8-10.

Maehr, D.S.; Hoctor, T.S.; Quinn, L.J.; Smith, J.S. 2001. Florida black bear habitat management guidelines for Florida. Tech. Rep. No. 17. Tallahassee, FL: Florida Fish and Wildlife Conservation Commission. 83 p.

Main, M.B.; Tanner, G.W. 1999. Effects of fire on Florida's wildlife and wildlife habitat. Fact Sheet WEC 137. Gainesville, FL: University of Florida Cooperative Extension Service. 4 p.

McKee, W.H., Jr. 1982. Changes in soil fertility following pre-scribed burning on Coastal Plain pine sites. Research Paper SE-234. Asheville, NC: U.S. Department of Agriculture, Forest Service, Southeastern Forest Experiment Station: 23 p.

McKee, W.H., Jr. 1987. Impacts of prescribed burning on Coastal Plain forest soils. In: Forests, the world, and the profession; proceedings; Society of American Foresters national convention; 1986; Bethesda, MD: Society of American Foresters: 107-111.

Means, D.B. 1997. Wiregrass restoration: probable shading effects in a slash pine plantation. Restoration and Management Notes. 15(1): 52-55.

Means, D.B.; Palis, J.G.; Baggett, M. 1996. Effects of slash pine silviculture on a Florida population of flatwoods salamander. Conservation Biology. 10: 426-437.

Mobley, H.E. 1991. Manage your smoke to save lives. Forest Farmer. 50: 46-48.

Monk, C.D. 1968. Successional and environmental relationships of the forest vegetation of north central Florida. American Midland Naturalist. 79(2): 441-457.

Monroe, M.; Jacobson, S.; Marynowski, S. 1999. Needs assessment report: Awareness and attitudes about fire in Florida. Unpublished report for the Florida Fish and Wildlife Conservation Commission. Gainesville, FL: University of Florida Cooperative Extension Service, School of Forest Resources and Conservation. 15 p. online: http://www.sfrc.ufl.edu/Extension/needsurv.htm

Monroe, M.C. 1999. Where there's fire, there's smoke: air quality and prescribed burning in Florida. Fact Sheet FOR 62. Gainesville, FL: University of Florida Cooperative Extension Service, School of Forest Resources and Conservation. 4 p.

Monroe, M.C.; Marynowski, S. 1999. Developing Florida with fire in mind. Fact Sheet FOR 63. Gainesville, FL: University of Florida Cooperative Extension Service, School of Forest Resources and Conservation. 4 p.

Moore, W.H.; Swindell, B.F.; Terry, W.S. 1982a. Vegetative response to clearcutting and chopping in a north Florida flatwoods forest. Journal of Range Management. 35(2): 214-218.

Moore, W.H.; Swindell, B.F.; Terry, W.S. 1982b. Vegetative response to prescribed fire in a north Florida flatwoods forest. Journal of Range Management. 35(3): 386-389.

Moser, W.K.; Palmer, W.E. 1997. Quail habitat and forest management: what are the opportunities? Forest Landowners Manual. March/April 1997, 56(2): 56-63.

Nowak, J.; Long, A. 2004. Slash pine in integrated timber, forage, and livestock silvopastoral systems. In: Dickens, E.D.; Barnett, J.P.; Hubbard, W.G.; Jokela, E.J., eds. Slash pine: still growing and growing! Proceedings of the slash pine symposium. Gen. Tech. Rep. SRS-76. Asheville, NC: U.S. Department of Agriculture, Forest Service, Southern Research Station: 98-104.

Ottmar, R.D.; Vihnanek, R.E. 2000. Stereo photoseries for quantifying natural fuels. Volume VI: Longleaf pine, pocosin, and marshgrass types in the southeast United States. PMS 835, Boise, ID: National Wildfire Coordinating Group, National Interagency Fire Center. 56 p.

Parry, J.; Humphrey, M.; Turnbull, B. [Date unknown]. Florida fire behavior training course. Tallahassee, FL: Florida Department of Agriculture and Consumer Services, Division of Forestry. 48 p.

Peroni, P.A.; Abrahamson, W.G. 1986. Succession in Florida sand ridge vegetation: a retrospective study. Florida Science. 49(3): 176-191.

Peterson, J.; Ward, D. 1990. An inventory of particulate matter and air toxic emissions from prescribed fires in the United States for 1989. Seattle, WA: U.S. Department of Agriculture, Forest Service, Pacific Northwest Research Station.

Platt, W.J.; Gottschak, R.M. 2001. Effects of exotic grasses on potential fine fuel loads in the groundcover of south Florida slash pine savannas. International Journal of Wildland Fire. 10: 155-159.

Plentovich, S.; Tucker, J.W.; Holler, N.R.; Hill, G.E. 1998. Enhancing Bachman's sparrow habitat via management for red-cockaded woodpeckers. Journal of Wildlife Management. 62(1): 347-354.

Provencher, L.; Litt, A.R.; Galley, K.E.M. [and others]. 2001. Restoration of fire-suppressed longleaf pine sandhills at Eglin Air Force Base, Florida. Interim final report to the Natural Resources Management Division, Eglin Air Force Base, Niceville, Florida. Gainesville, FL: The Nature Conservancy, Science Division.

Pyne, S.J.; Andrews, P.L.; Laven, R.D. 1996. Introduction to wildland fire. 2nd ed. New York, NY: John Wiley & Sons, Inc. 769 p.

Richter, D.D.; Ralston, C.W.; Harms, W.R. 1982. Prescribed fire: effects on water quality and forest nutrient cycling. Science. 215: 661-663.

Riekerk, H. 1985. Water quality effects of pine flatwoods silviculture. Journal of Soil and Water Conservation. 40: 306-309.

Robbins, L.A.; Myers, R.L. 1992. Seasonal effects of prescribed burning in Florida: a review. Misc. Pub. No. 8. Tallahassee, FL: Tall Timbers Research, Inc. 96 p.

Schaefer, J.; Sargent, M. 1990. Florida black bear: a threatened species. Fact Sheet SS-WIS-25. Gainesville, FL: University of Florida Cooperative Extension Service. 3 p.

Scholl, E.R.; Waldrop, T.A. 1999. Photos for estimating fuel loadings before and after prescribed burning in the upper Coastal Plain of the Southeast. Gen. Tech. Rep. SRS-26. Asheville, NC: U.S. Department of Agriculture, Forest Service, Southern Research Station. 25 p.

Shultz, R.P.; Wilhite, L.P. 1974. Changes in a flatwoods site following intensive site preparation. Forest Science. 20: 230-237.

Siegel, W.C. 1984. Legal implications of prescribed burning in the South. In: Wade, D.D., ed. Prescribed fires and smoke management in the south conference: proceedings; 1984 September 12-14; Atlanta, GA. Asheville, NC: U.S. Department of Agriculture, Forest Service, Southeastern Forest Experiment Station.

Stanton, R. 1995. Managing liability exposures associated with prescribed fires. Natural Areas Journal. 15(4): 347-352.

Stoddard, H. 1931. The bobwhite quail: its habits, preservation and increase. New York, NY: Charles Scribner's Sons. 559 p.

Swindel, B.F.; Marion, W.R.; Harris, L.D. [and others]. 1983. Multiresource effects of harvest, site preparation, and planting in pine flatwoods. Southern Journal of Applied Forestry. 7(1): 6-15.

U.S. Fish and Wildlife Service. 1995. Florida panther (*Felis concolor coryi*) recovery plan. Atlanta, GA: U.S. Fish and Wildlife Service. 69 p.

U.S. Fish and Wildlife Service. 2000. Technical/agency draft revised recovery plan for the red-cockaded woodpecker (*Picoides borealis*). Atlanta, GA: U.S. Fish and Wildlife Service. 283 p.

U.S. Forest Service. 1999. Revised land and resource management plan for National Forests in Florida. Management Bulletin R8-MB-83A. Atlanta, GA: U.S. Department of Agriculture, Forest Service, Southern Region. 130 p.

Wade, D.D. 1983. Fire management in the slash pine ecosystem. In: Stone, E.L., ed. The managed slash pine ecosystem symposium: proceedings; 1981 June 9-11; Gainesville, FL. Gainesville, FL: The University of Florida: 203-227.

Wade, D.D.; Brock, B.L.; Brose, P.H. [and others]. 2000. Fire in eastern ecosystems. In: Brown, J.K.; Smith, J.K. eds. Wildland fire in ecosystems: Effects of fire on flora. Gen. Tech. Rep. RMRS-42-vol. 2. Ogden, UT: U.S. Department of Agriculture, Forest Service, Rocky Mountain Research Station: 53-96.

Wade, D.D.; Lunsford, J.D. 1989. A guide for prescribed fire in southern forests. Technical Publication R8-TP 11. Atlanta, GA: U.S. Department of Agriculture, Forest Service, Southern Region: 56 p.

Weise, D.R.; Wade, D.D.; Johansen, R.W. 1990. Survival and growth of young southern pine after simulated crown scorch. In: 10th conference on fire and forest meteorology: proceedings; 1989 April 17-21; Ottawa, Canada. Bethesda, MD: Society of American Foresters: 161-168.

Williams, R.A. 1985. Use of prescribed fire on industrial lands in the gulf Coastal Plain and uplands. In: Wade, D.D., ed. Prescribed fires and smoke management in the south conference: proceedings; 1984 September 12-14; Atlanta, GA. Asheville, NC: U.S. Department of Agriculture, Forest Service, Southeastern Forest Experiment Station.

Wright, H.A.; Bailey, A.W. 1982. Fire ecology: United States and Southern Canada. New York, NY: John Wiley and Sons. 528 p.

WILDLIFE MANAGEMENT ISSUES AND OPPORTUNITIES IN SLASH PINE FORESTS

Michael T. Mengak and Steven B. Castleberry[1]

Abstract—The slash pine (*Pinus elliottii*)-longleaf pine (*P. palustris*) cover type currently occupies over 13 million acres (8.7 percent of total forested acres) in the southeastern United States. Despite the large acreage and numerous studies in longleaf forests, only a limited number of studies have examined wildlife utilization and management of slash pine stands. Natural slash pine sites are low in soil phosphorous and have low potential as white-tailed deer (*Odocoileus virginianus*) habitat. Regular prescribed fire improves the palatability and nutritional content of forage for deer. Similarly, thinning and burning slash pine plantations improves habitat for turkey (*Meleagris galapavo*) and quail (*Colinus virginianus*). The gopher tortoise (*Gopherus polyphemus*) is a keystone species found in the slash pine ecosystem. Burrows dug by gopher tortoises are used by over 50 other species of vertebrates and invertebrates. The flatwoods salamander (*Ambystoma cingulatum*), a federally threatened species, has experienced a rangewide population decline that is thought to be related to habitat conversion and fragmentation as longleaf pine stands are converted to slash and loblolly pine. Management for slash pine and wildlife are compatible but managers and landowners should manipulate vegetation to mimic natural conditions. Unfortunately, few studies examine the financial trade-offs between timber production and wildlife.

INTRODUCTION

Slash pine (*Pinus elliottii*) has been a favorite tree species for plantation management in Georgia with some plantations dating back to 1925 (Jones 1979). From 1956 to 1960, slash pine was widely planted in the Soil Bank Program. Slash pine often grows with longleaf pine (*Pinus palustris*) and currently the longleaf-slash pine cover type occupies over 13.17 million acres (8.7 percent of total forested acres) in the southeastern United States (USFS 2002). The majority of the acreage is in the south Atlantic Coastal Plain (87.1 percent).

The range of slash pine extends from east Texas to Georgetown County, South Carolina (USDA Forest Service 1965). Slash pine occurs naturally in all or part of 179 counties across the south and is more restricted than that of other major southern pines (Critchfield and Little 1966). Slash pine grows naturally on sandy soils that are poorly drained with 18-24 inches (46-61 cm) to a clay hardpan. Pond margins are well suited to slash pine whereas pure sand or poorly drained sites are least productive. Slash pine seedlings and young trees are susceptible to fire damage. Frequent fires tend to favor longleaf, but slash pine may out compete longleaf if given adequate fire protection (Jones 1979).

Because of the regional coverage of the slash pine type, wildlife managers frequently encounter both planted and natural stands. Wildlife rarely uses slash pine trees directly. Direct use includes cavity construction by woodpeckers in mature trees and feeding on cones by squirrels. Information on wildlife use of slash pine stands is important for managers. However, only a limited number of studies have examined wildlife utilization of slash pine stands. In the

absence of specific information from slash pine stands, inferences often are drawn from studies where the dominant pine type was loblolly (*P. taeda*) or longleaf.

WILDLIFE NEEDS

Wildlife management activities are often directed toward supplying target species with the necessary resources to meet their survival needs. For any species of wildlife, the fundamental rules of survival are: 1) get energy; 2) store or conserve energy; and 3) reproduce. Generally, wildlife management involves increasing populations or decreasing populations. Increasing the population size has more often been the objective for most wildlife management. Examples include threatened and endangered species management, stocking to reestablish populations and management to increase hunting or viewing opportunities. Often habitat management is the means for increasing population size. Habitat management techniques include burning, thinning, conversion to another forest type, food plot establishment, fertilization, herbicide treatment or a combination of techniques.

Wildlife habitat must supply space, cover, food and water. Space means an adequate area for obtaining life needs and avoiding stress from crowding. Cover includes the vegetative or physical features of a landscape that are used for hiding (adults and young or nests) and protection for weather (wind, rain, sun or snow). Food must be adequate in calories (energy) and nutrients to insure growth and survival and to maintain good health. Water is necessary but rarely limiting in the southeast. Increasing these elements raises carrying capacity of the environment. Decreasing the population size balances the number of animals with the available resources. Either strategy, alone

---

[1] M.T. Mengak, Assistant Professor of Wildlife Service and Outreach; and S.B. Castleberry, Assistant Professor of Wildlife Management in the Daniel B. Warnell School of Forest Resources at the University of Georgia, Athens, GA 30602.

Citation for proceedings: Dickens, E.D.; Barnett, J.P.; Hubbard, W.G.; Jokela, E.J., eds. 2004. Slash pine: still growing and growing! Proceedings of the slash pine symposium. Gen. Tech. Rep. SRS-76. Asheville, NC: U.S. Department of Agriculture, Forest Service, Southern Research Station. 148 p.

or in combination, can be employed in a wildlife management plan.

SUCCESSION

Succession involves the gradual change in plant and animal communities over time. Many wildlife species of the southeast such as deer, northern bobwhite, eastern cottontail (*Sylviligus floridana*), mourning dove (*Zenaida macroura*) and many small mammal species are considered early successional species and require frequent disturbances to the forest cover. These species respond well to forest management activities such as clearcutting or selection harvest.

Other species are late successional species that require less frequently disturbed vegetation or undisturbed vegetation. Examples include wild turkey, eastern gray squirrel (*Sciurus carolinensis*), fox squirrel (*S. niger*), red cockaded woodpeckers (*Picoides borealis*), and many songbirds. Hawks, owls and meso-mammalian predators require a mix of early and late successional habitat for hunting and nesting or denning. In reality, most species also utilize a variety of forest cover types in various stages of plant succession.

Succession occurs at both a forest stand and landscape level. At the stand level, succession is localized and impacts fewer species. At the landscape level the impacts are larger, involve more species, last longer and are more difficult to manage. From a management perspective, part of the difficulty in managing wildlife species arises from diverse ownership patterns and an incomplete knowledge of the life history requirements of many species, especially non-game species including threatened and endangered species. While forest cover type is important to the abundance and distribution of wildlife species, other factors are involved. These include such concepts as edge and interspersion or juxtaposition of habitats. Thus, wildlife management is an inexact science and wildlife managers often work behind forest managers especially when the landowners' objectives include financial returns from timberland.

WILDLIFE MANAGEMENT ACTIVITIES

Numerous tools are available to the wildlife manager or landowner for manipulating forest stands to enhance or decrease wildlife populations. These tools include prescribed burning, thinning, regeneration method, increasing snags and down material (course woody debris – CWD), use of herbicides in site preparation or intermediate stand management, fertilizing often at time of stand establishment, maintaining streamside management zones (SMZ's), and more. Each tool can be used alone or in combination. Each will have different results depending on the site, season and wildlife species involved.

Numerous researchers have examined the impacts of intensive pine plantation management on wildlife. In general, wildlife populations are abundant in the first few years following stand establishment. Wildlife populations, both small mammals and game species, decline as the stand ages and canopy closure occurs. Closed canopy pine plantations limit sunlight from reaching the forest floor that in turn prevents grasses, forbs, or woody understory from

developing. A thinning and burning regime is required in order to maintain habitat conditions favorable for wildlife. This level of management could decrease overall timber yield but may increase income from lease fees and non-consumptives uses. However, the financial trade-offs between timber production and wildlife management are largely unknown.

WILDLIFE SPECIES

Game

White-tailed deer—Natural slash pine forests typically occur on sites low in soil phosphorous and have low potential as deer habitat (Buckner 1983). The understory contains many xeric species due to prolonged dry periods and low fertility to mesic and hydric species as landscape position changes to lower lying areas. There is abundant food biomass but of low quality due to soil phosphorous deficiency or an imbalance in the calcium: phosphorous (Ca:P) ratio. The Ca:P ratio could be as high as 5:1 in slash pine flatwoods sites whereas the optimum ratio for deer diet is 2:1 or 1:1 (Buckner 1983). Buckner (1983) concluded that available phosphorous is not sufficient to maintain a "large healthy herd" (p. 370).

Fertilization of slash pine stands with phosphate fertilizers may improve forage quality. Wood (1986) reported that growing season applications of phosphate fertilizer improved the nutritional value of selected forage species for one to two seasons. He also found that the nutritional gain was greater on Coastal Plain than Piedmont sites in South Carolina. However, fertilizer uptake and competition between planted pines and understory forage have not been tested.

Time to crown closure affects use by deer in plantation slash pine. Clearcuts make large amounts of browse available to deer. Most deer use of clearcuts is only along the outer 100 yards (Buckner 1983). Additionally, shape of the clearcut determines the amount of edge created and influences deer utilization. Edge is important because most activity is concentrated in the transition zone between stands. After crown closure, most plantations provide little more than escape cover because the pine canopy shades out understory vegetation. Time to crown closure is inversely related to pine density in planted stands.

Thinned plantations can resemble natural stands and thinning will improve the site for use by deer. Thinning opens the canopy allowing sunlight to reach the forest floor, which in turn stimulates understory growth. Thinning plantations to 60 to 70 feet of basal area is recommended for deer.

Burning alters vegetation by controlling density and composition (Buckner 1983). Regular prescribed fire improves forage quality by setting back succession and stimulating new growth following the fire and promotes many fire-adapted species. This improves the palatability and nutritional content of forage for deer (Wood 1981, 1988). As a rule of thumb, understory production peaks in 2 to 3 years following fire while browse production peaks in five years. Burning at 3 to 4 year intervals is recommended.

Frequent prescribed burns will control hardwood midstory (Tanner 1987), which improves pine growth by reducing competition, and stimulating understory development. Understory shrubs can produce 200 to 300 lbs per ac of forage. Common shrubs include gallberry (*Ilex vomitoria*), runner oak (*Quercus pumila*) and greenbrier (*Smilax* spp.) Herbaceous biomass can reach 2500 lb per ac in natural slash pine (Tanner 1987). Biomass production tends to decrease following establishment of planted slash on cut-over sites because of changes in overstory composition and light intensity at the forest floor. Browse cover was greatest in plantations greater than 38 years old but herbaceous cover was greatest in natural slash pine stands (Tanner 1987). Tanner (1987) reported that overstory cover in natural slash pine was 58 percent. This level of canopy allows light to reach the forest floor and increases the production on herbaceous and woody browse.

In addition to thinning, burning and fertilizing plantations and natural stands, maintaining openings is beneficial to deer populations. Wildlife plantings can be established in utility rights-of-way, logging roads and decks, old house sites or similar areas. Mowing and maintaining edges improves cover and forage for deer and other early successional wildlife.

Quail—Quail (*Colinus virginiana*) are weak scratchers and need open ground for travel and foraging but with clumps of taller vegetation. However, they require moderately dense cover for nesting. Overhead cover is critical in reducing avian predation. Foraging, nesting, loafing, and dusting cover must be provided in close proximity to each other.

Burning pine stands at 1 to 2 year intervals often provides the necessary cover especially on the sandy soils where slash pine is the dominant overstory pine. Management should favor natural vegetation and succession. Food plot establishment and maintenance (usually on an annual basis) is costly and not always successful in increasing quail abundance. Newer research seems to indicate that food plots reduce the population lows frequently seen in quail population dynamics but do not substantially increase carrying capacity (Personal communication. 2002. Dr. L.M. Connor, Associate Scientist, Joseph W. Jones Ecological Research Center at Ichauway, Rt. 2, Box 2324, Newton, GA 39870). Management activities that encourage weeds and early successional stages include burning and rotational disking and rotational mowing (Jackson 1993, Thackston and Whitney 2001). These activities can take place in slash pine plantations especially if pine stem density is reduced through a thinning regime.

Turkey—Turkey (*Meleagris galapavo*) respond to many of the same management activities as deer and, to a lesser degree, quail. Turkeys consume the green succulent new growth of grasses, forbs, and legumes especially in winter and early spring (Hurst 1981). Food plots, along with thinning and burning can provide significant habitat improvement for turkeys. However, tree density in plantations also has a significant impact on turkey habitat quality.

Turkeys nest in openings or along the edge of clearcuts, forest roads, old fields and utility rights-of-way (Speake

1975). In slash pine plantations, tree seedlings should be planted on an 8 x 10 ft or 8 x 12 ft (545 or 455 trees per acre, respectively) spacing. Logging operations should leave streamside management zones (SMZ) at least 300 feet wide. A general management recommendation is to maintain 20 to 30 percent of the ground in direct sunlight at noon. Timber density objectives should maintain basal area at 10 to 15 ft² below site index (SI) at base age 50 years. In plantations, this can be achieved by maintaining a 12-foot wide skidder corridor at 70-foot intervals among the pine rows.

Thinning and burning regimes for turkey management in slash pine plantations should be similar to those recommended for deer. Numerous studies indicate that prescribed fire is an important management tool for maintaining turkey habitat in the southeastern Coastal Plain (Hurst 1981). Burning reduces cover making seeds and insects more readily available especially to poults. Burning also improves the nutritional status of forage including palatability, digestibility, nutrient content and mineral ratios.

WILDLIFE SPECIES

Non-game
Small mammals—Small mammals (for example, mice, voles, shrews and rats) are abundant in the early years of pine stands. The origin of the stand, natural or planted, has little influence on the mammal community (Mengak 1987). In managed stands (in other words plantations), herbaceous seed production is greatly reduced compared to natural stands and the granivore (seed eaters) and herbivore (grazers) community is missing or greatly altered compared to natural stands. Insectivores (shrews and some birds) are more dominant in managed stands (Buckner 1983, Mengak and others 1989). Small mammal populations may reach their peak between stand age 2 to 3 years depending on site factors and then decline steadily through canopy closure (fig. 1).

Songbirds—Songbird management is very difficult to summarize in relation to pine plantations. Songbirds are often characterized as early successional, edge species, or forest interior species. While mammals often show similar preference, songbirds have not been as widely studied. Slash pine plantations will provide suitable habitat for early successional songbirds. Those species that nest or forage on or near the ground will utilize pine plantations and young natural stands. Plantation management favors edge and early successional species. Cavity nesters can be accommodated if sufficient snags are left during logging. Canopy nesters will be eliminated from the harvest area until stands reach maturity.

Management recommendations vary by species but include such general guidelines as maintain a range of stand ages; keep harvest areas small (< 50 acres); maintain SMZ's; maintain snags; and, maintain dense understory. Generally, excluding fire can enhance songbird habitat.

Reptiles—Many reptiles are found on sites associated with slash pine. However, relatively little literature exists on management guidelines for reptiles. The indigo snake (*Drymarchon corais*) and gopher tortoise are significant

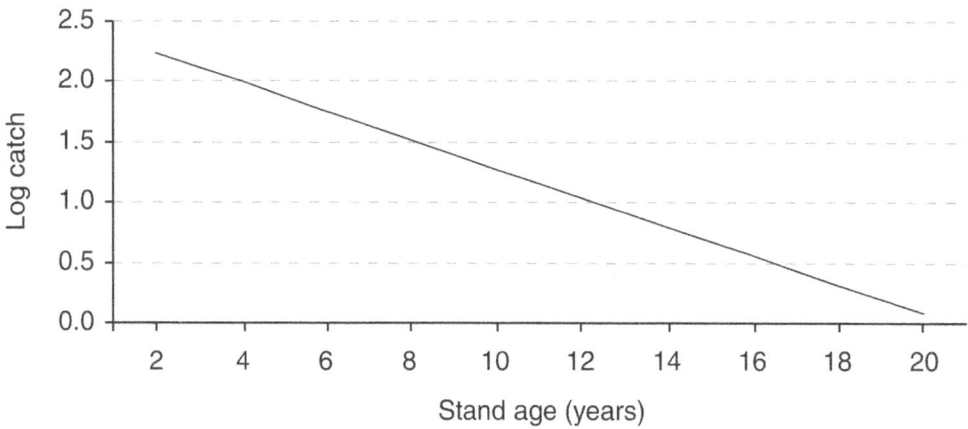

Figure 1—General model showing the decline in small mammal capture success with increasing age of the pine stand, either natural or plantation (from Mengak 1987).

inhabitants of slash pine stands because of their conservation status. Gopher tortoises (*Gopherus polyphemus)* are the more conspicuous and frequently studied of the two species.

The gopher tortoise is considered a keystone species in the Southeastern Coastal Plain. Burrows dug by gopher tortoises are used by over 50 other species of vertebrates and invertebrates. The tortoise itself is long-lived reaching ages of 50-60 years. Gophers are herbivores that prefer an open understory and well-drained loose soil (Breininger and others 1994). Foods include wiregrass, broad-leaf grasses, succulent forbs and fruit. Their limited mobility prevents them from venturing far from their burrows.

Gopher tortoises are most commonly found on the driest sites in southern Georgia where sand depth exceeds 3 ft. (Landers and Speake 1980). Slash pine plantations with wide spacing of trees and abundant ground cover can provide suitable habitat. Tortoise home range is inversely related to ground cover density (Landers and Speake 1980).

Burrow activity and burrow abandonment is related to tree density and canopy closure. In south-central Alabama, Aresco and Guyer (1999) found that total tree basal area was two times greater at abandoned burrows than at active burrows (305 ft^2 per ac versus 125 ft^2 per ac, respectively). Slash pine made up one-half of the total basal area. Tree density was one and one-half times greater at abandoned burrows vs. active burrows (590 trees per ac versus 323 trees per ac, respectively). Hardwood basal area was four times greater at abandoned burrows versus active burrows (Aresco and Guyer 1999). Canopy shading also contributes to abandonment as the understory is lost (Aresco and Guyer 1999). In fact, burrows were abandoned at the same rate as canopy closure. Burning without thinning was found to eliminate understory thus reducing the suitability of the site for tortoises. Burning and thinning should be used in combination for gopher tortoise management.

Management objectives for gopher tortoises should be to mimic natural canopy and understory conditions. For example, thinning stands improves overstory by removing hardwood competition and allowing light to reach the ground surface and burning is essential to control understory density and composition (Aresco and Guyer 1999). Gopher tortoise habitat should be burned during the growing season at 1 to 3 year intervals (Aresco and Guyer 1999).

Amphibians—The southeastern United States supports a rich amphibian fauna and the highest number of species in the country (Harris 1984:45). Hanlin and others (2000) working on the Savannah River Site (SRS) in the South Carolina upper coastal plain collected 1,788 individual amphibians from 12 species during 3 summers (1994 through 1996). Fifty-seven percent of individuals were collected from an oak-hickory forest (7.9 acre), 24 percent from a loblolly pine forest (405. acre) and 19 percent from a slash pine forest (42 acre). Amphibians were more numerous in the mixed hardwood forest but slash pine had the highest diversity of species in all 3 years of their study.

The flatwoods salamander (*Ambystoma cingulatum*) is a federally threatened species that inhabits mesic longleaf/ slash pine flatwoods. This species has experienced a rangewide population decline that is thought to be related to habitat conversion and fragmentation of the longleaf pine ecosystem (Palis 1997). It is now considered rare in Georgia, Florida and Alabama; endangered in South Carolina; and is a federally listed species (Palis 1997).

The flatwoods salamander is an autumn breeder. Breeding migration from upland sites to ponds is correlated with rainfall and air temperature. The salamander inhabits fire-maintained, open canopy longleaf and slash pine savannahs. Dense stands, roads, and lack of fire reduce site suitability for this salamander. In 1987, slash pine accounted for 69 percent of all commercial pine forest in Florida; two-thirds in plantations. This degree of habitat conversion from mature open stands to short-rotation plantations is considered detrimental to flatwoods salamander populations. Means and others (1996) found that converting native longleaf pine savannah to bedded slash pine on the Apalachicola National Forest may interfere with migration, successful hatching, larval life, feeding and location of suitable post-metamorphosis cover. They concluded that longleaf pine-wiregrass flatwoods have been severely reduced and degraded throughout the coastal plain and this has contributed to the decline in flatwoods salamander populations.

CONCLUSION

Slash pine and longleaf/slash pine forests once occupied a large area in the Atlantic Coastal Plain. Agriculture, development and intensive plantation forestry have replaced much of the original forest. Wildlife can survive and, perhaps, thrive in managed forests but landowners and foresters must manipulate the vegetation to mimic natural conditions. Manipulations include thinning, burning, and creating openings in forest stands. Fertilization can also improve habitat for some wildlife species. Large-scale conversion with or without site preparation can have negative impacts on vegetation and associated wildlife.

Landowners and foresters, who include wildlife in their management plan, must be willing to forego some timber revenue in exchange for increased wildlife populations. Other papers in this volume examine financial returns from slash pine for timber and supplemental products like pine straw. Unfortunately, few studies examine the trade-offs in timber production and wildlife. Such studies must include non-timber revenue such as non-consumptive recreation, hunting leases and aesthetic considerations. We acknowledge that such variables are not easily measured. Additional research is suggested to address non-timber values associated with southern pines in general and slash pine in particular.

ACKNOWLEDGMENTS
We thank Mac Lentz for obtaining the literature.

LITERATURE CITED

Aresco, M.J.; Guyer, C. 1999. Burrow abandonment by gopher tortoises in slash pine plantations of the Conecuh National Forest. Journal of Wildlife Management 63: 26-35.

Breininger, D.R.; Schmalzer, P.A.; Hinkle, C.R. 1994. Gopher tortoise (*Gopherus polyphemus*) densities in coastal scrub and slash pine flatwoods in Florida. Journal of Herpetology 28: 60-65.

Buckner, J.L. 1983. Wildlife concerns in the managed slash pine ecosystem. Pp. 369-374, In: E.L. Stone, editor. The Managed Slash Pine Ecosystem Symposium. School of Forest Resources and Conservation, University of Florida, Gainesville, FL.

Critchfield, W.B.; Little, E.L., Jr. 1966. Geographic distribution of the pines of the world. USDA Forest Service, Misc. Pub. 991, 97 p. Hanlin, H.G.; Martin, F.D.; Wike, L.D.; Bennett, S.H. 2000. Terrestrial activity, abundance, and species richness of amphibians in managed forests in South Carolina. American Midland Naturalist 143: 70-83.

Harris, L.D. 1984. The fragmented forest: island biogeography theory and the preservation of biotic diversity. University of Chicago Press, Chicago, IL. 211 pp.

Hurst, G.A. 1981. Effects of prescr bed burning on the eastern wild turkey. Pp. 81-88. In: Gene. W. Wood, editor. Prescribed fire and wildlife in southern forests. Belle Baruch Forest Science Institute, Clemson University, Georgetown, S.C. 170 pp.

Jackson, J.J. 1993. Bobwhite quail on your land: tips on management for Georgia and the Southeast. Cooperative Extension Service, College of Agricultural and Environmental Sciences, University of Georgia, Athens, Ga. Bulletin 1013. 23 pp.

Jones, E.P., Jr. 1979. Slash pine. Pages 6-10. In: Brender, E.V.; McComb, W.H.; and Hofeldt, V.H., editors. Silvicultural guidelines for forest owners in Georgia. Georgia Forest Research Paper-6, Research Division, Georgia Forestry Commission.

Landers, J.L.; Speake, D.W. 1980. Management needs of sandhill reptiles in southern Georgia. Proc. Annual Conf. SE Assoc. Fish and Wildlife Agencies 34: 515-529.

Means, B.D.; Palis, J.G.; Baggett, M. 1996. Effects of slash pine silviculture on a Florida population of flatwoods salamander. Conservation Biology 10: 426-437.

Mengak, M.T. 1987. Impacts of natural and artificial regeneration of loblolly pine on small mammals in the South Carolina Piedmont. Ph.D. Dissertation, Clemson University, Clemson, SC. 97 pp.

Mengak, M.T.; Guynn, David, C., Jr.; Van Lear, D.H. 1989. Ecological implications of loblolly pine regeneration for small mammal communities. Forest Science 15: 503-514.

Palis, J.G. 1997. Breeding migration of *Ambystoma cingulatum* in Florida. Journal of Herpetology 31:71-78.

Speake, D.W.; Lynch, T.E.; Fleming, W.J. [and others]. 1975. Habitat use and seasonal movements of wild turkey in the Southeast. Pp. 122-130. In: Halls, L.K., editor, Proc. Third National Wild Turkey Symposium, Texas Chapter, The Wildlife Society.

Tanner, G.W. 1987. Soils and vegetation of the longleaf/slash pine forest type, Apalachicola National Forest, Florida. Pages 186-200. In: USDA Forest Service, GTR-SO-68. Asheville, NC.

Thackston, R.; Whitney, M. 2001. The bobwhite quail in Georgia: history, biology and management. Ga. Department of Natural Resources, Wildlife Resources Division, Game Management Section, Social Circle, GA. 48 pp.

USDA Forest Service. 1965. Slash pine. Pages 458-463, In: Fowells, H.A. compiler. Silvics of forest trees of the United States, Agric. Handbook No. 271, USDA Forest Service, Washington, D.C.

USDA Forest Service. 2002. FIA data, www.cast.uark.edu/pif/tables/10.html.

Wood, G.W., ed. 1981. Prescribed fire and wildlife in southern forests. Belle Baruch Forest Science Institute, Clemson University, Georgetown, S. C. 170 pp.

Wood, G.W. 1986. Influences of forest fertilization on South Carolina deer forage quality. Southern Journal of Applied Forestry 10: 203-206.

Wood, G.W. 1988. Effects of prescribed fire on deer forage and nutrients. Wildlife Society Bulletin 16: 180-186.

INSECT ENEMIES OF SLASH PINE

Terry S. Price[1]

Abstract—Slash pine is attacked by many species of insects but only a few cause economic losses in growth and mortality. The five species of southern pine bark beetles are without a doubt the most damaging insects affecting slash pine. These include: the southern pine engravers (*Ips avulsus, Ips calligraphus, Ips grandicollis*), the black turpentine beetle (*Dendroctonus terebrans*), and the southern pine beetle, *Dendroctonus frontalis*.

THE ENGRAVERS AND DENDROCTONUS BEETLES

The small southern pine engraver (*Ips avulsus*), prefers to attack the upper portions of large trees and the main stem of sapling-sized trees as well as logging slash. It is often associated with *Ips calligraphus* which prefers the main bole of pulpwood and sawtimber-sized trees. *Ips grandicollis* prefers logging slash and the main stems of pulpwood to sawtimber-sized trees (fig. 1). Lightning strikes, drought

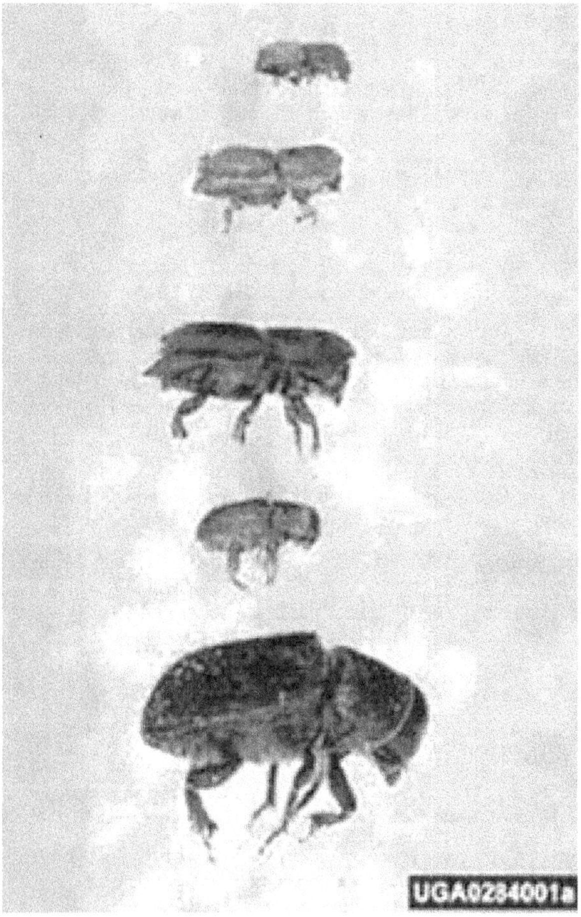

Figure 1—From top to bottom; *Ips avulsus, Ips grandicollis, Ips calligraphus, Dendroctonus frontalis, D. terebrans.* (Photo by Gerald Lenhard LSU) www.forestryimages.org.

stressed trees, fire damaged timber and stands infected with annosum root disease are often focal points for *Ips* infestations. Maintaining healthy stands (proper stocking, treating stumps with Sporax® to prevent annosum root rot), keeping stands burned and removing lightning strikes are ways to prevent Ips infestations.

The black turpentine beetle, *Dendroctonus terebrans*, is another bark beetle that frequents slash pine. This beetle is attracted to lightning struck trees, recently thinned stands, naval stores operations and stands damaged by fire.

The southern pine beetle, *Dendroctonus frontalis*, will attack slash pine but damage is greatest when slash is grown in mixture with loblolly. Pure stands of slash pine are more likely to be attacked by the *Ips* engraver beetles and black turpentine beetle than the southern pine beetle. Old growth slash pine is certainly more susceptible to southern pine beetles than young, fast growing stands. However, southern pine beetle spots don't grow at the phenomenal rates in slash pine as they do in loblolly.

Currently, Onyx® (bifenthrin), is a registered insecticide that is effective for control of pine bark beetles. Research is underway to find other suitable replacements for Lindane and chlorpyrifos (Dursban®, Cyren®). The new bark beetle insecticides of the future will be more environmentally friendly but the costs will limit the use of them.

Verbenone Pouch is an antiaggregation pheromone that works to reduce attacks by southern pine beetles. When too many southern pine beetles attack a tree, overcrowding can jeopardize brood development. To prevent overcrowding the resident beetles, particularly the males, produce verbenone that redirects incoming attacks to other nearby trees. This behavior pattern of redirecting incoming beetle attacks can now be used to disrupt spot growth. It is not effective for individual tree protection. The verbenone pouch method is currently registered by the Environmental Protection Agency as a management technique for southern pine beetles. Additional information may be found on the following website: http://www.bugwood.caes.uga.edu/

[1] Terry S. Price (retired), Associate Chief, Forest Management, Georgia Forestry Commission, Macon, GA 31202-0819.

Citation for proceedings: Dickens, E.D.; Barnett, J.P.; Hubbard, W.G.; Jokela, E.J., eds. 2004. Slash pine: still growing and growing! Proceedings of the slash pine symposium. Gen. Tech. Rep. SRS-76. Asheville, NC: U.S. Department of Agriculture, Forest Service, Southern Research Station. 148 p.

OTHER SLASH PINE INSECT PESTS

Several species of conifer sawflies are capable of causing severe defoliation and growth loss in slash pine but such outbreaks are sporadic and usually decline on their own in one to two years. The red-headed pine sawfly, *Neodiprion lecontei*, the slash pine sawfly, *N. merkeli*, and the black-headed pine sawfly, *N. excitans*, are common species in the South that feed on slash pine as well as other pine species (fig. 2). The red-headed and slash pine sawflies prefer to feed on young trees less than ten years of age and the blackheaded pine sawfly prefers sapling to mature, sawtimber-sized trees.

An interesting beetle that is often found attacking the charred bark of slash and other southern pines is the bostrichid beetle *Rhyzopertha dominica*. This insect is probably native to India and will feed on all kinds of stored grains and a wide variety of foods, chiefly cereals. When it attacks the bark of burned pines it produces a reddish-brown, powdery boring dust that resembles that of *Ips* species (fig. 3). The beetle does not harm trees and therefore, no control is necessary. It feeds only in the outer bark and does not enter the cambium.

Weevils that often debark slash pine seedlings are the pales, *Hylobius pales*, and pitch-eating, *Pachylobius picivorus*. These weevils damage seedlings by chewing bark from the stem above and below ground (figs. 4 and 5). Seedlings are often girdled and killed. Damage can be prevented or reduced when conditions favoring weevil development are avoided. Both species are attracted to recently logged areas with fresh pine stumps and buried logging slash. Adult weevils deposit eggs in the roots of freshly cut pine stumps or buried logging slash. The larvae hatch in a few days and begin feeding beneath the bark. Upon emergence the new adults will seek out seedlings to feed on. The newly emerging weevils and older adults attack seedlings planted on or adjacent to these cut over areas. The following guidelines will help reduce weevil damage:

- Delay planting one year on cutover pine sites if harvest cannot be completed before July.

- If planting cannot be delayed, the seedlings should be dipped in an approved insecticide or top sprayed in the nursery before lifting.

- Delay cuttings/thinnings that are adjacent to recently planted pines until seedlings are 3 to 4 years old.

- Planted seedlings can be sprayed in the field with an approved insecticide if weevils begin to appear.

In general, slash pine has two distinct forest health advantages over loblolly pine. Slash pine is less susceptible to attacks from the southern pine beetle and is seldom seriously damaged by the Nantucket pine tip moth. This should be considered when selecting a pine species to plant.

Figure 2—Red-headed pine sawfly larvae. Photo by Ron Billings, Texas Forest Service, www.forestryimages.org.

Figure 3—Boring frass *from Rhyzopertha dominica* (a bostrichid beetle). Photo by Stan Moore, GFC.

Forest Inventory and Analysis (FIA) data for 1972 and 1997 for a few selected Georgia counties indicate a decline in slash pine acreage and an increase in loblolly pine acreage (table 1). If this trend continues, that is, the replacement of slash with loblolly, we may see an increase in the incidence and severity of southern pine beetle outbreaks and other insects simply because we have changed the pine component from a less susceptible host to a more susceptible, one which is loblolly.

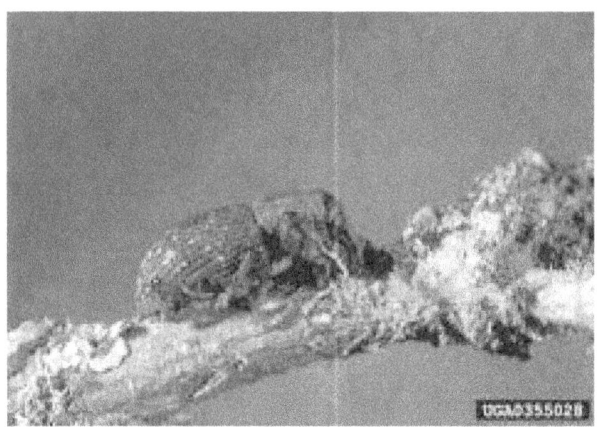

Figure 4—Pitch-eating weevil feeding on pine seedling. Photo by Robert L. Anderson, USDA Forest Service, www.forestryimages.org.

Figure 5—Pales weevil. Photo by Clemson University-USDA Cooperative Extension Slide Series, www.forestryimages.org.

Table 1—Change in loblolly and slash pine acreage in selected Georgia counties based on FIA data

County	Loblolly		+/-	Slash		+/-
	1972	1997	Change	1972	1997	Change
Appling	11,800	39,400	+27,600	128,342	99,578	-28,764
Atkinson	11,200	18,800	+7,600	88,958	71,762	-17,196
Bacon	4,400	18,000	+13,600	72,308	57,906	-14,402
Baker	17,600	14,200	- 3,400	17,036	12,313	-4,723
Ben Hill	10,000	37,800	+27,800	71,874	37,353	-34,521
Berrien	12,500	21,100	+8,600	77,483	68,169	-9,314
Brantley	4,100	10,800	+6,700	137,495	111,598	-25,897
Brooks	12,800	22,500	+9,700	18,061	34,671	+16,610
Charlton	14,100	11,200	- 2,900	187,245	227,707	+40,462
Clinch	24,800	28,300	+3,500	280,575	295,983	+15,408
Coffee	7,100	44,500	+37,400	124,521	91,056	-33,465
Cook	6,300	12,400	+6,100	15,810	11,379	-4,431
Echols	3,800	7,800	+4,000	128,324	122,106	-6,218
Irwin	10,000	15,300	+5,300	42,380	34,606	-7,774
Jeff Davis	16,600	35,700	+19,100	56,388	65,417	+9,029
Lanier	10,200	7,800	- 2,400	29,911	40,884	+10,973
Laurens	42,600	102,300	+59,700	111,509	48,012	-63,497
Lowndes	34,900	13,400	- 21,500	52,128	65,275	+13,147
Miller	0	10,100	+10,100	18,786	8,893	-9,893
Pierce	8,900	10,500	+1,600	59,330	52,539	-6,791
Seminole	4,100	12,200	+8,100	12,378	7,644	-4,734
Tift	0	8,500	+8,500	33,918	10,479	-23,439
Treutlen	0	19,400	+19,400	54,602	50,647	-3,955
Turner	7,700	17,200	+9,500	31,473	31,699	+226
Ware	15,900	31,100	+15,200	218,834	260,776	+41,942
Wheeler	3,300	50,000	+46,700	68,622	42,312	-26,310
Worth	10,100	36,700	+26,600	86,399	40,941	-45,458
Total	304,800	657,000	+352,200	2,224,690	2,001,705	-222,985

MAJOR DISEASE ISSUES WITH SLASH PINE MANAGEMENT

Robert A. Schmidt[1]

Abstract—The major disease problems related to slash pine management are well documented. However, as forest management practices evolve, pest management issues are changing. The potential effects of these changing issues on forest conditions are discussed.

INTRODUCTION AND HISTORICAL PERSPECTIVES

The previous slash pine symposium contained a comprehensive review of diseases of slash pine. Major disease occurrence was discussed by Blakeslee (1983) and disease management was detailed by Belanger and others (1983). These papers and an earlier report (Schmidt and Wilkinson 1979) serve slash pine disease management well today and here there is a need only to update the previous recommendations.

The 1970s, 1980s and early 1990s were dynamic and productive years for forest pathology in the South and for disease management of slash pine, in particular. The forest industry sought information on major diseases, especially in intensively managed pine plantations and they were significantly engaged in cooperative research in pest management (Miller and Schmidt 1987). State and federal agencies were responsive to public and private concerns and research and extension programs were staffed with forest pathologists. Now, priorities have changed. Public agencies are espousing forest health with the emphasis on the environment. They have renewed interests in longer rotation and restoration of longleaf pine and have relegated productivity to a lesser priority. Forest industry, while still interested in productivity, is now more driven by environmental issues, company image and business decisions and, collectively is less involved in woodland research, including research on tree diseases. Many companies no longer own the land necessary for long-term research. At educational institutions, once viable graduate programs in forest pathology now languish for lack of students, especially domestic students and those interested in the ecology of disease (epidemiology).

On the positive side, new technology, for example, biotechnology, is contributing to basic research, and researchers are attempting to understand the basic processes underlying the great store of empirical relations developed in the last four decades. If this quantum leap is successful, rapid advances can be made in forest management, including disease management.

DISEASE MANAGEMENT

While there has been significant research findings on several slash pine pathosystems since the 1981 Slash Pine Symposium, disease management recommendations have changed little in the interim. Current recommendations are available in recent research and extension publications and only a cursory treatment of new information which affects or could potentially affect disease management issues are noted herein.

Fusiform Rust

Fusiform rust, caused by *Cronartium quercuum* f. sp. *fusiforme* remains the most important disease in slash pine plantations. Updated regional rust hazard maps and associated analyses (Starkey and others 1997) show current rust distribution and recent changes occurring in rust incidence in the southeastern USA. Guidelines for rust hazard prediction at the stand level, including oak abundance, rust in adjacent stands, soil type and site quality are summarized by Schmidt (1998). Studies indicate that inoculum from surrounding oaks within one-half mile can cause significant rust incidence in adjacent pine plantations (Froelich and Snow 1986) and that removal of on-site oaks have little effect on disease incidence on pine in high-rust-hazard areas (Schmidt and others 1995). Genetic disease resistance has proven to be the best rust management practice (Powers and others 1976; Schmidt and others 1981, 1985; Schmidt and Allen 1997), and major advances have occurred in characterizing this resistance in both slash and loblolly pine (Walkinshaw and others 1980, Schmidt and others 2000), including the identification of major genes associated with resistance (Wilcox and others 1996). But it remains to determine the number and effects of genes associated with resistance and to determine the stability of host resistance and of pathogen adaptation and frequency of virulence in the slash pine ecosystem. Current rust management recommendations are published (Powers and others 1993, Schmidt 1998, Schmidt 2001), including guidelines for sanitation-salvage thinning of rust-infected stands (Belanger and others 2000). Bayleton® provides effective control of fusiform rust in nurseries and disease resistant planting stock provide the best control of rust in newly established plantations.

[1] Robert A. Schmidt, Professor of Forest Pathology, School of Forest Resources and Conservation, University of Florida, Gainesville FL 32611.

Citation for proceedings: Dickens, E.D.; Barnett, J.P.; Hubbard, W.G.; Jokela, E.J., eds. 2004. Slash pine: still growing and growing! Proceedings of the slash pine symposium. Gen. Tech. Rep. SRS-76. Asheville, NC: U.S. Department of Agriculture, Forest Service, Southern Research Station. 148 p.

Pitch Canker

Pitch canker of pines caused by *Fusarium subglutinens*, while of sporadic and unpredictable occurrence and incidence, is an important disease of slash pine, as it causes significant damage to seeds, seed orchards, nurseries and plantations of all ages (Blakeslee and others 1980). Genetic resistance to the pathogen occurs in slash pine (Blakeslee and Rockwood 1978) but resistant seedlings for planting are not readily available. Pitch canker occurrence, incidence and severity are often closely related to environmental factors such as fertilization and drought. Insects often can play an important role since wounds are required for infection. Infected stands have been associated with commercial chicken houses, where high levels of chemicals deposited in the soil or on needles may dispose trees to pitch canker. Precommercial thinning in loblolly plantations reduced subsequent pitch canker incidence and severity, especially during conditions of severe pitch canker outbreaks (Blakeslee and others 1999).

Annosum Root Decay

Short rotations and clear-cutting have all but eliminated annosum root decay from the slash pine plantation ecosystem. However, if longer rotations and associated thinning become more prevalent, this once feared and important disease will likely rear it's ugly head once again, especially on moderately to well-drained sandy soils common to slash pine cultivation. Spraying bonax on freshly-cut stumps is an effective control, (Froelich and others 1977) otherwise infected stands should be partially or completely harvested.

Planting Survival on Converted Agricultural Croplands

Planting previously cultivated fields, especially pasture land, as was often done during the Conservation Reserve Plantings (CRP), frequently resulted in poor seedling survival. "Scalping" down to bare soil in the planting row prior to planting alleviates this problem, as competitive vegetation, insects and fungal pests are removed from the near vicinity of young seedling stems and roots (Barnard and others 1995).

FUTURE SLASH PINE DISEASE ISSUES

As future forest management priorities and practices evolve, pest management issues will change. Witness the introduction of the red heart pathogen (*Phellinus pini*) into longleaf pine to create nesting cavities for the red cockaded woodpecker. Presently, several potential issues include:

Biotechnology

Biotechnology will create new synthetic genotypes improved for desired traits. These new plant materials should be field-tested for their reaction to forest pests.

Clonal Forestry

When clonal forestry becomes a reality, new pest issues will accompany vegetative propagation, container-grown planting material and genetic diversity. Clonal forestry without safeguards against pathogen adaptation will be risky.

Intensive Culture

Fertilization and competition control promote rapid, succulent growth, which in turn can predisposes pines to some pathogens and/or create physiological disorders. Faster-growing trees are not necessarily healthier trees.

Longer Rotations

Short rotations and clear-cutting have reduced or eliminated some diseases, for example, stem and root decays. Longer rotations with associated thinnings will likely see an increase in these problems, for example, annosum root rot.

Geographic Information Systems (GIS)

New technology in GIS will improve our ability to detect and inventory disease occurrence, thereby improving opportunities for timely pest management. The interactive capabilities of GIS can help to better understand disease ecology, that is, climatic, edaphic and biotic effects on forest tree diseases.

Global Forestry Markets

The global marketplace affects and, in turn, is affected by forest tree pathogens. Export markets take issue with southern pine products infected or potentially infected with pathogens, for example, the pinewood nematode and pitch canker. Likewise, the importation of wood and fiber raises issues of the potential introduction of exotic plant pathogens into the slash pine ecosystem. Such introductions can have significant, even disastrous impacts.

Slash Pine in the Urban Environment

Slash pine used as shade and landscape trees in yards, golf courses and municipal settings suffer unique diseases associated with anthropogenic effects, for example, wounding, excess or deficiencies of water, use of chemicals for weed control, soil compaction and soil nutrient and pH imbalance. As populations and urbanization expand these problems will become more prevalent.

Methyl Bromide Replacement

With the impending removal of methyl bromide from the marketplace, finding a replacement for use in slash pine nurseries is an important issue.

Wood Preservation

As chromated copper arsenate (CCA) is removed from the marketplace because of concerns regarding arsenic toxicity, a suitable replacement will be needed, especially for residential construction. Currently, disposal of CCA-treated wood is an important issue, especially for municipal landfills.

Climate Change

Who knows what evils lurk behind the potential threat of climate change? We do know that temperature and moisture (both soil and leaf surface moisture) can profoundly affect pathogens and the incidence and severity of the diseases they incite.

Education and Training of Forest Pathologists

Retirements have greatly thinned the ranks of forest pathologists. The educational pipeline for traditional forest pathologists in the South is essentially dry, appropriately so in view of the lack of jobs. If new positions become available, they will likely be filled with laboratory-oriented biotechnologists. Where will the traditional research forest pathologists come from, for example, those trained in etiology and epidemiology?

LITERATURE CITED

Barnard, E.L.; Dixon, W.N.; Ash, C.E. [and others]. 1995. Scalping reduces impact of soi borne pests and improves survival and growth of slash pine seedlings on converted agricultural croplands. South. J. Appl. For. 19: 49-59.

Belanger, R.P.; Miller, T.; Schmidt, R.A. 1983. Pest management in slash pine. Pp. 273-287 in: E. L. Stone (ed.). Proceedings June 1981, The Managed Slash Pine Ecosystem Symposium, School of Forest Resources and Conservation, University of Florida. 434 p.

Belanger, R.P.; Miller, T.; Zarnoch, S.J. [and others]. 2000. An integrated approach toward reducing losses from fusiform rust in merchantable slash and loblolly pine plantations. U.S. Department of Agriculture, Forest Service, Southern Research Station.

Blakeslee, G.M. 1983. Major diseases affecting slash pine. Pp. 257-272. In: E.L. Stone (ed.). Proceedings June 1981. The Managed Slash Pine Ecosystem Symposium, School of Forest Resources and Conservation, University of Florida. Fla. 434 p.

Blakeslee, G.M.; Dwinell, L.D.; Anderson, R.L. 1980. Pitch canker of southern pines: identification and management considerations. U.S. Department of Agriculture, Forest Service. Southeastern Area Forest Report SA-FR11.

Blakeslee, G.M.; Jokela, E.J.; Hollis, C.H. [and others]. 1999. Pitch canker in young loblolly pines: influence of precommercial thinning and fertilization on disease incidence and severity. South. J. Appl. For. 23: 139-143.

Blakeslee, G.M.; Rockwood, D.L. 1978. Pitch canker resistance in slash pine. Cooperative Forest Genetics Research Progress Report No. 28. School of Forest Resources and Conservation University of Florida, Gainesville.

Froelich, R.C.; Kuhlman, E.G.; Hodges, C.S. [and others]. 1977. *Fomes anosus* root rot in the South: guidelines for prevention. Southeastern Area. U. S. Department of Agriculture, Forest Service.

Froelich, R.C.; Snow, G.A. 1986. Predicting site hazard to fusiform rust. For. Sci. 32: 21-35.

Miller, T.; Schmidt, R.A. 1987. A new approach to forest pest management. Plant Dis. 71: 204-207.

Powers, H.R.; Kraus, J.F.; Duncan, H.J. 1976. Development of rust resistant slash and loblolly pines in Georgia. Georgia Forestry Research Council Paper No. 87.

Powers, H.R.; Miller, T.; Belanger, R.P. 1993. Management strategies to reduce losses from fusiform rust. South. J. Appl. For. 17: 146-149.

Schmidt, R.A. 1998. Fusiform rust disease of southern pines: biology, ecology and management. Technical Bulletin 903. Agricultural Experimental Station, Institute of Food and Agricultural Sciences, University of Florida. Gainesville.

Schmidt, R.A. 2001. Fusiform rust of southern pines: preventing and minimizing financial loss. For. Landow. 60(3): 18-21.

Schmidt, R.A.; Allen, J.E. 1997. Fusiform rust epidemics in family mixtures of suscept ble and resistant slash and loblolly pines. In: pp. 309-319, Proceedings 24th Biennial Southern Forest Tree Improvement Conference. Orlando FL.

Schmidt, R.A.; Allen, J.E.; Belanger, R.P.; Miller, T. 1995. Influence of oak control and pine growth on fusiform rust incidence in young slash and loblolly pine plantations. South. J. Appl. For. 19: 151-156.

Schmidt, R.A.; Gramacho, K.P.; Miller, T.; Young, C.H. 2000. Components of partial resistance in the slash pine - fusiform rust pathosystem. Phytopathology 90: 1005-1010.

Schmidt, R.A.; Holley, R.C.; Klapproth, M.C. 1985. Results from operational plantings of fusiform rust resistant slash and loblolly pines in high rust incidence areas in Florida and Georgia. In: pp. 33-41. J. Barrows-Broaddus and H.R. Powers (eds.). Proceedings of the International Union of Forest Research Organizations. Rust of hard pines Working.. Party Conference S2.06-10. Athens, Ga. 331 p.

Schmidt, R.A.; Powers, H.R., Jr.; Snow, G.A. 1981. Application of genetic disease resistance for the control of fusiform rust in intensively managed southern pine. Phytopathology 71: 993-997.

Schmidt, R.A.; Wilkinson, R.C. 1979. Prospects for integrated pest management in slash pine ecosystems in Florida. Proceedings August 5-11, Washington, D.C. Symposium of the Ninth International Congress Plant Protection.

Starkey, D.A.; Anderson, R.L.; Young, C.H. [and others]. 1997. Monitoring incidence of fusiform rust in the South and change over time. U.S. Department of Agriculture, Forest Service. Southern Region Forest Health Protection Report. PR-XXX. Atlanta, GA.

Walkinshaw, C.H.; Dell, T.R.; Hubbard, S.D. 1980. Predicting field performance of slash pine families from inoculated greenhouse seedlings. U. S. Department of Agriculture, Forest Service. Southern Forest Experiment Station Research Paper SO-160. 6 p.

Wilcox, P.L.; Amerson, H.V.; Kuhlman, E.J. [and others]. 1996. Detection of a major gene for resistance to fusiform rust disease in loblolly pine by genomic mapping. In: Proceedings p. 3859-3864. Applied Biological Sciences. National Academy of Sciences. U.S.A.

EFFECTS OF ANNUAL PINESTRAW REMOVAL AND MID-ROTATION FERTILIZATION ON PINE GROWTH IN UNTHINNED PLANTATIONS

E.A. Ogden and L.A. Morris[1]

Abstract—Harvesting of pinestraw in southern pine plantations provides landowners an opportunity to increase income but also may result in decreased growth due to nutrient removal. A factorial experiment combining two levels of pinestraw removal (none and annual) and two levels of fertilization (none and a single NPK fertilization) was replicated in five unthinned planted slash (*Pinus elliotii* Engelm.) or loblolly (*Pinus taeda* L.) pine stands located on cut-over and old-field sites. Fertilization in the first year with 224, 56 and 56 kg ha^{-1} of N, P and K, respectively, did not significantly increase stem volume growth, and on one site, was associated with reduced volume due to increased mortality. Pinestraw yields generally increased as a function of basal area. Although fertilized plots produced more pinestraw, increases in understory vegetation hampered pinestraw harvest. Annual pinestraw removal did not significantly reduce pine volume growth during the five-year period of study. Green foliar nutrient contents were above critical levels and did not differ among treatments.

INTRODUCTION

Demand for pinestraw for use in landscaping has resulted in a market niche for the procurement, harvest and distribution of pinestraw. Anticipated growth in the market for baled pinestraw, coupled with an attractive income opportunity prior to timber harvest, offers forest landowners an incentive to include pinestraw in their management plans. Potential benefits to the landowner do not come without potential costs to the site. Pinestraw plays an important role in maintaining the productivity of relatively infertile soils supporting southern pine forests. Harvest of pinestraw interrupts the cycling of nutrients in the forest ecosystem and may lead to reduced tree growth, reduced needle production and poor stand condition. The impacts of pinestraw removal and nutrient depletion have been observed and questioned for over a century (Ebermayer 1876), and it is generally accepted that repeated pinestraw removal without nutrient amendment can decrease growth (Jemison 1943). Although more recent studies have addressed the effects of forest floor removal on nutrient cycling (Blevins 1994) and management practices for pinestraw production (Duryea and Edwards 1984, Mills and Robertson 1991), few have specifically investigated shorter term growth responses to pinestraw removal in fertilized stands (McNeil and others 1984, McLeod and others 1979). Typically, southern pine plantations are thinned and fertilized at mid-rotation to encourage growth on the residual stand. When managed for pinestraw production, thinning is postponed or skipped entirely because of its detrimental effect on pinestraw production and recovery. Thinning drops limbs and debris, reduces basal area which results in reduced straw fall, and opens gaps in the canopy allowing for competing vegetation which interferes with the raking process. Without thinning, competition among trees for available resources is intensified, and growth of individual stems is not as responsive to fertilization as in less competitive environments.

The objective of this study was to measure the effects of annual pinestraw removal and mid-rotation fertilization on unthinned slash and loblolly stands. Comparisons of timber and pinestraw yields provide an economic analysis of one common approach to pinestraw management.

MATERIALS AND METHODS

The effects of straw removal and fertilization were assessed in replicated experiments during a 5-year period in slash and loblolly pine plantations. Experimental treatments consisted of a factorial combination of two levels of pinestraw removal (no removal and annual removal) and two fertilization treatments (no fertilization and fertilization with 224 kg ha^{-1} nitrogen (N), 56 kg ha^{-1} phosphorus (P), and 56 kg ha^{-1} potassium (K) for a total of four treatments. Each plantation began with at least three replications in complete blocks.

Five study sites were established in Georgia: two loblolly sites located in the Upper Coastal Plain, two slash pine sites also in the Upper Coastal Plain, and an additional loblolly site in the Lower Coastal Plain flatwoods (table 1). Areas determined to be commercially rakeable were selected, and 0.1 ha treatment plots were established. Responses were measured on plots of 0.04 ha nested within the gross treatment plots.

Foliar samples were collected from each plot prior to fertilization, and again at the end of the third growing season. Samples were oven dried at 70°C, ground and sieved to pass through a 1 mm mesh screen. Nitrogen and P concentrations were determined colorimetrically by the Technicon Auto Analyzer II (Industrial Method No.334-7A and 144-71a 1972) following block digestion (Isaac and Johnson 1976). Potassium, Ca, and Mg concentrations were determined following perchloric acid digest (Georgia Cooperative Extension Service 1970) by atomic absorption spectroscopy (Perkin-Elmer 1987).

[1] Lee Ogden, Research Coordinator; and Larry Morris, Professor of Forest Soils, University of Georgia, Daniel B. Warnell School of Forest Resources, Athens, GA 30602-2152.

Citation for proceedings: Dickens, E.D.; Barnett, J.P.; Hubbard, W.G.; Jokela, E.J., eds. 2004. Slash pine: still growing and growing! Proceedings of the slash pine symposium. Gen. Tech. Rep. SRS-76. Asheville, NC: U.S. Department of Agriculture, Forest Service, Southern Research Station. 148 p.

Table 1—Characteristics of five mid-rotation plantations used to evaluate growth response to pinestraw harvest with and without mid-rotation fertilization

| Location | Species | Soil series | Age | Status at study establishment | | |
				Site index	Stocking	Basal area
			years	*m @ age 25*	*stems/ha*	*m²/ha*
Rincon	Loblolly	Rigdon sand	21	19.2	1,262	32.35
		Olustee fine sand		18.3		
Louisville old-field	Loblolly	Dothan sandy loam	19	18.3	1,442	36.13
Louisville cut-over	Loblolly	Dothan sandy loam	16	18.3	1,670	29.88
		Faceville fine sandy loam		17.7		
Albany	Slash	Tifton sandy loam	15	18.3	1,764	23.71
Wrightsville	Slash	Dothan sandy loam	12	18.3	1,772	21.96
		Fuquay sand		18.3		

Soil series were determined from county soils maps and confirmed by on-site examination. Soil characteristics were considered when prescribing fertilizer and herbicide application rates. Fertilizer was applied at rates of 224-56-56 kg ha⁻¹ of N-P-K, respectively. These rates were close to rates applied in operational mid-rotation fertilization and exceeded the projected nutrient removal in five years of annual pinestraw harvest. Dry formulations of commercially available urea (46-0-0), triple superphosphate (0-46-0), and muriate of potash (0-0-60) were the applied in the first dormant season. Sites varied widely in severity of vegetative competition, especially after fertilization. Hardwood sprouts were cut repeatedly. Heavy grass and blackberry infestations were treated with backpack spray applications of Velpar® and Roundup®.

Manual raking was conducted by crews as part of commercial operations or by University personnel so as to emulate commercial harvesting. Only fresh, "clean" straw (free of leaves, sticks, cones, or weeds) from readily accessible areas was harvested. Raking occurred annually, usually in the fall. Bale counts and weights, or weights of straw raked from subplots randomly located within the measurement plots, were used to quantify removals from the sites. Sub-samples of straw from the harvest were collected for nutrient content analysis to determine actual nutrient removal from the site.

Height and diameter measurements were taken at the time of experimental blocking, and annually thereafter. Basal area and volume of individual stems were calculated based upon species and location, and used to compare growth over time (Bailey and others 1985, Belcher and Clutter 1977). Differences in growth and nutrient concentration among treatments were tested using a general linear models procedure (SAS 1987) with and without initial plot basal area as a covariate.

RESULTS AND DISCUSSION

Growth and Yield

Growth response to fertilization was expected to be most evident on sites that were not raked. These trees would benefit from additional nutrients without any losses from pinestraw removal. Since these plots were undisturbed after the fertilizer application, the trees may also have benefitted from the mulching effect of the intact forest floor and improved soil microclimate and moisture availability. Plots that were fertilized but also raked were expected to show some fertilizer response compared with the control plots, due to the addition of nutrients to supplement losses through pinestraw harvest. Any negative response to raking would have been most evident on plots which were raked but received no fertilization.

Generally, heights and diameters increased with fertilization, and were unaffected by raking (table 2). However, these differences were not statistically significant among any of the treatments at any of the sites. Loblolly pine growth at the Rincon and Louisville sites followed the hypothesized response to fertilization and raking. A non-significant positive diameter response to raking was observed in slash pines at Wrightsville and Albany. A negative response of average tree height to fertilization at Wrightsville was also observed. Basal area and stand volume calculations followed similar patterns (table 2). Volume response of loblolly pine to N or NP fertilization generally lasts for a five to seven year period with maximum response occurring during the first three years following application (Fisher and Garbett 1980). Observed volume responses were within documented ranges (McNeil and others 1984).

Analysis of variance for stand volume revealed that neither raking nor fertilization treatments were significantly different (at the .05 confidence level) from the control. The results were similar to findings reported by McKee and Mims (1995). The positive effect of raking at Wrightsville is not easily explained and may be spurious. Raking can reduce

**Table 2—Mean annual growth of unthinned loblolly and slash pine stands
with or without fertilization and annual raking for a 5-year period**

Management	Height	Diameter	Basal area	Volume	Mortality
	m/yr	cm/yr	m²/ha/yr	m³/ha/yr	trees/ha/yr
Rincon loblolly pine					
Not fertilized					
Not raked	0.58	0.43	0.66	12.3	28
Raked	0.52	0.43	0.78	9.0	41
Fertilized					
Not raked	0.76	0.59	1.25	18.7	14
Raked	0.74	0.60	0.75	14.2	48
Louisville old-field loblolly pine					
Not fertilized					
Not raked	0.82	0.29	0.75	16.8	41
Raked	0.79	0.28	0.82	19.4	70
Fertilized					
Not raked	0.87	0.38	0.81	15.7	41
Raked	0.77	0.31	0.61	14.7	74
Louisville cut-over loblolly pine					
Not fertilized					
Not raked	0.76	0.45	1.64	18.5	44
Raked	0.74	0.43	1.34	16.7	21
Fertilized					
Not raked	0.91	0.60	2.04	22.9	54
Raked	0.93	0.61	1.41	19.1	65
Albany slash pine					
Not fertilized					
Not raked	0.44	0.78	1.83	19.2	54
Raked	0.37	0.86	2.05	19.8	44
Fertilized					
Not raked	0.58	0.97	0.32	11.8	142
Raked	0.49	0.91	0.29	12.1	98
Wrightsville slash pine					
Not fertilized					
Not raked	0.55	0.82	1.82	19.4	25
Raked	0.80	0.85	2.31	24.1	33
Fertilized					
Not raked	0.73	0.82	1.43	17.0	49
Raked	0.83	0.81	2.47	23.3	33

interception of precipitation by the forest floor and increase soil temperatures leading to more rapid decomposition and nutrient mineralization potentially contributing to short-term improvements in tree growth.

Since tree growth is dependent upon various stand characteristics, a covariant analysis, using initial basal area as the covariant with subsequent basal area, was applied in an attempt to remove natural variation caused by initial differences in stocking or tree size at the start of the study. As in previous analyses, none of the treatments were statistically significantly different in height, diameter, basal area, or volume.

Mortality in several of the treatment plots decreased stand basal area and volume (table 2). On all sites except Rincon, mortality was higher on fertilized plots, with statistically significant losses occurring at the Albany site. Fertilization accelerates stand development (Allen 1987) and in these unthinned stands, some increased mortality was expected. A relationship between fertilization (tree vigor) and increased mortality due to fusiform rust also exists, particularly in slash pine (Dinus and Schmidtling 1971). Fusiform rust in the slash pines at Albany and Wrightsville caused high mortality and reductions in basal area and volume, especially after fertilization.

At the Louisville and Rincon loblolly sites, mortality increases were observed on raked plots. At the Albany and Wrightsville slash stands, there was no increase in mortality associated with raking.

Site Conditions

No soil erosion or compaction was observed as a result of either raking or fertilizing activity on any of these sites. This may be attributed to the low slope gradients (0-3 percent) and relatively sandy nature of the surface soils. It does not appear that pinestraw removal activity or the application of fertilizer or herbicide adversely affected the physical attributes of the soil. Although these experimental sites were fertilized by hand spreader, herbicided by backpack sprayer, and raked and baled by hand, machine operation would probably not be precluded.

Tree Nutrition

Pre-treatment foliar analyses showed that trees on all sites had sufficient concentrations of macro- and micro nutrients for tree growth (table 3). No significant changes in foliar nutrient concentrations could be attributed to either raking or fertilization before or after treatments. Foliar nutrient analysis performed in year 3 showed that on most sites and most treatments, trees had levels of N, P, K, Ca, and Mg at or above sufficiency levels considered necessary for tree growth (Allen 1987, NCSFNC 1991, Blevins 1994). The only exceptions were a slight nitrogen deficiency on control treatments at four of the five sites, and a slight potassium deficiency on control and rake-only treatments at the Louisville cut over site.

Table 3—Nutrient content of green foliar samples before and 3 years after treatment

Management	Period	N	P	K	Ca	Mg
	years	percent	- - - - - - parts per million - - - - - -			
Rincon loblolly pine						
Not fertilized						
Not raked	1990/91	0.85	1,017	2,967	2,230	692
	1993/94	0.98	1,017	3,000	2,175	648
Raked	1990/91	0.88	919	2,900	2,256	643
	1993/94	0.95	1,002	3,000	2,200	637
Fertilized						
Not raked	1990/91	0.87	976	2,933	2,250	747
	1993/94	0.95	1,006	3,033	2,175	733
Raked	1990/91	0.80	953	3,008	2,831	738
	1993/94	0.93	1,017	3,133	2,350	761
Louisville old field loblolly pine						
Not fertilized						
Not raked	1990/91	1.37	1,400	3,600	2,350	1,200
	1993/94	1.33	1,383	3,583	2,325	1,258
Raked	1990/91	1.31	1,450	3,650	2,200	1,200
	1993/94	1.21	1,400	3,467	2,092	1,192
Fertilized						
Not raked	1990/91	1.35	1,400	3,400	2,050	1,200
	1993/94	1.34	1,400	3,433	1,983	1,142
Raked	1990/91	1.40	1,350	3,700	2,150	1,250
	1993/94	1.42	1,300	3,708	2,267	1,275
Louisville cut-over loblolly pine						
Not fertilized						
Not raked	1990/91	0.98	1,450	2,567	2,525	1,200
	1993/94	1.03	1,450	2,542	2,475	1,217
Raked	1990/91	1.10	1,500	2,900	2,975	1,200
	1993/94	1.19	1,517	2,967	3,008	1,192
Fertilized						
Not raked	1990/91	1.18	1,300	3,500	3,117	1,200
	1993/94	1.23	1,300	3,683	3,142	1,150
Raked	1990/91	1.25	1,300	3,100	2,700	1,217
	1993/94	1.27	1,317	3,067	2,617	1,167

continued

Management	Period	N	P	K	Ca	Mg
	years	percent	- - - - - - parts per million - - - - - -			
Albany slash pine						
Not fertilized						
Not raked	1990/91	0.97	1,400	3,500	2,600	1,005
	1993/94	0.96	1,317	3,458	2,675	992
Raked	1990/91	1.00	1,400	3,700	3,200	1,175
	1993/93	1.05	1,300	4,058	3,325	1,200
Fertilized						
Not raked	1990/91	0.96	1,400	3,400	2,600	1,000
	1993/94	1.07	1,500	3,558	2,625	992
Raked	1990/91	1.00	1,400	3,300	2,400	900
	1993/94	1.07	1,300	3,200	2,008	875
Wrightsville slash pine						
Not fertilized						
Not raked	1990/91	0.90	1,300	3,200	2,300	1,000
	1993/94	0.92	1,300	3,100	2,200	1,167
Raked	1990/91	0.99	1,300	3,150	2,300	1,075
	1993/94	1.07	1,200	3,383	2,233	1,150
Fertilized						
Not raked	1990/91	1.00	1,300	3,350	2,000	1,003
	1993/94	1.09	1,250	3,617	1,875	958
Raked	1990/91	1.10	1,300	3,350	2,300	1,033
	1993/94	1.05	1,083	3,358	2,317	1,050
Sufficiency[a]		1.0– 1.1	1,000	3,000	1,000	600

[a] Source: Allen (1987), Blevins (1994), NCSFNC (1991).

Pinestraw Production

Fertilization of slash pine stands increases straw production approximately 1150 kg ha⁻¹ yr⁻¹ for the first three years following mid-rotation fertilization (NC State Forest Tree Nutrition Cooperative and Cooperative Research in Forest Fertilization (CRIFF) (NCSFNC 1991)). Pinestraw yield in young stands is closely correlated with basal area (Dalla-Tea and Jokela 1991). For slash pines grown in fully stocked plantations, there is an increase of about 1010 kg ha⁻¹ yr⁻¹ for every additional 1.7 m² of basal area, up to a maximum of about 5050 kg ha⁻¹ at around age 15 (Gholz and others 1985). In loblolly pines, straw production will reach 5050 to 5615 kg ha⁻¹ at 9.3 to 10.2 m² of basal area (Gresham 1982, Switzer and Nelson 1972). For less intensively managed or more mature stands, the rates are lower for a given basal area (Hennessey and others 1992).

Since only the RAKE-ONLY and RAKE&FERT plots were actually raked, only a fertilizer response can be evaluated here. Significant differences between the RAKE&FERT plots (mean 696 kg ha⁻¹ increase) compared with the RAKE-ONLY plots (mean 414 kg ha⁻¹ increase) occurred.

Straw yield response varied significantly between sites: the only sites not statistically significantly different were the two Louisville sites. Loblolly pines at the Rincon site exhibited the largest response to fertilization, yielding 2140 kg ha⁻¹ in the third year in conjunction with a 5 m² increase in basal area (table 4). Non-fertilized plots yielded 1010 kg ha⁻¹ of straw and a basal area increase of 3 m² in the same period. At the two Louisville sites, loblolly pines responded less dramatically: fertilized plots on old field and cut-over sites increased only 110 and 680 kg ha⁻¹, respectively, despite basal area gains of 1.7 and 6.2 m². Although the Rincon and Louisville old field sites were the oldest stands in the study, and past what would normally be considered the peak of pinestraw production (Gresham 1982), non-fertilized plots at the old field site still yielded 650 kg ha⁻¹.

Slash pines at Wrightsville exhibited a similar straw yield response to fertilization (table 4). Though the RAKE&FERT plots gained 5.7 m² of basal area over 3 years, they yielded 960 kg ha⁻¹ more straw in the third year. The RAKE-ONLY plots gained 9.5 m² of basal area in the same period, but yielded only 560 kg ha⁻¹ more straw. Differences in basal

Table 4—Pinestraw yields from raked plots before and 3 years after fertilization

	Treatment			
Site	Raked		Raked and fertilized	
	Basal area	Yield	Basal area	Yield
	m^2/ha	kg/ha	m^2/ha	kg/ha
Rincon				
1991	33.1	4380	31.3	3590
1994	36.1	5390	36.3	5730
Louisville old-field				
1991	34.5	3930	33.1	4040
1994	36.8	4580	34.8	4150
Louisville cut-over				
1991	29.0	4210	30.6	3700
1994	33.1	4150	36.8	4380
Albany				
1991	22.8	3260	23.2	2920
1994	29.0	3030	24.4	2530
Wrightsville				
1991	21.6	2250	21.9	3030
1994	31.1	2810	27.6	3990

area growth are attributed to higher mortality on the fertilized plots. Pinestraw theft confounded straw yield estimates here and at Albany. At Albany, where tree mortality was high and severe weed infestation prevented optimal straw recovery, slash pines showed decreased straw yield on both treatments despite gains of 6.2 m^3 and 1.2 m^2 of basal area over 3 years on the RAKE-ONLY and RAKE&FERT treatments, respectively. The slash pines at Albany and Wrightsville were the youngest stands in the study, and should have been near their maximum straw yield (Gholz and others 1985).

Nutrient Removal

Based upon the nutrient content of grab samples of straw raked from the Rincon, Albany, and Louisville sites, an average of 38.2 kg of N, 1.4 kg of P, 3.1 kg of K, 9.2 kg of Ca, and 3.6 of Mg ha^{-1} yr^{-1} were removed in pinestraw harvest. These amounts are within the ranges observed in previous research (Morris and others 1992). Assuming that volatile losses and leaching of N were low, the application of 224-56-56 kg ha^{-1} NPK fertilizer more than adequately compensated for the removal of these elements over the 5 years of raking involved in this study.

Economic Considerations

On healthy, well-stocked sites, the value of pinestraw sales alone or in conjunction with the value of increased wood volume can exceed the cost of fertilizer application, and produce an attractive return on investment. To compare the economic returns from management for pinestraw production with traditional timber management (mid-rotation thinning and fertilization), one must consider a number of factors including stand characteristics, management costs and value of increased straw and wood volume.

On the Rincon site, for example, fertilization cost approximately $180 ha^{-1} at the time of treatment (1990). An additional cost of about $5 ha^{-1} was incurred for foliar sampling and analysis. These loblolly pines, age 17 at treatment, showed significant increases in both straw production and volume growth following fertilization. Assuming 7.5 kg bales of straw at $0.40 bale^{-1}, pulpwood prices of $35 cord^{-1}, and a discount rate of 4 percent, the value of the additional 4500 kg per ha of straw harvested and estimated 11.7 cords of wood produced at the end of the 5 year period (stand age 22-years) was $147.50 ha^{-1}. If chip&saw prices of $81 cord^{-1} were applied to the increased volume, the value of the additional wood and straw would be $256 ha^{-1}. This is an uninflated (nominal) return on the investment of 42 percent.

Had this stand not been raked and fertilized for pinestraw production, but instead, thinned at age 17 and then fertilized, a GAPPS analysis (Burgan and others 1989) predicted a yield at thinning of approximately 27.2 cords ha^{-1}, worth $1,478 ha^{-1} (table 5). The yield of the residual stand 5 years later, at harvest age 22, would be approximately 81 cords ha^{-1}, valued at $6,079 ha^{-1}. If the same stand had not been raked or thinned, there would be 116 cords ha^{-1} at age 22, at a value of $8,265 ha^{-1}. Depending upon the landowner's cash flow needs, pinestraw management appears to be a viable economic option for a stand such as this one.

Table 5—Cash flows associated with traditional vs. pinestraw management at two contrasting sites (rotation age 22)

Management	12	13	14	15	16	17	18	19	20	21	22
						net revenue ($/ha)					
Rincon loblolly site[a]											
None						0	0	0	0	0	8265
Raked						137	166	197	240	279	8265
Fertilized						-180	0	0	0	0	8676
Fertilized/raked						-180	191	227	267	306	8676
Thinned						1478	0	0	0	0	6079
Thinned/fertilized						1297	0	0	0	0	6489
Louisville cut-over loblolly site[b]											
None	0	0	0	0	0	0	0	0	0	0	4585
Raked	165	171	170	167	174	165	171	171	171	171	4585
Fertilized	-180	0	0	0	0	0	0	0	0	0	5180
Fertilized/raked	-180	197	208	221	234	229	224	224	224	224	5180
Thinned	0	0	0	676	0	0	0	0	0	0	4047
Thinned/fertilized	0	0	0	496	0	0	0	0	0	0	4646

[a] Based on 3590, 4250, 5000, and 5730 kg/ha straw harvested during the years following fertilization (increases of 1015, 1235, 1125, and 1125 kg/ha); mean bale weight of 7.5 kg; price per bale of $0.40. Assumes a 5-year timber volume response to fertilization at 11.7 cords/ha at $35.00 per cord.

[b] Based on 3700, 3900, 4140, 4380, 4300, and 4200 kg/ha straw harvested during the first 6 years following fertilization (increases of 500, 700, 1000, 1120, 1200, and 1000), returning to an annual yield of 3500 kg/ha. Assumes a 5-year timber volume response to fertilization of 17 cords/ha.

At the Louisville old-field site, fertilization at age 15-years did not produce statistically significantly different treatment means. Although fertilized trees grew slightly larger than non-fertilized trees, there was no increase in pinestraw yield (tables 2 and 4). The lower return on fertilizer investment, and the lack of increased needle production indicates that fertility was good and foliage yield at or near its expected maximum.

At the Louisville cut-over site, age 12 at treatment, the observed fertilizer response of 3.4 additional cords ha^{-1} yr^{-1} (1.4 cords ac^{-1} yr^{-1}) is not expected to continue through rotation age 22-years. The value of additional wood and straw produced during the first 5 years after fertilization would still offset the initial investment cost of the fertilizer and foliar testing. Under the current recommendation of fertilization at mid-rotation (Morris and others 1992), this site would not have been fertilized until four years later in the rotation, shortening the length of time over which the investment would be held, and increasing the return on the investment.

The potential for timber volume losses due to increased mortality from fusiform rust and pitch canker associated with fertilization should be considered in financial analysis of fertilizer investment. Stands with high fusiform infection should be considered higher risk for fertilization in conjunction with raking due to their propensity to lose trees, which opens gaps in the canopy, permitting understory invasion, and reduces straw production and recovery. Fertilization and raking should be avoided in slash pine stands with rust incidence greater than 25 percent. Although fertilization can increase straw yields there is little additional volume growth benefit associated with fertilization in unthinned pine plantations that are candidates for pinestraw harvesting. Such sites appear to be self-selecting for sites that already have high fertility, high leaf areas and canopy closure which allows for little understory. On these sites, raking can be safely conducted without fertilization.

Managers are encouraged to monitor the progress and health of stands after treatment. The flexibility to adjust raking frequency, herbicide prescriptions, and other activities with changing stand conditions should be part of the pinestraw management plan.

ACKNOWLEDGMENT
This research was initially funded by the Georgia Forestry Commission, with continued support from the University of Georgia Daniel B. Warnell School of Forest Resources. A special thanks to Union Camp Corporation for providing manpower, data and research sites, and to F & W Forestry Services, and Drs. Cubbage and Newman for use of their lands.

LITERATURE CITED

Allen, H.L. 1987. Forest fertilizers: nutrient amendments, stand productivity, and environmental impact. J. For. 85(2): 37-46.

Bailey, R.L.; Grider, G.E.; Rheney, J.W.; Pienaar, L.V. 1985. Volume, weight and diameter distribution and yield equations for site-prepared loblolly pine plantations in the Piedmont and upper Coastal Plain of Alabama, Georgia, and South Carolina. Univ. Ga., Sch. of For. Resources Plantation Management Research Coop. Tech. Rep. No. 1985-3, Sch. of Forest Resources, Univ. Ga., Athens, Ga.

Belcher, D.M.; Clutter, J.L. 1977. Yield of slash pine plantations in the Georgia and north Florida Coastal Plain. Univ. Ga., Sch. of For. Resources Plantation Management Research Coop. Tech. Rep. No. 1977-2, revised Feb. 15, 1979. Sch. of Forest Resources, Univ. Ga., Athens, GA.

Blevins, D.P. 1994. Pinestraw raking and fertilization impacts on the nutrition and productivity of longleaf pine. Thesis. North Carolina State University, Sch. of For. Resources, Raleigh, NC.

Burgan, T.B.; Bailey, R.L.; Brooks, J.R. 1989. GAPPS (Georgia Pine Plantation Simulator). Version 3.0. Sch. of Forest Resources, Univ. Ga., Athens, GA.

Dalla-Tea, F.; Jokela, E.J. 1991. Needle fall canopy light interception and productivity of young intensively managed slash and loblolly pine stands. For. Sci. 37: 1298-1313.

Dinus, R.J.; Schmidtling, R.C. 1971. Fusiform rust in loblolly and slash pine after cultivation and fertilization. USDA For. Serv. Res. Pap. 50-68. 10 p.

Duryea, M.L.; Edwards, J.C. 1989. Pine-straw management in Florida's forests. Fla. Coop. Ext. Serv. Circ. 831, Univ. Florida, Gainesville.

Ebermayer, E. 1876. Die gesamte lehre der waldstreu mit ruchsicht auf die chemische statik des waldbaues. J. Spring, Berlin.

Fisher, R.F.; Garbett, W.S. 1980. Response of semimature slash and loblolly pine plantations to fertilization with nitrogen and phosphorus. Soil Sci. Soc. Amer. J. 44: 850-854.

Georgia Cooperative Extension Service. 1970. Lab procedures - soil testing and plant analysis laboratory.

Gholz, H.L.; Perry, C.S.; Cropper, W.P.; Hendry, L.C. 1985. Litterfall decomposition and nitrogen and phosphorus dynamics in a chronosequence of slash pine (*Pinus eliottii*) plantations. For. Sci. 31: 463-478.

Gresham, C.A. 1982. Litterfall patterns in mature loblolly and long-leaf pine stands in coastal South Carolina. Forest Science. 28: 223-231.

Hennessey, T.C.; Dougherty, P.M.; Cregg, B.M.; Wittwer, R.F. 1992. Annual variation in needle fall of a loblolly pine stand in relation to climate and stand density. For. Ecol. and Manage. 51: 329-338.

Isaac, R.A.; Johnson, W.C. 1976. Determination of total nitrogen in plant tissue using a block digestor. Journal of the Association of Official Analytical Chemists. 59: 98-100.

Jemison, G.M. 1943. Effects of litter removal on diameter growth of shortleaf pine. Journal of Forestry. 41(3) 213-214.

McKee, W.H., Jr.; Mims, M. 1995. Effect of forest floor removal and nitrogen fertilization. Center for Forested Wetlands Research, SE For. Exp. Station, Charleston, SC. Submitted to Biennial Silviculture Conference Proceedings.

McLeod, K.W.; Sherrod, C., Jr.; Porch, T.E. 1979. Response of longleaf pine plantations to litter removal. For. Ecol. and Manage. 2(1): 1-12.

McNeil, R.C.; Ballard, R.; Duzan, H.W., Jr. 1984. Prediction of mid-term from short-term fertilizer responses for southern pine plantations. Forest Science 30(1): 264-269.

Mills, R.; Robertson, D.R. 1991. Production and marketing of Louisiana pinestraw. Preliminary report. Louisiana Cooperative Extension Service, Louisiana State University Agricultural Center, Baton Rouge, LA. 11 pp.

Morris, L.A.; Jokela, E.J.; O'Connor, J.B., Jr. 1992. Silvicultural guidelines for pinestraw management in the Southeastern United States. Georgia For. Res. Paper No. 88, Jul 1992.

NCSFNC. 1991a. Descriptive statistics and relationships among soil and foliar characteristics in mid-rotation loblolly pine plantations. NCSFNC Res. Note No. 7. North Carolina State Forest Nutrition Cooperative. College of Forest Resources. North Carolina State University. Raleigh, NC.

NCSFNC. 1991b. Leaf area variation in mid rotation loblolly pine plantations. NCSFNC Research Note 6. North Carolina State Forest Nutrition Cooperative. North Carolina State University, Raleigh, NC. 25 p.

Perkin-Elmer. 1987. Analytical methods for atomic absorption spectrophotometry.

SAS Institute, Inc. 1987. SAS/STAT guide for personal computers. version 6 edition. SAS Institute, Inc. Cary, NC.

Switzer, G.L.; Nelson, L.E. 1972. Nutrient accumulation and cycling in loblolly pine (*Pinus taeda* L.) plantation ecosystems: the first twenty years. Soil Sci. Soc. Amer. Proc. 36:143-147.

Technicon Industrial Systems. 1972. Preliminary for Technicon Auto Analyzer II.

SLASH PINE IN INTEGRATED TIMBER, FORAGE, AND LIVESTOCK SILVOPASTORAL SYSTEMS

Jarek Nowak and Alan Long[1]

Abstract—Establishment of slash pine-based silvopastoral systems either by (1) planting trees on agricultural lands, or (2) thinning of mid-rotation age pine plantations has been reviewed. The high suitability of typical slash pine variety in silvopastoral systems is contrasted to that of south Florida slash pine and other commonly planted southern pine species. Lack of apparent long-term impact of cattle grazing on slash pine growth and quality is discussed. Past research has shown that silvopastures established in 12x12 ft spacing produced twice as much wood and 33 percent less total beef cattle liveweight gains than those planted in 20x20 ft spacing (Lewis and others 1983). Wood volume was higher in bahiagrass silvopastures than when dallisgrass was grown under slash pine canopies. Total beef cattle liveweight gains were higher in bahia- and dallisgrass than in bermudagrass silvopastures. Silvopastures planted at 12x12 ft produced 39 percent and those planted at 20x20 ft, 59 percent of total beef cattle liveweight gains attained on open pastures. The 4x8x40 ft tree spacing has been shown to facilitate simultaneous timber and forage production from the same acreage (Lewis and others 1985). This spacing continues to be popular in Florida for silvopasture planting. To date no other viable tree spacing configurations or forage species/varieties have been experimentally tested in silvopastures established in the southeastern U.S. Conversion of mid-rotation age slash pine plantations to silvopastures is deemed possible based on documented similar conversions in loblolly pine plantations. However, this also requires experimental testing.

INTRODUCTION

Grazing of slash pine (*Pinus elliottii* Engelm.) forests in the Lower Coastal Plain dates back to around 1520, when cattle were first brought to Florida by Ponce de Leon from Spain (Lewis 1983). However, the history of modern day silvopasture in the Southeast began in the early 1950s, when pine trees were first planted in improved pastures as part of the Conservation Reserve Soil Bank Program. In this paper, silvopasture is defined as intentional combination of trees, forage plants and livestock in an integrated, and intensively managed system (fig. 1). Once known as tree-pasture, or pine-pasture, this agroforestry practice continues to attract

Figure 1—Seventeen-year-old slash pine, bahiagrass, crimson clover, and cattle silvopasture near Chipley, Florida. Trees were planted in double-row 4x8 ft spacing with 40 ft pasture alleys between the double rows. Bahiagrass dominates alleys during summer and crimson clover during winter months. Credits: Todd Groh, August 2001.

non-industrial private forest landowners as well as livestock operators who want to diversify their enterprise (Kalmbacher 2000, Nowak and Blount 2002). Production of high quality timber is usually the ultimate goal in silvopastures located in temperate climates (Sharrow 1999).

Pine-based silvopasture has potential to be more profitable than traditional plantation forestry under most economic circumstances and management regimes studied to date (Dangerfield and Harwell 1990, Clason 1995, Grado and others 2001, Husak and Grado 2002). The key to improved cash flow of combined enterprise is the annual income derived from livestock, forage and hunting leases, which supplements long-term, periodic income from timber sales. The multi-product nature of silvopastoral systems provides safeguards against unfavorable single-commodity markets, weather conditions, or agricultural policy decisions (Sharrow 1999). Silvopasture can be practiced on small tracts or large landholdings. It could be a stand-alone operation, or part of a mosaic of land-uses that include improved pastures and diverse timberlands. There is also a potential for partnerships between forestland and livestock owners. The forest owners could gain annual income; the livestock owners would have access to an additional grazing resource.

Silvopasture is different than forest range, or woodlot grazing in that it employs improved forages. Forest range management relies on native forages. Open forest range grazing and management were thoroughly investigated into the mid-1980s (for example, Pearson and others 1971, Pearson and Whitaker 1974, Clary 1979, Byrd and others 1984, Lundgren and others 1984, Grelen and others 1985). Prescribed grazing of young slash pine and other coniferous

[1] J. Nowak, Assistant Professor of Forestry, University of Florida, North Florida Research and Education Center, Quincy, FL 32351-5677; and A.J. Long, Associate Professor of Forestry, University of Florida, School of Forest Resources and Conservation, Gainesville, FL 32611-0410.

Citation for proceedings: Dickens, E.D.; Barnett, J.P.; Hubbard, W.G.; Jokela, E.J., eds. 2004. Slash pine: still growing and growing! Proceedings of the slash pine symposium. Gen. Tech. Rep. SRS-76. Asheville, NC: U.S. Department of Agriculture, Forest Service, Southern Research Station. 148 p.

plantations has also been used for understory vegetation control in the stand establishment phase (Pearson and others 1971, Doescher and others 1987, Karl and Doescher 1993). While grazing of public and industrial forestlands is generally a practice of the past, farmers and other private landowners continue to use their forests and small woodlots for livestock. Silvopasture offers an opportunity for a more intensive management of integrated timber, forage and livestock resources than the systems employed in the previous decades and centuries.

The objective of this paper is to familiarize practicing foresters, non-industrial private forest landowners, livestock operators, and other natural resource managers, with slash pine-based silvopasture establishment and basic management considerations, based on the available literature on this subject.

SUITABILITY OF SLASH PINE VARIETIES FOR SILVOPASTURE

Among the southern pine species commercially grown in the South, the typical slash pine variety (*Pinus elliottii* Engelm. var. *elliottii*) possesses traits that make it uniquely suitable for silvopastures. When mature, slash pine has a straight, long and clear bole. These traits make it an excellent species for high value timber production. This variety is known for fast height growth in early years. This contributes to successful stand establishment even in the presence of onsite competition from grasses or other vegetation. Branches are relatively few, thin, and they self-prune easily, which results in short and narrow crowns. The branching habits and crown characteristics contribute to high timber value, but also facilitate forage production underneath the tree canopy. On the other hand, the south Florida slash pine variety (*Pinus elliottii* var. *densa* Little and Dorman) has many undesirable traits for use in silvopastures. Seedlings of this variety undergo a dwarf stage similar to the "grass stage" of longleaf pine (*Pinus palustris* Mill.). When the height growth resumes, south Florida slash pine often forms forks or lacks the straightness of the typical slash pine variety. In later years, south Florida slash pine stems tend to divide into large spreading branches, which produce flat-topped or rounded crowns (Barnett and Sheffield 2004). Such crowns are likely to impede forage production underneath the tree canopy.

Other commonly planted southern pines can be used in silvopastures; however, they do not display traits as desirable as the typical slash pine variety. Loblolly pine (*Pinus taeda* L.) produces more volume than other southern pines. This species tends to have more and thicker branches than slash pine, which makes it less suitable for silvopastures. Longleaf pine has good crown characteristics and can produce high value timber; however, it is also the hardest species to establish, especially in grass. Discussion in the reminder of this article is concerned with typical slash pine variety, unless stated otherwise.

ESTABLISHMENT OF SILVOPASTURE

Silvopasture establishment requires a number of different management steps depending on previous land use. Planting trees in an existing improved pasture is the easiest way to start the system. Slash pine-based silvopastures have also been established on forest cutover sites by planting trees first, and establishing improved forages in the fourth growing season (Lewis and others 1983). Establishment of silvopastures on old agricultural fields is also possible. Old-fields do not need as intensive site preparation as cutover sites, but may require vigorous herbaceous weed control. On both, cutover sites and old-fields, improved grasses should be established in the spring following tree planting, or as soon after tree planting as practical. Another possible scenario is to thin existing timber stands and plant or seed forage species among the remaining trees. Although this approach to silvopasture establishment has been documented in mid-rotation loblolly pine stands in Louisiana (Clason 1995, 1999), similar conversions of slash pine stands were not attempted or documented in the available literature. Most of this review concentrates on pasture to silvopasture conversion, as this is the most straight-forward, and cost effective process in which many of the same general plantation forestry concepts apply.

Converting Pastures to Silvopastures

Silvopastures are the easiest to establish by planting trees in existing pastures. This eliminates costs of forage planting, shrub and brush control, and removal of timber harvest residues. Well-established and managed bahiagrass, bermudagrass or other similar pastures are most suitable. Tree planting density varies from 100 to 450 stems per acre depending on product objectives, and anticipated level of management intensity (Lewis and others 1983, 1985). If fewer trees are planted, thinning of pulpwood size trees may not be necessary. However, trees grown at wider spacings require pruning for quality timber production (Lewis and others 1983). Standard tree planting methods and equipment can be used, as described below.

Site preparation—Site preparation before tree planting improves seedling survival and early growth by reducing competition from grasses and other vegetation for water, nutrients and light. Proper site preparation can be achieved by chemical, mechanical or prescribed fire treatments applied alone or in combination. The method of choice depends on site conditions, vegetation to be controlled, treatment costs, and other considerations such as herbicide acceptability or objections to smoke from prescribed fires.

Chemical site preparation consists of herbicide applications before trees are planted. Herbicides are most often sprayed in bands along planting rows or around planting spots. Pre-planting treatments allow for higher application rates, and therefore greater possibility of success in controlling unwanted vegetation. Chemical site preparation offers the longest lasting competition control where it is needed most, within rows of planted trees. Reduction of competition is essential to rapid seedling establishment. Broadcast herbicide application is usually not necessary, unless the current pasture is to be replaced with more suitable forage species. Under most circumstances, banded application, or even spot application, should be sufficient to control vegetation competing with trees at a lower cost than broadcast application. Some common herbicide treatments include: Arsenal®, or Velpar® with Oust® in the spring, or tank mixes of Accord® with Arsenal® in the fall. In bermudagrass pastures, Arsenal® or Accord® must be used. One should read the herbicide label prior to application for recommended rates, mixing instructions, and species recommendations.

Scalping is a very effective mechanical site preparation technique on pastures. By exposing the mineral soil, scalping prepares a furrow for tree planting machines and generally reduces weed competition during the next growing season. Sod and grass are stripped along intended tree rows by a tractor-pulled scalping plow. Some sites may also require subsoiling before planting to break existing "plow pans" or other "hard pans". This is accomplished by a metal shank pulled behind a tractor at soil depths up to 24 inches. As a result, increased tree root penetration leads to better tree survival and establishment after planting. Scalping and subsoiling, or scalping and tree planting are sometimes combined into one operation with the right implements attached to a tractor. Disked strips can also be used to break up sod and prepare planting rows. As with scalping, untreated areas are left between planting rows to protect soil and provide forage. On slopes, disking and scalping should always follow contours to limit the possibility of soil erosion.

Prescribed fire recycles nutrients and temporarily reduces competition from herbaceous and other vegetation. It has an added benefit of increasing forage palatability. It should be applied shortly before tree planting. Fire alone has been shown to be sufficient site preparation for good slash pine survival and growth (Lewis 1985). Prescribed fire is usually the cheapest site preparation option (Dubois and others 1999), but most pasture grasses resprout quickly after it is applied.

Combination of methods, such as broadcast herbicide application followed by prescribed fire, or banded herbicide application along scalped rows, may be necessary if shrubs, undesirable perennials and/or vines need to be controlled. Prescribed fire (with or without prior herbicide application) may be followed by mechanical site preparation.

Seedling types—Genetically improved tree seedlings are preferred for establishment of silvopastures. Planting stock recommended for typical slash pine plantations (White and Byram 2004) is also best for silvopasture establishment. It is especially important to use fusiform rust resistant seedlings whenever slash pine is planted. Large caliper seedlings have much more desirable shoot and root characteristics than seedlings produced at high sowing densities, such as once common 28 seedlings per ft^2 of nursery bed (Rowan 1986). Well-developed, fibrous root systems allow rapid seedling establishment, increasing survival and growth in the field. Bareroot slash pine seedlings 0.4 inch in diameter at the root collar (the juncture between seedling tap root and the shoot) have been found to survive and grow better than typically produced 0.2 inch caliper seedlings (South and Mitchell 1999). Planting of large caliper seedlings has been more likely to result in better early survival and growth compared to application of either double bedding or Arsenal herbicide to control competition on flatwoods sites in Georgia. Bareroot seedlings are cheaper than those produced in containers, but they need to be planted during winter. Containerized seedlings work well, and they can be planted either during winter or after the start of the summer rainy season.

Tree spacing at planting—Silvopasture requires tree spacing that allows for sufficient timber and forage yields. A 4x8 ft tree spacing with 40 ft forage alleys between pairs of tree rows has been found to best satisfy these requirements in previous Georgia and Florida experiments (Lewis and others 1985). The double-row 4x8x40 ft tree spacing (fig. 2) produced both high wood volumes and forage yields (table 1). This tree-planting configuration continues to be popular for establishment of silvopastures in Florida (Kalmbacher 2000).

Other tree arrangements in silvopastures are also possible. Trees have been planted in single wide-spaced rows such as 12x12 or 20x20 ft in Georgia experiments (Lewis and others 1983). In the northwestern U.S., tree planting in multiple rows with wide alleys between the sets, or in clusters have been suggested by Sharrow (1999). In any tree arrangement, open areas between trees allow for forage production. Planting trees in rows facilitates access for future forage and silvicultural operations, and therefore is preferred over random tree placement or planting tree clusters. Generally, wider spacing between single rows, or wider alleys between sets of multiple rows support higher levels of forage production. However, too much open pasture space also means less wood production on a per acre basis. The trade-offs between timber and forage production are well illustrated by comparing yields of both commodities in double-row 4x8x40 and 2x8x88 ft spacings. The 4x8x40 ft tree pattern produced twice as much wood as the 2x8x88 tree spacing, whereas the opposite was true for forage production (table 1).

Tree spacing at planting for silvopasture establishment requires further experimental testing. Besides single- and double-row configurations used by Lewis and others (1983, 1985), no other silvopastoral tree spacings have been documented in the Southeastern U.S. to date.

Tree planting—Trees are best planted with a mechanical planter, but hand planting is also possible, especially on smaller or irregular tracts of land. Machine planting produces straight rows and uniform spacings, which is

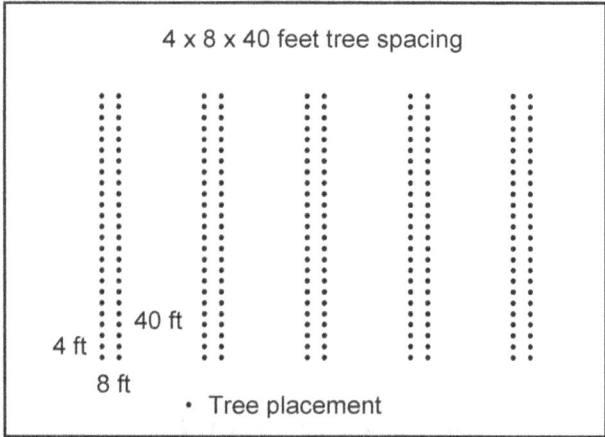

Figure 2—Double-row 4x8 ft tree spacing with 40 ft wide alleys between pairs of tree rows was found to satisfy both timber and forage growth requirements as documented by Lewis and others (1985).

Table 1—Average tree and forage responses of slash pine at age 13 years[a]

	Tree spacing (feet)					
	8 x 12	4 x 24	2 x 48	6 x 8 x 24	4 x 8 x 40	2 x 8 x 88
Tree survival (percent)	61	68	68	67	67	74
Tree height (feet)	35	35	36	32	36	34
Tree diameter (inches)	5.7	5.2	5.1	5.0	5.5	4.3
Stand basal area (square feet per acre)	50	49	52	40	59	33
Wood volume (cubic feet per acre)	903	866	973	658	1086	580
Total forage yield[b] (pounds per acre per year)	1,138	542	1,069	1,347	1,264	2,573

[a] Trees were planted in single (8 x 12, 4 x 24, or 2 x 48 feet) and double-row (6 x 8 x 24, 4 x 8 x 40, or 2 x 8 x 88 feet) configurations at 454 trees per acre (modified table adopted from Tanner and Lewis 1984).
[b] Native forage yields are reported, yields would most likely be higher if improved fertilized forages were employed.

important in silvopastoral systems. General guidelines for planting trees in silvopastures are the same as for establishing tree plantations. Plant trees on the contour wherever pastures are on slopes to limit the possibility of soil erosion. Staying in scalps and furrows while planting trees should not pose any difficulties. However, more effort may be needed to plant trees within herbicided bands if the treated vegetation has not yet discolored. At planting, care needs to be exercised not to bend roots upwards, which causes "j-rooting", and may lead to low seedling survival. Soil should be firmly packed around roots of each seedling to avoid air pockets, and the seedlings should be planted deep enough to cover root collars. If planting bareroot stock, keep seedlings and roots moist and in the shade from the time they are lifted from nursery beds until planted in the field (Duryea and Edwards 1987).

Tree survival and establishment—Post-planting treatments are often necessary for best tree survival and establishment results. Grasses and weeds often quickly reoccupy scalped or disked rows and they need to be controlled with herbicides during the first and/or second year after planting. Banded or spot herbicide applications along tree rows (up to 4 feet across) are most effective in controlling unwanted vegetation. The following herbicides can be used: (1) Oust®, Arsenal® or Accord® on bahiagrass; (2) Arsenal®, Accord®, or Fusilade® 2000 on bermudagrass; (3) Arsenal®, Oust®, or Oustar®, as single herbicide treatments; or (4) tank mixes of Oust® with Velpar®, Arsenal®, or Accord® for other grasses and herbaceous vegetation. Consult labels prior to herbicide applications for appropriate rates, mixing instructions and plant species that can be controlled with each herbicide. It is best to protect tree seedlings from direct contact with the herbicides, although some are labeled for "over the top applications". Stressed seedlings are more prone to herbicide-caused damage than healthy and vigorous ones. Tank mixes may be more damaging than any of the herbicides applied alone. For example, applying Velpar® or Arsenal® with Oust® may increase damage to young slash pine seedlings.

Mowing between the rows of trees is advised several times a year during the first three growing seasons after tree planting. Mowing helps to further reduce the competition from grasses and increase light available to tree seedlings. If the grass yield is sufficient, mowing can be part of haying operations to provide revenue or forage during the years before livestock are allowed to graze on the site. Avoid hitting the seedlings or scuffing off the bark when mowing, hay cutting or during any other operation that requires driving equipment between the rows of trees.

Preventing livestock injury to young trees—Livestock is best introduced into the system when the trees reach sufficient heights to prevent damage to terminal buds from browsing. Seedling mortality is most likely when the terminal bud and needles are both browsed off (Pearson and others 1990). In one study, up to 34.5 percent of planted slash pine seedlings showed moderate to severe damage, and 4 percent were dead in the first growing season after planting under yearlong grazing regime (Pearson and others 1971). The remaining 61.5 percent of seedlings showed none-to-light damage. In all, this study showed that slash pine height growth was negatively impacted by grazing for the first five years. However, differences in wood volume between grazed and ungrazed treatments were not significant in the same plantations at 18 years (Grelen and others 1985). This was attributed to larger diameters of the fewer remaining trees in the heavily grazed plots. None of the parameters measured at 30 years: tree height, diameter at breast height, diameter growth rate, tree grade, amount of latewood, wood specific gravity or fiber length were statistically different between grazed and ungrazed plots (Cutter and others 1999). The reader is cautioned that these slash pine plantations were established at 908 trees per acre, twice the number of trees in 4x8x40 ft spacing. Therefore, they could absorb more initial cattle-caused damage than silvopastures planted at lower initial tree densities, and still produced wood volumes and quality comparable to ungrazed plantations. Nevertheless, slash pine is quite resilient and is able to recover from physical damage. Hughes (1976) and Lewis (1980a, 1980b, 1980c) studied simulated cattle injury to planted slash pine, and generally found that trees survived and recovered from all but the most severe types of artificially inflicted injuries. Young pine plantations suffer little damage if cattle stocking rates are in balance with forage available for grazing (Lewis 1984). However, injuries repeated over an extended period of time can potentially reduce wood volume production, especially when fewer trees are planted per acre. Therefore, the lower the number of trees, the greater care needs to be exercised to protect young trees from cattle inflicted damage or mortality. It follows, that grazing could be initiated earlier where cattle-caused damage to timber can be offset by greater number of trees per acre.

Establishment of Silvopasture on Forest Cutover Sites

Silvopasture establishment on forest cutover sites requires a considerable amount of site preparation work followed by tree and forage planting. Lewis and others (1983) prepared a cutover site intended for silvopasture in the following manner. First, trees and stumps were removed with a bulldozer. Other woody material worked to the surface by repeated disk harrowing and raking with farm implements was also removed from the site. Liming and N-P-K fertilizer requirements were determined by soil testing. Appropriate amounts of lime and mineral fertilizer were incorporated into the soil during the final disking and leveling. Slash pine seedlings were planted in one of two spacings: 12x12 or 20x20 ft. In the fourth growing season, coastal bermudagrass (*Cynodon dactylon* (L.) Pers.), dallisgrass (*Paspalum dilatatum* Poiret) or Pensacola bahiagrass (*Paspalum notatum* Flügge) were established between rows of trees and in a tree-less area. The silvopastures and open pastures were fertilized (100-22-42 lbs per acre of elemental N-P-K, respectively), grazed by yearling heifers, and burned annually every March for 15 years. Some of the results of this study are summarized in table 2. In short, silvopastures planted in 12x12 ft spacing produced twice as much wood, but 33 percent less cattle beef liveweight gains compared to those planted in 20x20 ft spacing. Cattle grazed on bahiagrass and dallisgrass under slash pine canopies,

gained more liveweight than when grazed on bermudagrass. More wood was produced when bahiagrass was grown under tree canopies compared to dallisgrass. Wood volume in bermudagrass silvopastures was not significantly different from the bahiagrass or dallisgrass silvopastures (table 1). Total beef cattle liveweight gains on open pasture were 1.7 and 2.6 times more than those in silvopastures with 100 and 300 trees per acre, respectively (table 1). Forage available for grazing was declining with the passage of time in all treatments. However, only in silvopastures planted at 12x12 ft, and thinned to spacing of 18x18 ft at age 10, there was not enough forage to support cattle in the 19th year since trees were planted (table 2). The acceptable trade-offs between wood, forage and livestock production need to be decided on a case by case basis by landowners, who will be financially affected by these decisions.

Establishment of Silvopasture on Old-Fields

Specific examples of slash pine silvopasture establishment on old-field sites were not found in the subject literature. However, one can assume that similar procedures to those described above for the forest cutover sites could be followed for tree and forage establishment on old-fields. Scalping before tree planting and other site preparation techniques recommended for pastures would be suitable for old-fields as well. Barnard and others (1995) found scalping to be especially effective site preparation technique on old-fields. In their study, slash pine seedlings in scalped rows almost always survived and grew better than seedlings in nine other treatments. Those results were based on five different slash pine plantations established in two different years across western half of Florida's panhandle. Barnard and others (1995) attributed the improved seedling performance in scalped rows to the combined effects of reduced weed competition, improved moisture regimes, reduced pressure from root pathogens, reduced insect-caused seedling damage, and improved tree planting quality facilitated by exposed mineral soil. Recent cropping history that includes leguminous and other row crops such as soybeans, peanuts, and cotton, often creates

Table 2—Tree survival, wood yield, beef cattle stocking, and liveweight gains in slash pine-based silvopastures at two tree spacings (20x20 or 12x12 ft) with bermudagrass, dallisgrass or bahiagrass under tree canopies[a]

	Tree spacing (feet)			Forage grasses		
	None[b]	20 x 20	12 x 12	Bermuda	Dallis	Bahia
Tree survival at age 10-years (percent)	—	61	66	65	71	55
Wood yield at age 20-years (cubic feet per acre)	—	1,296	2,593	1,979	1,728	2,124
Cattle stocking 7th year[c] (animals per acre)	1.9	1.6	1.4	1.6	1.6	1.7
Cattle stocking 19th year[d] (animals per acre)	1.3	0.2	0.0	0.2	0.5	0.8
Total liveweight gains[e] (pounds per acre)	3,506	2,053	1,353	1,905	2,348	2,656

[a] The silvopasture results are contrasted to cattle stocking and liveweight gains on open pastures. (Based on results of Lewis and others 1983).

[b] None refers to open pasture condition, averages for the three improved grasses are reported.

[c] Cattle stocking in the 7th year of the study reached maximum number of animals per acre in all treatments (based on forage availability).

[d] Cattle stocking in different treatments based on forage availability at the end of the study.

[e] Sum of cattle liveweight gains starting in year 5 through year 19 in each treatment are reported.

conditions favorable to buildup of certain soilborne agricultural pests linked to slash pine seedlings mortality. Among those pests, whitefringed beetles (*Graphognathus* spp.) and the charcoal root rot fungus (*Macrophomina phaseolina* [Tassi] Goid.) seem to be successfully neutralized by scalping before tree planting (Barnard and others 1995).

Similarly to other silvopastures, trees may be planted in the 4x8x40 ft or other suitable configurations as described in the section on pasture to silvopasture conversion. Improved forages could be established in the spring following tree planting, or as soon as practical thereafter. Soil cultivation will generally be needed before grasses can be seeded or sprigged between the rows of trees. Pine plantations established on freshly converted croplands often look "clean" of herbaceous weeds. This should not be misleading, as the weeds will develop and interfere with survival and growth of newly planted pines in the vegetative season following planting. Appropriate herbaceous weed control measures as described above for converted pastures will be needed on old-fields as well.

Conversion of Pine Plantation to Silvopasture

First thinning of a pine plantation offers an excellent opportunity for conversion of timber only operations into a silvopasture. This conversion into a silvopasture is a multi-step process composed of tree harvest, understory suppression, debris removal, seedbed preparation and forage planting. The overall objective is to open up the stand and create conditions for forage production underneath the tree canopy. There are no documented examples of mid-rotation slash pine plantation conversion into a silvopasture through thinning and forage establishment in the available literature. However, such conversions were successfully attempted in loblolly pine plantations (Clason 1995, 1999). Twenty-year-old overstocked loblolly pine stands in northwest Louisiana were thinned in two steps, first to 250 and five years later to 125 trees per acre (Clason 1999). Appropriate tree density through thinning is the first step in creating conditions for improved forage planting or seeding. Understory vegetation suppression is achieved by herbicide applications, as needed. Seedbed is prepared by prescribed fire and/or mechanical debris removal and disking. Warm season forages are sown in the spring, followed by N, P, K fertilization, and top dressing with N in early summer. Local fertilization rates will vary depending on soil testing results, species planted and other considerations. Costs of forage establishment will also depend on forage species and other local factors. If a legume is desired, it could be seeded in the fall, after the warm-season forage is grazed or harvested, to facilitate seed contact with the soil. In cases where trees were planted in improved pastures, understory vegetation removal or suppression after thinning may promote the return of the forage to grazing condition.

Introduction of Livestock and Silvopasture Management

The introduction of livestock into a tree and forage system needs to be carefully planned with respect to timing, appropriate animal species or variety, stocking rates, and grazing management scheme. To a large extent these decisions depend on the kind and quality of forage available for grazing. Water availability in each pasture and appropriate fencing are also important before livestock is integrated into the system. There are many other livestock management considerations dependent on the animal species that are beyond the scope of this publication. Beef cattle management in pine-pasture systems is described by a number of authors (Byrd and others 1984, Lundgren and others 1984, Tyree and Kunkle 1995). Lundgren and others (1984) pointed out that among five forest-grazing management systems studied, multi-pasture rotational grazing was more economical than yearlong, continuous grazing. After livestock are integrated into the silvopasture, continued intensive management of all three components: livestock, forage(s) and trees is needed. Trees do not need to be fertilized separately if the forage is routinely fertilized. Additional nutrients are supplied from animal wastes by livestock utilizing the site. Weed suppression may be needed if not enough grazing pressure exists to eliminate unwanted vegetation. In wider spacings, trees need to be pruned for quality timber production. Timing and number of thinnings depends mostly on the tree species planted, initial spacing and product objectives. To avoid overgrazing, silvopastures must not be overstocked or grazed too close to the ground. Damage to forage, trees, soils, and water resources might result if proper animal husbandry practices are not followed. On the other hand, if designed and managed wisely silvopasture can provide many of the economic and environmental benefits of the integrated system (Nowak and Blount 2002).

CONCLUSIONS

Silvopastures are intentional, integrated and intensively managed systems designed to optimize timber, forage and livestock production from the same acreage at the same time. Silvopastoral systems offer the possibility of forestland-derived annual revenue and diversification of farm income. A silvopasture can be most easily established by planting trees in an existing improved pasture. Planting trees on well prepared forest cutover sites, or old-fields and establishing forages in subsequent years is also possible. Conversion of mid-rotation loblolly pine plantations to silvopastoral systems has been shown to be successful in northwest Louisiana. Similar conversions are deemed possible in mid-rotation slash pine plantations, but that requires further experimental testing. Open forest range grazing was thoroughly investigated in the past; however, more research is needed to test optimal tree configurations, forage and livestock selections, as well as overall management of integrated silvopastoral systems employing improved forages. No matter what approach is taken, continuous intensive management of tree, forage and livestock components is needed if the potential economic and environmental benefits of a silvopasture are to be realized.

ACKNOWLEDGMENTS

The reviews and improvements suggested to the original manuscript by Drs. Bob Myer, Michael Bannister, and Ann Blount are greatly appreciated.

LITERATURE CITED

Barnard, E.L.; Dixon, W.N.; Ash, E.C. [and others]. 1995. Scalping reduces impact of soilborne pests and improves survival and growth of slash pine seedlings on converted agricultural croplands. Southern Journal of Applied Forestry. 19(2): 49-59.

Barnett, J.P.; Sheffield, R.M. 2004. Slash pine: characteristics, history, status, and trends. In: Dickens, E.D.; Barnett, J.P.; Hubbard, W.G.; Jokela, E.J., eds. Slash pine: still growing and growing! Proceedings of the slash pine symposium. Gen. Tech. Rep. SRS-76. Asheville, NC: U.S. Department of Agriculture, Forest Service, Southern Research Station: 1-6.

Byrd, N.A.; Lewis, C.E.; Pearson, H.A. 1984. Management of southern pine forests for cattle production. General Report R8-GR4. Atlanta, GA: US Department of Agriculture, Forest Service, Southern Region 22 p.

Clary, W.P. 1979. Grazing and overstory effects on rotationally burned slash pine plantation ranges. Journal of Range Management. 32(4): 264-266.

Clason, T.R. 1995. Economic implications of silvipastures on southern pine plantations. Agroforestry Systems. 29: 227-238.

Clason, T.R. 1999. Silvopastoral practices sustain timber and forage production in commercial loblolly pine plantations of northwest Louisiana, USA. Agroforestry Systems. 44: 293-303.

Cutter, B.E.; Hunt, K.; Haywood, J.D. 1999. Tree/wood quality in slash pine following longterm cattle grazing. Agroforestry Systems. 44: 305-312.

Dangerfield, C.W.; Harwell, R.L. 1990. An analysis of a silvopastoral system for the marginal land in the Southeast United States. Agroforestry Systems. 10: 187-197.

Doescher, P.S.; Tesch, S.D.; Alejandro-Castro, M. 1987. Livestock grazing: a silvicultural tool for plantation establishment. Journal of Forestry. 85: 29-37.

Dubois, M.R.; McNabb, K.; Straka, T.J. 1999. Costs and cost trends for forestry practices in the South. Forest Landowner. 58(2): 3-8.

Duryea, M.L.; Edwards, J.C. 1987. Planting southern pines. Florida Cooperative Extension Service, IFAS, University of Florida. Circular 767. 14 p.

Grado, S.C.; Hovermale, C.H.; St. Louis, D.G. 2001. A financial analysis of silvopasture system in southern Mississippi. Agroforestry Systems. 53: 313-322.

Grelen, H.E.; Pearson, H.A.; Thill, R.E. 1985. Establishment and growth of slash pine on grazed cutover range in central Louisiana. Southern Journal of Applied Forestry. 9: 232-236.

Hughes, R.H. 1976. Response of planted south Florida slash pine to simulated cattle damage. Journal of Range Management. 29(3): 198-201.

Husak, A.L.; Grado, S.C. 2002. Monetary benefits in a southern silvopastoral system. Southern Journal of Applied Forestry. 26(3): 159-164.

Kalmbacher, R.S. 2000. Planting pines in bahiagrass pastures. Ona Reports. The Florida Cattleman and Livestock Journal. http://www.ifas.ufl.edu/~ona/or/7-00.html

Karl, M.G.; Doescher, P.S. 1993. Regulating competition on conifer plantations with prescribed cattle grazing. Forest Science. 39(3): 405-418.

Lewis, C.E. 1980a. Simulated cattle injury to planted slash pine: combination of defoliation, browsing, and trampling. Journal of Range Management. 33(5): 340-345.

Lewis, C.E. 1980b. Simulated cattle injury to planted slash pine: defoliation. Journal of Range Management. 33(5): 345-348.

Lewis, C.E. 1980c. Simulated cattle injury to planted slash pine: girdling. Journal of Range Management. 33(5): 337-340.

Lewis, C.E. 1983. Forage resources and integrated management in the slash pine ecosystem. In: Stone, E.L., ed. The managed slash pine ecosystem: symposium proceedings; 1981 June 9-11; Gainesville, FL: School of Forest Resources and Conservation, University of Florida: 360-368.

Lewis, C.E. 1984. Warm season forage under pine and related cattle damage to young pines. In: Linnartz, N.E.; Johnson, M.K., eds. Agroforestry in the southern United States. 33rd Annual Forestry Symposium. School of Forestry, Wildlife, and Fisheries. Louisiana Agricultural Experiment Station. Louisiana State University Agricultural Center: 66-78.

Lewis, C.E. 1985. Planting slash pine in a dense pasture sod. Agroforestry Systems. 3: 267-274.

Lewis, C.E.; Burton, G.W.; Monson, W.G.; McCormick, W.C. 1983. Integration of pines, pastures, and cattle in south Georgia, USA. Agroforestry Systems. 1: 277-297.

Lewis, C.E.; Tanner, G.W.; Terry, W.S. 1985. Double vs. single-row pine plantations for wood and forage production. Southern Journal of Applied Forestry. 9(1): 55-61.

Lundgren, G.K.; Conner, J.R.; Pearson, H.A. 1984. An economic analysis of five forest-grazing management systems in the southeastern United States. MP-1551. College Station, TX The Texas Agricultural Experiment Station, The Texas A&M University System. 8 p.

Nowak, J.; Blount, A. 2002. Silvopasture-more than cattle grazing in pine plantations. Forest Landowner. 61(2): 10-14.

Pearson, H.A.; Baldwin, V.C.; Barnett, J.P. 1990. Cattle grazing and pine survival and growth in subterranean clover pasture. Agroforestry Systems 10: 161-168.

Pearson, H.A.; Whitaker, L.B. 1974. Yearlong grazing of slash pine ranges: effects on herbage and browse. Journal of Range Management. 27(3): 195-197.

Pearson, H.A.; Whitaker, L.B.; Duvall, V.L. 1971. Slash pine regeneration under regulated grazing. Journal of Forestry. 69: 744-746.

Rowan, S.J. 1986. Seedbed density affects performance of slash and loblolly pine in Georgia. International symposium on nursery management practices for the southern pines: proceedings; 1985 August 4-9; Montgomery, AL: Auburn University: 126-135.

Sharrow, S.H. 1999. Silvopastoralism: competition and facilitation between trees, livestock and improved grass-clover pastures on temperate rainfed lands. In: Buck, L.E.; Lassoie, J.P.; Fernandes, E.C.M., eds. Agroforestry in Sustainable Agricultural Systems. Boca Raton, FL: CRC Press LLC. 416 p.

South, D.B.; Mitchell, R.J. 1999. Determining the "optimum" slash pine seedling size for use with four levels of vegetation management on a flatwoods site in Georgia, U.S.A. Canadian Journal of Forest Research. 29: 1039-1046.

Tanner, G.W.; Lewis, C.E. 1984. Alternative tree spacings for wood and forage production in Florida. Florida Cooperative Extension Service, Forest Resources and Conservation Fact Sheet FRC-36. IFAS, University of Florida, Gainesville. 2 p.

Tyree, A.B.; Kunkle, W.E. 1995. Managing pine trees and bahiagrass for timber and cattle production. Florida Cooperative Extension Service, IFAS, University of Florida. Circular 1154. 10 p.

White, T.L.; Byram, T.D. 2004. Slash pine tree improvement. In: Dickens, E.D.; Barnett, J.P.; Hubbard, W.G.; Jokela, E.J., eds. Slash pine: still growing and growing! Proceedings of the slash pine symposium. Gen. Tech. Rep. SRS-76. Asheville, NC: U.S. Department of Agriculture, Forest Service, Southern Research Station: 7-19.

SLASH PINE *PINUS ELLIOTTII* VAR. *ELLIOTTII* SELECT BIBLIOGRAPHY

Bryan C. McElvany, Kim D. Coder, and E. David Dickens[1]

INTRODUCTION

Slash pine (*Pinus elliottii* var. *elliottii*) is a major forest product species. The research literature is voluminous and diverse. This publication was compiled to assist slash pine managers and forest landowner consultants to better appreciate and access important information in the literature. This is not a comprehensive review but a selection from among papers in the last 22 years (1981 through 2002 inclusive). These citations were checked and proofed to assure minimal errors, but undoubtedly some errors remain. Also note that inclusion or exclusion of a paper is not a judgement upon value, but a selection by the authors for the most germane papers on slash pine culture and an avenue into the literature.

BIBLIOGRAPHY

Abbott, J.E. 1982. Operational planting of container grown slash pine seedlings on problem sites. Gen. Tech. Rep. SO-GTR-37. New Orleans, LA: U.S. Department of Agriculture, Forest Service, Southern Forest Experiment Station. 115-116.

Abrahamson, W.G. 1991. South Florida slash pine mortality in seasonal ponds. Florida Scientist. 54(2): 80-83.

Adams, D.E.; Lenhart, J.D.; Vaughn, A.B.; Lapongan, J. 1996. Predicting survival of east Texas loblolly and slash pine plantations infected with fusiform rust. Southern Journal of Applied Forestry. 20(1): 30-35.

Airhart, D.L.; Natarella, N.J.; Pokorny, F.A. 1981. Electron microprobe analysis of calcium solution penetration into milled pine bark particles. Communications in Soil Science and Plant Analysis. 12(4): 319-329.

Alig, R.J.; Kurtz, W.B.; Mills, T.J. 1981. Financial return estimates of alternative management strategies for 9- to 15-year-old southern pine plantations in Mississippi. Southern Journal of Applied Forestry. 5(1): 3-7.

Allan, R. 1998. A report on pit size treatments and how these impact on tree growth and survival. ICRF Bulletin Series. 4: 18p.

Allen, P.J. 1985. Estimation of genetic parameters for wood properties in slash pine in south east Queensland. Research Note, Department of Forestry, Queensland. 41: 15p.

Allen, P.J. 1993. Stem profile and form factor comparisons for *Pinus elliottii*, *P. caribaea* and their F1 hybrid. Australian Forestry. 56(2): 140-144.

Anderson, R.L. 1986. New method for assessing contamination of slash and loblolly pine seeds by *Fusarium moniliforme* var *subglutinans*. Plant Disease. 70(5): 452-453.

Anderson, R.L.; Belcher, E.; Miller, T. 1984. Occurrence of seed fungi inside slash pine seeds produced in seed orchards in the United States. Seed Science and Technology. 12(3): 797-799.

Anderson, R.L.; Cost, N.D.; McClure, J.P.; Ryan, G. 1986. Predicting severity of fusiform rust in young loblolly and slash pine stands in Florida, Georgia and the Carolinas. Southern Journal of Applied Forestry. 10(1): 38-41.

Anderson, R.L.; Knighten, J.L.; Powers, H.R., Jr. 1984. Field survival of loblolly and slash pine seedlings grown in trays and leach containers. Tree Planters' Notes. 35(2): 3-4.

Anderson, R.L.; McCartney, T.C.; Cost, N.D. [and others]. 1988. Fusiform-rust-hazard maps for loblolly and slash pines. Res. Note. SE-RN-351. Ashville, NC: U.S. Department of Agriculture, Forest Service, Southeastern Forest Experiment Station. 7p.

Anderson, R.L.; McClure, J.P.; Cost, N.; Uhler, R.J. 1986. Estimating fusiform rust losses in five Southeast States. Southern Journal of Applied Forestry. 10(4): 237-240.

Anderson, R.L.; Mistretta, P.A. 1982. Integrated pest management handbook. Management strategies for reducing losses caused by fusiform rust, annosus root rot and littleleaf disease. Agriculture Handbook 597. Asheville, NC: U.S. Department of Agriculture, Forest Service, Southeastern Area State and Private Forestry. 30p.

Aoki, H.; Cruz, S.F. 1998. New methods for resin tapping in *Pinus*. Revista do Instituto Florestal. 10(2): 123-126.

Arabatzis, A.A.; Gregoire, T.G.; Lenhart, J.D. 1991. Fusiform rust incidence in loblolly and slash pine plantations in east Texas. Southern Journal of Applied Forestry. 15(2): 79-84.

Arvanitis, L.G.; Godbee, J.F., Jr.; Porta, I. 1984. Pitch canker impact on volume growth: a case study in slash pine plantations. Southern Journal of Applied Forestry. 8(1): 43-47.

---

[1] Bryan C. McElvany, Research Coordinator; Kim D. Coder, Forest Ecology Professor; and E. David Dickens, Forest Productivity Associate Professor, Daniel B. Warnell School of Forest Resources, The University of Georgia, Athens, GA 30602-2152.

Citation for proceedings: Dickens, E.D.; Barnett, J.P.; Hubbard, W.G.; Jokela, E.J., eds. 2004. Slash pine: still growing and growing! Proceedings of the slash pine symposium. Gen. Tech. Rep. SRS-76. Asheville, NC: U.S. Department of Agriculture, Forest Service, Southern Research Station. 148 p.

Atkinson, P.R.; Laing, M.D. 1996. First results of investigations into fungal diseases of pines at establishment. ICFR Bulletin Series. 6: 13.

Atkinson, T.H.; Foltz, J.L.; Connor, M.D. 1988. Bionomics of *Pissodes nemorensis* Germar (Coleoptera: Curculionidae) in northern Florida. Annals of the Entomological Society of America. 81(2): 255-261.

Atkinson, T.H.; Foltz, J.L.; Connor, M.D. 1988. Flight patterns of phloem- and wood-boring Coleoptera (Scolytidae, Platypodidae, Curculionidae, Buprestidae, Cerambycidae) in a north Florida slash pine plantation. Environmental Entomology. 17(2): 259-265.

Auer, C.G.; Grigoletti, A., Jr. 1997. The occurrence of *Sphaeropsis sapinea* on *Pinus* in the states of Parana and Santa Catarina. Boletim de Pesquisa Florestal. 34: 99-101.

Bacon, G.J.; Hawkins, P.J.; Ward, J.P. 1982. Productivity of commercial thinning operations in Queensland plantations: influence of alternative silvicultural options. New Zealand Journal of Forestry Science. 12(2): 308-323.

Bailey, R.L. 1986. Rotation age and establishment density for planted slash and loblolly pines. Southern Journal of Applied Forestry. 10(3): 162-168.

Bailey, R.L. 1994. A compatible volume-taper model based on the Schumacher and Hall generalized constant form factor volume equation. Forest Science. 40(2): 303-313.

Bailey, R.L.; Abernethy, N.C.; Jones, E.P., Jr. 1981. Diameter distribution models for repeatedly thinned slash pine plantations. Gen. Tech. Rep. SO-GTR-34. New Orleans, LA: U.S. Department of Agriculture, Forest Service, Southern Forest Experiment Station. 115-126.

Bailey, R.L.; Borders, R.E.; Ware, K.D.; Jones, E.P., Jr. 1985. A compatible model relating slash pine plantation survival to density, age, site index, and type and intensity of thinning. Forest Science. 31(1): 180-189.

Bailey, R.L.; Brooks, J.R. 1994. Determining site index and estimating timber volumes without measuring heights. Southern Journal of Applied Forestry. 18(1): 15-18.

Bailey, R.L.; Burgan, T.M.; Jokela, E.J. 1989. Fertilized midrotation-aged slash pine plantations - stand structure and yield prediction models. Southern Journal of Applied Forestry. 13(2): 76-80.

Bailey, R.L.; Da Silva, J.A. Aleixo. 1988. Compatible models for survival, basal area growth, and diameter distributions of fertilized slash pine plantations. Gen. Tech. Rep. NC-GTR-120. St. Paul, MN: U.S. Department of Agriculture, Forest Service, North Central Research Station. 538-546.

Bailey, R.L.; Pienaar, L.V. 1983. An experiment to evaluate row, selection, and combination thinning: design and installation results. Gen. Tech. Rep. SE-GTR-24. Ashville, NC: U.S. Department of Agriculture, Forest Service, Southeastern Forest Experiment Station. 213-216.

Bailey, R.L.; Ware, K.D. 1983. Compatible basal-area growth and yield model for thinned and unthinned stands. Canadian Journal of Forest Research. 13(4): 563-571.

Baker, F.A.; Verbyla, D.L.; Hodges, C.S., Jr.; Ross, E.W. 1993. Classification and regression tree analysis for assessing hazard of pine mortality caused by *Heterobasidion annosum*. Plant Disease. 77(2): 136-139.

Baldwin, V.C., Jr. 1985. Survival curves for unthinned and early-thinned direct-seeded slash pine stands. Gen. Tech. Rep. SO-GTR-54. New Orleans, LA: U.S. Department of Agriculture, Forest Service, Southern Forest Experiment Station. 460-465.

Baldwin, V.C., Jr.; Busby, R.L. 1993. A comparison of predicted mensurational and economic performance of thinned Louisiana loblolly and slash pine plantations. Gen. Tech. Rep. SO-GTR-93. New Orleans, LA: U.S. Department of Agriculture, Forest Service, Southern Forest Experiment Station. 573-584.

Baldwin, V.C., Jr.; Feduccia, D.P.; Haywood, J.D. 1989. Post-thinning growth and yield of row-thinned and selectively thinned loblolly and slash pine plantations. Canadian Journal of Forest Research. 19(2): 247-256.

Ball, M.J., III; Hunter, D.H.; Swindel, B.F. 1981. Understory biomass response to microsite and age of bedded slash pine plantations. Journal of Range Management. 34(1): 38-42.

Ballard, R. 1981. Urea and ammonium nitrate as nitrogen sources for southern pine plantations. Southern Journal of Applied Forestry. 5(3): 105-108.

Balmer, W.E.; Mobley, H.E. 1983. Damaged stands: appraisal of damages, recovery potential and management decisions. In: The Managed Slash Pine Ecosystem. Proceedings of a symposium held at the University of Florida. June 9-11, 1981. 288-303.

Banfield, D.W. 1983. Direct seeding of pines by machine in rows on lignite mine-spoils and abandoned agricultural fields. Forestry Abstracts. 44(11): 706.

Bao, F.C.; Jiang, Z.H.; Jiang, X.O. [and others]. 1998. Comparative studies on wood properties of juvenile vs. mature wood and plantation vs. natural forest of main plantation tree species in China. Scientia Silvae Sinicae. 34(2): 63-76.

Barnard, E.L.; Dixon, W.N.; Ash, E.C. [and others]. 1995. Scalping reduces impact of soilborne pests and improves survival and growth of slash pine seedlings on converted agricultural croplands. Southern Journal of Applied Forestry. 19(2): 49-59.

Barnard, E.L.; Gilly, S.P.; Dixon, W.N. 1991. Incidence of *Heterobasidion annosum* and other root-infecting fungi in residual stumps and roots in thinned slash pine plantations in Florida. Plant Disease. 75(8): 823-828.

Barnard, E.L.; Hollis, C.A.; Pritchett, W.L. 1981. A comparative evaluation of seedling quality in commercial forest nurseries in Florida. Tech. Pub. SA-TP-17. Atlanta, GA: U.S. Department of Agriculture, Forest Service, Southeastern Area State and Private Forestry. 34-41.

Barnard, E.L.; Kannwischer-Mitchell, M.E.; Mitchell, D.J.; Fraedrich, S.W. 1997. Development and field performance of slash and loblolly pine seedlings produced in fumigated nursery seedbeds and seedbeds amended with organic residues. In: National Proceedings: Forest and Conservation Nursery Association. 32-37.

Barnard, E.L.; Miller, T. 1999. Southern cone rust: a growing problem in need of attention? Gen. Tech. Rep. SRS-GTR-30. Ashville, NC: U.S. Department of Agriculture, Forest Service, Southern Research Station. 569-572.

Barnard, E.L.; Yin, M.; Ash, E.C., III [and others]. 1996. Aerial application trial for control of southern cone rust in a slash pine seed orchard using triadimefon. Tree Planters' Notes. 47(4): 126-131.

Barnes, R.D.; Plumptre, R.A.; Quilter, T.K. [and others]. 1999. The use of stem dissection to sample trees of different ages for determining pulping properties of tropical pines. IAWA Journal. 20(1): 37-43.

Barnett, J.P. 1981. Imbibition temperatures affect seed moisture uptake, germination and seedling development. Gen. Tech. Rep. SO-GTR-34. New Orleans, LA: U.S. Department of Agriculture, Forest Service, Southern Forest Experiment Station. 41-45.

Barnett, J.P. 1983. Freeze- and kiln-drying of slash pine cones and seeds. Gen. Tech. Rep. SE-GTR-24. Asheville, NC: U.S. Department of Agriculture, Forest Service, Southeastern Forest Experiment Station. 387-389.

Barnett, J.P. 1996. How seed orchard culture affects seed quality: experience with the southern pines. Forestry Chronicle. 72(5): 469-473.

Barnett, J.P.; Brissette, J.C.; Kais, A.G.; Jones, J.P. 1988. Improving field performance of southern pine seedlings by treating with fungicides before storage. Southern Journal of Applied Forestry. 12(4): 281-285.

Barnett, J.P.; McLemore, B.F. 1984. Germination speed as a predictor of nursery seedling performance. Southern Journal of Applied Forestry. 8(3): 157-162.

Barnett, J.P.; Vozzo, J.A. 1985. Viability and vigor of slash and shortleaf pine seeds after 50 years. Forest Science. 31(2): 316-320.

Barrett, R.L. 1983. Raising pines in planter flats. South African Forestry Journal. 125: 58-67.

Barrows-Broaddus, J.; Dwinell, L.D. 1983. Histopathology of Fusarium moniliforme var. sublgutinans in four species of southern pines. Phytopathology. 73(6): 882-889.

Barrows-Broaddus, J.; Dwinell, L.D.; Kerr, T.J. 1985. Evaluation of Arthrobacter sp. for biological control of the pitch canker fungus on slash pine. Canadian Journal of Microbiology. 31(10): 888-892.

Barrows-Broaddus, J.B. 1981. Histopathology of Fusarium moniliforme var. sublutinans in slash and loblolly pine. Phytopathology. 71(8): 858.

Baynes, J.; Dunn, G.M. 1997. Estimating foliage surface area index in 8-year-old stands of Pinus elliottii var. elliottii x Pinus caribaea var. hondurensis of variable quality. Canadian Journal of Forest Research. 27(9): 1367-1375.

Beeson, R.C., Jr. 1993. Benefits of progressively increasing container size during nursery production depend on fertilizer regime and species. Journal of the American Society of Horticultural Science. 118(6): 752-756.

Belanger, R.P. 2001. An integrated approach toward reducing losses from fusiform rust in merchantable slash and loblolly pine plantations. Res. Pap. SRS-RP-23. Asheville, NC: U.S. Department of Agriculture, Forest Service, Southern Research Station. 14p.

Belanger, R.P.; Godbee, J.F.; Miller, T.; Webb, R.S. 1983. Salvage cutting in southern pine forests. Gen. Tech. Rep. SE-GTR-24. Asheville, NC: U.S. Department of Agriculture, Forest Service, Southeastern Forest Experiment Station. 382-386.

Belanger, R.P.; Miller, T.; Godbee, J.F. 1985. Fusiform rust: guidelines for selective cutting of rust-infected trees in merchantable slash pine plantations. Gen. Tech. Rep. SO-GTR-56. New Orleans, LA: U.S. Department of Agriculture, Forest Service, Southern Forest Experiment Station. 254-257.

Belanger, R.P.; Miller, T.; Schmidt, R.A. 1983. Pest management in slash pine. In: The Managed Slash Pine Ecosystem. Proceedings of a symposium held at the University of Florida. June 9-11, 1981. 273-287.

Belcher, E.W.; Leach, G.N.; Gresham, H.H. 1984. Sizing slash pine seeds as a nursery procedure. Tree Planter's Notes. 35(3): 5-10.

Belmont, R.A.; Habeck, D.H. 1983. Parasitoids of Diooryctira spp. (Pyralidae: Lepidoptera) coneworms in slash pine seed production areas of north Florida. Florida entomologist. 66(4): 399-407.

Bengston, G.W.; Smart, G.C., Jr. 1981. Slash pine growth and response to fertilizer after application of pesticides to the planting site. Forest Science. 27(3): 487-502.

Bennett, F.A. 1983. Managing natural stands. In: The Managed Slash Pine Ecosystem. Proceedings of a symposium held at the University of Florida. June 9-11, 1981. 314-326.

Bennett, F.A.; Jones, E.P., Jr. 1983. Thinning and its effect on growth. In: The Managed Slash Pine Ecosystem. Proceedings of a symposium held at the University of Florida. June 9-11, 1981. 304-313.

Berisford, C.W.; Turnbow, R.H., Jr.; Brady, U.E. 1982. Selective application of insecticides for prevention of southern pine beetle attack. Journal of Economic Entomology. 75(3): 458-461.

Berry, C.R. 1981. Sewage sludge affect soil properties and growth of slash pine seedlings in a Florida nursery. Tech. Pub. SA-TP-17. Atlanta, GA: U.S. Department of Agriculture, Forest Service, Southeastern Area State and Private Forestry. 46-51.

Biblis, E.J. 1990. Properties and grade yield of lumber from a 27-year-old slash pine plantation. Forest Products Journal. 40(3): 21-24.

Binkley, D.; Johnson, D.W. 1992. Regional evaluations of acid deposition effects on forest. Ecological Studies: analysis and synthesis. 91: 534-543.

Birchem, R.; Sommer, H.E.; Brown, C.L. 1981. Comparison of plastids and pigments of *Pinus palustris* Mill. and *Pinus elliottii* Engelm. in callus tissue culture. International Journal of Plant Physiology. 102(2): 101-107.

Birchfield, W.B.; McGawley, E.C.; Jones, J.P.; Yik, C.P. 1982. Pinewood nematode identified in Louisiana. Louisiana Agriculture. 25(3): 22-23.

Birdsey, R.A.; Van Hees, W.W.S.; Beltz, R.C. 1981. Pine regeneration in southwest Arkansas. Res. Pap. SO-RP-165. New Orleans, LA: U.S. Department of Agriculture, Forest Service, Southern Forest Experiment Station. 10 p.

Blakeslee, G.M. 1983. Major diseases affecting slash pine. In: The Managed Slash Pine Ecosystem. Proceedings of a symposium held at the University of Florida. June 9-11, 1981. 257-272.

Blanche, C.A.; Elam, W.W.; Hodges, J.D. [and others]. 1989. Accelerated aging: a potential vigor test for longleaf and slash pine seedlings. Gen. Tech. Rep. SO-GTR-74. New Orleans, LA: U.S. Department of Agriculture, Forest Service, Southern Forest Experiment Station. 107-114.

Boden, D.I. 1982. The relationship between timber density of the three major pine species in the Matal Midlands and various site and tree parameters. Report - Wattle Research Institute. 35: 120-126.

Bonner, F.T. 1986. Measurement of seed vigor for loblolly and slash pines. Forest Science. 32(1): 170-178.

Bonner, F.T. 1987. Effect of storage of loblolly and slash pine cones on seed quality. Southern Journal of Applied Forestry. 11(1): 59-65.

Boomsma, B.D.; Burger, J.A. 1981. Factors affecting nitrogen mineralization in an acid sandy forest soil. In: Proceedings: Managing Nitrogen Economics of Natural and Man Made Forest Ecosystems. 250-258.

Borders, B.E.; Bailey, R.L. 1986. A compatible system of growth and yield equations for slash pine fitted with restricted three-stage least squares. Forest Science. 32(1): 185-201.

Borders, B.E.; Bailey, R.L.; Ware, K.D. 1984. Slash pine site index from a polymorphic model by joining (splining) non-polynomial segments with an algebraic difference method. Forest Science. 30(2): 411-423.

Borders, B.E.; Harrison, W.M. 1989. Comparison of slash pine and loblolly pine performance on cutover site-prepared sites in the Coastal Plain of Georgia and Florida. Southern Journal of Applied Forestry. 13(4): 204-207.

Borders, B.E.; Jordan, J.B. 1999. Loblolly and slash pine growth and yield prediction for regional timber supply projection algorithms. Southern Journal of Applied Forestry. 23(4): 230-237.

Borders, B.E.; Shiver, B.D. 1995. Board foot volume estimation for southern pines. Southern Journal of Applied Forestry. 19(1): 23-28.

Borders, B.E.; Souter, R.A.; Bailey, R.L.; Ware, K.D. 1987. Percentile-based distributions characterize forest stand tables. Forest Science. 33(2): 570-576.

Bower, R.C.; McKinley, C.R. 1987. Effects of related and unrelated graft partners in slash pine (*Pinus elliottii* Engelm.). In: Proceeding of the Southern Forest Tree Improvement Conference. 41: 269-274.

Bramlett, D.L. 1984. Inventory-monitoring system for southern pine seed orchards. In: Proceedings of the Cone and Seed Insects Working Party Conference. 102-111.

Bramlett, D.L. 1997. Genetic gain from mass controlled pollination and topworking. Journal of Forestry. 95(3): 15-19.

Brasil, M.A.M.; Montagna, R.G.; Coelho, L.C.C.; Veiga, R.A. 1982. Basic wood density of *Pinus elliottii*, var. *elliottii* in three regions of the state of Sao Paulo. Boletim tecnico - Instituto Florestal. 36(1): 9-17.

Brasil, M.A.M.; Veiga, R.A.; Coelho, L.C.C. 1982. Yield in weight of dry matter of *Pinus elliottii* Engelm. var. *elliottii* trees. Boletim tecnico - Instituto Florestal. 36(1): 1-8.

Brawner, J.T.; Carter, D.R.; Huber, D.A.; White, T.L. 1999. Projected gains in rotation-age volume and value from fusiform rust resistant slash and loblolly pines. Journal of Forest Research. 29(6): 737-742.

Bredendkamp, B.V.; Loveday, N.C. 1984. Volume equations for diameter measurements in millimeters. South African Forestry Journal. 130: 40.

Breininger, D.R.; Duncan, B.W.; Dominy, N.J. 2002. Relationships between fire frequency and vegetation type in pine flatwoods of east-central Florida. Natural Areas Journal. 22(3): 186-193.

Brewer, J.S. 1998. Patterns of plant species richness in a wet slash-pine (*Pinus elliottii*) savanna. Journal of Torrey Botanical Society. 125(3): 216-224.

Brissette, J.C.; Lantz, C.W. 1983. Seedling quality: summary of a workshop. Tech. Pub. R8-TP-4. Atlanta, GA: U.S. Department of Agriculture, Forest Service, Southern Region. 303-305.

Brissette, J.C.; Vande Linde, F.; Barnett, J.P. 1983. Producing, storing, and handling quality of slash pine seedlings. In: The Managed Slash Pine Ecosystem. Proceedings of a symposium held at the University of Florida. June 9-11, 1981. 150-164.

Broerman, F.S.; Sarigumba, T.I.; Immel, M.J. 1983. Site preparation and slash pine productivity. In: The Managed Slash Pine Ecosystem. Proceedings of a symposium held at the University of Florida. June 9-11, 1981. 131-149.

Bronson, M.R.; Dixon, R.K. 1988. *In-vitro* plantlet formation from embryonic cotyledons of *Pinus elliottii* Engelm. In: Proceedings, 10th North American Forest Biology Workshop, pages 261-267.

Bronson, M.R.; Dixon, R.K. 1991. Cultural factors influencing adventitious shoot and plantlet formation from slash pine cotyledons. New Forests. 5(4): 277-288.

Bronson, M.R.; Li, Y.A.; Dixon, R.K. [and others]. 1992. *In vitro* host-pathogen interactions of *Pinus elliottii* calli and *Fusarium moniliforme* var. *subglutinans*. European Journal of Forest Pathology. 22(6): 432-440.

Brooks, J.R.; Borders, B.E.; Bailey, R.L. 1992. Predicting diameter distributions for site-prepared loblolly and slash pine plantations. Southern Journal of applied forestry. 16(3): 130-133.

Brown, C.L.; Pienaar, L.V. 1981. Observations on growth of paraquat-treated slash pine. Southern Journal of Applied Forestry. 5(3): 145-150.

Buckner, J.L. 1983. Wildlife concerns in the managed slash pine ecosystem. In: The Managed Slash Pine Ecosystem. Proceedings of a symposium held at the University of Florida. June 9-11, 1981. 369-374.

Bunse, G.G. 1992. Conference on subtropical pines. In: Jornadas sobre pinos subtropicales, Eldorado, Misiones, Argentian, 5-7 de Agosto de 1992. 407p.

Burger, J.A.; Pritchett, W.L. 1984. Effects of clearfelling and site preparation on nitrogen mineralization in a southern pine stand. Soil Science Society of America Journal. 48: 1432-1437.

Burger, J.A.; Pritchett, W.L. 1988. Site preparation effects on soil moisture and available nutrients in a pine plantation in the Florida flatwoods. Forest Science. 34(1): 77-87.

Burns, J.A.; Schwarz, O.J. 1996. Bacterial stimulation of adventitious rooting on *in vitro* cultured slash pine (*Pinus elliottii* Engelm.) seeding explants. Plant Cell Reports. 15(6): 405-408.

Burns, J.A.; Schwarz, O.J.; Schlarbaum, S.E. 1991. Multiple shoot production from seedling explants of slash pine (*Pinus elliottii,* Engelm.). Plant Cell Reports. 10(9): 439-443.

Burns, P.Y.; Hu, S.C. 1985. Effects of fusiform rust on growth of planted slash pines. Gen. Tech. Rep. SO-GTR-54. New Orleans, LA: U.S. Department of Agriculture, Forest Service, Southern Forest Experiment Station. 231-234.

Burns, P.Y.; Hu, S.C.; Awang, J.B. 1981. Relationship of fusiform rust infection to intensive culture of slash pine. Gen. Tech. Rep. SO-GTR-34. New Orleans, LA: U.S. Department of Agriculture, Forest Service, Southern Forest Experiment Station. 366-369.

Burton, J.D.; Shoulders, E.; Snow, G.A. 1985. Incidence and impact of fusiform rust vary with silviculture in slash pine plantations. Forest Science. 31(3): 671-680.

Burton, J.D.; Snow, G.A. 1983. Triadimefon controls fusiform rust in young slash pine outplantings. Plant Disease. 67(8): 853-854.

Burton, J.D.; Snow, G.A. 1985. Intensive culture gives slash pine plantations a fast start. Gen. Tech. Rep. SO-GTR-54. New Orleans, LA: U.S. Department of Agriculture, Forest Service, Southern Forest Experiment Station. 321-326.

Busby, R.L.; Haines, T.K. 1988. Determining the value of a fusiform rust-infected stand. Res. Pap. SE-RP-245. Asheville, NC: U.S. Department of Agriculture, Forest Service, Southeastern Forest Experiment Station. 5p.

Busby, R.L.; Ward, K.B. 1989. MERCHOP: a dynamic programming model for estimating the harvest value of unthinned loblolly and slash pine plantations. Res. Pap. SO-RP-254. New Orleans, LA: U.S. Department of Agriculture, Forest Service, Southern Forest Experiment Station. 19p.

Bush, P.B.; Merka, W.; Morris, L.A.; Torrance, R. 1999. Chicken litter as a nutrient source for slash pine establishment in the Georgia Coastal Plain. Gen. Tech. Rep. SRS-GTR-30. Asheville, NC: U.S. Department of Agriculture, Forest Service, Southern Research Station. 469-473.

Byrd, N.A.; Lewis, C.E.; Pearson, H.A. 1984. Management of southern pine forests for cattle production. Gen. Rep. R8-GR-4. Atlanta, GA: U.S. Department of Agriculture, Forest Service, Southern Region. 22p.

Byres, D.P.; Dean, T.J.; Johnson, J.D. 1992. Long-term effects of ozone and simulated acid rain on the foliage dynamics of slash pine (*Pinus elliotti* var. *elliottii* Engelm.). New Phytologist. 120(1): 61-67.

Byres, D.P.; Johnson, J.D.; Dean, T.J. 1992. Photosynthesis to long-term exposure to ozone and acidic precipitation. New Phytologist. 122(1): 91-96.

Byrne, P.J.; Just, T.E. 1982. Exotic pine plantation prescribed burning using a helicopter. Technical Paper, Department of Forestry, Queensland. 28: 13p.

Cai, J.; Pan, W.; Feng, S. [and others]. 2002. Effects of thinning intensity on wood properties of slash pine. Forest Research, Beijing. 15(3): 297-303.

Caldeira, M.V.W.C.; Tonini, H.; Hoppe, J.M. [and others]. 1996. Site definition for a *Pinus elliottii* Engelm. population at Encruzilhada do Sul, RS. Ciencia Florestal. 6(1): 1-13.

Cameron, R.S.; Billings, R.F. 1988. Southern pine beetle: factors associated with spot occurrence and spread in young plantations. Southern Journal of Applied Forestry. 12(3): 208-214.

Campbell, M.S.F.; Comer, C.W.; Rockwood, D.L.; Henry, C. 1984. Biomass yields of young heavily stocked slash pine stands in north Florida. In: Proceedings of the 1983 Southern Forest Biomass Workshop. 77-82.

Campbell, T.E. 1981. Growth and development of loblolly and slash pines direct-seeded or planted on a cutover site. Southern Journal of Applied Forestry. 5(3): 115-119.

Campbell, T.E. 1981. Spot seeding is effective and inexpensive for reforesting small acreage. Gen. Tech. Rep. SO-GTR-34. New Orleans, LA: U.S. Department of Agriculture, Forest Service, Southern Forest Experiment Station. 50-53.

Campbell, T.E. 1982. Imbibition, desiccation, and reimbibition effects of light requirements for germinating southern pine seeds. Forest Science. 28(3): 539-543.

Campbell, T.E. 1983. Effects of initial seedling density on spot-seeded loblolly and slash pines at age 15 years. Gen. Tech. Rep. SE-GTR-24. Asheville, NC: U.S. Department of Agriculture, Forest Service, Southeastern Forest Experiment Station. 118-127.

Campbell, T.E. 1985. Development of direct-seeded and planted loblolly and slash pines through age 20. Southern Journal of Applied Forestry. 9(4): 205-211.

Campbell, T.E. 1985. Sprouting of slash, loblolly, and shortleaf pines following a simulated precommercial thinning. Res. Note SO-RN-320. New Orleans, LA: U.S. Department of Agriculture, Forest Service, Southern Forest Experiment Station. 3p.

Campbell, T.E. 1987. Pine growth response to chemical release from woody competition. In: Proceedings - Southern Weed Science Society. 40: 249-254.

Cannell, M.G.R. 1986. Physiology of southern pine seedlings. In: Proceedings of the International Symposium on Nursery Management Practices for the Southern Pines. 251-274.

Cao, Q.V.; Dean, T.J.; Baldwin, V.C., Jr. 2000. Modeling the size-density relationship in direct-seeded slash pine stands. Forest Science. 46(3): 317-321.

Carey, W.A.; Kelley, W.D. 1993. Seedling production trends and fusiform rust control practices at southern nurseries. Southern Journal of Applied Forestry. 17(4): 207-211.

Carino, H.F.; Bilish, E.J. 1991. Profit potential of producing lumber from 27-year-old slash pine plantation timber. Forest Products Journal. 41(11): 50-54.

Carlson, C.A. 2001. A summary of the literature concerning the fertilization of pines at planting in the summer rainfall region of South Africa, and some current thoughts on fertilizer recommendations. ICFR Bulletin Series. 3: 19p.

Carter, F.L.; Beal, R.H. 1982. Termite responses to susceptible pine wood treated with antitermitic wood extracts. International Journal of Wood Preservation. 2(4): 185-191.

Carter, G.A. 1998. Reflectance wavebands and indices for remote estimation of photosynthesis and stomatal conductance in pine canopies. Remote Sensing of Environment. 63(1): 61-72.

Carter, G.A.; Cibula, W.G.; Miller, R.L. 1996. Narrow-band reflectance imagery compared with thermal imagery for early detection of plant stress. Journal of Plant Physiology. 148(5): 515-522.

Carter, G.A.; Dell, T.R.; Cibula, W.G. 1996. Spectral reflectance characteristics and digital imagery of a pine needle blight in the Southeastern United States. Canadian Journal of Forest Research. 26(3): 402-407.

Carter, G.A.; Young, D.R. 1993. Foliar spectral reflectance and plant stress on a barrier island. International Journal of Plant Sciences. 154(2): 298-308.

Castro, M.S.; Gholz, H.L.; Clark, K.L.; Steudler, P.A. 2000. Effects of forest harvesting on soil methane fluxes in Florida slash pine plantations. Canadian Journal of Forest Research. 30(10): 1534-1542.

Castro, M.S.; Peterjohn, W.T.; Melillo, J.M. [and others]. 1994. Effects of nitrogen fertilization on the fluxes of N_2O, CH_4, and CO_2 from soils in a Florida slash pine plantation. Canadian Journal of Forest Research. 24(1): 9-13.

Catchpoole, K.J.; Nester, M.R. 2002. Decision support software tools for pine plantations. New Zealand Journal of Forestry. 46(4): 15-18.

Caulfield, J.P.; Shoulders, E.; Lockaby, B.G. 1989. Methods for including risk in species-site selection decisions. Gen. Tech. Rep. SO-GTR-74. New Orleans, LA: U.S. Department of Agriculture, Forest Service, Southern Forest Experiment Station. 181-186.

Caulfield, J.P.; Shoulders, E.; Lockaby, B.G. 1989. Risk-efficient species-site selection decisions for southern pines. Canadian Journal of Forest Research. 19(6): 743-753.

Caulfield, J.P.; South, D.B.; Boyer, J.N. 1987. Nursery seedbed density is determined by short-term or long-term objectives. Southern Journal of Applied Forestry. 11(1): 9-14.

Cawse, J.C.L. 1983. Industrial wood regimes for plantations of *Pinus patula, P. taeda* and *P. elliottii.* South African Forestry Journal. 125: 35-57.

Chai, X.M.; Li, T.S.; Wu, Z.D. 1985. Studies on fatal factors of the pine-moth (*Dendrolimus punctatus*) in the winter generation in the forest of slash pine. Journal of Nanjing Institute of Forestry. 3: 103-113.

Chappelka, A.H., III; Schmidt, R.A. 1983. The phenology of inoculum production by *Cronartium quercuum* f.sp. *fusiform* on slash pine in north Florida and south Georgia. Forest Science. 29(2): 253-262.

Chappelka, A.H., III; Schimdt, R.A.; Patterson, H.D. 1984. Dynamics of aeciospore inoculum production by *Cronartium quercuum* f.sp. *fusiforme* on slash pine. Forest Science. 30(3): 787-792.

Charpentier, B.A.; Cowles, J.R. 1981. Rapid method of analyzing phenolic compounds in *Pinus elliottii* using high-performance liquid chromatography. Journal of Chromatography. 208(1): 132-136.

Chen, H.J.; Li, Y.Q.; Chen, D.D.; Hu, S.C. 1997. Growth responses of young slash pine (*Pinus elliotti* Engelm.) to N, P and K fertilizers in red-yellow soil in Jiangxi Province, China. Pedosphere. 7(3): 243-249.

Chen, J.; Tauer, C.G.; Huang, Y. 2002. Paternal chloroplast inheritance patterns in pine hybrids detected with *trnL-trnF* intergenic region polymorphism. Theoretical and Applied Genetics. 104(8): 1307-1311.

Chen, Y.G. 1999. Mineral element features of artificial slash pine plantation in Qianzanzhou Experiment Area. Journal of Beijing Forestry University. 21(6): 40-44.

Chen, Z.H.; Dai, F.Q.; Pan, X.Y.; Jin, S.W. 1996. Test of new improved seedling cultivation technique for *Pinus elliotti* and *Pinus taeda.* Journal of Zhejiang Forestry Science and Techonology. 16(4): 37-40.

Chirenje, T.; Ma, L.Q. 1999. Greenhouse study of slash pine response to fertilizer in a papermill-ash amended soil. In: Proceedings, Soil and Crop Science Society of Florida. 58: 44-51.

Choong, E.T.; Fogg, P.J.; Shoulders, E. 1989. Effect of cultural treatment and wood-type on some physical properties of longleaf and slash pine wood. Wood and Fiber Science. 21(2): 193-206.

Christie, S.I.; Tallon, N.B. 1991. The influence of nursery and planting practice on the incidence of resin-infiltrated heart shake in *Pinus elliottii* plantations in the eastern Transvaal. South African Forestry Journal. 157: 7-11.

Cibula, W.G.; Carter, G.A. 1992. Identification of a far-red reflectance response to ectomycorrhizae in slash pine. International Journal of Remote Sensing. 13(5): 925-932.

Cilliers, A.J.; Swart, W.J.; Wingfield, M.J. 1995. The occurrence of *Lasiodiplodia theobromae* on *Pinus elliottii* seeds in South Africa. Seed Science and Technology. 23(3): 851-860.

Clark, A., III; Saucier, J.R. 1989. Influence of initial planting density, geographic location, and species on juvenile wood formation in southern pine. Forest Product Journal. 39(7): 42-48.

Clark, A., III; Saucier, J.R. 1990. Tables for estimating total-tree weights, stem weights, and volumes of planted and natural southern pines in the Southeast. Georgia Forest Research Paper. 19: 27p.

Clark, A., III; Saucier, J.R. 1991. Influence of planting density, intensive culture, geographic location, and species on juvenile wood formation in southern pine. Georgia Forest Research Paper. 85: 13p.

Clark, A., III; Schmidtling, R.C. 1989. Effect of intensive culture on juvenile wood formation and wood properties of loblolly, slash, and longleaf pine. Gen. Tech. Rep. SO-GTR-74. New Orleans, LA: U.S. Department of Agriculture, Forest Service, Southern Forest Experiment Station. 211-217.

Clark, A., III; Souter, R.A. 1996. Stem cubic-foot volume tables for tree species in the Deep South area. Res. Pap. SRS-RP-293. Asheville, NC: U.S. Department of Agriculture, Forest Service, Southern Research Station. 131p.

Clark, K.L.; Cropper, W.P., Jr.; Gholz, H.L. 2001. Evaluation of modeled carbon fluxes for a slash pine ecosystem: SPM2 simulations compared to eddy flux measurements. Forest Science. 47(1): 52-59.

Clason, T.R.; Caro, Q.V. 1983. Comparing growth and yield between 31-year-old slash and loblolly pine plantations. Gen. Tech. Rep. SE-GTR-24. Asheville, NC: U.S. Department of Agriculture, Forest Service, Southeastern Forest Experiment Station. 291-297.

Clough, M.E. 1991. Comparison of aluminium, basic cations and acidity in the soil of indigenous forests and pine stands in the southern Cape. South African Journal of Plant and Soil. 8(4): 177-183.

Clutter, J.L.; Dell, T.R.; Brister, G.H. 1983. Application of available growth and yield data for management decisions. In: The Managed Slash Pine Ecosystem. Proceedings of a symposium held at the University of Florida. June 9-11, 1981. 349-359.

Coelho, M.C.B.; Finger, C.A.G. 1997. Growth height of *Pinus elliottii* Engelm. originating from different regeneration methods in Canela, RS. Ciencia Florestal. 7(1): 139-155.

Colbert, S.R.; Jokela, E.J.; Neary, D.G. 1990. Effects of annual fertilization and sustained weed control on dry matter partitioning, leaf area, and growth efficiency of juvenile loblolly and slash pine. Forest Science. 36(4): 995-1014.

Coleman, S.S.; Mace, A.C., Jr.; Swindel, B.F. 1982. Impacts of intensive forest management practices. In: Fourteenth Annual Spring Symposium. IMPAC Report, Intensive Management Practices Assessment Center. 7: 110p.

Comerford, N.B.; Fisher, R.F. 1984. Using foliar analysis to classify nitrogen-deficient sites. Soil Science Society of America Journal. 48(4): 910-913.

Comerford, N.B.; Fiskell, J.G.A. 1983. Profile of metal movement and plant uptake of an industrial sewage sludge for a slash pine stand. In: Soil and Crop Science Society of Florida Proceedings. 42: 176-180.

Comerford, N.B.; Mollitor, A.V.; McFee, W. 1987. Late season changes in fascicle nutrient content, weight, and phosphorus uptake by slash pine. Soil Science Society of America Journal. 51(3): 806-808.

Comerford, N.B.; Porter, P.S.; Escamilla, J.A. 1994. Use of Theissen areas in models of nutrient uptake in forested ecosystems. Soil Science Society of America Journal. 58(1): 210-215.

Comerford, N.B.; Smethurst, P.J. 1993. Potential for leaching of potassium and phosphorus from pine and grass roots. Communications in Soil Science and Plant Analysis. 24(13): 1577-1581.

Conde, L.F.; Swindel, B.F.; Smith, J.E. 1983. Plant species cover, frequency, and biomass: early responses to clear-cutting, burning and windrowing, discing, and bedding in Pinus elliottii flatwoods. Forest Ecology and Management. 6(4): 319-331.

Conde, L.F.; Swindel, B.F.; Smith, J.E. 1983. Plant species cover, frequency, and biomass: early responses to clear-cutting, chopping, and bedding in Pinus elliottii flatwoods. Forest Ecology and Management. 6(4): 307-317.

Conde, L.F.; Swindel, B.F.; Smith, J.E. 1986. Five years of vegetation changes following conversion of pine flatwoods to Pinus elliottii plantations. Forest Ecology and Management. 15(4): 295-300.

Cooksey, T.E.; Comerford, N.B.; Neary, D.G. 1988. Equilibrium patterns of slash pine water potentials using thermocouple psychrometry as influenced by bath temperature. Plant and Soil. 110(1): 153-155.

Costantini, A. 1995. Impacts of Pinus plantation management on selected physical properties of soils in the coastal lowlands of southeast Queensland, Australia. Commonwealth Forestry Review. 74(3): 211-223, 264-266.

Cowles, J.R.; Lemay, R.; Jahns, G. [and others]. 1989. Lignification in young plant seedlings grown on Earth and aboard the space shuttle. In: ACS Symposium series - American Chemical Society. 399: 203-213.

Cozzo, D. 1994. Conversion of forest plantations of exotic species into sustainable system in Argentina. Invesitgacion Agraria, Sistemas y Recursos Forestales. 3(1): 31-42.

Creighton, J.L.; Zutter, B.R.; Glover, G.R.; Gjerstad, D.H. 1987. Planted pine growth and survival responses to herbaceous vegetation control, treatment duration, and herbicide application technique. Southern Journal of Applied Forestry. 11(4): 223-227.

Crevatin, M.A. 1989. Grinder mesh size and exhaust systems and their effect on C.C.A. analytical results. Technical Note - Department of Forestry, Queensland, Australia. 13, 5 p.

Cropper, W.P., Jr. 1988. Labile carbon dynamics in a Florida slash pine plantation. Gen. Tech. Rep. NC-GTR-120. St. Paul, MN: U.S. Department of Agriculture, Forest Service, North Central Research Station. 278-284.

Cropper, W.P., Jr. 1997. Modeling the potential sensitivity of slash pine stem growth to increasing temperature and carbon dioxide. In: The Productivity and Sustainability of Southern Forest Ecosystems in a Changing Environment. 353-366.

Cropper, W.P., Jr. 2000. SPM2: a simulation model for slash pine (Pinus elliottii) forests. Forest Ecology and Management. 126(2): 201-212.

Cropper, W.P., Jr.; Ewel, K.C. 1983. Computer simulation of long-term carbon storage patterns in Florida slash pine plantations. Forest Ecology and Management. 6(2): 101-114.

Cropper, W.P., Jr.; Ewel, K.C. 1987. A regional carbon storage simulation for large-scale biomass plantations. Ecological Modelling. 36(3): 171-180.

Cropper, W.P., Jr.; Gholz, H.L. 1991. In situ needle and fine root respiration in mature slash pine (Pinus elliottii) trees. Canadian Journal of Forest Research. 21(11): 1589-1595.

Cropper, W.P., Jr.; Gholz, H.L. 1993. Simulation of carbon dynamics of a Florida slash pine plantation. Ecological Modelling. 66(3): 231-249.

Cubbage, F.W.; Pye, J.M.; Holmes, T.P.; Wagner, J.E. 2000. An economic evaluation of fusiform rust protection research. Southern Journal of Applied Forestry. 24(2): 77-85.

Cuevas, E.; Lugo, A.E. 1998. Dynamics of organic matter and nutrient return from litterfall in stands of ten tropical tree plantation species. Forest Ecology and Management. 112(3): 263-279.

Cunningham, M.E.; Van Buijtenen, J.P. 1983. Effect of shortened auxin treatments on the rooting of girdled slash pine shoots. Canadian Journal of Forest Research. 13(5): 917-920.

Curran, P.J.; Dungan, J.L.; Gholz, H.L. 1990. Exploring the relationship between reflectance red edge and chlorophyll content in slash pine. Tree Physiology. 7(1): 33-48.

Curran, P.J.; Dungan, J.L.; Gholz, H.L. 1992. Seasonal LAI in slash pine estimated with Landsat TM. Remote Sensing of Environment. 39(1): 3-13.

Curran, P.J.; Dunga, J.L.; Peterson, D.L. 2001. Estimating the foliar biochemical concentration of leaves with reflectance specotrometry. Testing the Kokaly and Clark methodologies. Remote Sensing of Environment. 76(3): 349-359.

Curran, P.J.; Windham, W.R.; Gholz, H.L. 1995. Exploring the relationship between reflectance red edge and chlorophyll concentration in slash pine leaves. Tree Physiology. 15(3): 203-206.

Cutter, B.E.; Hunt, K.; Haywood, J.D. 1999. Tree/wood quality in slash pine following longterm cattle grazing. Agroforestry Systems. 44(2): 305-312.

Czaplewski, R.L.; Reich, R.M.; Bechtold, W.A. 1994. Spatial autocorrelation in growth of undisturbed natural pine stands across Georgia. Forest Science. 40(2): 314-328.

Da Cruz, S.F.; Boas, O.V.; Garrido, L.M. do A.G.; Franco, F.S. 1996. Associations of *Pinus* species and agricultural species. Revista do Instituto Florestal. 8(2): 135-144.

Dalla-Tea, F.; Jokela, E.J. 1991. Needlefall, canopy light interception, and productivity of young intensively managed slash and loblolly pine stands. Forest Science. 37(5): 1298-1313.

Dalla-Tea, F.; Jokela, E.J. 1994. Needlefall returns and resorption rates of nutrients in young intensively managed slash and loblolly pine stands. Forest Science. 40(4): 650-662.

Darfus, G.H.; Fisher, R.F. 1984. Site relations of slash pine on dredge mine spoils. Journal of Environmental Quality. 13(3): 487-492.

Darrow, W.K. 1983. Pine oleoresin: a minor forest product of major importance? South African Forestry Journal. 125: 97-99.

Darrow, W.K. 1984. The origin of imported *Pinus elliottii* seedlots planted in South Africa, a historical investigation. South African Forestry Journal. 131: 25-27.

Darrow, W.K. 1992. Heart shake in South African-grown *Pinus elliottii*. Wood and Fiber Science: Journal of the Society of Wood Science and Technology. 24(3): 241-251.

Da Silva, H.M.; De Garrido, M.A.; Vaz, F.A.J.; Do Garrido, L.M. 1984. Resin production of *Pinus elliottii* var. *densa* and *Pinus oocarpa*. Boletim Tecnico do Instituto Florestal. 38(2): 177-185.

Da Silva, J.A.A. 1987. Dynamics of stand structure in fertilized slash pine plantations. Dissertation Abstracts International. 47(8): 3189.

Da Silva, J.A.A.; Machado, S.A.; Meunier, I.M.J.; Ferreira, R.L.C. 2000. Modeling volumes of *Pinus elliottii* Engelm. in the Santa Catarina state plateau. Revista Arvore. 24(1): 91-96.

Da Silva, J.R.; De Oliveira, F.F.; Sebastiani, E.E.G.; Lunardi, A.L. 2000. Soil compaction due to forestry traffic and engineering work. Engenharia Agricola. 20(3): 243-249.

Dawson, T.P.; Curran, P.J.; Plummer, S.E. 1998. The biochemical decomposition of slash pine needles from reflectance spectra using neural networks. International Journal of Remote Sensing. 19(7): 1433-1438.

Dean, T.J. 1991. Effect of growth rate and wind sway on the relation between mechanical and water-flow properties in slash pine seedlings. Canadian Journal of Forest Research. 21(10): 1501-1506.

Dean, T.J.; Johnson, J.D. 1992. Growth response of young slash pine trees to simulated acid rain and ozone stress. Canadian Journal of Forest Research. 22(6): 839-848.

Dean, T.J.; Jokela, E.J. 1992. A density-management diagram for slash pine plantations in the lower Coastal Plain. Southern Journal of Applied Forestry. 16(4): 178-185.

Dees, C.S.; Clark, J.D.; Van Manen, F.T. 2001. Florida panther habitat use in response to prescribed fire. Journal of Wildlife Management. 65(1): 141-147.

De Guth, E. Bonvaia. 1983. Variation in wood density of *Pinus elliottii* in relation to locality in Misiones and Corrientes provinces. Trabajos Tecnicos, 19 deg Congreso Tecnico sobre Celulosa y Papel, ATIPCA. 1: 79-91.

Delabraze, F.; Otto, H.J. 1982. Fire risk evaluation and development of forest fires, silvicultural measures to reduce the fire risk. Forest fire prevention and control. 62-84, 173-207.

Deng, Q.; Tan, S.S.; Su, K.J.; Li, J.P. 1994. The occurrence of shoot dieback of exotic pines in relation to stand growth and site conditions. Forest Research. 7(3): 346-350.

De Pinheiro, G.; De Pontinha, A.; De Souza, W.A. 1983. Determination of basic density of *Pinus elliottii* var. *elliottii* at three different stages in Itapteininga. Boletim Tecnico do Instituto Florestal. 37: 19-29.

De Pinheiro, G.; De Veiga, R.A.; Buzatto, O. 1984. Comparison of volume equations for *Pinus* species at the Moji Guacu experiment Station, Sao Paulo. Boletim Tecnico do Instituto Florestal. 38(1): 83-93.

De Pinheiro, G.; Mariano, G.; Coelho, L.C.C.; Muller, S.S. 1982. Volume determination in *Pinus elliottii* var. *elliottii* trees from basal diameter. Boletim Tecnico do Instituto Florestal. 36(1): 43-51.

De Pinheiro, G.; Romanelli, R.C.; De Souza, W.A. 1982. Volume tables for young stands of *Pinus elliottii* var. *elliottii*. Boletim Tecnico do Instituto Florestal. 36(3): 127-136.

De Ronde, C. 1982. The resistance of *Pinus* species to fire damage. South African Forestry Journal. 122: 22-27.

De Ronde, C. 1983. Controlled burning in pine stands in the Cape: the influence of crown scorch on tree growth and litterfall. South African Forestry Journal. 127: 39-41.

De Ronde, C. 1993. Spatial variation of forest floor loading in pine stands of the Tsitsikamma. South African Forestry Journal. 166: 1-7.

De Souza, M.L.; De Souza, D.M.; Lucchesi, L.A.C. 1982. Field capacity in two soil types under *Pinus elliottii* forest and native grassland. Revista do Setor de Ciencias Agrarias. 4(1): 17-22.

De Souza, S.M.; Hodge, G.R.; White, T.L. 1992. Indirect prediction of breeding values for fusiform rust resistance of slash pine parents using greenhouse tests. Forest Science. 38(1): 45-60.

De Souza, S.M.; White, T.L.; Hodge, G.R.; Schmidt, R.A. 1991. Genetic parameter estimates for greenhouse traits of slash pine artificially inoculated with fusiform rust fungus. Forest Science. 37(3): 836-848.

De Souza, S.M.; White, T.L.; Schmidt, R.A. [and others]. 1990. Evaluating fusiform rust symptoms on greenhouse-grown slash pine seedlings to predict field resistance. Plant Disease. 74(12): 969-974.

Devine, O.W.; Clutter, J.L. 1985. Prediction of survival in slash pine plantations infected with fusiform rust. Forest Science. 31(1): 88-94.

Dewald, L.; White, T.L.; Duryea, M.L. 1992. Growth and phenology of seedlings of four contrasting slash pine families in ten nitrogen regimes. Tree Physiology. 11(3): 255-269.

Dhakal, L.P.; White, T.L.; Hodge, G.R. 1996. Realized genetic gains from slash pine tree improvement. Silvae Genetica. 45(4): 190-197.

Dickens, E.D.; Van Lear, D.H.; Marsinko, A.P.C.; Sarigumba, T.I. 1989. Long-term effects of soil drainage, spacing, and site preparation on height and stand volume growth of slash pine. Gen. Tech. Rep. SO-GTR-74. New Orleans, LA: U.S. Department of Agriculture, Forest Service, Southern Forest Experiment Station. 225-230.

Dieters, M.J. 1996. Genetic parameters for slash pine (*Pinus elliottii*) grown in south-east Queensland, Australia: growth, stem straightness and crown defects. Forest genetics. 3(1): 27-36.

Dieters, M.J.; Hodge, G.R.; White, T.L. 1996. Genetic parameter estimates for resistance to rust (*Cronartium quercuum*) infection from full-sib tests of slash pine (*Pinus elliottii*), modeled as functions of rust incidence. Silvae Genetica. 45(4): 235-242.

Dieters, M.J.; White, T.L.; Hodge, G.R. 1995. Genetic parameter estimates for volume from full-sib tests of slash pine (*Pinus elliottii*). Canadian Journal of Forest Research. 25(8): 1397-1408.

Diner, A.M. 1991. Sterilization and germination processes for improving micropropagation efficiency of three southern pines. In: Proceedings - Southern Forest Tree Improvement Conference. 169-173.

Ding, A.F.; Yu, Y.C.; Chen, P.P. 2001. Effects of aluminum in soil on the tree root growth. Journal of Zhejiang Forestry College. 18(2): 119-122.

Dippon, D.R.; Shelton, J.T. 1983. Rate of return from fertilization of semimature slash pine plantations. Gen. Tech. Rep. SE-GTR-24. Asheville, NC: U.S. Department of Agriculture, Forest Service, Southeastern Forest Experiment Station. 302-311.

Dissmeyer, G.E.; Greis, J.G. 1983. Sound soil and water management is good economics. In: The Managed Slash Pine Ecosystem. Proceedings of a symposium held at the University of Florida. June 9-11, 1981. 194-202.

Distefano, J.F.; Gholz, H.L. 1989. Controls over net inorganic nitrogen transformations in an age sequence of *Pinus elliottii* plantations in north Florida. Forest Science. 35(4): 920-934.

Distefano, J.F.; Gholz, H.L. 1989. Nonsymbiotic biological dinitrogen fixation (acetylene reduction) in an age sequence of slash pine plantations in north Florida. Forest Science 35(3): 863-869.

Dixon, W.N. 1983. Clonal specificity of *Ips* and *Pityophthorus* spp. (Coleoptera: Scolytidae) on a slash pine seed orchard. Florida entomologist. 66(4): 515-517.

Dixon, W.N. 1983. Damage of slash pine female strobili by reproduction weevils. Florida Entomologist. 66(3): 364-365.

Dixon, W.N.; Corneil, J.A.; Wilkinson, R.C.; Foltz, J.L. 1984. Using stem char to predict mortality and insect infestation of fire-damaged slash pines. Southern Journal of Applied Forestry. 8(2): 85-88.

Dodge, R.E.; Fairbanks, R.G.; Benninger, L.K.; Maurrasse, F. 1983. Plant cover and biomass response to clear-cutting, site preparation, and planting in *Pinus elliottii* flatwoods. Science, USA. 219: 1421-1425.

Donald, D.G.M. 1982. The use of paraquat to stimulate resin production in pine trees. Wood, Southern Africa. 7(8): 11, 13-14, 16, 19, 21.

Donald. D.G.M. 1983. The application of fertilizer to pole stage pine crops. In: Forestry Quo Vadis? A proceedings of a symposium of the Southern African Institute of Forestry. Pp. 59-71.

Donald, D.G.M. 1983. Plant characteristics affecting survival and early growth. Mededeling, Fakulteit Bosbou, Universiiteit Stellenbosch. 98(1): 246-268.

Donald, D.G.M. 1984. A study in nursery efficiency and plant quality. South African Forestry Journal. 128: 12-14.

Donald, D.G.M. 1986. The separation of full dead seed from live seed in *Pinus elliottii*. In: Proceedings of the International Symposium on Nursery Management Practices for the Southern Pines. 83-88.

Donald, D.G.M.; Jacobs, C.B. 1990. The effect of storage time, temperature and container on the viability of the seed of four pine species. South African Forestry Journal. 154: 41-46.

Donald, D.G.M.; Kirby-Smith, J.H. 1982. Chemical weed control in the production of pines. South African Forestry Journal. 123: 14-18.

Donald, D.G.M.; Visser, L.B. 1989. The effects of Nitroacta (urea formaldehyde) on the survival and growth of *Pinus elliottii*. South African Forestry Journal. 151: 36-38.

Donald, D.G.M.; Young, I. 1982. The growth of pine seedlings in South African forest nurseries. South African Forestry Journal. 123: 36-50.

Dong, J.W.; Tu, Y.H.; Fan, H.H.; Zhang, X.Z. 1999. Appropriate management densities and cultivation patterns of slash pine forests for paper-pulp and resin. Ciencia Florestal. 9(2): 55-73.

Dorado, M.; Astini, E.; Verzino, G. [and others]. 1997. Growth curves for *Pinus elliottii*, *Pinus taeda* and *Pinus radiata* in two areas of the Calamuchita Valley (Argentina). Forest Ecology and Management. 95(2): 173-181.

Doren, R.F.; Platt, W.J.; Whiteaker, L.D. 1993. Density and size structure of slash pine stands in the everglades region of south Florida. Forest Ecology and Management. 59(3): 295-311.

Doudrick, R.L. 1996. Genetic recombinational and physical linkage analyses on slash pine. In: Unifying Plant Genomes. 53-60.

Doudrick, R.L.; Heslop-Harrison, J.S.; Nelson, C.D. [and others]. 1995. Karyotype of slash pine (*Pinus elliottii* var *elliottii*) using patterns of fluorescence *in situ* hybridization and fluorochrome banding. Journal of Heredity. 86(4): 289-296.

Doudrick, R.L.; Schmidtling, R.C.; Nelson, C.D. 1996. Host relationships of fusiform rust disease. I. Infection and pycnial production of slash pine and nearby tropical relatives. Silvae Genetica. 45(2): 142-149.

Doyle, J.H.; Botha, A.M.; Wingfield, B.D. 2002. Identification of pine hybrids using SSR loci. Southern African Forestry Journal. 193: 25-30.

Drooz, A.T.; Neunzig, H.H. 1988. Notes on the biology of two phycitines (Lepidoptera: Pyralidae) associated with *Toumeyella pini* (Homoptera: Coccidae) on pine. In: Proceedings of the Entomological Society of Washington. 90(1): 44-46.

Duncan, D.V.; Terry, T.A. 1983. Water management. In: The Managed Slash Pine Ecosystem. Proceedings of a symposium held at the University of Florida. June 9-11, 1981. 91-111.

Duncan, P.D.; White, T.L.; Hodge, G.R. 1996. First-year freeze hardiness of pure species and hybrid taxa of *Pinus elliottii* (Engelmann) and *Pinus caribaea* (Morelet). New Forests. 12(3): 223-241.

Dungey, H.S. 2001. Pine hybrids - a review of their use performance and genetics. Forest Ecology and Management. 148(1): 243-258.

Du Plooy, A.B.J. 1981. Growth rate and pulp quality of South African grown *Pinus caribeae* and *Pinus elliottii*. Australian Pulp and Paper Industry Technical Association. 35(3): 230-236.

Duryea, M.L. 1990. Nursery fertilization and top pruning of slash pine seedlings. Southern Journal of Applied Forestry. 14(2): 73-76.

Dwinell, L.D. 1985. Relative susceptibilities of five pine species to three populations of the pinewood nematode. Plant Disease. 69(5): 440-442.

Eccles, N.S.; Kritzinger, J.L.; Little, K.M. 1996. Appropriateness of non-destructive measures of young pine tree performance in weeding experiments. Southern African Forestry Journal. 178: 25-29.

Edwards, G.J.; Arvanitis, L.G. 1992. Reflection measurements of slash pine trees grown in an ozone atmosphere. In: Color Aerial Photography in Plant Sciences and Related Fields: Proceedings of the Thirteenth Biennial Workshop. 80-86.

Edwards, M.B.; McNab, W.H. 1981. Biomass prediction for young southern pines - an addendum. Journal of Forestry. 79(5): 291.

Ellis, T.H.; Mace, A.C., Jr. 1981. Forest research in Florida. Journal of Forestry. 79(8): 502-505, 515.

Enebak, S.A.; Wei, G.; Kloepper, J.W. 1998. Effects of plant growth-promoting rhizobacteria on loblolly and slash pine seedlings. Forest Science. 14(1): 139-144.

Epp, E.A.; Anderson, T.M. 1982. The effects of directional thinning to slash pine plantations. Research Note, Department of Forestry, Queensland. 33: 8p.

Escamilla, J.A.; Comerford, N.B. 1998. Phosphorus and potassium depletion by roots of field-grown slash pine: aerobic and hypoxic conditions. Forest Ecology and Management. 110(1): 25-33.

Escamilla, J.A.; Comerford, N.B. 2000. Phosphorus and potassium uptake by woody roots of twelve-year-old slash pine trees. Forest Ecology and Management. 129(1): 153-166.

Escamilla, J.A.; Comerford, N.B.; Neary, D.G. 1991. Spatial pattern of slash pine roots and its effect on nutrient uptake. Soil Science Society of America Journal. 55(6): 1716-1722.

Evans, J. 1999. Sustainability of plantation forestry: impact of species change and successive rotations of pine in the Usutu Forest, Swaziland. Southern African Forestry Journal. 184: 63-70.

Evans, L.S.; Fitzgerald, G.A. 1993. Histological effects of ozone on slash pine (Pinus elliottii var. densa). Environmental and Experimental Botany. 33(4): 505-513.

Evans, P.D.; Wingate-Hill, R.; Cunningham, R.B. 1997. The ability of physical treatments to reduce checking in preservative treated slash pine posts. Forest Products Journal. 47(5): 51-55.

Ewel, K.C.; Cropper, W.P., Jr.; Gholz, H.L. 1987. Soil CO_2 evolution in Florida slash pine plantations. I. Changes through time. Canadian Journal of Forest Research. 17(4): 325-329.

Ewel, K.C.; Cropper, W.P., Jr.; Gholz, H.L. 1987. Soil CO_2 evolution in Florida slash pine plantations. II. Importance of root respiration. Canadian Journal of Forest Research. 17(4): 330-333.

Exum, J.H.; McGlincy, J.A.; Speake, D.W. [and others]. 1987. Ecology of the eastern wild turkey in an intensively managed pine forest in southern Alabama. Bulletin, Tall Timbers Research Station. 23: 70p.

Falkenhagen, E.R. 1986. Reliability of measurement of open pollinated progency tests of Pinus elliottii in South Africa. South African forestry Journal. 136: 39-42.

Falkenhagen, E.R. 1989. Influences of testing sites on the genetic correlations in open-pollinated family trials of Pinus elliottii in South Africa. Theoretical and Applied Genetics. 77(6): 873-880.

Falkenhagen, E.R. 1989. Relationships between some genetic parameters and test environments in open-pollinated family trials of Pinus elliottii in South Africa. Theoretical and Applied Genetics. 77(6): 857-866.

Fang, C.; Moncrieff, J.B.; Gholz, H.L.; Clark, K.L. 1998. Soil CO_2 efflux and spatial variation in a Florida slash pine plantation. Plant and Soil. 205(2): 135-146.

Fang, S.Q.; Fu, Z.J.; Zhu, L.H. [and others]. 1998. A study on techniques for regulating pine seedling growth in the field. Journal of Zhejiang Forestry Science and Technology. 18(2): 15-21.

Fang, S.Z.; Cao, F.L.; Dai, P.Y. 1997. Effects of seed pretreatment methods on improving the salt tolerance of seedlings of three tree species. Journal of Plant Resources and Environment. 6(1): 35-40.

Fang, Z.; Bailey, R.L. 2001. Nonlinear mixed effects modeling for slash pine dominant height growth following intensive silvicultural treatments. Forest Science. 47(3): 287-300.

Fang, Z.; Bailey, R.L.; Shiver, B.D. 2001. A multivariate simultaneous prediction system for stand growth and yield with fixed and random effects. Forest Science. 47(4): 550-562.

Fang, Z.X.; Borders, B.E.; Bailey, R.L. 2000. Compatible volume-taper models for loblolly and slash pine based on a system with segmented-stem form factors. Forest Science. 46(1): 1-12.

Farrar, R.M., Jr. 1998. Fundamentals of uneven-aged management in southern pine. Misc. Publication - Tall Timbers Research Station. Tallahassee, FL. 9: 63p.

Fatzinger, C.W.; Dixon, W.N. 1996. Degree-day models for predicting levels of attack by slash pine flower thrips. (Thysanoptera: Phlaeothripidae) and the phenology of female strobilus development on slash pine. Environmental Entomology. 25(4): 727-735.

Fatzinger, C.W.; Merkel, E.P.; Mantie, R.; Goldman, S.E. 1984. Control of cone and seed insects in slash pine seed orchards with acephate sprays. Journal of the Georgia Entomological Society. 19(1): 102-110.

Fatzinger, C.W.; Muse, H.D.; Miller, T.; Bhattacharyya, H. 1990. Survey and pest monitoring system for southern pine seed orchards. Southern Journal of Applied Forestry. 14(3): 147-159.

Fatzinger, C.W.; Wilkinson, R.C.; Berisford, C.W. 1983. Insects affecting the managed slash pine ecosystem. In: The Managed Slash Pine Ecosystem. Proceedings of a symposium held at the University of Florida. June 9-11, 1981. 228-256.

Fatzinger, C.W.; Yates, H.O., III; Barber, L.R. 1992. Evaluation of aerial applications of acephate and other insecticides for control of cone and seed insects in southern pine seed orchards. Journal of Entomological Science. 27(2): 172-184.

Ferraz, L.C.C.B. 1981. Nematode parasites of Eucalyptus, Pinus and other species of forest trees cultivated in Sao Paulo State, Brazil. Dissertation abstracts. 110-113.

Fight, R.D.; Dutrow, G.F. 1981. Financial comparison of forest fertilization in the Pacific Northwest and the Southeast. Journal of Forestry. 79(4): 214-215.

Figueiredo Fihlo, A.; Machado, S.A.; Carneiro, M.R.A. 2000. Testing accuracy of log volume calculation procedures against water displacement techniques (xylometer). Canadian Journal of Forest Research. 30(6): 990-997.

Figueiredo Filho, A.; Schaaf, L.B. 1999. Comparison between predicted volumes estimated by taper equations and true volumes obtained by the water displacement technique (xylometer). Canadian Journal of Forest Research. 29(4): 451-461.

Fisher, H.M.; Stone, E.L. 1990. Active potassium uptake by slash pine roots from O_2-depleted solutions. Forest Science. 36(3): 582-598.

Fisher, H.M.; Stone, E.L. 1990. Air-conducting porosity in slash pine roots from saturated soils. Forest Science. 36(1): 18-33.

Fisher, H.M.; Stone, E.L. 1991. Iron oxidation at the surfaces of slash pine roots from saturated soils. Soil Science Society of America Journal. 55(4): 1123-1129.

Fisher, R.F. 1983. Silvical characteristics. In: The Managed Slash Pine Ecosystem. Proceedings of a symposium held at the University of Florida. June 9-11, 1981. 48-55.

Fisher, R.F.; Adrian, F. 1981. Bahiagrass impairs slash pine seedling growth. Tree Planters' Notes. 32(2): 19-21.

Fisher, R.F.; Garbett, W.S.; Underhill, E.M. 1981. Effects of fertilization on healthy and pitch canker-infected pines. Southern Journal of Applied Forestry. 5(2): 77-79.

Fisher, R.F.; Pritchett, W.L. 1982. Slash pine growth response to different nitrogen fertilizers. Soil Science Society of America Journal. 46(1): 133-136.

Fiskell, J.G.A.; Pritchett, W.L.; Maftoun, M. 1984. Effects of three sewage sludges on slash pine seedlings grown in three acid sandy soils. In: Soil and Crop Science Society of Florida Proceedings. 43: 71-76.

Foltz, J.L.; Corneil, J.A.; Reich, R.M. 1985. Procedures for sampling six-spined Ips populations in slash pine. Gen. Tech. Rep. SO-GTR-56. New Orleans, LA: U.S. Department of Agriculture, Forest Service, Southern Forest Experiment Station. 6-12.

Fontaine, M.S.; Foltz, J.L. 1982. Field studies of a male-released aggregation pheromone in Pissodes nemorensis Deodar weevil, pest of southern pines. Environmental entomology. 11(4): 881-883.

Ford-Logan, J.L.; Foster, G.S.; Van Buijtenen, J.P. 1991. Early field performance of rust-resistant clones of slash pine: a combination of direct and indirect selection. In: Proceedings - Southern Forest Tree Improvement Conference. 225-232.

Foster, T.E.; Brooks, J.R. 2001. Long-term trends in growth of Pinus palustris and Pinus elliottii along a hydrological gradient in central Florida. Canadian Journal of Forest Research. 31(10): 1661-1670.

Fraedrich, B.R.; Witcher, W. 1982. Influence of fertilizations on pitch canker development on three southern pine species. Plant Disease. 66(10): 938-940.

Fraedrich, S.W.; Miller, T. 1995. Mycroflora associated with slash-pine seeds from cones collected at seed orchards and cone-processing facilities in the South-eastern USA. European Journal of Forest Pathology. 25(2): 73-82.

Fraedrich, S.W.; Miller, T.; Zarnoch, S.J. 1994. Factors affecting the incidence of black seed rot in slash pine. Canadian Journal of Forest Research. 24(8): 1717-1725.

Frampton, L.J., Jr.; Hodges, J.F. 1989. Nursery rooting of cuttings from seedlings of slash and loblolly pine. Southern Journal of Applied Forestry. 13(3): 127-132.

Frampton, L.J., Jr.; Rockwood, D.L. 1983. Genetic variation in traits important for energy utilization of sand and slash pines. Silvae Genetica. 32(1): 18-23.

Francis, P.J. 1984. The role of cultivation in plantation establishment in subtropical Eastern Australia. In: Proceedings IUFRO Symposium on Site and Productivity of Fast Growing Plantations. 2: 579-587.

Francis, P.J.; Bacon, G.J.; Gordon, P. 1984. Effect of ripping and nitrogen fertilizer on the growth and windfirmness of slash pine on a shallow soil of the Queensland coastal lowlands. Australian Forestry. 47(2): 90-94.

Friemond, S. 1997. Fertilizing pines at planting in the summer rainfall forestry region: Mpumalanga trial series. ICRF Bulletin Series. 12: 20p.

Froelich, R.C. 1987. Sawtimber as an alternative forest management strategy for sites with a high fusiform rust hazard. Southern Journal of Applied Forestry. 11(4): 228-231.

Froelich, R.C. 1988. Determining the effects of fusiform rust on forest productivity. In: Proceedings of the Society of American Foresters National Convention. Pp. 68-71.

Froelich, R.C. 1989. Annual variation in fusiform rust infection of slash and loblolly pine seed lots in time-replicated plantings. Canadian Journal of Forest Research. 19(12): 1531-1537.

Froelich, R.C.; Nance, W.L.; Snow, G.A. 1981. Growth of slash pine seedlings and saplings after infection with the fusiform rust fungus. Phytopathology. 71(8): 875.

Froelich, R.C.; Nance, W.L.; Snow, G.A. 1983. Size and growth of planted slash pines infected with fusiform rust. Forest Science. 29(3): 527-534.

Froelich, R.C.; Schmidtling, R.C. 1998. Survival of slash pine having fusiform rust disease varies with year of first stem infection and severity. Southern Journal of Applied Forestry. 22(2): 96-100.

Froelich, R.C.; Snow, G.A. 1986. Predicting site hazard to fusiform rust. Forest Science. 32(1): 21-35.

Gagne, R.J.; Beavers, G.M. 1984. Contarinia spp. (Diptera: Cecidomyiidae) from shoots of slash pine (Pinus elliottii Engelm.) with the description of a new species injurious to needles. Florida Entomologist. 67(2): 221-228.

Gagnon, K.G.; Johnson, J.D. 1988. Bud development and dormancy in slash and loblolly pine. I. Speed of budbreak and second year height as related to lifting date. New Forests. 2(4): 261-268.

Gagnon, K.G.; Johnson, J.D. 1988. Bud development and dormancy in slash and loblolly pine. II. Effect of ethephon applications. New Forests. 2(4): 269-274.

Gao, Q.; Zhao, P.; Zeng, X. [and others]. 2002. A model of stomatal conductance to quantify the relationship between leaf transpiration, microclimate and soil water stress. Plant, Cell and Environment. 25(11): 1373-1381.

Gao, Z.H.; Chen, S.W.; Jiang, M.D. [and others]. 1999. Water and soil conservation effectiveness of different types of vegetation of subtropical rocky coast. Journal of Xhejiang Forestry College. 16(4): 380-386.

Gao, Z.H.; Chen, S.W.; Lu, T.G. [and others]. 2000. Studies on variation in growth of *Pinus elliottii* under different terraced conditions along a rocky coast. Journal of Zhejiang Forestry Science and Technology. 20(6): 16-20.

Gaskin, J.W.; Nutter, W.L.; McMullen, T.M. 1989. Comparison of nutrient losses by harvesting and site preparation practices in the Georgia Piedmont and Coastal Plain. Georgia Forest Research Paper. 77: 7p.

Gatch, J.A.; Harrington, T.B.; Price, T.S.; Edwards, M.B. 1999. Stem sinuosity, tree size, and pest injury of machine-planted trees with and without bent taproots: a comparison of loblolly and slash pine. Gen. Tech. Rep. SRS-GTR-30. Asheville, NC: U.S. Department of Agriculture, Forest Service, Southern Research Station. 359-361.

Ge, Z.H. 1981. A study on the resistance of several pine species to the bast scale (*Matsucoccus matsumurae* Kuwana). Scientia Silvae Sinicae. 17(4): 400-405.

Geldenhuys, C.J. 1997. Native forest regeneration in pine and eucalypt plantations in Northern Province, South Africa. Forest Ecology and Management. 99(1): 101-115.

Gering, L.R.; Pienaar, L.V. 1988. Stand density effects for site-prepared slash pine plantations in the flatwoods of Georgia and north Florida. Gen. Tech. Rep. NC-GTR-120. St. Paul, MN: U.S. Department of Agriculture, Forest Service, North Central Research Station. 596-603.

Germishuizen, P.J.; Smale, P.J. 1982. The use of controlled burning in an established pine stand as a means of fire protection at Usutu Pulp Company Limited (Swaziland). In: Usutu Pulp Company fire seminar. 10-12.

Gholz, H.L.; Clark, K.L. 2002. Energy exchange across a chronosequence of slash pine forests in Florida. Agricultural and Forest Meteorology. 112(2): 87-102.

Gholz, H.L.; Cropper, W.P., Jr. 1991. Carbohydrate dynamics in mature *Pinus elliottii* var. *elliottii* trees. Canadian Journal of Forest Research. 21(12): 1742-1747.

Gholz, H.L.; Fisher, R.F. 1982. Organic matter production and distribution in slash pine plantations. Ecology. 63(6): 1827-1839.

Gholz, H.L.; Fisher, R.F. 1984. The limits of productivity: fertilization and nutrient cycling in Coastal Plain slash pine forests. In: Proceedings, Sixth North American Forest Soils Conference, University of Tennessee. 105-120.

Gholz, H.L.; Fisher, R.F.; Pritchett, W.L. 1985. Nutrient dynamics in slash pine plantation ecosystems. Ecology. 66(3): 647-659.

Gholz, H.L.; Guerin, D.N.; Cropper, W.P., Jr. 1999. Phenology and productivity of saw palmetto (*Serenoa repens*) in a north Florida slash pine plantation. Canadian Journal of Forest Research. 29(8): 1248-1253.

Gholz, H.L.; Hendry, L.C.; Cropper, W.P., Jr. 1986. Organic matter dynamics of fine roots in plantations of slash pine (*Pinus elliottii*) in north Florida. Canadian Journal of Forest Research. 16(3): 529-538.

Gholz, H.L.; Perry, C.S.; Cropper, W.P., Jr.; Hendry, L.C. 1985. Litterfall, decomposition, and nitrogen and phosphorus dynamics in chronosequence of slash pine (*Pinus elliottii*) plantations. Forest Science. 31(2): 463-478.

Gholz, H.L.; Vogel, S.A.; Cropper, W.P., Jr. [and others]. 1991. Dynamics of canopy structure and light interception in *Pinus elliottii* stands, north Florida. Ecological Monographs. 61(1): 33-51.

Gholz, H.L.; Wedin, D.A.; Smitherman, S.M. [and others]. 2000. Long-term dynamics of pine and hardwood litter in contrasting environments: toward a global model of decomposition. Global Change Biology. 6(7): 751-765.

Gibson, M.D.; McMillin, C.W.; Shoulders, E. 1986. Moisture content and specific gravity of the four major southern pines under the same age and site conditions. Wood and Fiber Science. 18(3): 428-435.

Gjerstad, D.H.; South, D.B. 1981. Preemergence weed control in loblolly, slash, shortleaf, and eastern white pine nursery seedbeds. Canadian Journal of Forest Research. 11(4): 848-853.

Glufke, C.; Finger, C.A.G.; Schneider, P.R. 1997. Growth of *Pinus elliottii* Engelm. under different thinning intensities. Ciencia Florestal. 7(1): 11-25.

Goddard, R.E.; Rockwood, D.L. 1981. Cooperative forest genetics research program. Research report - University of Florida, School of Forest Resources and Conservation. 31: 17p.

Goddard, R.E.; Rockwood, D.L.; Kok, H. 1982. Cooperative forest genetics research program. Twenty-fourth progress report. Research report-University of Florida, School of Forest Resources and Conservation. 33: 25p.

Goddard, R.E.; Wells, O.O.; Squillace, A.E. 1983. Genetic improvements of slash pine. In: The Managed Slash Pine Ecosystem. Proceedings of a symposium held at the University of Florida. June 9-11, 1981. 56-68.

Goldammer, J.G. 1983. Controlled burning as a method of fire management in pine plantations in Southern Brazil. Friburger Waldschutz-Abhandlungen. 4: 211-239.

Goncalves, R.; Bartholomeu, A. 2000. Assessment of the performance of non destructive tests in beams of *Eucalyptus citriodora* and *Pinus elliottii* wood. Revista Brasileira de Engenharia Agricola e Ambiental. 4(2): 269-274.

Gong, P.C.; Yin, R.S. 2001. Slash pine plantation management with stochastic prices: optimal harvest strategy and silvicultural regime. Arbetsrapport - Institution for Skogsekonomi, Sveriges Lantbruksuniversitet. 304: 18p.

Gong, X.D.; Liang, Z.C. 1988. The resistance of slash pine to brown spot needle blight. Journal of South China Agricultural University. 9(1): 54-59.

Gonzalez, F.E. 1983. Southern pine release with hexazinone formulations. In: Proceedings, Southern Weed Science Society, 36th Annual Meeting. 223-229.

Gorden, R.; Miller, J.H.; Brewer, C. 1981. Site preparation treatments and nutrient loss following complete harvest using the Nicholson-Koch mobile chipper. Gen. Tech. Rep. SO-GTR-34. New Orleans, LA: U.S. Department of Agriculture, Forest Service, Southern Forest Experiment Station. 79-84.

Gordon, P. 1984. Height/diameter relationships for slash pine in south east Queensland. Technical Note, Department of Forestry, Queensland. 12: 10.

Gough, G.; Barnes, R.D. 1984. A comparison of three methods of wood density assessment in a *Pinus elliottii* progency test. South African Forestry Journal. 128: 22-25.

Gous, S.F. 2000. Targeted spot vegetation management in *Pinus radiata* and *P. elliottii* plantations, Tsitsikamma, South Africa. Southern African Forestry Journal. 188: 7-11.

Green, E.J.; Straswderman, W.E. 1996. Predictive posterior distributions from a Bayasian version of a slash pine yield model. Forest Science. 42(4): 456-464.

Greene, W.D.; Lanford, B.L. 1985. Potential for second thinnings in southern pine plantations. Gen. Tech. Rep. SO-GTR-54. New Orleans, LA: U.S. Department of Agriculture, Forest Service, Southern Forest Experiment Station. 212-215.

Grelen, H.E. 1983. Comparison of seasons and frequencies of burning in a young slash pine plantation. Res. Pap. SO-RP-185. New Orleans, LA: U.S. Department of Agriculture, Forest Service, Southern Forest Experiment Station. 5p.

Grelen, H.E.; Pearson, H.A.; Thill, R.E. 1985. Establishment and growth of slash pine on grazed cutover range in central Louisiana. Southern Journal of Applied Forestry. 9(4): 232-236.

Grelen, H.E.; Pearson, H.A.; Thill, R.E. 1985. Response of slash pines to grazing from generation to the first pulpwood thinning. Gen. Tech. Rep. SO-GTR-54. New Orleans, LA: U.S. Department of Agriculture, Forest Service, Southern Forest Experiment Station. 523-527.

Grider, G.E. 1984. A computer simulation model for stand structure, yield, growth, and financial analysis of thinned, site-prepared, slash pine plantations. University of Georgia Research bulletin 308: 90p.

Griggs, M.M.; Dinus, R.J.; Snow, G.A. 1984. Inoculum source and density influence assessment of fusiform rust resistance in slash pine. Plant Disease. 9: 770-774.

Griggs, M.M.; Squillace, A.E. 1982. Inheritance of yellow oleoresin in shortleaf and slash pine. The Journal of Heredity. 73(6): 405-407.

Griggs, M.M.; Walkinshaw, C.H. 1981. Inheritance of seedling resistance to fusiform rust *Cronartium quercuum fusiforme* in five slash pine parents. Phytopathology. 71(2): 221.

Griggs, M.M.; Walkinshaw, C.H. 1982. Diallel analysis of genetic resistance to *Cronartium quercuum*, f.sp. *fusiforme* in slash pine. Phytopathology. 72(7): 816-818.

Guldin, R.W. 1982. Nursery costs and benefits of container-grown southern pine seedlings. Southern Journal of Applied Forestry. 6(2): 93-99.

Guldin, R.W. 1983. Regeneration costs using container-grown southern pine seedlings. Res. Pap. SO-RP-187. New Orleans, LA: U.S. Department of Agriculture, Forest Service, Southern Forest Experiment Station. 29p.

Guldin, R.W. 1984. Site characteristics and preparation practices influence costs of hand-planting southern pine. Journal of Forestry. 82(2): 97-100.

Guldin, R.W.; Farrar, R.M., Jr. 1983. Computation of southern pine site index using a TI-59 calculator. Gen. Tech. Rep. SO-GTR-48. New Orleans, LA: U.S. Department of Agriculture, Forest Service, Southern Forest Experiment Station. 8p.

Guo, D.; Mou, P.; Jones, R.H.; Mitchell, R.J. 2002. Temporal changes in spatial patterns of soil moisture following disturbance: an experimental approach. Journal of Ecology. 90(2): 338-347.

Gurgel Garrido, L.M.; Cruz, S.F.; Ribas, C. 1999. Genotype environment interactions in *Pinus elliottii* var. *elliottii*. Revista do Instituto Florestal. 11(1): 1-12.

Gurumurti, K.; Srivastava, V.K. 1982. Estimation of needle area in pines. Indian Journal of Forestry. 5(1): 52-54.

Gurumurit, K.; Srivastava, V.K. 1984. Studies on growth correlations in *Pinus elliottii*. Indian Forester. 110(3): 269-273.

Gwaze, D.P. 1999. Performance of some interspecific F$_1$ pine hybrids in Zimbabwe. Forest Genetics. 6(4): 283-289.

Gwaze, D.P. 2001. Interspecific hybrids in Zimbabwe: status review and future challenges. Southern African Forestry Journal. 192: 85-91.

Haack, R.A. Growth and survival of slash pine seedlings in a Florida nursery. Tree Planters' Notes. 39(2): 30-36.

Haack, R.A.; Foltz, J.L.; Wilkinson, R.C. 1984. Longevity and fecundity of *Ips calligraphus* (Coleoptera: Scolytidae) in relation to slash pine phloem thickness. Annals of the Entomological Society of America. 77(6): 657-662.

Haack, R.A.; Foltz, J.L.; Wilkinson, R.C. 1985. Effects of temperature and slash pine phloem thickness on *Ips calligraphus* life processes. Gen. Tech. Rep. SO-GTR-56. New Orleans, LA: U.S. Department of Agriculture, Forest Service, Southern Forest Experiment Station. 102-113.

Haack, R.A.; Wilkinson, R.C. 1987. Phoresy by *Dendrochernes* pseudoscorpions on Cerambycidae (Coleoptera) and Aulacidae (Hymenoptera). American Midland Naturalist. 117(2): 369-373.

Haack, R.A.; Wilkinson, R.C.; Foltz, J.L. 1987. Plasticity in life-history traits on the bark beetle *Ips calligraphus* as influenced by phloem thickness. Oecologia 72(1): 32-38.

Haack, R.A.; Wilkinson, R.C.; Foltz, J.L.; Corneil, J.A. 1984. Gallery construction and oviposition by *Ips calligraphus* (Coleoptera: Scolytidae) in relation to slash pine phloem thickness and temperature. Canadian Entomologist. 116(4): 625-632.

Haack, R.A.; Wilkinson, R.C.; Foltz, J.L.; Corneil, J.A. 1987. Spatial attack pattern, reproduction, and brood development of *Ips calligraphus* (Coleoptera: Scolytidae) in relation to slash pine phloem thickness: a field study. Environmental Entomology. 16(2): 428-436.

Hacker, W.D.; Bilan, M.V. 1991. Site index curves for loblolly and slash pine plantations in the post oak belt of east Texas. Southern Journal of Applied Forestry. 15(2): 97-100.

Hacker, W.D.; Bilan, M.V. 1997. Site factors affecting growth of slash pine in the Texas post oak belt. Southern Journal of Applied Forestry. 21(2): 71-74.

Hain, F.P.; Mawby, W.D.; Cook, S.P.; Arthur, F.H. 1983. Host conifer reaction to stem invasion. Zeitschrift fur Angewandte Entomologie. 96(3): 247-256.

Haines, L.W.; Gooding, J. 1983. Site selection: slash pine versus other species. In: The Managed Slash Pine Ecosystem. Proceedings of a symposium held at the University of Florida. June 9-11, 1981. 112-130.

Hamilton, R.B.; Yurkunas, V.G. 1987. Avian use of habitats in the longleaf-slash pine forests of Louisiana. Gen. Tech. Rep. SO-GTR-68. New Orleans, LA: U.S. Department of Agriculture, Forest Service, Southern Forest Experiment Station.125-137.

Han, N.L.; Zhao, J.N.; Liu, Z.X. [and others]. 1997. The high seed yield tests in slash pine (*Pinus elliottii* Engelm.) orchard in Changle Forest Farm. Forest Research. 10(1): 70-75.

Hanlin, H.G.; Martin, F.D.; Wike, L.D.; Bennett, S.H. 2000. Terrestrial activity, abundance and species richness of amphibians in managed forests in South Carolina. American Midland Naturalist. 143(1): 70-83.

Hansen, R.S. 1987. Growth and development of southern pine plantations in the northern post oak tension zone of Texas. Dissertation Abstracts International. 47(9): 3606.

Hansen, R.S.; Bilan, M.V. 1989. Height growth of loblolly and slash pine plantations in the northern post-oak belt of Texas. Southern Journal of Applied Forestry. 13(1): 5-8.

Hanula, J.L.; DeBarr, G.L.; Harris, W.M.; Berisford, C.W. 1984. Factors affecting catches of male coneworms, *Diorcytria* spp. (Lepidoptera: Pyralidae) in pheromone traps in southern pine seed orchards. Journal of Economic Entomology. 77(6): 1449-1453.

Harding, R.B.; Hollis, C.A. 1993. Growth response of slash pine to intensive drainage and bedding. Gen. Tech. Rep. SO-GTR-93. New Orleans, LA: U.S.Department of Agriculture, Forest Service, Southern Forest Experiment Station. 243-246.

Harding, R.B.; Jokela, E.J. 1994. Long-term effects of forest fertilization on site organic matter and nutrients. Soil Science Society of America Journal. 58(1): 216-221.

Hare, R.C. 1981. Nitric acid promotes pine seed germination. Res. Note. SO-RN-281. New Orleans, LA: U.S. Department of Agriculture, Forest Service, Southern Forest Experiment Station. 2p.

Hare, R.C. 1982. Effect of nine growth retardants applied to loblolly and slash pine. Canadian Journal of Forest Research. 12(1): 112-114.

Hare, R.C. 1984. Application method of timing of gibberllin a 4/7 treatments for increasing pollen conebud production in southern pines. Canadian Journal of Forest Research. 14(1): 128-131.

Hare, R.C. 1984. EL-500: an effective growth retardant for dwarfing southern pine seedlings. Canadian Journal of Forest Research. 14(1): 123-127.

Hare, R.C. 1984. Nitrapyrin (2-chloro-6-(trichloromethyl)-pyridine), a nitrification inhibitor, may replace fertilizers for promoting cone bud production in southern pine seed orchards. Canadian Journal of Forest Research. 14(2): 206-208.

Hare, R.C.; Snow, G.A. 1983. Control of fusiform rust in slash pine with Bayleton (triadimefon) seed treatment. Res. Note SO-RN-288. New Orleans, LA: U.S. Department of Agriculture, Forest Service, Southern Forest Experiment Station. 4 p.

Harms, W.R. 1996. An old-growth definition for wet pine forests, woodlands, and savannas. Gen. Tech. Rep. SRS-GTR-2. Asheville, NC: U.S. Department of Agriculture, Forest Service, Southern Research Station. 7p.

Harrell, J.B. 1987. The development of techniques for the use of trees in the reclamation of phosphate lands. FIPR Publication No.03-001-049: 78p.

Harrington, T.B.; Hendrick, R.L. 1999. Tree growth and resource availability in response to simulated canopy gaps in mature slash pine forest. Gen. Tech. Rep. SRS-GTR-30. Asheville, NC: U.S. Department of Agriculture, Forest Service, Southern Research Station. 374-376.

Harrington, T.B.; Minogue, P.J.; Lauer, D.K.; Ezell, A.W. 1998. Two-year development of southern pine seedlings and associated vegetation following spray-and-burn site preparation. New Forests. 15(1): 89-106.

Hart, R.; Biggs, R.H.; Webb, P.G. 1986. Effect of simulated acid rain on growth and yield of Valencia orange, Flordade tomato and slash pine in Florida. Environmental Toxicology and Chemistry. 5(1): 79-85.

Hayes, J.L.; Meeker, J.R.; Foltz, J.L.; Strom, B.L. 1996. Suppression of bark beetles and protection of pines in the urban environment: a case study. Journal of Arboriculture. 22(2): 67-74.

Haywood, J.D. 1981. Discontinuous mounding as a site treatment on a flatwoods soil. Gen. Tech. Rep. SO-GTR-34. New Orleans, LA: U.S. Department of Agriculture, Forest Service, Southern Forest Experiment Station. 88-91.

Haywood, J.D. 1983. Response to planted pines to site preparation on a Beauregard-Caddo soil. Gen. Tech. Rep. SE-GTR-24. Asheville, NC: U.S. Department of Agriculture, Forest Service, Southeastern Forest Experiment Station. 14-17.

Haywood, J.D. 1983. Small topographic differences affect slash pine response to site preparation and fertilization. Southern Journal of Applied Forestry. 7(3): 145-148.

Haywood, J.D. 1987. Response of slash pine planted on mounds in central and southwestern Louisiana. New Forests. 1(4): 291-300.

Haywood, J.D. 1994. Early growth reductions in short rotation loblolly and slash pine in central Louisiana. Southern Journal of Applied Forestry. 18(1): 35-39.

Haywood, J.D. 1995. Responses of young slash pine on poorly drained to somewhat poorly drained silt loam soils to site preparation and fertilization treatments. Res. Note. SO-RN-379. New Orleans, LA: U.S. Department of Agriculture, Forest Service, Southern Forest Experiment Station. 5p.

Haywood, J.D.; Barnett, J.P. 1994. Comparing methods of artificially regenerating loblolly and slash pines: container planting, bareroot planting, and spot seeding. Tree Planters' Notes. 45(2): 63-67.

Haywood, J.D.; Tiarks, A.E.; Shoulders, E. 1990. Loblolly and slash pine height and diameter are related to soil drainage in winter on poorly drained silt loams. New Forests. 4(2): 81-96.

Haywood, J.D.; Tiarks, A.E.; Snow, G.A. 1994. Combinations of fungicide and cultural practices influence the incidence and impact of fusiform rust in slash pine plantations. Southern Journal of Applied Forestry. 18(2): 53-59.

Hedman, C.W.; Grace, S.L.; King, S.E. 2000. Vegetation composition and structure of southern Coastal Plain pine forests: an ecological comparison. Forest Ecology and Management. 134(1): 233-247.

Hendry, L.C.; Gholz, H.L. 1986. Aboveground phenology in north Florida slash pine plantations. Forest Science. 32(3): 779-788.

Highsmith, M.T.; Frampton, J.; O'Malley, D. [and others]. 2001. Susceptibility of parent and interspecific F1 hybrid pine trees to tip moth damage in a coastal North Carolina planting. Canadian Journal of Forest Research. 31(5): 919-923.

Hillig, É.; Haselein, C.R.; Santini, E.J. 2002. Mechanical properties of flakeboard made from pine, eucalypts and wattle wood. Ciencia Florestal. 12(1): 59-70.

Hodge, G.R.; Purnell, R.C. 1993. Genetic parameter estimates for wood density, transition age, and radial growth in slash pine. Canadian Journal of Forest Research. 23(9): 1881-1891.

Hodge, G.R.; Schmidt, R.A.; White, T.L. 1990. Substantial realized gains from mass selection of fusiform rust-free trees in highly infected stands of slash pine. Southern Journal of Applied Forestry. 14(3): 143-146.

Hodge, G.R.; White, T.L. 1992. Genetic parameter estimates for growth traits at different ages in slash pine and some implications for breeding. Silvae Genetica. 41(4): 252-262.

Hodge, G.R.; White, T.L.; Powell, G.L.; De Souza, S.M. 1989. Predicted genetic gains from one generation of slash pine tree improvement. Southern Journal of Applied Forestry. 13(1): 51-56.

Hodge, G.R.; White, T.L.; Schmidt, R.A.; Allen, J.E. 1993. Stability of rust infection ratios for resistant and susceptible slash and loblolly pine across rust hazard levels. Southern Journal of Applied Forestry. 17(4): 188-192.

Hodges, A.W.; Johnson, J.D. 1997. Borehole oleoresin production from slash pine. Southern Journal of Applied Forestry. 21(3): 108-115.

Hodges, A.W.; Williams, G. 1993. Pine gum in a bottle? A sealed collection system for production of high purity oleoresin. Naval Stores Review. 103(3): 2-8.

Hodgson, T.J. 1983. The relationship between heat unit accumulation and the growth and development of tree seedlings. Mededeling, Fakulteit Bosbou, Uiversiteit Stellenbosch. 98(1): 221-232.

Hof, J.G. 1983. Comparing management alternatives with low and high energy input levels for Florida slash pine plantations. Forest Science. 29(1): 78-84.

Hogsett, W.E.; Plocher, M.; Wildman, V. [and others]. 1985. Growth response of two varieties of slash pine seedlings to chronic ozone exposures. Canadian Journal of Botany. 63(12): 2369-2376.

Holder, C.D. 2000. Geography of *Pinus elliottii* Engelm. and *Pinus palustris* Mill. Journal of Biogeography. 27(2): 311-318.

Hollis, C.A.; Smith, J.E.; Fisher, R.F. 1982. Allelopathic effects of common understory species on germination and growth of southern pines. Forest Science. 28(3): 509-515.

Hong, S.S.; Hu, B.T.; Huang, X.Q. [and others]. 1997. Five years' growth response of slash pine to fertilization. Forest Research. 10(6): 624-628.

Hood, I.A.; Ramsden, M. 1997. Sapstain and decay following fire in stands of *Pinus elliottii* var. *elliottii* near Beerburrum, south east Queensland. Australian Forestry. 60(1): 715.

Hood, W.M.; Berisford, C.W.; Hedden, R.L. 1985. Oviposition preferences of the Nantucket pine tip moth (Lipedoptera: Tortricidae) on loblolly and slash pine. Journal of Entomological Science. 20(2): 204-206.

Hough, W.A. 1982. Phytomass and nutrients in the understory and forest floor of slash/longleaf pine stands. Forest Science. 28(2): 359-372.

Howell, R.A.; Leach, G.N.; Nutter, D.E.; Steltencamp, M.S. 1984. Some age-associated trends of planted slash pines as related to kraft pulping. In: Proceedings of the Symposium on Utilization of the Changing Wood Source in the Southern United States. 243-260.

Hu, S.C.; Burns, P.Y.; Liliholm, R.J. 1985. Slash pine. A bibliography 1816-1982. Research Report, School of Forestry, Wildlife and Fisheries, Louisiana State University. 4: 152p.

Huang, J.W.; Kuhlman, E.G. 1989. Recovery and pathogenicity of *Rhizoctonia solani* and binucleate Rhizoctonia-like fungi in forest nurseries. Plant Disease. 73(12): 968-972.

Huang, J.W.; Kuhlman, E.G. 1990. Fungi associated with damping-off of slash pine seedlings in Georgia. Plant Disease. 74(1): 27-30.

Huang, J.W.; Kuhlman, E.G. 1991. Formulation of a soil amendment to control damping-off of slash pine seedlings. Phytopathology. 81(2): 163-170.

Huang, J.W.; Kuhlman, E.G. 1991. Mechanisms inhibiting damping-off pathogens of slash pine seedlings with a formulated soil amendment. Phytopathology. 81(2): 171-177.

Hubbard, S.D.; Walkinshaw, C.H.; Anderson, R.L. 1981. Selecting field resistant slash pine families through greenhouse inoculation. Phytopathology. 71(8): 882.

Huber, C.M.; Hain, F.P. 1984. Oviposition and survival of the introduced pine sawfly, *Diprion similis* (Hymenoptera: Diprionidae), on selected conifers in North Carolina. Journal of the Georgia Entomological Society. 19(2): 158-165.

Hunt, E.V., Jr.; Lenhart, J.D. 1986. Fusiform rust trends in east Texas. Southern Journal of Applied Forestry. 10(4): 215-216.

Hunt, S.M.; Simpson, J.A. 1985. Effects of low intensity prescribed fire on the growth and nutrition of a slash pine plantation. Australian Forest Research. 15(1): 67-77.

Irntoto, B.; Tan, K.H.; Sommer, H.E. 1993. Effect of humic acid on callus culture of slash pine (*Pinus elliottii* Engelm.). Journal of Plant Nutrition. 16(6): 1109-1118.

Irwin, K.M.; Duryea, M.L.; Stone, E.L. 1998. Fall-applied nitrogen improves performance of 1-0 slash pine nursery seedlings after outplanting. Southern Journal of Applied Forestry. 22(2): 111-116.

Jack, S.B.; Stone, E.L.; Swindel, B.F. 1988. Stem form changes in unthinned slash and loblolly pine stands following midrotation fertilization. Southern Journal of Applied Forestry. 12(2): 90-97.

Jain, S.M.; Dong, N.; Newton, R.J. 1989. Somatic embyogenesis in slash pine (*Pinus elliottii*) from immature embryos culture *in vitro*. Plant Science. 65(2): 233-241.

Jewell, F.F. 1994. Histopathology of *Pinus elliottii* var. *elliottii* needles infected by *Ploiodema hedgcockii*. European Journal of Forest Pathology. 24(6): 323-334.

Jewell, F.F.; Jewell, D.C.; Walkinshaw, C.H. 1982. Histopathology of anatomical mechanisms for resistance to fusiform rust in slash pine. In: Proceedings 3rd International Workshop on Genetics of Host-Parasite Interactions in Forestry. 110-118.

Jha, M.N.; Pande, P.; Rathore, R.K. 1984. Soil fertility status under different tropical pine plantations. India Journal of Forestry. 7(4): 287-290.

Ji, J.S.; Zhong, Q.P.; Hu, B.T. [and others]. 1997. The response of young slash pine plantation to fertilizing on a red shale soil. Forest Research. 10(4): 408-414.

Jia, H.J.; Zheng, H.M.; Hua, X.M.; Li, J.N.; Wan, X.R. 1997. Effects of steady-state mineral nutrition on Pt ectomycorrhizae formation and growth of container-grown seedlings of slash pine. Scientia Silvae Sinicae. 33(1): 51-58.

Jian, M.D.; Gao, Z.X.; Chen, S.W. [and others]. 1996. Study on the afforestation technique for *Pinus elliottii* in subtropical coastal bedrock. Journal of Zhejiang Forestry Science and Technology. 15(3): 1-6.

Jiang, J.M.; Hu, S.C.; Yu, M.L. [and others]. 1997. A study on the conditioning effects of undercutting and top pruning on slash pine bare rooted. Forest Research. 10(2): 182-188.

Jiang, J.M.; Yu, M.K.; Hu, S.C. [and others]. 1996. Effect of seed sorting on germination and seedling quality of slash pine. Forest Research. 9(3): 290-295.

Jiang, J.M.; Yu, M.K.; Tong, F.P. 2000. On the thinning scheme for industrial timber stands of slash pine and loblolly pine. Forest Research, Beijing. 13(4): 397-406.

Jiang, J.M.; Yu, M.K.; Tong, F.P. [and others]. 2000. Study on the initial planting density of industrial timber stands of slash pine and loblolly pine. Forest Research, Beijing. 13(2): 167-176.

Jing, Y.; Sun, D.P. 1994. Studies on the biological characteristics of the pathogen causing slash pine dieback. *Diplodia pinea*. Forest Research. 7(1): 72-77.

Johansen, R.W. 1984. Prescribed burning spot fires in the Georgia Coastal Plain. Georgia Forest Research Paper. 49: 7p.

Johansen, R.W.; Wade, D.D. 1985. Response of slash pine to severe crown scorch. In: Proceedings, Fire management: the challenge of protection and use. 31-34.

Johansen, R.W.; Wade, D.D. 1987. Effects of crown scorch on survival and diameter growth of slash pines. Southern Journal of Applied Forestry. 11(4): 180-184.

Johnson, D.W.; Knoepp, J.D.; Swank, W.T. [and others]. 2002. Effects of forest management on soil carbon: results of some long-term resampling studies. Environmental Pollution. 116(supplement): S201-S208.

Johnson, D.W.; Sogn, T.; Kvindesland, S. 2000. The nutrient cycling model: lessons learned. Forest Ecology and Management. 138(1): 91-106.

Johnson, J.D.; Byres, D.P.; Dean, T.J. 1995. Diurnal water relations and gas exchange of two slash pine (*Pinus elliottii*) families exposed to chronic ozone levels of acidic rain. New Phytologist. 131(3): 381-392.

Johnson, J.D.; Seiler, J.R.; McNabb, K.L. 1986. Manipulation of pine seedling physiology by water stress conditioning. In: Proceedings of the International Symposium on Nursery Management Practices for the Southern Pines. 290-302.

Johnson, M.K.; Davis, L.G. 1983. Potentials for forest grazing in the Southeastern United States. International Tree Crops Journal. 2(2): 121-131.

Jokela, E.J.; Harding, R.B.; Nowak, J.A. 1989. Long-term effects of fertilization on stem form, growth relations, and yield estimates of slash pine. Forest Science. 35(3): 832-842.

Jokela, E.J.; Martin, T.A. 2000. Effects of ontogeny and soil nutrient supply on production, allocation, and leaf area efficiency in loblolly and slash pine stands. Canadian Journal of Forest Resources. 30(10): 1511-1524.

Jokela, E.J.; McFee, W.W.; Stone, E.L. 1991. Micronutrient deficiency in slash pine: response and persistence of added manganese. Soil Science Society of America Journal. 55(2): 492-496.

Jokela, E.J.; Smith, W.H.; Colbert, S.R. 1990. Growth and elemental content of slash pine 16 years after treatment with garbage composted with sewage sludge. Journal of Environmental Quality. 19(1): 146-150.

Jokela, E.J.; Stearns-Smith, S.C. 1993. Fertilization of established southern pine stands: effects of single and split nitrogen treatments. Southern Journal of Applied Forestry. 17(3): 135-138.

Jokela, E.J.; Wilson, D.S.; Allen, J.E. 2000. Early growth responses of slash and loblolly pine following fertilization and herbaceous weed control treatments at establishment. Southern Journal of Applied Forestry. 24(1): 23-30.

Jones, E.P., Jr. 1985. Direct seeding slash pine before clearcutting. Gen. Tech. Rep. SO-GTR-54. New Orleans, LA: U.S. Department of Agriculture, Forest Service, Southern Forest Experiment Station. 105-109.

Jorge, L.A.B. 1983. Height equation for stands of *Pinus elliottii* in the Tres Barras National Forest, Santa Catarina Brazil. Brasil Florestal. 13(56): 41-47.

Jorge, L.A.B. 1984. Assortment tables for *Pinus elliottii* in the Tres Barras National Forest, Santa Catrina, Brazil. Floresta. 15(1): 61-80.

Kainer, K.A.; Duryea, M.L. 1990. Root wrenching and lifting date of slash pine: effects on morphology, survival and growth. New Forests. 4(3): 207-221.

Kainer, K.A.; Duryea, M.L.; White, T.L.; Johnson, J.D. 1991. Slash pine bud dormancy as affected by lifting date and root wrenching in the nursery. Tree Physiology. 9(4): 479-489.

Kamm, A.; Doudrick, R.L.; Heslop-Harrison, J.S.; Schmidt, T. 1996. The genomic and physical organization of Ty 1-copia-like sequences as a component of large genomes in *Pinus elliottii* var. *elliottii* and other gynmnosperms. In: Proceedings of the National Academy of Sciences of the United States of America. 93(7): 2708-2713.

Kamra, S.K. 1987. Studies on seed of *Pinus elliottii* by x-ray contrast method. Report - Swedish University of Agricultural Sciences. 110-123.

Karrafalt, R.P. 1983. Fungus-damaged seeds can be removed from slash pine seedlots. Tree Planters' Notes. 34(2): 38-40.

Kasuya, M.C.M.; Muchovej, R.M.C.; Bellei, M.M.; Borges, A.C. 1992. *In vitro* ectomycorrhizal formation in six varieties of pine. Forest Ecology and Management. 47(1): 127-134.

Kaul, O.N.; Singh, R.P.; Srivastava, V.K.; Gurumurti, K. 1982. Distribution of organic matter in *Pinus elliottii* plantations. Indian Forester. 108(1): 39-50.

Kaul, O.N.; Srivastava, V.K. 1985. Energy budgets in slash pine (*Pinus elliottii*) plantations at Dehra Dun. Indian Journal of Forestry. 8(1): 1-5.

Kelley, W.D. 1982. Effects of triadimefon (Bayleton) on ectomycorrhizae of loblolly and slash pines in Alabama. Forest Science. 28(2): 232-236.

Kelley, W.D.; Rowan, S.J. 1986. Fusiform rust and its control in southern forest tree nurseries. In: Proceedings of the International Symposium on Nursery Management Practices for Southern Pines. 454-459.

Kellison, R.C. 1986. Seed procurement and nursery management of the southern pines in the People's Republic of China. In: Proceedings of the International Symposium on Nursery Management Practices for Southern Pines. 20-24.

Kewley, S.; Kollegg, L. 2001. Mechanical feller-buncher felling: an example study on timber value recovery in South Africa. Southern African Forestry Journal. 192: 59-64.

Kidder, G.; Comerford, N.B.; Mollitor, A.V. 1987. Fertilization of slash pine plantations. Circular - Florida Cooperative Extension Service. No. 735: 5p.

Kilpatrick, P.P. 1987. Soils of the loblolly/shortleaf and longleaf/slash pine project: Grand and Vernon Parishes, Louisiana. Gen. Tech. Rep. SO-GTR-68. New Orleans, LA: U.S. Department of Agriculture, Forest Service, Southern Forest Experiment Station. 67-72.

Knowe, S.A. 1984. Herbaceous weed control in slash pine and cottonwood plantations. In: Proceedings, Southern Weed Science Society, 37th Annual Meeting. 214-217.

Kokaly, R.F. 2001. Investigating a physical basis for spectroscopic estimates of leaf nitrogen concentration. Remote Sensing of Environment. 75(2): 153-161.

Kossuth, S.V. 1981. Pretreatment for cloning slash and scotch pine. In: Proceedings of the annual meeting of the Florida State Horticultural Society. 93: 112-114.

Kossuth, S.V. 1984. Multipurpose slash pine-genetics and physiology of gum naval stores production. Gen. Tech. Rep. NE-GTR-90. Newton Square, PA: U.S. Department of Agriculture, Forest Service, Northeastern Research Station. 77-83.

Kossuth, S.V.; Bernard, E.L.; Squillace, A.E.; Kratka, S. 1981. Effects of sand pine scion on monterpene composition of slash pine rootstocks. Canadian Journal of Forest Research. 11(4): 857-859.

Kossuth, S.V.; Biggs, R.H. 1981. Role of apophysis and outer scale tissue in pine cone opening. Forest Science. 27(4): 828-836.

Kossuth, S.V.; McReynolds, R.D. 1987. Induced changes in monoterpene composition of slash and longleaf pines. In: Proceedings of the Plant Growth Regulator Society of America Fourteenth Annual Meeting. 268-277.

Kossuth, S.V.; Muse, H.D. 1986. Cortical monoterpene variation among slash pine ramets by season, aspect, crown position, and bud vigor. Forest Science. 32(3): 605-613.

Kossuth, S.V.; Peters, W.J.; Gansel, C.R. 1982. High-gum-yielding slash pines survive and grow well. Res. Note. SE-RN-315. Asheville, NC: U.S. Department of Agriculture, Forest Service, Southeastern Forest Experiment Station. 3p.

Kossuth, S.V.; Roberts, D.R.; Huggman, J.B.; Wang, S.C. 1982. Resin acid, turpentine and caloric content of paraquat-treated slash pine. Canadian Journal of Forest Research. 12(3): 489-492.

Kraus, J.F.; La Farge, T. 1982. Georgia's seed orchard trees. A report on the first-generation selections. Georgia Forest Research Paper. 37: 10p.

Kraus, J.F.; La Farge, T. 1984. Early results of a slash pine variety trial. Southern Journal of Applied Forestry. 8(1): 41-43.

Kraus, J.F.; Sluder, E.R. 1981. Fifth-year performance of progencies of selected South African slash and loblolly pine clones. Southern Journal of Applied Forestry. 5(2): 62-65.

Kraus, J.F.; Sluder, E.R. 1982. Fifth-year performance of progencies of selected South African slash and loblolly pine clones. South African Forestry Journal. 121: 84-87.

Kroll, J.C.; Deauman, W.C.; Foster, C.D. [and others]. 1985. Survival of pines on droughty soils: two year results. Gen. Tech. Rep. SO-GTR-54. New Orleans, LA: U.S. Department of Agriculture, Forest Service, Southern Forest Experiment Station. 128-131.

Kronka, S.do N.; Barbin, D.; Cortarelli, A. 1982. Components of variance in height and diameter data for *Pinus* spp. Cientifica. 10(2): 173-179.

Kubisiak, T.L.; Nelson, C.D.; Nowak, J.; Friend, A.L. 2000. Genetic linkage mapping of genomic regions conferring tolerance to high aluminum in slash pine. Journal of Sustainable Forestry. 10(1): 69-78.

Kuhlman, E.G. 1981. Parasite interaction with sporulation by *Cronartium quercuum*, f.sp. *fusiforme* on loblolly and slash pine. Phytopathology. 71(3): 348-350.

Kuhlman, E.G. 1981. Sporulation by *Cronartium quercuum* f.sp. *fusiforme* on loblolly and slash pine. Phytopathology. 71(3): 345-347.

Kuhlman, E.G. 1987. Effects of inoculation treatment with *Fusarium moniliforme* var. *subglutinans* on dieback of loblolly and slash pine seedlings. Plant Disease. 71(2): 161-162.

Kuhlman, E.G.; Pepper, W.D. 1994. Temperature effects on basidopspore germination and on infection of slash pine seedlings by *Cronartium quercuum* f.sp. *fusiforme*. Phytopathology. 84(7): 735-739.

Kuhlman, E.G.; Powers, H.R.; Pepper, W.D. 1995. Relative fusiform rust resistance of loblolly and slash pine sources and families in Georgia and South Carolina. Res. Pap. SRS-RP-291. Asheville NC: U.S. Department of Agriculture, Forest Service, Southern Research Station. 12p.

Kuo, P.C. 1984. Phytotoxic study of Velpar and Roundup on the seedlings of eight Taiwan important conifers. Technical Bulletin, Experimental Forest, National Taiwan University. 147: 8p.

Labisky, R.F.; Hovis, J.A. 1987. Comparison of vertebrate wildlife communities in longleaf pine and slash pine habitats in north Florida. Gen. Tech. Rep. SO-GTR-68. New Orleans, LA: U.S. Department of Agriculture, Forest Service, Southern Forest Experiment Station. 201-228.

Lai, D. 2001. Culture techniques of cutting seedlings of *Pinus taeda*, *Pinus elliottii* and *Pinus massoniana*. Journal of Fujian College of Forestry. 21(3): 249-252.

Land, D.; Marion, W.R.; O'Meara, T.E. 1989. Snag availability and cavity nesting birds in slash pine plantations. Journal of Wildlife Management. 53(4): 1165-1171.

Landers, J.L.; Boyer, W.D. 1999. An old-growth definition for upland longleaf and south Florida slash pine forests, woodlands, and savannas. Gen. Tech. Rep. SRS-GTR-29. Asheville, NC: U.S. Department of Agriculture, Forest Service, Southern Research Station. 15 p.

Lantz, C.W. 1986. Handling and care of southern pine seedlings. In: Proceedings of the International Symposium on Nursery Management Practices for Southern Pines. 549-556.

Lappi, J.; Bailey, R.L. 1988. A height prediction model with random stand and tree parameters: an alternative to traditional site index methods. Forest Science. 34(4): 907-927.

Larrieu, M.R.; Slavare, F.D.; Medvescig, M.; Clemente, N.I. 1998. Use of a geographical information system to locate and enumerate forest plantations of *Eucalyptus* sp. and *Pinus* sp. in the department of Concordia, province of Entre Rios. SAGPyA Forestal. 6: 2-16.

La Torraca, S.M.; Haag, H.P.; Miglionhi, A.J. 1984. Uptake and removal of nutrients by *Pinus elliottii* var. *elliottii* on a dark red latosol in the Agudos region, Sao Paulo. IPEF, Institute de Pesquisas e Estudos Florestais. 27: 41-47.

Lauer, D.K.; Glover, G.R. 1998. Early pine response to control of herbaceous and shrub vegetation in the flatwoods. Southern Journal of Applied Forestry. 22(4): 201-208.

Lauer, D.K.; Glover, G.R. 1999. Relating stand level pine response to shrub and herbaceous vegetation following vegetation control treatments. In: Proceedings, Southern Weed Science Society. 52: 122-123.

Lauer, D.K.; Glover, G.R. 1999. Stand level pine response to occupancy of woody shrub and herbaceous vegetation. Canadian Journal of Forest Research. 29(7): 979-984.

Lauer, D.K.; Zutter, B.R. 1999. Pine response and vegetation control following mechanical bedding and chemical site-preparation methods. In: Proceedings, Southern Weed Science Society. 52: 90.

Lauer, D.K.; Zutter, B.R. 2001. Vegetation cover response and second-year loblolly and slash pine response following bedding and pre- and post-plant herbicide applications in Florida. Southern Journal of Applied Forestry. 25(2): 75-83.

Layton, P.A.; Goddard, R.E. 1983. Low level inbreeding effects on germination, survival, and early height growth of slash pine. In: Proceedings of the Southern Forest Tree Improvement Conference. 39: 106-115.

Ledbetter, J.R.; Matney, T.G. 1983. Merchantable volume predictions for slash pine trees. Technical bulletin - Mississippi Agricultural and Forestry Experiment Station. 118: 29p.

Lee, R.S.; Pritchett, W.L.; Smith, W.H. 1983. Forest floor characteristics under longleaf-slash pine on two Spodosols. Forest Ecology and Management. 5(3): 193-205.

Lee, Y.J.; Lenhart, J.D. 1997. Estimating crown height for unthinned planted pines in east Texas. Southern Journal of Applied Forestry. 21(1): 130-133.

Lee, Y.J.; Lenhart, J.D. 1998. Influence of planting density on diameter and height in east Texas pine plantations. Southern Journal of Applied Forestry. 22(4): 241-244.

Leightley, L.E. 1986. The use of CCA treated slash pine as a pole series. Technical Paper, Department of Forestry, Queensland. 41: 8p.

Lenhart, J.D. 1988. Diameter-distribution yield-prediction system for unthinned loblolly and slash pine plantations on non-old-fields in east Texas. Southern Journal of Applied Forestry. 12(4): 239-242.

Lenhart, J.D. 1988. Evaluation of explicit and implicit yield prediction in loblolly and slash pine plantations in east Texas. Gen. Tech. Rep. NC-GTR-120. St. Paul, MN: U.S. Department of Agriculture, Forest Service, North Central Research Station. 747-753.

Lenhart, J.D. 1996. Total and partial stand-level yield protection for loblolly and slash pine plantations in east Texas. Southern Journal of Applied Forestry. 20(1): 36-41.

Lenhart, J.D.; Gregoire, T.G.; Kronard, G.D.; Holley, A.G. 1994. Characterizing fusiform rust incidence and distribution in east Texas. Southern Journal of Applied Forestry. 18(1): 29-34.

Lenhart, J.D.; Hackett, T.L.; Laman, C.J. [and others]. 1987. Tree content and taper functions for loblolly and slash pine trees planted on non-old-fields in east Texas. Southern Journal of Applied Forestry. 11(3): 147-151.

Lenhart, J.D.; Hunt, E.V., Jr.; Blackard, J.A. 1985. Establishment of permanent growth and yield plots in loblolly and slash pine plantations in east Texas. Gen. Tech. Rep. SO-GTR-54. New Orleans, LA: U.S. Department of Agriculture, Forest Service, Southern Forest Experiment Station. 436-437.

Lenhart, J.D.; Hunt, E.V., Jr.; Blackard, J.A. 1986. Site index equations for loblolly and slash pine plantations on non-old-fields in east Texas. Southern Journal of Applied Forestry. 10(2): 109-112.

Lenhart, J.D.; Kronrad, G.D.; Fountain, M.S. 1993. Comparison of planted loblolly and slash pine performance in southeast Texas. Southern Journal of Applied Forestry. 17(1): 26-31.

Lenhart, J.D.; McGrath, W.T.; Hackett, T.L. 1988. Fusiform rust trends in east Texas: 1969-1987. Southern Journal of Applied Forestry. 12(4): 259-261.

Lesney, M.S. 1989. Growth responses and lignin production in cell suspensions of *Pinus elliottii* 'elicited' by chitin, citosan or mycelium of *Cronartium quercuum* f.sp. *fusiforme*. Plant Cell, Tissue and Organ Culture. 19(1): 23-31.

Lesney, M.S. 1990. Effect of 'elicitors' on extracellular peroxidase activity in suspension-cultured slash pine (*Pinus elliottii* Engelm.). Plant Cell, Tissue and Organ Culture. 20(3): 173-175.

Lesney, M.S. 1990. Polycation-like behavior of chitosan on suspension-culture derived protoplasts of slash pine. Phytochemistry. 29(4): 1123-1125.

Lesney, M.S. 1991. Slash pine (*Pinus elliottii* Engelm.). Biotechnology in Agriculture and Forestry. 16: 288-303.

Lesney, M.S.; Johnson, J.D.; Korhnak, T.; McCaffery, M.W. 1988. *In vitro* manipulation of slash pine (*Pinus elliottii*). Genetic Manipulation of Woody Plants. p.43-55.

Lewis, C.E. 1983. Forage resources and integrated management in slash pine ecosystems. In: The Managed Slash Pine Ecosystem. Proceedings of a symposium held at the University of Florida. June 9-11, 1981. 360-368.

Lewis, C.E. 1985. Planting slash pine in a dense pasture sod. Agroforestry Systems. 3(3): 267-274.

Lewis, C.E. 1989. Herbage yield response to the maturation of a slash pine plantation. Journal of Range Management. 42(3): 191-195.

Lewis, C.E.; Burton, G.W.; Monson, W.G.; McCormick, W.C. 1983. Integration of pines, pastures, and cattle in south Georgia, USA. Agroforestry Systems. 1(4): 227-297.

Lewis, C.E.; Burton, G.W.; Monson, W.G.; McCormick, W.C. 1984. Integration of pines and pastures for hay and grazing. Agroforestry Systems. 2(1): 34-41.

Lewis, C.E.; Swindel, B.F.; Conde, L.F.; Smith, J.E. 1984. Forage yields improved by site preparation in pine flatwoods of north Florida. Southern Journal of Applied Forestry. 8(4): 181-185.

Lewty, M.J.; Frodsham, T.M. 1983. Post-emergence weed control efficacy of Caragard in *Pinus* nursery. Technical Note, Department of Forestry, Queensland. 11: 4p.

Li, C.D.; Han, Z.M.; Ye, J.R. [and others]. 1987. Development of brown-spot needle blight in slash pine plantations. Journal of Nanjing Forestry University. 1: 1-7.

Li, C.D.; Han, Z.M.; Zhang, Z.H. [and others]. 1986. Biology of brown-spot disease fungus (*Mycosphaerella deamessi*) in slash pine (*Pinus elliottii*) plantations. Journal of Nanjing Institute of Forestry. 2: 19-26.

Li, S.F. 1999. Study on the relationship between the height of *P. elliottii* plantation and site condition. Journal of Fujian College of Forestry. 19(3): 276-278.

Li, W.H.; Guo, J.S.; Guo, Y.Q.; Luo, R.Y. 1983. Results of application labeled ^{15}N and ^{32}P fertilizers to younglings of slash pine and four clones of hybrid poplars. Journal of Nanjing Technological College of Forest Products. 3: 141-146.

Li, X.A.; Xia, X.M.; Zhou, J.W. [and others]. 1996. Study on variation in wood density in slash pine and loblolly pine and selection of elite trees. Scientia Silvae Sinicae. 32(3): 248-253.

Li, Z.S.; Liu, Y.S.; Peng, J.F. [and others]. 1998. Study on the biology and control of *Hylobitelus xiaoi* Zhang. Forest Research. 11(2): 198-202.

Liang, Y.Z. 1984. Growth differences of slash, loblolly and Masson's pines at seedling stage. Forest Science and Technology. 2: 11-13.

Liao, Y.K.; Amerson, H.V. 1995. Slash pine (*Pinus elliottii* Engelm.) somatic embryogenesis I. Initiation of embryogenic cultures from immature zygotic embryos. New Forests. 10(2): 145-163.

Liao, Y.K.; Amerson, H.V. 1995. Slash pine (*Pinus elliottii* Engelm.) somatic embryogenesis II. Maturation of somatic embryos and plant regeneration. New Forests. 10(2): 165-182.

Lie, Z.P.; Tang, J.A.; Zhang, L.H.; Zou, Y.Q. 1995. The influence of nutritional supplements on the growth of ectomycorrhizal fungi in cultural and associated tree seedlings in the nursery and field. In: Mycorrhizas for Plantation Forestry in Asia: Proceedings of an International Symposium and Workshop, Kaiping, Guangdong Province, P.R. China. Pp. 57-61.

Lin, Q.L. 2002. Growth characteristics analysis of *Pinus taeda*, *Pinus elliottii* and *Pinus massoniana*. Journal of Fujian College of Forestry. 22(2): 133-136.

Lin, W.L. 2001. Observation of growth on *Pinus elliottii* in sands of seashore. Journal of Zhejiang Forestry Science and Technology. 21(1): 54-56.

Lister, A.J.; Mou, P.O.; Jones, R.H.; Mitchell, R.J. 2000. Spatial patterns of soil and vegetation in a 40-year-old slash pine (*Pinus elliottii*) forest in the Coastal Plain of South Carolina, U.S.A. Canadian Journal of Forest Research. 30(1): 145-155.

Little, K.M.; Rolando, C.A. 2001. The impact of vegetation control on the establishment of pine at four sites in the summer rainfall region of South Africa. Southern African Forestry Journal. 192: 31-39.

Liu, A.; Xiang, W.H.; Cai, B.Y.; Zhong, J.D. 1998. Studies on nutrient elements cycling and density effect in slash pine plantations. Scientia Silvae Sinicae. 34(3): 11-17.

Liu, S.G.; Riekerk, H.; Gholz, H.L. 1995. Simulation of stomatal conductances of pond cypress and slash pine in Florida flatwoods. In: Proceedings - Soil and Crop Science Society of Florida. 54: 72-80.

Liu, S.G.; Riekerk, H.; Gholz, H.L. 1998. Simulation of evapotranspiration from Florida pine flatwoods. Ecological Modelling. 114(1): 19-34.

Liu, X.Y. 1984. Biomass measurement of *Pinus elliottii* in hilly red soil areas. Forest Science and Technology. 9: 10-13.

Lloyd, F.T.; Jones, E.P., Jr. 1981. A thinning rule for slash pine plantations on a medium site. Gen. Tech. Rep. SO-GTR-34. New Orleans, LA: U.S. Department of Agriculture, Forest Service, Southern Forest Experiment Station. 131-136.

Lloyd, F.T.; Jones, E.P., Jr. 1983. Density effects on height growth and its implications for site index prediction and growth prediction. Gen. Tech. Rep. SE-GTR-24. Asheville, NC: U.S. Department of Agriculture, Forest Service, Southeastern Forest Experiment Station. 329-333.

Locklear, W.G. 1983. Current costs of even-aged methods of regenerating loblolly pine and slash pine in the west Gulf Coastal Plain. Forestry Abstracts. 44(11): 708.

Loescher, H.W. 1997. Non-methane hydrocarbon fluxes from *Pinus elliottii* and *Sereonoa repens*: comparing enclosure and above-canopy measurements. US Imprint. 112.

Lohrey, R.E. 1985. Stem volume, volume ratio, and taper equations for slash pine in the west gulf region. Gen. Tech. Rep. SO-GTR-54. New Orleans, LA: U.S. Department of Agriculture, Forest Service, Southern Forest Experiment Station. 451-459.

Lohrey, R.E. 1987. Site index curves for direct-seeded slash pines in Louisiana. Southern Journal of Applied Forestry. 11(1): 15-17.

Lohrey, R.E.; Jones, E.P., Jr. 1983. Natural regeneration and direct seeding. In: The Managed Slash Pine Ecosystem. Proceedings of a symposium held at the University of Florida. June 9-11, 1981. 183-193.

Long, A.J.; Flinchum, D.M. 1992. Slash pine response to spot applications of hexazinone pellets for release from oak competition. Southern Journal of Applied Forestry. 16(3): 133-138.

Lopez-Upton, J.; Blakeslee, G.M.; White, T.L.; Huber, D.A. 2000. Effects of cultural treatments and genetics on tip moth infestation of loblolly pine, slash pine, and some slash pine hybrids. Forest Genetics. 7(4): 275-286.

Lopez-Upton, J.; White, T.L.; Huber, D.A. 1999. Effects of site and intensive culture on family differences in early growth and rust incidence of loblolly and slash pine. Silvae Genetica. 48(6): 284-293.

Lopez-Upton, J.; White, T.L.; Huber, D.A. 1999. Taxon and family differences in survival, cold hardiness, early growth, and rust incidence of loblolly pine, slash pine and some pine hybrids. Silvae Genetica. 48(6): 303-313.

Lopez-Upton, J.; White, T.L.; Huber, D.A. 2000. Species differences in early growth and rust incidence of loblolly and slash pine. Forest Ecology and Management. 132(2): 211-222.

Lopez-Zamora, I.; Duryea, M.L.; Wild, C.M. [and others]. 2001. Effect of pine needle removal and fertilization on tree growth and soil P availability in a *Pinus elliottii* Engelm. var. *elliottii* stand. Forest Ecology and Management. 148(1): 125-134.

Lotan, J.E. 1981. The forest soil environment. Gen. Tech. Rep. WO-GTR-16. Washington DC: U.S. Department of Agriculture, Forest Service, Washington DC Office. 52-56.

Lowe, W.J.; Barber, L.R.; Cameron, R.S. [and others]. 1994. A southwide test of bifenthrin (Capture) for cone and seed insect control in seed orchards. Southern Journal of Applied Forestry. 18(2): 72-75.

Loxton, R.F.; Donald, D.G.M. 1987. The effect of Nitroacta (urea formaldehyde) on the growth and development of *Eucalyptus grandis* and *Pinus elliottii*. South African Forestry Journal. 142: 68-70.

Lundquist, J.E.; Luttrell, E.S. 1982. Early symptomatology of fusiform rust on pine seedlings. Phytopahtology. 72(1): 54-57.

Lundquist, J.E.; Miller, T. 1984 . Development of stem lesions on slash pine seedlings infected by *Cronartium quercuum*, f.sp. *fusiforme*. Phytopathology. 17(5): 514-518.

Lundquist, J.E.; Miller, T.; Powers, H.R., Jr. 1982. A rapid technique for determining resistance of slash pine to fusiform rust. Phytopathology. 72(6): 613-615.

Lutrick, M.C.; Riekerk, H.; Cornell, J.A. 1986. Soil and slash pine response to sludge applications in Florida. Soil Science Society of America Journal. 50(2): 447-451.

Luzzi, M.A.; Wilkinson, R.C.; Tarjan, A.C. 1984. Transmission of the pinewood nematode, *Bursaphelenchus xylophilus*, to slash pine trees and log bolts by a cerambycid beetle, *Monochamus titillator*, in Florida. Journal of Nematology. 16(1): 37-40.

Lynch, R.O.; Militor, A.V.; Comerford, N.B. 1985. Modeling effects of mid-rotation fertilization on slash pine plantation diameter distributions. Gen. Tech. Rep. SO-GTR-54. New Orleans, LA: U.S. Department of Agriculture, Forest Service, Southern Forest Experiment Station. 445-450.

Mabvurira, D. 1995. The comparative profitability of *P. patula*, and *P. elliottii* stands in Zimbabwe. ForMat. 7(1): 1-3.

MacFall, J.S.; Spaine, P.; Doudrick, R.; Johnson, G.A. 1994. Alterations in growth and water-transport processes in fusiform rust gall infected slash pine, determined by magnetic resonance microscopy. Phytopathology. 84(3): 288-293.

Mackenzie, A.A. 1983. Weed control and fertilizer use in South African forest establishment. Mededeling, Fakulteit Bosbou, Universiteit Stellenbosch. 98(1): 295-304.

MacLean, J.T. 1983. Regeneration of southern pines (1970-1983). Quick bibliography series - National Agricultural Library. 24p.

MacPeak, M.D.; Burkhart, L.F.; Weldon, D. 1990. Comparison of grade, yield, and mechanical properties of lumber produced from young fast-grown and older slow-grown planted slash pine. Forest Products Journal. 40(1): 11-14.

Maggs, J. 1985. Litterfall and retranslocation of nutrients in a refertilized and prescribed burned *Pinus elliottii* plantation. Forest ecology and management. 12(3): 253-268.

Maggs, J.; Hewett, R.K. 1986. Nitrogenase activity (C_2H_2 reduction) in the forest floor of a *Pinus elliottii* plantation following superphosphate addition and prescribed burning. Forest Ecology and Management. 14(2): 91-101.

Main, M.B.; Richardson, L.W. 2002. Response of wildlife to prescribed fire in southwest Florida pine flatwoods. Wildlife Society Bulletin. 30(1): 213-221.

Malan, F.S. 1994. The wood properties and quality of *Pinus pringlei* Shaw and *P. greggii* Engel. compared with that of *P. patula* and *P. elliottii* grown in South Africa. South African Forestry Journal. 171: 43-52.

Malan, F.S. 1995. The basic wood properties and sawtimber quality of South African grown *Pinus Elliotti* x *Pinus caribaea*. South African Forestry Journal. 173: 35-41.

Malan, F.S. 1998. Variation in the incidence of resin-filled shakes and wood density among open-pollinated families of *Pinus elliottii* planted at four different sites. Southern African Forestry Journal. 182: 21-26.

Mann, W.F., Jr.; Musselman, L.J. 1981. Small infestations of *Seymeria cassioides* (Scrophulariaceae) reduce growth of potted slash pine. Plant Disease. 65(9): 748-749.

Manrich, S.; Agnelli, J.A.M. 1989. The effect of chemical treatment of wood and polymer characteristics or properties of wood-polymer composites. Journal of Applied Polymer Science. 37(7): 1777-1790.

Maradei, D. 1982. Herbicides in plantations of *Pinus elliottii* var. *elliottii* Argentina. Malezas - Association Agentina para el Control de Malezas. 10(3): 12-21.

Marino, T.M. 1981. Propagation of southern pines by cuttings. In: Combined Proceedings, International Plant Propagator's Society. 31: 518-528.

Marquez-Millano, A.; Elam, W.W.; Blanche, C.A. 1991. Influence of accelerated aging on fatty acid composition of slash pine (*Pinus elliottii* Engelm. var. *elliottii*) seeds. Journal of Seed Technology. 15(1): 29-41.

Martin, S.W.; Bailey, R.L.; Jokela, E.J. 1999. Growth and yield predictions for lower Coastal Plain slash pine plantations fertilized at mid-rotation. Southern Journal of Applied Forestry. 23(1): 39-45.

Martin, T.A. 2000. Winter season tree sap flow and stand transpiration in an intensively managed loblolly and slash pine plantation. Journal of Sustainable Forestry. 10(1): 155-163.

Marx, D.H.; Cordell, C.E. 1986. Bayleton (triadimefon) affects ectomycorrhizal development on slash and loblolly pine seedlings in nurseries. Proceedings of the International Symposium on Nursery Management Practices for Southern Pines. 460-475.

Marx, D.H.; Cordell, C.E. 1987. Triadimefon affects *Pisolithus* ectomycorrhizal development, fusiform rust, and growth of loblolly and slash pines in nurseries. Res. Pap. SE-RP-267. Asheville NC: U.S. Department of Agriculture, Forest Service, Southeastern Forest Experiment Station. 14p.

Marx, D.H.; Cordell, C.E.; France, R.C. 1986. Effects of triadimefon on growth and ectomycorrhizal development of loblolly and slash pines in nurseries. Phytopathology. 76(8): 824-831.

Marx, D.H.; Cordell, C.E.; Maul, S.B.; Ruehle, J.L. 1989. Ectomycorrhizal development on pine by *Pisolithus tinctorius* in bare-rooted and container seedling nurseries. I. Efficacy of various vegetative inoculation formulations. New Forests. 3(1): 45-56.

Marx, D.H.; Jarl, K.; Ruehle, J.L.; Bell, W. 1984. Development of *Pisolithus tinctorius* ectomycorrhizae on pine seedlings using basidiospore-encapsulated seeds. Forest Science. 30(4): 897-907.

Mason, M.E.; Davis, J.M. 1997. Defense response in slash pine: chitosan treatment alters the abundance of specific mRNAs. Molecular Plant-Microbe Interactions. 10(1): 135-137.

Matheson, A.C.; White, T.L.; Powell, G.R. 1995. Effects of inbreeding on growth, stem form and rust resistance in *Pinus elliottii*. Silvae Genetica. 44(1): 37-46.

Matlack, G.R. 2001. Factors determining the distribution of soil nematodes in a commercial forest landscape. Forest Ecology and Management. 146(1): 129-143.

Matney, T.G.; Ledbetter, J.R.; Sullivan, A.D. 1987. Diameter distribution yield systems for unthinned cutover site-prepared slash pine plantations in southern Mississippi. Southern Journal of Applied Forestry. 11(1): 32-36.

Matney, T.G.; Sullivan, A.D. 1981. Estimation of merchantable volume and height of natural grown slash pine trees. Gen. Tech. Rep. WO-GTR-28. Washington DC: U.S. Department of Agriculture, Forest Service, Washington DC Office. 464-470.

Matney, T.G.; Sullivan, A.D. 1982. Variable top volume and height predictors for slash pine trees. Forest Science. 28(2): 274-282.

Matney, T.G.; Sullivan, A.D. 1982. Volume and height to any top diameter limit for slash pine tress planted on "cut-over" prepared sites in the coastal plain and flatwoods of Mississippi. Technical bulletin - Mississippi Agricultural and Forestry Experiment Station. 112: 9p.

Mattie, V.L. 2000. Transformation of abandoned agricultural areas with *Pinus elliottii* Engelm. plantations using direct sowing. Revista Cientifica Rural. 5(2): 117-125.

Mattie, V.L.; Romano, C.M.; Teixeira, M.C.C. 2001. Shelters for direct seeding of *Pinus elliottii* Engelm. Ciencia Rural. 31(5): 775-780.

Mauldin, J.K.; Kard, B.M. 1996. Disodium ocaborate tetrahydrate treatments to slash pine for protection against Formosa subterranean termite and eastern subterranean termite. Journal of Economic Entomology. 89(3): 682-688.

McAlister, R.H.; Clark, A., III; Saucier, J.R. 1997. Effect of initial spacing on mechanical properties of lumber sawn from unthinned slash pine at age 40. Forest Products Journal. 47(7): 107-109.

McAlister, R.H.; Powers, H.R., Jr. 1992. Physical and mechanical properties of half-sib families of rust resistant loblolly and slash pine. Forest Products Journal. 42(11): 15-20.

McCarthy, J.W.; Stone, E.L. 1991. Changes in soil water tables following phosphorus fertilization of young slash pine. Soil Science Society of America Journal. 55(5): 1440-1446.

McGrath, D.A.; Duryea, M.L. 1994. Initial moisture stress, budbreak and two-year field performance of three morphological grades of slash pine seedlings. New Forests. 8(4): 335-350.

McKee, W.H., Jr. 1982. Changes in soil fertility following prescribed burning on coastal plain pine sites. Res. Pap. SE-RP-234. Asheville, NC: U.S. Department of Agriculture, Forest Service, Southeastern Forest Experiment Station. 23p.

McKee, W.H., Jr.; Lewis, C.E. 1983. Influence of burning and grazing on soil nutrient properties and tree growth on a Georgia Coastal Plain site after 40 years. Gen. Tech. Rep. SE-GTR-24. Asheville, NC: U.S. Department of Agriculture, Forest Service, Southeastern Forest Experiment Station. 79-86.

McKelvey, K.S. 1988. A geometric model of sunlight penetration for slash pine in northern Florida. Gen. Tech. Rep. NC-GTR-120. St. Paul, MN: U.S. Department of Agriculture, Forest Service, North Central Research Station. 323-330.

McKinley, C.R. 1987. A southern pine seed orchard in the lower Rio Grande Valley of Texas. In: Proceeding of the Southern Forest Tree Improvement Conference. 41: 247-252.

McMinn, J.W. 1981. Site preparation for natural regeneration of slash pine. Southern Journal of Applied Forestry. 5(1): 10-12.

McNeil, R.C.; Ballard, R.; Duzan, H.W., Jr. 1984. Prediction of mid-term from short-term fertilizer responses for southern pine plantations. Forest Science. 30(1): 264-269.

McReynolds, R.D. 1983. Gum naval stores production from slash pine. In: The Managed Slash Pine Ecosystem. Proceedings of a symposium held at the University of Florida. June 9-11, 1981. 375-384.

McReynolds, R.D.; Gansel, C.R. 1985. High-gum yielding slash pine: performance to age 30. Southern Journal of Applied Forestry. 9(1): 29-32.

McReynolds, R.D.; Kossuth, S.V. 1984. CEPA in sulfuric acid paste increases oleoresin yields. Southern Journal of Applied Forestry. 8(3): 168-172.

McReynolds, R.D.; Kossuth, S.V. 1985. CEPA in liquid sulfuric acid increases oleoresin yields. Southern Journal of Applied Forestry. 9(3): 170-173.

Meadows, D.G. 1999. Growing the forest in South Africa. Tappi Journal. 82: 60-66.

Means, D.B.; Palis, J.G.; Baggett, M. 1996. Effects of slash pine silviculture on a Florida population of flatwoods salamander. Conservation Biology. 10(2): 426-437.

Mente, R.F.; Brack-Hanes, S.D. 1990. Scale development in ovuliferous cones of *Pinus elliottii* Englem., Pinaceae. Florida Scientist. 53(14): 274-279.

Merkel, E.P.; Clark, E.W. 1981. Insecticides for preventing insect-caused mortality of paraquat-treated slash pines. Res. Pap. SE-RP-219. Asheville, NC: U.S. Department of Agriculture, Forest Service, Southeastern Forest Experiment Station. 6p.

Merkel, E.P.; Fatzinger, C.W.; Dixon, W.N. 1994. Keys for distinguishing thrips (Thysanoptera) commonly found on slash pine in Florida. Journal of Entomological Science. 29(1): 92-99.

Meyer, H.J. 1998. *In vitro* formation of adventitious buds on mature embryos of *Pinus elliottii* Engelm X *P. caribaea* Morelet hybrids. South African Journal of Botany. 64(3): 220-225.

Michelozzi, M.; Squillace, A.E.; White, T.L. 1990. Monoterpene composition and fusiform rust resistance in slash pine. Forest Science. 36(2): 470-475.

Michelozzi, M.; White, T.L.; Squillace, A.E.; Lowe, W.J. 1995. Monoterpene composition and fusiform rust resistance in slash and loblolly pines. Canadian Journal of Forest Research. 25(2): 193-197.

Miller, T.; Belanger, R.P.; Webb, R.S.; Godbee, J.F. 1985. Pest assessments after sanitation-salvage cutting in fusiform rust-infected slash pine plantations. Gen. Tech. Rep. SO-GTR-56. New Orleans, LA: U.S. Department of Agriculture, Forest Service, Southern Forest Experiment Station. 258-262.

Miller, T.; Blakeslee, G.M.; Bramlett, D.L.; Matthews, F.R. 1987. The effects of using pollen contaminated with conidia of *Fusarium moniliforme* var. *subglutinans* on control-pollinated strobili of slash pine. In: Proceeding of the Southern Forest Tree Improvement Conference. 41: 232-239.

Mims, C.W.; Doudrick, R.L. 1996. Ultrastructure of spermatia and spermatium ontogeny in the rust fungus *Cronartium quercuum* f.sp. *fuisforme*. Canadian Journal of Botany. 74(7): 1050-1057.

Minogue, P.S.; Zutter, B.R. 1986. Second-year results of herbicide screening trials for forest site preparation in the flatwoods. In: Proceedings, Southern Weed Science Society. 39th Annual Meeting. 219.

Misra, M.K.; Mahapatra, D.K.; Nisanka, S.K. 1997. Comparative dimensional analysis of plantations of five pines at Kalinga Hills of Orissa. Journal of Hill Research. 10(2): 113-120.

Mollitor, A.V.; Comerford, N.B. 1985. Fertilizer placement in young slash pine plantations. Gen. Tech. Rep. SO-GTR-54. New Orleans, LA: U.S. Department of Agriculture, Forest Service, Southern Forest Experiment Station. 360-362.

Mollitor, A.V.; Comerford, N.B.; Fisher, R.F. 1983. Prescribed burning and nitrogen fertilization of slash pine plantations. Gen. Tech. Rep. SE-GTR-24. Asheville, NC: U.S. Department of Agriculture, Forest Service, Southeastern Forest Experiment Station. 66-69.

Moncrieff, J.B.; Fang, C. 1999. A model for soil CO_2 production and transport 2: application to a Florida *Pinus elliotte* [*P. elliottii*] plantation. Agricultural and Forest Meterology. 95(4): 237-256.

Moore, W.H.; Swindel, B.F.; Terry, W.S. 1982. Vegetation response to prescribed fire in a north Florida flatwoods forest. Journal of Range Management. 35(3): 386-389.

Moorhead, D.J. 1988. Selecting and planting pine seedlings. Bulletin - Cooperative Extension Service, University of Georgia, College of Agriculture 983. 22p.

Morris, A.R.; Palmer, E.R.; Barnes, R.D. [and others]. 1997. The influence of felling age and site altitude on pulping properties of *Pinus patula* and *Pinus elliottii*. Tappi Journal. 80(6): 133-138.

Morris, L.A.; Pritchett, W.L. 1983. Effects of site preparation on *Pinus elliottii-P. palustris* flatwoods forest soil properties. Gen. Tech. Rep. PNW-GTR-163. Portland, OR: U.S. Department of Agriculture, Forest Service, Pacific Northwest Forest and Range Experiment Station. 243-251.

Morris, L.A.; Pritchett, W.L.; Swindel, B.F. 1983. Displacement of nutrients into windrows during site preparation of a flatwood forest. Soil Science Society of American Journal. 47(3): 591-594.

Mullin, K.; Williams, K.L. 1987. Mammals of longleaf-slash pine stands in central Louisiana. Gen. Tech. Rep. SO-GTR-68. New Orleans, LA: U.S. Department of Agriculture, Forest Service, Southern Forest Experiment Station. 121-124.

Nance, W.L. 1985. Making management decisions before establishing slash pine plantation in areas where fusiform rust is a hazard. In: 34th Annual Forestry Symposium, Louisiana State University, Division of continuing Education. 120-135.

Nance, W.L.; Froelich, R.C.; Dell, T.R.; Shoulders, E. 1983. A growth and yield model for unthinned slash pine plantations infected with fusiform rust. Gen. Tech. Rep. SE-GTR-24. Asheville, NC: U.S. Department of Agriculture, Forest Service, Southeastern Forest Experiment Station. 275-282.

Nance, W.L.; Froelich, R.C.; Shoulders, E. 1981. Effects of fusiform rust on survival and structure of Mississippi and Louisiana slash pine plantations. Res. Pap. SO-RP-172. New Orleans, LA: U.S. Department of Agriculture, Forest Service, Southern Forest Experiment Station. 11p.

Nance, W.L.; Shoulders, E.; Dell, T.R. 1985. Predicting survival and yield of unthinned slash and loblolly pine plantations with different levels of fusiform rust. Gen. Tech. Rep. SO-GTR-56. New Orleans, LA: U.S. Department of Agriculture, Forest Service, Southern Forest Experiment Station. 62-72.

Neary, D.G. 1988. Effect of gallberry on early slash and loblolly pine growth. In: Proceedings - Southern Weed Science Society. 41: 251-255.

Neary, D.G.; Comerford, N.B. 1983. Herbicidal weed reduction on slash pine beds amended with mill sludge. In: Proceedings, Southern Weed Science Society, 36th Annual Meeting. 250-258.

Neary, D.G.; Conde, L.F.; Smith, J.E. 1984. Effects of sulfometruon methyl on six important competing species in Coastal Plain flatwoods. In: Proceedings-Southern Weed Science Society. 193-199.

Neary, D.G.; Cooksey, T.E.; Comerford, N.B.; Bush, P.B. 1985. Slash and loblolly pine response to weed control and fertilization at establishment. In: Proceedings-Southern Weed Science Society. 38: 246-253.

Nelson, C.D. 1991. Fusiform rust incidence and volume growth in a first-generation backcross population, (shortleaf X slash) X slash. Proceedings - Southern Forest Tree Improvement Conference. 152-159.

Nelson, C.D.; Linghai, Z.; Hamaker, J.M. 1992. Propagation of loblolly, slash and longleaf pine from needle fascicles. Tree Planters' Notes. 43(4): 67-71.

Nelson, C.D.; Nance, W.L.; Doudrick, R.L. 1993. A partial genetic linkage map of slash pine (*Pinus elliottii* Engelm. var. *elliottii*) based on random amplified polymorphic DNAs. Theoretical and Applied Genetics. 87(1): 145-151.

Nelson, C.D.; Nance, W.L.; Wagner, D.B. 1994. Chloroplast DNA variation among and within taxonomic varieties of *Pinus caribeae* and *Pinus elliottii*. Canadian Journal of Forest Research. 24(2): 424-426.

Nelson, C.D.; Schmidtling, R.C.; Doudrick, R.L. 1996. Host relationships of fusiform rust disease. II. Genetic variation and heritability in typical and south Florida varieties of slash pine. Silvae Genetica. 45(2): 149-153.

Nelson, R.; Krabill, W.; Tonelli, J. 1988. Estimating forest biomass and volume using airborne laser data. Remote Sensing of Environment. 24(2): 247-267.

Nester, M.R. 1981. Assessment and measurement errors in slash pine research plots (in Queensland). Technical Paper, Department of Forestry, Queensland. 26: 10p.

Newton, R.J.; Dong, N.; Sen, S. [and others]. 1997. Genetic transformation in *Pinus elliottii* Engelm. In: Plant Protoplasts and Genetic Engineering VII. 280-296.

Newton, R.J.; Marek-Swize, K.A.; Magallanes-Cedeno, M.E. [and others]. 1995. Somatic embryogenesis in slash pine (*Pinus elliottii* Engelm.). Forestry Sciences. 44: 183-195.

Nix, L.E.; Brown, C.L. 1987. Cellular kinetics of compression wood formation in slash pine. Wood and Fiber Science. 19(2): 126-134.

Nix, L.E.; Villiers, K. 1985. Tracheid differentiation in southern pines during the dormant season. Wood and Fiber Science. 17(3): 397-403.

Nord, J.C.; DeBarr, G.L.; Overgaard, N.A. [and others]. 1984. High-volume applications of axinphosmethyl, fenvalerate, permethrin, and phosmet for control of coneworms (Lepidoptera: Pyralidae) and seed bugs (Hemiptera: Coreidae and Pentatomidae) in southern pine seed orchards. Journal of Economic Entomology. 77(6): 1589-1595.

Nowak, J.; Friend, A.L. 1995. Aluminum sensitivity of loblolly pine and slash pine seedlings grown in solution culture. Tree Physiology. 15(9): 605-609.

Oak, S.W.; Blakeslee, G.M.; Rockwood, D.L. 1987. Pitch canker resistant slash pine identified by greenhouse screening. In: Proceedings of the Southern Forest Tree Improvement Conference. 41: 132-139.

Olmsted, I.; Dunevitz, H.; Platt, W.J. 1993. Effects of freezes on tropical trees in Everglades National Park Florida, USA. Tropical Ecology. 34(1): 17-34.

Ombir, S.; Paramjeet, S. 1997. Accelerated ageing of slash pine seed. Van Vigyan. 35(1): 17-20.

Oppenheimer, M.J.; Shiver, B.D.; Rheney, J.W. 1989. Ten-year growth response of midrotation slash pine plantations to control of competing vegetation. Canadian Journal of Forest Research. 19(3): 329-334.

Osborne, D. 1991. Long-term response of slash pine to phosphorus fertilizer application. Research Results - Queensland Department of Forestry. 3: 2p.

Oscroft, D.G.; Little, K.M.; Viero, P.W.M. 2000. The effects of soil-amended hydrogel on the establishment of *Pinus elliottii x caribaea* rooted cuttings on the Zululand coastal sands. ICRF Bulletin Series. 19: 8p.

Ostrosina, W.J.; Hess, N.J.; Zarnoch, S.J. [and others]. 1997. Blue-stain fungi associated with roots of southern pine trees attacked by the southern pine beetle, *Dendroctonus frontalis*. Plant Disease. 81(8): 942-945.

Outcalt, K.W. 1982. Selecting pine species for flatwoods sites. Tree Planters' Notes. 33(1): 18-19.

Outcalt, K.W. 1983. Mechanical site preparation improves growth of genetically improved and unimproved slash pine on a Florida flatwoods site. Gen. Tech. Rep. SE-GTR-24. Asheville, NC: U.S. Department of Agriculture, Forest Service, Southeastern Forest Experiment Station. 11-13.

Outcalt, K.W. 1984. Influence of bed height on the growth of slash and loblolly pine on a Leon fine sand in the northeast Florida. Southern Journal of Applied Forestry. 8(1): 29-31.

Outcalt, K.W. 1985. Direct seeding versus planting for establishment of pines on west Florida sandhills. Gen. Tech. Rep. SO-GTR-54. New Orleans, LA: U.S. Department of Agriculture, Forest Service, Southern Forest Experiment Station. 122-127.

Outcalt, K.W. 1993. Southern pines performance on sandhills sites in Georgia and South Carolina. Southern Journal of Applied Forestry. 17(2): 100-102.

Paliwal, D.P.; Thaper, H.S.; Paliwal, G.S. 1984. A simplified seed identification key for nine species of *Pinus* on the basis of morphological and anatomical characters. Journal of Tree Sciences. 3(1): 134-139.

Pallett, R. 2000. Growth and fiber yield of *Pinus patula* and *Pinus elliottii* pulpwood plantations at high altitude in Mpumalanga. Southern African Forestry Journal. 187: 11-17.

Palmer, E.R.; Ganguli, S.; Gibbs, J.A. 1984. Pulping properties of *Pinus caribaea*, *Pinus elliottii* and *Pinus patula* growing in Tanzania. Report, Tropical Development and Research Institute. L66: 32p.

Pan, Y.; McGuire, A.D.; Melillo, J.M. [and others]. 2002. A biogeochemistry-based dynamic vegetation model and its application along a moisture gradient in the continental United States. Journal of Vegetation Science. 13(3): 369-382.

Pan, Z.G. 1995. Twelve year provenance test of slash and loblolly pine in China. Forest Genetic Resources. 23: 33-40.

Pan, Z.G.; Guan, N.; Wei, S.H. [and others]. 1999. Research on the growth and wood properties of hybrid pine in South China. Forest Research, Beijing. 12(4): 398-402.

Panow, S.; Nester, M.R. 1985. Drying end point determination during high-temperature drying. Forest Products Journal. 35(10): 51-55.

Parker, S.R.; White, T.L.; Hodge, G.R.; Powell, G.L. 1998. The effects of scion maturation on growth and reproduction of grafted slash pine. New Forests. 15(3): 243-259.

Parresol, B.R. 2001. Additivity of nonlinear biomass equations. Canadian Journal of Forest Research. 31(5): 865-878.

Parresol, B.R.; Thomas, C.E. 1996. A simultaneous density-integral system for estimating stem profile and biomass: slash pine and willow oak. Canadian Journal of Forest Research. 26(5): 773-781.

Pearson, H.A.; Baldwin, V.C. 1993. Agroforestry: southern pines and subterranean clover cultural treatments. Agroforestry Systems. 22(1): 49-58.

Pearson, H.A.; Grelen, H.E.; Parresol, B.R.; Wright, V.L. 1987. Detailed vegetative description of the longleaf-slash pine type, Vernon District, Kisatchie National Forest, Louisiana. Gen. Tech. Rep. SO-GTR-68. New Orleans, LA: U.S. Department of Agriculture, Forest Service, Southern Forest Experiment Station. 107-115.

Pearson, H.A.; Lewis, C.E. 1989. Agroforestry in the Southeastern United States. In: Proceedings of the XVI International Grassland Congress. Pp. 1637-1638.

Pearson, H.A.; Lohoefener, R.R.; Wolfe, J.L. 1987. Amphibians and reptiles on longleaf-slash pine forests in southern Mississippi. Gen. Tech. Rep. SO-GTR-68. New Orleans, LA: U.S. Department of Agriculture, Forest Service, Southern Forest Experiment Station. 157-165.

Pearson, H.A.; Smeins, F.E.; Thill, R.E. 1987. Ecological, physical and socioeconomic relationships within southern national forests. Proceedings of the Southern Evaluation Project Workshop. Gen. Tech. Rep. SO-GTR-68. New Orleans, LA: U.S. Department of Agriculture, Forest Service, Southern Forest Experiment Station. 293p.

Pedersen, C.T.; Sylvia, D.M.; Shilling, D.G. 1999. *Pisolithus arhizus* ectomycorrhiza affects plant competition for phosphorus between *Pinus elliottii* and *Panicum chamaelonche*. Mycorrhiza. 9(4): 199-204.

Pehl, C.E.; Shellnutt, H.E., Jr. 1986. Forest floor and soil nutrient conditions in the Georgia sandhills. Georgia Forest Research Paper. 62: 11p.

Pereira, J.C.D.; Barrichelo, L.E.G.; Do Couto, H.T.Z. [and others]. 1983. Effect of growth rate on the density of wood from *Pinus elliottii* var. *elliottii*. In: ABCP 16th Annual meeting/3rd Latin-American cellulose and paper congress. 139-146.

Perkins, T.E.; Matlack, G.R. 2002. Human-generated pattern in commercial forests of southern Mississippi and consequences for the spread of pests and pathogens. Forest Ecology and Management. 157(1/3): 143-154.

Permar, T.A.; Fisher, R.F. 1983. Nitrogen fixation and accretion by wax myrtle *(Myrica cerifera)* in slash pine (*Pinus elliottii*) plantations. Forest Ecology and Management. 5(1): 39-46.

Pestana, M. 1993. Characterization of turpentine from five species of pine. Silva Lusitana. 1(1): 109-112.

Pezeshki, S.R.; DeLaune, R.D. 1998. Responses of seedlings of selected woody species to soil oxidation-reduction conditions. Environmental and Experimental Botany. 40(2): 123-133.

Phillips, D.R.; McNab, W.H. 1982. Total-tree green weights of sapling-size pines in Georgia. Georgia Forest Research Paper. 39: 18.

Phillips, T.W.; Atkinson, T.H.; Foltz, J.L. 1989. Pheromone-based aggregation in *Orthotomicus caelatus* (Eichhoff) (Coleoptera: Scolytidea). Canadian Entomologist. 121(11): 933-940.

Pienaar, L.V. 1989. A stand table projection approach to yield predictions in plantations. South African Forestry Journal. 149: 44-47.

Pienaar, L.V.; Bailey, R.L.; Clutter, M.L. 1984. Pine plantation thinning practices. Georgia Forest Research Paper. 51: 5.

Pienaar, L.V.; Harrison, W.M. 1988. A stand table projection approach to yield prediction in unthinned even-aged stands. Forest Science. 34(3): 804-808.

Pienaar, L.V.; Harrison, W.M. 1989. Simultaneous growth and yield prediction equations for *Pinus elliottii* plantations in Zululand. South African Forestry Journal. 149: 48-53.

Pienaar, L.V.; Harrison, W.M.; Rheney, J.W. 1990. Volume, weight and yield tables for slash pine plantations in the southeastern Coastal Plain. Georgia Forest Research Paper. 78: 47p.

Pienaar, L.V.; Page, H.H.; Rheney, J.W. 1990. Yield prediction for mechanically site-prepared slash pine plantations. Southern Journal of Applied Forestry. 14(3): 104-109.

Pienaar, L.V.; Rheney, J.W. 1993. The effect of different site preparation treatments on slash pine plantation growth in the Atlantic Coastal Plain. Gen. Tech. Rep. SO-GTR-93. New Orleans, LA: U.S.Department of Agriculture, Forest Service, Southern Forest Experiment Station. 431-436.

Pienaar, L.V.; Rheney, J.W. 1993. Yield prediction for mechanically site-prepared slash pine plantations in the southeastern Coastal Plain. Southern Journal of Applied Forestry. 17(4): 163-173.

Pienaar, L.V.; Rheney, J.W. 1995. Modeling stand level growth and yield response to silvicultural treatments. Forest Science. 41(3): 629-638.

Pienaar, L.V.; Rheney, J.W. 1996. Results of slash pine spacing and thinning study in the southeastern Coastal Plain. Southern Journal of Applied Forestry. 20(2): 94-98.

Pienaar, L.V.; Rheney, J.W.; Shiver, B.D. 1983. Response to control of completing vegetation in site-prepared slash pine plantations. Southern Journal of Applied Forestry. 7(1): 38-45.

Pienaar, L.V.; Shiver, B.D. 1981. Survival functions for site-prepared slash pine plantations in the flatwoods of Georgia and northern Florida. Southern Journal of Applied Forestry. 5(2): 59-62.

Pienaar, L.V.; Shiver, B.D. 1984. An analysis and models of basal area growth in 45-year-old unthinned and thinned slash pine plantation plots. Forest Science. 30(4): 933-942.

Pienaar, L.V.; Shiver, B.D. 1984. The effect of planting density on dominant height in unthinned slash pine plantations. Forest Science. 30(4): 1059-1066.

Pienaar, L.V.; Shiver, B.D. 1986. Basal area prediction and projection equations for pine plantations. Forest Science. 32(2): 626-633.

Pienaar, L.V.; Shiver, B.D.; Grider, G.E. 1985. Predicting basal area growth in thinned slash pine plantations. Forest Science. 31(3): 731-741.

Platt, W.J.; Doren, R.F.; Armentano, T.V. 2000. Effects of Hurricane Andrew on stands of slash pine (*Pinus elliottii* var. *densa*) in the everglades region of south Florida (USA). Plant Ecology. 146(1): 43-60.

Platt, W.J.; Gottschalk, R.M. 2001. Effects of exotic grasses on potential fine fuel loads in the groundcover of south Florida slash pine savannas. International Journal of Wildland Fire. 10(2): 155-159.

Polglase, P.J.; Comerford, N.B.; Jokela, E.J. 1992. Leaching of inorganic phosphorus from litter of southern pine plantations. Soil Science Society of America Journal. 56(2): 573-577.

Polglase, P.J.; Comerford, N.B.; Jokela, E.J. 1992. Mineralization of nitrogen and phosphorus from soil organic matter in southern pine plantations. Soil Science Society of America Journal. 56(3): 921-927.

Polglase, P.J.; Jokela, E.J.; Comerford, N.B. 1992. Nitrogen and phosphorus release from decomposing needles of southern pine plantations. Soil Science Society of America Journal. 56(3): 914-920.

Polglase, P.J.; Jokela, E.J.; Comerford, N.B. 1992. Phosphorus, nitrogen, and carbon fractions in litter and soil of southern pine plantations. Soil Science Society of America Journal. 56(2): 566-572.

Popp, M.P.; Johnson, J.D.; Lesney, M.S. 1995. Changes in ethylene production and monterpene concentration in slash pine and loblolly pine following inoculation with bark beetle vectored fungi. Tree Physiology. 15(12): 807-812.

Popp, M.P.; Johnson, J.D.; Lesney, M.S. 1995. Characterization of the induced response of slash pine to inoculation with bark beetle vectored fungi. Tree Physiology. 15(9): 619-623.

Popp, M.P.; Johnson, J.D.; Massey, T.L. 1991. Stimulation of resin flow in slash and loblolly pine by bark beetle vectored fungi. Canadian Journal of Forest Research. 21(7): 1124-1126.

Popp, M.P.; Wilkinson, R.C.; Jokela, E.J. [and others]. 1989. Effects of slash pine phloem nutrition on the reproductive performance of *Ips calligraphus* (Coleoptera: Scolytidae). Environmental Entomology. 18(5): 795-799.

Powell, G.L.; White, T.L. 1994. Cone and seed yields from slash pine seed orchards. Southern Journal of Applied Forestry. 18(3): 122-127.

Powers, H.R., Jr. 1981. Developing fusiform rust-resistant seed orchards using survivors of artificial inoculation tests. Gen. Tech. Rep. SO-GTR-34. New Orleans, LA: U.S. Department of Agriculture, Forest Service, Southern Forest Experiment Station. 34-37.

Powers, H.R., Jr. 1984. Control of fusiform rust of southern pines in the USA. European Journal of Forest Pathology. 14(7): 426-431.

Powers, H.R., Jr.; Hubbard, S.D.; Anderson, R.L. 1982. Testing for resistance to fusiform rust of pine. In: Proceedings 3rd International Workshop on Genetics of Host-Parasite Interactions in Forestry. 427-434.

Powers, H.R., Jr.; Kraus, J.F. 1983. Developing fusiform rust-resistant loblolly and slash pines. Plant Disease. 67(2): 187-189.

Powers, H.R., Jr.; Matthews, F.R. 1987. Five fusiform rust-resistant seed sources in coastal South Carolina: a field comparison. Southern Journal of Applied Forestry. 11(4): 198-201.

Powers, H.R., Jr.; Miller, T.; Belanger, R. 1989. Silvicultural practices that reduce losses from fusiform rust. In: Proceedings of the Society of American Foresters National Convention. 182-186.

Powers, H.R., Jr.; Miller, T.; Belanger, R.P. 1993. Management strategies to reduce losses from fusiform rust. Southern Journal of Applied Forestry. 17(3): 146-149.

Powers, H.R., Jr.; Zoerb, M. 1983. Field resistance of slash pine families affected by interactions with local rust populations. Gen. Tech. Rep. SE-GTR-24. Asheville, NC: U.S. Department of Agriculture, Forest Service, Southeastern Forest Experiment Station. 427-430.

Pritchett, W.L.; Comerford, N.B. 1982. Long-term response to phosphorus fertilization on selected southeastern Coastal Plain soils. Soil Science Society of America Journal. 46(3): 640-644.

Pritchett, W.L.; Comerford, N.B. 1983. Nutrition and fertilization of slash pine. In: The Managed Slash Pine Ecosystem. Proceedings of a symposium held at the University of Florida. June 9-11, 1981. 69-90.

Pswarayi, I.Z.; Barnes, R.D. 1994. Genetic gains expected from phenotypic and combined index selection in *Pinus elliottii*. Research Paper - Zimbabwe Forestry Commission. 5(11): 36.

Pswarayi, I.Z.; Barnes, R.D.; Birks, J.S.; Kanowski, P.J. 1996. Genetic parameter estimates for production and quality traits of *Pinus elliottii* Engelm. var. *elliottii* in Zimbabwe. Slivae Genetica. 45(4): 216-222.

Pswarayi, I.Z.; Barnes, R.D.; Birks, J.S.; Kanowski, P.J. 1997. Genotype-environment interaction in a population of *Pinus elliottii* Engelm. var. *elliottii*. Silvae Genetica. 46(1): 35-40.

Putz, F.E. 1992. Reduction of root competition increases growth of slash pine seedlings on a cutover site in Florida. Southern Journal of Applied Forestry. 16(4): 193-197.

Ranasinghe, M.A.S.K.; Wilkinson, R.C. 1988. Seasonal occurrence of *Gnophothrips fuscus* (Thysanoptera: Phlaeothripidae) on slash pine in Florida. Florida Entomologist. 71(3): 384-387.

Reams, G.A.; Sullivan, A.D.; Matney, T.G. 1982. Estimating above-ground biomass of slash pine and sweetgum. Technical bulletin - Mississippi Agricultural and Forestry Experiment Station. 110: 11.

Red, J.T.; Nutter, W.L. 1986. Wastewater renovation in slash pine plantations subjected to prescribed burning. Journal of Environmental Quality. 15(4): 351-356.

Reddy, M.S.; Natarajan, K. 1996. *In vitro* ectomycorrhizal formation of *Pinus patula, P. pseudostrobus, P. oocarpa*, and *P. elliottii* grown in Southern India. New Forests. 11(2): 149-153.

Redmond, C.H.; Anderson, R.L. 1986. Economic benefits of using the resistance screening center to assess relative resistance to fusiform rust. Southern Journal of Applied Forestry. 10(1): 34-37.

Reich, R.; Dippon, D. 1984. Stand level optimization via a dynamic simulation model for slash pine plantations. In: Proceedings of the Convention of the Society of American Foresters. 520-524.

Reich, R.M.; Webb, R.S.; Arvanitis, L.G.; Patterson, H.D. 1986. Estimation of growing space for young slash pines and the association of spatial patterns of fusiform rust in Florida plantations. Applied Agricultural Research. 1(2): 124-129.

Reissman, C.B.; Zottl, H.W. 1984. Mineral nutrition and yield of pine plantations in Southern Brazil. In: Proceedings IUFRO Symposium on Site and Productivity of Fast Growing Plantations. 2: 647-658.

Reissmann, C.B. 1983. Humus horizon morphology in exotic conifer forests in South Brazil. Revista do Setor de Ciencias Agrarias. 5(1): 11-16.

Relihan, M.D.; Laing, M.D. 1996. Incidence of natural ectomycorrhizal infection of pine and eucalypt seedlings in three KwaZulu-Natal nurseries. South African Forestry Journal. 177: 31-38.

Rheney, J.W.; Shiver, B.D. 1986. Site preparation impacts on growth and yield of slash pine. In: Proceedings of the Society of American Foresters National Convention. 85-88.

Rheney, J.W.; Shiver, B.D.; Pienaar, L.V. 1986. Response to removal of competing vegetation in slash pine plantations. In: Proceedings, Southern Weed Science Society, 39th Annual Meeting. 246-250.

Ribas, C.; Assini, J.L.; De Garrido, M.A.; Do Garrido, L.M. 1982. Mass selection of phenotypes for high resin production in *Pinus elliottii* var. *elliottii*. Boletim Tecnico do Instituto Florestal. 36(3): 137-147.

Ribas, C.; Do Garrido, L.M.; De Garrido, M.A. [and others]. 1984. Resin production and influence on dendrometric growth in *Pinus elliottii* var. *elliottii* of different diameters. Boletim Technico do Instituto Florestal. 38(2): 155-163.

Ribas, C.; Do Garrido, L.M.; De Garrdio, M.A. [and others]. 1984. Resin production in *Pinus* - comparison between operational techniques and chemical stimulants. Boletim Technico do Instituto Florestal. 38(1): 35-46.

Richmond, G.B.; McKinley, C.R. 1986. An experimental seed orchard in south Texas. Journal of Forestry. 84(7): 19.

Riekerk, H. 1983. Impacts of silviculture on flatwoods runoff, water quality, and nutrient budgets. Water Resources Bulletin. 19(1): 73-79.

Riekerk, H. 1985. Lysimetric evaluation of pine forest evapotranspiration. In: Proceedings of the forest environmental measurements conference held at Oak Ridge, Tennessee. 293-308.

Riekerk, H. 1985. Lysimetric measurement of pine evapotranspiration for water balances. In: Proceedings of the National Conference on Advances in Evapotranspiration. 276-281.

Riekerk, H. 1985. Water quality effects of pine flatwoods silviculture. Journal of soil and water conservation. 40(3): 306-309.

Riekerk, H. 1989. Forest fertilizer and runoff-water quality. In: Proceedings - Soil and Crop Science Society of Florida. 48: 99-102.

Riekerk, H. 1989. Influence of silvicultural practices on the hydrology of pine flatwoods in Florida. Water Resources Research. 25(4): 713-719.

Riekerk, H.; Lutrick, M.C. 1986. Slash pine growth and yield responses to sludge applications. Southern Journal of Applied Forestry. 10(3): 142-145.

Riekerk, H.; Mace, A.C.; Neary, D.G.; Swindel, B.F. 1986. Hydrologic responses to forest management in pine flatwoods and Florida's water. In: Proceedings - Soil and Crop Science Society of Florida. 45: 163-169.

Riley, M.A.; Goyer, R.A. 1986. Impact of beneficial insects on Ips. spp. (Coleoptera: Scolytidae) bark beetles in felled loblolly and slash pines in Louisiana. Environmental Entomology. 15(6): 1220-1224.

Riley, M.A.; Goyer, R.A. 1988. Seasonal abundance of beneficial insects and Ips spp. engraver beetles (Coleoptera: Scolytidae) in felled loblolly and slash pines in Louisiana. Journal of Entomological Science. 23(4): 357-365.

Roberts, D.R.; Outcalt, K.W. 1983. Optimum paraquat treatments for inducing resin-soaking in slash and loblolly pines. Southern Journal of Applied Forestry. 7(1): 31-33.

Roberts, D.R.; Williams, I.L.; Kossuth, S.V. 1982. Double application of paraquat for production of lightwood with high oleoresin content. Forest Products Journal. 32(10): 74-78.

Robinson, J.L.; Clason, T. 2000. From a pasture to a silvo-pasture system. Agroforestry Notes. 22: 4p.

Rockwood, D.L. 1981. Volume prediction for genetically improved slash pine trees. Bulletin, Agricultural Experiment Stations, University of Florida. 819: 17p.

Rockwood, D.L. 1983. Alternative designs for progency testing slash pine. In: Proceedings of the Southern Forest Tree Improvement Conference. 39: 179-185.

Rockwood, D.L. 1984. Genetic improvement potential for biomass quality and quantity. Biomass. 6(1): 37-45.

Rockwood, D.L.; Blakeslee, G.M.; Lowerts, G.A. [and others]. 1988. Genetic stategies for reducing pitch canker incidence in slash pine. Southern Journal of Applied Forestry. 12(1): 28-32.

Rockwood, D.L.; Dippon, D.R. 1989. Biological and economic potentials of Eucalyptus grandis and slash pine as biomass energy crops. Biomass. 20(3): 155-165.

Rockwood, D.L.; Harding, K.J.; Nikles, D.G. 1991. Variation in the wood properties of the Pinus elliottii X Pinus caribaea, var. hondurensis F1 hybrid, its parental species, and back-cross to Pinus elliottii in Australia. In: Proceedings, Southern Forest Tree Improvement Conference. 21: 233-240.

Rockwood, D.L.; Huber, D.A.; White, T.L. 2001. Provenance and family variability in slash pine (Pinus elliottii var. elliottii Engelm.) grown in Southern Brazil and Northeastern Argentina. New Forests. 21(2): 115-125.

Rockwood, D.L.; Windsor, C.L.; Hodges, J.F. 1985. Response of slash pine progenies to fertilization. Southern Journal of Applied Forestry. 9(1): 37-40.

Rolando, C.A.; Little, K.M. 2000. The impact of vegetation control on the establishment of pine at four sites in the summer rainfall region of South Africa. ICFR Bulletin Series. 21: 29p.

Rosado, S.C.S.; Kropp, B.R.; Piche, Y. 1994. Genetics of ectomycorrhizal symbiosis: I. Host plant variability and heritability of ectomycorrhizal and root traits. New Phytologist. 126(1): 105-110.

Rosado, S.C.S.; Kropp, B.R.; Piche, Y. 1994. Genetics of ectomycorrhizal symbiosis: II. Fungal variability and heritability of ectomycorrhizal traits. New Phytologist. 126(1): 111-117.

Rose, C.E., Jr.; Shiver, B.D. 2002. An assessment of first and second rotations average dominant codominant height growth for slash pine plantations in south Georgia and north Florida. Southern Journal of Applied Forestry. 26(2): 61-71.

Rosen, D.; Bennett, F.D.; Capinera, J.L. 1996. Chemical ecology of bark beetles in the Florida slash pine ecosystem. In: Pest Management in the Subtropics: Integrated Pest Management a Florida Perspective. 209-222.

Ross, D.W.; Birgersson, G.; Espelie, K.E.; Berisford, C.W. 1995. Monterpene emissions and cuticular lipids of loblolly and slash pines: potential bases for oviposition preference of the Nantucket pine tip moth. Canadian Journal of Botany. 73(1): 21-25.

Ross, E.W.; Hodges, C.S., Jr. 1981. Control of Heterobasidion annousum colonization in mechanically sheared slash pine stumps treated with Peniophora gigantea. Res. Pap. SE-RP-229. Asheville, NC: U.S. Department of Agriculture, Forest Service, Southeastern Forest Experiment Station. 3p.

Rost, A.A.; Arvanitis, L.G. 1984. Estimation of woody biomass in slash pine plantations using color aerial photography feasibility study. In: Proceedings. American Society of Photogrammetry. 121-128.

Roundtree, K.R. 1988. The decline of the south Florida slash pine. In: Proceedings of the Florida State Horticultural Society, 101: 118-120.

Rowan, S.J. 1981. Efficacy of five fungicidal compounds for control of fusiform rust of pine seedlings. In: Fungicide and Nematicide Tests, Results - American Phytopathological Society, 36: 130.

Rowan, S.J. 1982. Effects of rate and kind of seedbed mulch and sowing depth on germination of southern pine seed. Tree Planters' Notes. 33(2): 9-21.

Rowan, S.J. 1982. Influence of method and rate of application of Bayleton on fusiform rust on slash pine seedlings. Tree Planters' Notes. 33(1): 15-17.

Rowan, S.J. 1982. Tip dieback in southern pine nurseries. Plant Disease. 66(3): 258-259.

Rowan, S.J. 1983. Loss of feeder roots lowers seedling survival more than severe black root rot. Tree Planters' Notes. 34(1): 18-20.

Rowan, S.J. 1984. Bayleton (R) seed treatment combined with foliar spray improves fusiform rust control in nurseries. Southern Journal of Applied Forestry. 8(1): 51-54.

Rowan, S.J. 1986. Seedbed density affects performance of slash and loblolly pine in Georgia. In: Proceedings of the International Symposium on Nursery Management Practices for the Southern Pines. 126-135.

Rowan, S.J. 1986. Triademefon controls fusiform rust in young slash pine plantations. Southern Journal of Applied Forestry. 10(2): 112-114.

Rowan, S.J.; Kelley, W.D. 1986. Survival and growth of outplanted pine seedlings after mycorrhizae were inhibited by use of triadimefon in the nursery. Southern Journal of Applied Forestry. 10(1): 21-23.

Rowan, S.J.; Muse, D. 1981. Latent fusiform rust infections in slash and loblolly pine nursery stock. Gen. Tech. Rep. SO-GTR-34. New Orleans, LA: U.S. Department of Agriculture, Forest Service, Southern Forest Experiment Station. 38-40.

Ruark, G.A.; Thomas, C.E.; Becthold, W.A.; May, D.M. 1991. Growth reductions in naturally regenerated southern pine stands in Alabama and Georgia. Southern Journal of Applied Forestry. 15(2): 73-79.

Sage, R.D. 1985. Chemical vs. mechanical site preparation for east Florida flatwoods - a pilot scale trial. In: Proceedings, Southern Weed Science Society, 38th Annual Meeting. 213-215.

Salom, S.M. 1997. Status and management of pales weevil in the Eastern United States. Tree Planters' Notes. 48(1): 4-11.

Samuelson, L.J. 2000. Effects of nitrogen on leaf physiology and growth of different families of loblolly and slash pine. New Forests. 1: 95-107.

Sands, R. [and others]. 1983. Effects of management on physical and chemical properties of soil and on yield. Gen. Tech. Rep. PNW-GTR-163. Portland, OR: U.S. Department of Agriculture, Forest Service, Pacific Northwest Forest and Range Experiment Station. 146-279.

Sanz, J.A. 1989. Naval stores status in South America with a focus on Brazil. Naval Stores Review. 99(5): 6-9.

Sarigumba, T.I. 1985. Sustained response of planted slash pine to spacing and site preparation. Gen. Tech. Rep. SO-GTR-54. New Orleans, LA: U.S. Department of Agriculture, Forest Service, Southern Forest Experiment Station. 79-84.

Saucier, J.R.; Clark, A.C., III. 1992. New evidence on the role of the environmental factors associated with the length of juvenile wood formation in the southern pines. IAWA Bulletin Series. 13(3): 262.

Saucier, J.R.; Phillips, D.R.; Williams, J.G., Jr. 1981. Green weight, volume, board-foot, and cord tables for the major southern pine species. Georgia Forest Research Paper. 19: 63p.

Schafer, G.N. 1988. A site growth model for Pinus elliottii in the southern Cape. South African Forestry Journal. 146: 12-17.

Schilling, A.C.; Schneider, P.R.; Haselein, C.; Finger, C.A.G. 1997. Influence of pruning on wood density of the first thinning of Pinus elliottii Engelm. Ciencia Florestal. 7(1): 77-89.

Schilling, A.C.; Schneider, P.R.; Haselein, C.R.; Finger, C.A.G. 1998. Influence of different pruning intensities on the percentage of latewood and quantity of knots from the first thinning of Pinus elliottii Engelman. Ciencia Florestal. 8(1): 115-127.

Schmidt, R.A.; Allen, J.E.; Belanger, R.P.; Miller, T. 1995. Influence of oak control and pine growth on fusiform rust incidence in young slash and loblolly pine plantations. Southern Journal of Applied Forestry. 19(4): 151-156.

Schmidt, R.A.; Gramacho, K.P.; Miller, T.; Young, C.H. 2000. Components of partial resistance in the slash pine-fusiform rust pathosystem. Phytopathology. 90(9): 1005-1010.

Schmidt, R.A.; Holley, R.C.; Klapproth, M.C.; Miller, T. 1986. Temporal and spatial patterns of fusiform rust epidemics in young plantations of susceptible and resistant slash and loblolly pines. Plant Disease. 70(7): 661-666.

Schmidt, R.A.; Jokela, E.J.; Allen, J.E.; Belanger, R.P.; Miller, T. 1990. Association between fusiform rust incidence and CRIFF soil classification for slash pine plantations in the Coastal Plain of Florida and Georgia. Southern Journal of Applied Forestry. 14(1): 39-43.

Schmidt, R.A.; Klapproth, M.C. 1982. Delineation of fusiform rust hazard based on estimated volume loss as a guide to rust management decisions in slash pine plantations. Southern Journal of Applied Forestry. 6(1): 59-63.

Schmidt, R.A.; Miller, T. 1999. Influence of inoculum concentration on production of r and aecia on pine seedlings infected by basidiospores of Cronartium quercuum f. sp. fuisorme. Plant Disease. 83(4): 367-370.

Schmidt, R.A.; Miller, T.; Holley, R.C. [and others]. 1988. Relation of site factors in fusiform rust incidence in young slash and loblolly pine plantations in the Coastal Plain of Florida and Georgia. Plant Disease. 72(8): 710-714.

Schmidt, R.A.; Wilkinson, R.C. 1981. Prospects for integrated pest management in slash pine ecosystems in Florida. In: Proceedings of Symposia, IX International Congress of Plant Protection. 610-615.

Schmidtling, R.C. 1983. Timing of fertilizer application important for management of southern pine seed orchards. Southern Journal of Applied Forestry. 7(2): 76-81.

Schmidtling, R.C. 1988. Influence of rootstock on flowering, growth, and foliar nutrients of slash pine grafts. In: Proceedings, 10th North American Forest Biology Workshop. 120-127.

Schneider, P.R.; Finger, C.A.G.; Hope, J.M. 1999. The effect of pruning intensity on the production of *Pinus elliottii* Engelm., planted in a poor soil in the state of Rio Grande do Sul. Ciencia Florestal. 9(1): 35-46.

Schreiber, J.D.; Duffy, P.D. 1982. Organic carbon and oxygen demand relationships in stormflow from southern pine watersheds. Soil Science of America Journal. 46: 142-148.

Schroeer, A.E.; Hendrick, R.L.; Harrington, T.B. 1999. Root, ground cover, and litterfall dynamics within canopy gaps in a slash pine (*Pinus elliotti* Englem.) dominated forest. Ecoscience. 6(4): 548-555.

Schultz, R.P. 1983. The original slash pine forest - an historic view. In: The Managed Slash Pine Ecosystem. Proceedings of a symposium held at the University of Florida. June 9-11, 1981. 24-48.

Segal, D.S.; Neary, D.G.; Best, G.R.; Michael, J.L. 1987. Effect of ditching, fertilization, and herbicide application on groundwater levels and groundwater quality in a flatwood Spodosol. In: Proceedings, Soil and Crop Science Society of Florida. 46: 107-112.

Semke, L.K. 1984. Effects of juvenile pine fibers on kraft paper properties. In: Proceedings of the Symposium on utilization of the changing wood resource in the southern United States. 160-177.

Sequeira, W.; Gholz, H.L. 1991. Canopy structure, light penetration and tree growth in a slash pine (*Pinus elliottii*) silvo-pastoral system at different stand configurations in Florida. The Forestry Chronicle. 67(3): 263-267.

Sferrazza, M.J. 1987. A comparison of thermomechanical pulps from Queensland slash pine and Southern US slash and loblolly pine. Appita Journal. 40(3): 201-207.

Shan, J.P.; Morris, L.A.; Hendrick, R.L. 2001. The effects of management on soil and plant carbon sequestration in slash pine plantations. Journal of Applied Ecology. 38(5): 932-941.

Sharma, N.K.; Dwinell, L.D.; Noe, J.P. 1989. *Helicotylenchus multicinctus* found in a slash pine seed orchard in Georgia. Plant Disease. 73(6): 518.

Sheffield, R.M.; Knight, H.A.; McClure, J.P. 1983. The slash pine resource. In: The Managed Slash Pine Ecosystem. Proceedings of a symposium held at the University of Florida. June 9-11, 1981. 4-23.

Shen, X.N.; Jiang, J.M.; Wu, C.Z.; Hu, S.C. 1998. Effects of different thinning intensities on slash pine plantations. Forest Research. 11(5): 513-517.

Shepard, R.K., Jr. 1981. Ice damage to slash and loblolly pine in northern Louisiana. Tree Planters' Notes. 32(1): 6-8.

Sheridan, J.M.; Lowrance, R.; Bosch, D.D. 1999. Management effects on runoff and sediment transport in riparian forest buffers. Transactions of the ASAE. 42(1): 55-64.

Shimizu, J.Y.; Spir, I.H.Z. 1999. Selection of slash pine on breeding values for high resin production. Boletim de Pesquisa Florestal. 38: 103-117.

Shiver, B.D. 1988. Sample size and estimation methods for the Weibull distribution for unthinned slash pine plantation diameter distributions. Forest Science. 34(3): 809-814.

Shiver, B.D. 1994. Response and economics of mid-rotation competition control in southern pine plantations. Weed Science Education: the cost of Ignorance. In: Proceedings of the 4th Annual Meeting of the Southern Weed Science Society. 85-92.

Shiver, B.D.; Rheney, J.W. 1993. Effect of genetic improvement and vegetation control on loblolly and slash pine plantations after three growing seasons. Gen. Tech. Rep. SO-GTR-93. New Orleans, LA: U.S.Department of Agriculture, Forest Service, Southern Forest Experiment Station. 299-302.

Shiver, B.D.; Rheney, J.W.; Hitch, K.L. 2000. Loblolly pine outperforms slash pine in southeastern Georgia and northern Florida. Southern Journal of Applied Forestry. 24(1): 31-36.

Shiver, B.D.; Rheney, J.W.; Oppenheimer, M.J. 1990. Site-preparation method and early cultural treatments affect growth of flatwoods slash pine plantations. Southern Journal of Applied Forestry. 14(4): 183-188.

Shiver, B.D.; Rheney, J.W.; Pienaar, L.V.; Fortson, J.C. 1986. Effect of site preparation and vegetation control on slash pine plantation growth. In: Proceedings, Southern Weed Science Society, 39th Annual Meeting. 210-216.

Shoulders, E. 1981. Concentration and distribution of selected elements in aboveground biomass of 8-year-old slash pine. Gen. Tech. Rep. SO-GTR-34. New Orleans, LA: U.S. Department of Agriculture, Forest Service, Southern Forest Experiment Station. 154-158.

Shoulders, E. 1982. Comparison of growth and yield of four southern pines on uniform sites on the Gulf Coastal Plain. In: Annual Forestry Symposium, Louisiana State University, Division of Continuing Education. 31: 75-100.

Shoulders, E.; Baldwin, V.C.; Tiarks, A.E. 1989. Mid-rotation fertilization affects stem form in planted slash pine. Gen. Tech. Rep. SO-GTR-74. New Orleans, LA: U.S. Department of Agriculture, Forest Service, Southern Forest Experiment Station. 455-459.

Shoulders, E.; Tiarks, A.E. 1990. Nine year response of thinned slash pine to nitrogen, phosphorus, and potassium. Soil Science Society of America Journal. 54(1): 234-237.

Shukla, A.N.; Schmidt, R.A.; Miller, T. 2001. Symptoms in slash pine seedlings following inoculation with the cone rust fungus *Cronartium strobilinum*. Forest Pathology. 31(6): 345-352.

Siegfried, B.D.; Fatzinger, C.W.; Wilkinson, R.C.; Nation, J.L. 1986. In-flight responses of the black turpentine beetle (Coleoptera:Scolytidae) to individual monoterpenes, turpentine, and paraquat-treated slash pines. Environmental Entomology. 15(3): 710-714.

Simpson, J.A.; Osborne, D.O. 1993. Relative fertilizer requirements and foliar nutrient levels of young slash pine, Honduras Caribbean pine and the hybrid in Queensland. Commonwealth Forestry Review. 72(2): 105-113.

Simpson, J.A.; Osborne, D.O.; Xu, Z.H. 1998. Pine plantations on the coastal lowlands of subtropical Queensland, Australia. In: Site Management and Productivity in Tropical Plantation Forests, Workshop Proceedings. 61-67.

Simpson, J.A.; Xu, Z.H.; Smith, T. [and others]. 2000. Effects of site management in pine plantations on the coastal lowlands of subtropical Queensland, Australia. In: Site Management and Productivity in Tropical Plantation Forests: a Progress Report. 73-81.

Simpson, W.T. 2002. Effect of wet bulb depression on heat sterilization time of slash pine lumber. Res. Pap. FPL-RP-604. Madison, WI: U.S. Department of Agriculture, Forest Service, Forest Products Laboratory. 6p.

Skoog, P.J.; Harris, L.D. 1981. Utilization of pine *Pinus elliottii* plantations by white-tailed deer in north Florida. IMPAC reports. Gainesville, FL: U.S. Department of Agriculture, Forest Service, Southeastern Forest Experiment Station, Intensive Management Practices Assessment Center. 6: 19p.

Slansky, F., Jr.; Haack, R.A. 1986. Age-specific flight behavior in relation to body weight and lipid content of *Ips calligraphus* reared in slash pine bolts with thick or thin inner bark (phloem). Entomologia Experimentalis et Applicata. 40(2): 197-207.

Slee, M.U.; Abbott, D.C. 1990. Pollination investigations for production of the hybrid between slash and Caribbean pines. South African Forestry Journal. 152: 7-16.

Sluder, E.R. 1983. Three increments of gain from three stages of selection in slash and longleaf pines and heritabilities at age 21 years. In: Proceedings of the Southern Forest Tree Improvement Conference. 39: 253-261.

Sluder, E.R. 1986. Gains from first-cycle selection in slash and longleaf pines. Silvae Genetica, 35(4): 155-159.

Sluder, E.R. 1989. Fusiform rust in crosses among resistant and susceptible loblolly and slash pines. Southern Journal of Applied Forestry. 13(4): 174-177.

Sluder, E.R. 1989. Gain and variation after two generations of selection in slash pine in Georgia. Research Report - Georgia Forestry Commission 5: 5.

Sluder, E.R. 1991. Seed and seedling size grading of slash pine has little effect on long-term growth of trees. Tree Planters' Notes. 42(3): 23-27.

Sluder, E.R. 1994. Gains in fusiform rust resistance and height growth in a second generation slash pine seedling orchard. Silvae Genetica. 43(1): 41-48.

Sluder, E.R. 1996. Two-stage selection in slash pine produces good gains in fusiform rust resistance. Southern Journal of Applied Forestry. 20(3): 143-147.

Sluder, E.R.; Powers, H.R., Jr. 1982. Fusiform rust infection of loblolly and slash pines after artificial inoculation and natural exposure in plantations. Res. Note. SE-RN-318. Asheville, NC: U.S. Department of Agriculture, Forest Service, Southeastern Forest Experiment Station. 5p.

Sluder, E.R.; Powers, H.R., Jr. 1986. Further comparisons between infection of loblolly and slash pines in fusiform rust after artificial inoculation or planting. Res. Note. SE-RN-342. Asheville, NC: U.S. Department of Agriculture, Forest Service, Southeastern Forest Experiment Station. 4p.

Smethurst, P.J.; Comerford, N.B. 1993. Potassium and phosphorus uptake by competing pine and grass: observations and model verification. Soil Science Society of America Journal. 57(6): 1602-1610.

Smethurst, P.J.; Comerford, N.B. 1993. Simulating nutrient uptake by single or competing and contrasting root systems. Soil Science Society of America Journal. 57(5): 1361-1367.

Smethurst, P.J.; Comerford, N.B.; Neary, D.G. 1993. Predicting the effects of weeds on K and P uptake by young slash pine on a Spodosol. Forest Ecology and Management. 60(1): 27-39.

Smethurst, P.J.; Comerford, N.B.; Neary, D.G. 1993. Weed effects on early K and P nutrition and growth of slash pine on a Spodosol. Forest Ecology and Management. 60(1): 15-26.

Smith, C.K.; White, T.L.; Hodge, G.R. 1993. Genetic variation in second-year slash pine shoot traits and their relationship to 5- and 15-year volume in the field. Silvae Genetica. 42(4): 266-275.

Smith, C.K.; White, T.L.; Hodge, G.R. [and others]. 1993. Genetic variation in first-year slash pine shoot components and their relationship to mature field performance. Canadian Journal of Forest Research. 23(8): 1557-1565.

Smith, G.P.; Shelburne, V.B.; Walker, J.L. 1999. Structure and composition of vegetation on longleaf pine (*Pinus palustris*) and slash pine (*Pinus elliottii*) plantation sites in the hilly Coastal Plain of South Carolina. Gen. Tech. Rep. SRS-GTR-30. Asheville, NC: U.S. Department of Agriculture, Forest Service, Southern Research Station. 228-231.

Smith, H.; Wingfield, M.J.; Crous, P.W.; Coutinho, T.A. 1996. *Sphaeropsis sapinea* and *Botryosphaeira dothidea* endophytic in *Pinus* spp. *Eucalyptus* spp. in South Africa. South African Journal of Botany. 62(2): 86-88.

Smith, W.H.; Dowd, M.L. 1981. Biomass production in Florida. Journal of Forestry. 79(8): 508-511, 515.

Snow, G.A. 1986. A needle blight of slash and loblolly pines in south Mississippi. Gen. Tech. Rep. WO-GTR-50. Washington DC: U.S. Department of Agriculture, Forest Service, Washington DC Office. Pp. 20-21.

Snow, G.A. 1990. Current status of slash and loblolly pine needlecast diseases in the Gulf States. Gen. Tech. Rep. WO-GTR-56. Washington, DC: U.S. Department of Agriculture, Forest Service, Washington DC office. 69-70.

Snow, G.A.; Feduccia, D.P. 1983. Bayleton tested against fusiform rust on 3-year old slash pine. In: Fungicide and Nematicide Tests: Results - American Phytopathological Society. v38: 181.

Snowdon, P. 1981. Estimation of height from diameter measurements in fertilizer trials. Australian Forest Research, 11(3): 223-230.

Snowdon, P.; Waring, H.D.; Woollons, R.C. 1981. Effect of fertilizer and weed control on stem form and average taper in plantation-grown pines. Australian Forest Research. 11(3): 209-221.

Sohlenius, B. 1997. Fluctuations of nematode populations in pine forest soil. Fundamental and Applied Nematology. 20(2): 103-114.

Sommer, H.E.; Wetzstein, H.Y.; Stine, M.; Lee, N. 1984. Differentiation in tissue culture of sweetgum and southern pines. In: Proceedings of the Technical Association of the Pulp and Paper Industry. 35-37.

Sorrentino, F.A. 1990. Yield of exotic forest species in Uruguay. Boletin de Investigacion - Facultad de Agronomia, Montevideo. 27: 36.

Sorrentino, F.A. 1991. Provisional site indexes for the main forest species cultivated in Uruguay. Boletin de Investigacion - Facultad de Agronomia. 33: 52.

Sorrentino, Fattoruso, I. 1983. Local merchantable volume tables for *Pinus pinaster, P. elliottii* and *P. taeda*. Boletin, Facultad de Agronomia, Universidad de la Repulica. 135: 34.

South, D.B. 1986. Diphenylether herbicides in southern pine nurseries. In: Proceedings of the International Symposium on Nursery Management Practices for the Southern Pines. 441-445.

South, D.B. 1987. A re-evaluation of Wakeley's "critical tests" of morphological grades of southern pine nursery stock. South African Forestry Journal. 142: 56-59.

South, D.B. 1988. Diphenylether herbicides used on southern pine seedlings in the United States. Aspects of Applied Biology. 16: 215-222.

South, D.B. 1997. Fomesaen: a herbicide of pine seedbeds. Southern Journal of Applied Forestry. 21(3): 143-145.

South, D.B. 1998. Effects of top-pruning on survival of southern pines and hardwoods. Gen. Tech. Rep. SRS-GTR-20. Asheville, NC: U.S. Department of Agriculture, Forest Service, Southern Research Station. 3-8.

South, D.B. 2000. Tolerance of southern pine seedlings to clopyralid. Southern Journal of Applied Forestry. 24(1): 51-56.

South, D.B.; Donald, D.G.M.; Rakestraw, J.L. 1993. Effect of nursery culture and bud status on freeze injury to *Pinus taeda* and *P. elliottii* seedlings. South African Forestry Journal. 166: 37-45.

South, D.B.; Gjerstad, D.H. 1983. Postemergence weed control in loblolly, slash, longleaf, and eastern white pine nursery seedbeds. Canadian Journal of Forest Research. 13(6): 1257-1261.

South, D.B.; Mitchell, R.J. 1999. Determining the "optimum" slash pine seedling size for use with four levels of vegetation management on a flatwoods site in Georgia, U.S.A. Canadian Journal of Forest Research. 29(7): 1039-1046.

South, D.B.; Zwolinski, J.B. 1997. Transplant stress index: a proposed method of quantifying planting check. New Forests. 13(1): 315-328.

Spathelf, P.; Schneider, P.R. 2000. Development of a density management diagram as a decision tool for growth control of *Pinus elliottii* Engelm. stands. Forstwissenschaftliches Centralblatt. 119(3): 89-99.

Spathelf, P.; Seling, I. 2000. Economic effects of different thinning programmes in *Pinus elliottii* stands. Ciencia Florestal. 10(1): 21-44.

Squillace, A.E.; Goddard, R.E. 1982. Selfing in clonal seed orchards of slash pine. Forest Science. 28(1): 71-78.

Squillace, A.E.; Layton, P.A.; Goddard, R.E. 1983. Relation between height and fusiform rust infection in slash pine. In: Proceedings of the Southern Forest Tree Improvement Conference. 39: 262-270.

Stanger, T.K.; Shaw, M.J.P.; Braunstein, R.; Nikles, D.G. 1999. A comparison of the kraft pulp properties of *P. elliottii* and the *P. elliottii* x *P. caribaea* var. *hondurensis* hybrid grown in Queensland, Australia. Southern African Forestry Journal. 186: 9-14.

Stearns-Smith, S.C.; Jokela, E.J.; Abt, R.C. 1992. Thinning and fertilizing southern pine stands of the lower Coastal Plain: biological and economic effects. Southern Journal of Applied Forestry. 16(4): 186-193.

Stelzer, H.E.; Doudrick, R.L.; Kubisiak, T.L.; Nelson, C.D. 1999. Slash pine and *Cronartium* pedigrees for evaluation of complementary gene action in fusiform rust disease. Plant Disease. 83(4): 385-389.

Stewart, A.W.; Hurst, G.A. 1987. Vegetation in the longleaf-slash pine forest, Biloxi District, DeSoto National Forest, Mississippi. Gen. Tech. Rep. SO-GTR-68. New Orleans, LA: U.S. Department of Agriculture, Forest Service, Southern Forest Experiment Station. 149-155.

Stine, M.; Sommer, H.E. 1985. Comparison of adventitious shoot formation from mature embryos of longleaf pine, slash pine, and the hybrid, longleaf pine X slash pine. In: Proceedings of the North Central Tree Improvement Conference. 6-11.

Stone, C. 1993. Survey of arthropods from billets on *Pinus* following infestation by *Ips grandicollis* (Eichloff) (Coleoptera: Scolytidae) in Northeastern New South Wales. Journal of Australian Entomological Society. 32(4): 289-296.

Stone, C.; Simpson, J.A. 1991. Influence of cell viability of freshly felled *Pinus elliottii* on the subcortical community associated with *Ips grandicollis* (Coleoptera: Scolytidae). Canadian Journal of Forest Research. 21(7): 1006-1011.

Stone, E.L., ed. 1983. The managed slash pine ecosystem. Proceedings of a symposium held at the University of Florida. June 9-11, 1981. 434p.

Stone, E.L.; Hollis, C.A.; Barnard, E.L. 1982. Boron deficiency in a southern pine nursery. Southern Journal of Applied Forestry. 6(2): 108-112.

Strub, M.R.; Sprinz, P.T. 1988. Comparisons of southern pine height growth. Gen. Tech. Rep. NC-GTR-120. St. Paul, MN: U.S. Department of Agriculture, Forest Service, North Central Research Station. 428-434.

Stubbs, J. 1983. Paraquat-induced lightwood in southern pine. In: The Managed Slash Pine Ecosystem. Proceedings of a symposium held at the University of Florida. June 9-11, 1981. 385-393.

Stubbs, J.; Roberts, D.R.; Outcalt, K.W. 1984. Chemical stimulation of lightwood in southern pines. Gen. Tech. Rep. SE-GTR-25. Asheville, NC: U.S. Department of Agriculture, Forest Service, Southeastern Forest Experiment Station. 51p.

Sun, G. 1981. Studies on the types of slash pine. Forest Science and Technology 3: 1-4.

Sun, G.; Riekerk, H.; Comerford, N.B. 1996. FLATWOODS- a distributed hydrologic simulation model for Florida pine flatwoods. In: Proceedings - Soil and Crop Science Society of Florida. 55: 23-32.

Sun, G.; Riekerk, H.; Korhnak, L.V. 1995. Shallow groundwater table dynamics of cypress wetland/pine upland systems in Florida flatwoods. In: Proceedings - Soil and Crop Science Society of Florida. 54: 66-71.

Surles, S.E.; White, T.L.; Hodge, G.R. 1995. Genetic parameter estimates for seedling dry weight traits and their relationship with parental breeding values in slash pine. Forest Science. 41(3): 546-563.

Surles, S.E.; White, T.L.; Hodge, G.R.; Duryea, M.L. 1993. Relationships among seed weight components, seedling growth traits, and predicted field breeding values in slash pine. Canadian Journal of Forest Research. 23(8): 1550-1556.

Suzuki, K. 1984. General effect of water stress on the development of pine wilting disease caused by *Bursaphelenchus xylphilus*. In: Bulletin, Forestry and Forest Products Research Institute, Japan. 325: 97-126.

Swindel, B.F.; Conde, L.F.; Smith, J.E. 1983. Plant cover and biomass response to clear-cutting, site preparation, and planting in *Pinus elliottii* flatwoods of Florida. Science. 219: 1421-1422.

Swindel, B.F.; Conde, L.F.; Smith, J.E. 1984. Species diversity: concept, measurement, and response to clearcutting and site-preparation. Forest Ecology and Management. 8(1): 11-22.

Swindel, B.F.; Conde, L.F.; Smith, J.E. 1986. Successional changes in *Pinus elliottii* plantations following two regeneration treatments. Canadian Journal of Forest Research. 16(3): 630-636.

Swindel, B.F.; Conde, L.F.; Smith, J.E. 1986. Windrowing affects early growth of slash pine. Southern Journal of Applied Forestry. 10(2): 81-84.

Swindel, B.F.; Conde, L.F.; Smith, J.E. 1987. Index-free diversity orderings: concept, measurement, and observed response to clearcutting and site-preparation. Forest Ecology and Management. 20(3): 195-208.

Swindel, B.F.; Conde, L.F.; Smith, J.E.; Hollis, C.A., III. 1982. Green weights of major tree species in north Florida pine flatwoods. Southern Journal of Applied Forestry. 6(2): 74-78.

Swindel, B.F.; Lassiter, C.J.; Riekerk, H. 1982. Effects of clearcutting and site preparation on water yields from slash pine forests. Forest Ecology and Management. 4(2): 101-113.

Swindel, B.F.; Lassiter, C.J.; Riekerk, H. 1983. Effects of clearcutting and site preparation on stormflow volumes of streams in *Pinus elliottii* flatwood forests. Forest Ecology and Management. 5(4): 245-253.

Swindel, B.F.; Lassiter, C.J.; Riekerk, H. 1983. Effects of different harvesting and site preparation operations on the peak flows of streams in *Pinus elliottii* flatwoods forests. Forest Ecology and Management. 5(2): 77-86.

Swindel, B.F.; Smith, J.E.; Neary, D.G.; Comerford, N.B. 1989. Recent research indicates plant community responses to intensive treatments including chemical amendments. Southern Journal of Applied Forestry. 13(3): 152-156.

Swindel, B.F.; Smith, J.E.; Outcalt, K.W. 1989. Long-term response of competing vegetation to mechanical site preparation in pine plantations. Gen. Tech. Rep. SO-GTR-74. New Orleans, LA: U.S. Department of Agriculture, Forest Service, Southern Forest Experiment Station. 123-127.

Sylvia, D.M. 2000. Short root densities and surface phosphatase activities of ectomycorrhizal morphotypes in a slash pine plantation. Journal of Sustainable Forestry. 11(3): 83-93.

Sylvia, D.M.; Jarstfer, A.G. 1997. Distribution of mycorrhiza on competing pines and weeds in a southern pine plantation. Soil Science Society of America Journal. 61(1): 139-144.

Tam, P.C.F. 1994. Mycorrhizal associations in *Pinus massoniana* Lamb. and *Pinus elliottii* Engel. inoculated with *Pisolithus tinctorius*. Mycorrhiza. 4(6): 255-263.

Tang, C.Y. 1996. Interception and recharge processes beneath a *Pinus elliottii* forest. Hydrological Processess. 10(11): 1427-1434.

Tang, R.N.; Tang, X.L. 1987. Studies of ecological benefits of interplanting slash pine in a tea plantation. Journal of Nanjing Forestry University. 2: 35-44.

Tang, W.; Fan, O.Y.; Guo, Z.C. 1997. Plantlet regeneration via somatic embryogenesis in slash pine. Journal of Plant Resources and Environment. 6(2): 8-11.

Tankersley, L.; Bongarten, B.; Brister, G.; Zoerb, M. 1983. Operational plantations of improved slash pine: age 15 results. In: Proceedings of the Southern Forest Tree Improvement Conference. 39: 271-280.

Tanner, G.W. 1987. Soils and vegetation of the longleaf/slash pine forest type, Apalachicola National Forest, Florida. Gen. Tech. Rep. SO-GTR-68. New Orleans, LA: U.S. Department of Agriculture, Forest Service, Southern Forest Experiment Station. 186-200.

Teare, I.D.; Wright, D.L.; Stanley, R.L., Jr.; Kidd, B.T. 1987. Bahiagrass response to lime and nitrogen under pines. Agronomy Journal. 79(1): 1-4.

Terry, W.S.; Tanner, G.W. 1986. Nutritive value of two major grasses on north Florida slash pine plantations. In: Proceedings, Soil and Crop Science Society of Florida. 45: 151-157.

Teskey, R.O.; Gholz, H.L.; Cropper, W.P., Jr. 1994. Influence of climate and fertilization on net photosynthesis of mature slash pine. Tree Physiology. 14(11): 1215-1227.

Thomas, H.A.; Richmond, J.A.; Bradley, E.L. 1981. Bioassay of pine bark extracts as biting stimulants for the southern pine beetle. Research Note SE-RN-302. Asheville, NC: U.S. Department of Agriculture, Forest Service, Southeastern Forest Experiment Station. 5p.

Tiarks, A.E. 1983. Effect of site preparation and fertilization on slash pine growing on a good site. Gen. Tech. Rep. SE-GTR-24. Asheville, NC: U.S. Department of Agriculture, Forest Service, Southeastern Forest Experiment Station. 34-39.

Tiarks, A.E. 1990. Growth of slash pine planted in soil disturbed by wet-weather logging. Journal of Soil and Water Conservation. 45(3): 405-408.

Tiarks, A.E.; Baldwin, V.C., Jr. 1999. Validation of volume and taper equations for loblolly, shortleaf and slash pine. Gen. Tech. Rep. SRS-GTR-30. Asheville, NC: U.S. Department of Agriculture, Forest Service, Southern Research Station. 497-500.

Tiarks, A.E.; Haywood, J.D. 1981. Response of newly established slash pine to cultivation and fertilization. Res. Note SO-RN-302. New Orleans, LA: U.S. Department of Agriculture, Forest Service, Southern Forest Experiment Station. 4p.

Tiarks, A.E.; Haywood, J.D. 1996. Site preparation and fertilization effects on growth of slash pine for two rotations. Soil Science Society of America Journal. 60(6): 1654-1663.

Tiarks, A.E.; Shoulders, E. 1982. Effects of shallow water tables on height growth and phosphorus uptake by loblolly and slash pines. Res. Note. SO-RN-285. New Orleans, LA: U.S. Department of Agriculture, Forest Service, Southern Forest Experiment Station. 5p.

Tonini, H.; Finger, C.A.G.; Schneider, P.R.; Spathelf, P. 2001. Height growth of *Pinus elliottii* Engelm., in the region of Pirantini, Rio Grande do Sul State, Brazil. Ciencia Rural. 31(3): 417-422.

Tonini, H.; Finger, C.A.G.; Schneider, P.R.; Spathelf, P. 2002. Graphical comparison among site index curves for *Pinus elliottii* and *Pinus taeda*, built at South Brazil. Ciencia Florestal. 12(1): 143-152.

Trumble, W.P.; Messina, E.E. 1985. CCA-PEG pole preservative research. In: Proceedings of the American Wood-Preservers' Association Annual Meeting. 81: 203-212.

Tu, Y.H. 1999. A study on cultivation patterns of industrial raw material forest of slash pine (*Pinus elliottii*): 1. Definition on the appropriate management density of paper pulp forest. Journal of Fujian College of Forestry. 19(3): 242-245.

Tucker, J.W., Jr.; Hill, G.E.; Holler, N.R. 1998. Managing mid-rotation pine plantations to enhance Bachman's sparrow habitat. Wildlife Society Bulletin. 26(2): 342-348.

Turvey, N.D.; Attiwill, P.M.; Cameron, J.N.; Smethurst, P.J. 1983. Growth of planted pine trees in response to variation in the densities of naturally regenerated acacias. Forest Ecology and Management. 7(2): 103-117.

Valluri, J.V.; Castillon, J.; Newton, R.J.; Soltes, E.J. 1989. Water stress-induced changes in protein synthesis of slash pine hypocotyls. Journal of Plant Physiology. 135(3): 355-360.

Valluri, J.V.; Soltes, E.J. 1990. Callose formation during wound-inoculated reaction of *Pinus elliottii* to *Fusarium subglutinans*. Phytochemistry. 29(1): 71-72.

Valluri, J.V.; Soltes, E.J.; Newton, R.J.; Cobb, B.G. 1987. Induction of new host-coded proteins in *Pinus elliottii* seedlings in response to pathogen and water stress. In: Proceedings of the Southern Forest Tree Improvement Conference. 41: 152-158.

Valluri, J.V.; Treat, W.J.; Newton, R.J. [and others]. 1988. Protein synthesis in slash pine callus cultures exposed to water stress. Tree Physiology. 4(2): 181-186.

Van Buijtenen, J.P. 1981. Insecticides for seed orchards - a case study in applied research. Southern Journal of Applied Forestry. 5(1): 33-37.

Vanclay, J.K. 1982. Optimum sampling of sample trees for volume equations. Research Note, Department of Forestry, Queensland. 35: 15p.

Vanclay, J.K. 1982. Stem form and volume slash pine thinnings in south east Queensland. Technical Paper, Department of Forestry, Queensland. 34: 17p.

Vanclay, J.K.; Anderson, T.M. 1982. Initial spacing effects on thinned stem volumes of slash pine in south east Queensland. Research Note, Department of Forestry, Queensland. 34: 9p.

Vanclay, J.K.; Shepherd, P.J. 1983. Compendium of volume equations for plantation species used by the Queensland Department of Forestry. Technical Paper, Department of Forestry, Queensland. 36: 21p.

Van Der Sijde, H.A. 1984. Results of an establishment trial with *Pinus elliottii* on the Transvaal Highveld. South African Forestry Journal. 131: 44-47.

Van Deusen, P.C.; Snow, G.A. 1991. Paired-tree study suggests 20-year current slash pine blight. Canadian Journal of Forest Research. 21(7): 1145-1148.

Van Rees, K.C.J. 1994. Michaelis-Mentan kinetics: calculation and use in nutrient uptake models. New Zealand Journal of Forestry Science. 24(2): 226-233.

Van Rees, K.C.J.; Comerford, N.B. 1986. Vertical root distribution and strontium uptake of a slash pine stand on a Florida Spodosol. Soil Science Society of America Journal. 50(4): 1042-1046.

Van Rees, K.C.J.; Comerford, N.B. 1990. The role of woody roots of slash pine seedlings in water and potassium absorption. Canadian Journal of Forest Research. 20(8): 1183-1191.

Van Rees, K.C.J.; Comerford, N.B.; McFee, W.W. 1990. Modeling potassium uptake in slash pine seedlings from low-potassium-supplying soils. Soil Science Society of America Journal. 54(5): 1413-1421.

Van Wyk, G.; Van Der Sijde, H.A. 1983. The economic benefits of forest tree breeding. South African Forestry Journal. 126: 48-54.

Vellidis, G.; Lowrance, R.; Gay, P.; Wauchope, R.D. 2002. Herbicide transport in a restored riparian forest buffer system. Transactions of the ASAE. 45(1): 89-97.

Viljoen, A.; Wingfield, M.J.; Kemp, G.H.J.; Marasas, W.F.O. 1995. Susceptibility of pines in South Africa to the pitch canker fungus *Fusarium subglutinans* f.sp. *pini*. Plant Pathology. 44(5): 877-882.

Vlok, J.H.J.; De Ronde, C. 1989. The effect of low-intensity fires on forest floor vegetation in mature *Pinus elliottii* plantations in the Tsitsikamma. South African Journal of Botany. 55(1): 11-16.

Voth, R.D. 1987. Pine responses to glyphosate plus sulfometuron methyl treatments. In: Proceedings, Southern Weed Science Society. 40: 167-174.

Wade, D.D. 1983. Fire management in the slash pine ecosystem. In: The Managed Slash Pine Ecosystem. Proceedings of a symposium held at the University of Florida. June 9-11, 1981. 203-227.

Wade, D.D.; Wilhite, L.P. 1981. Low intensity burn prior to bedding and planting slash pine is of little value. Gen. Tech. Rep. SO-GTR-34. New Orleans, LA: U.S. Department of Agriculture, Forest Service, Southern Forest Experiment Station. 70-74.

Wagner, D.B.; Nance, W.L.; Neslon, C.D. [and others]. 1992. Taxonomic patterns and inheritance of chloroplast DNA variation in a survey of *Pinus echinata, Pinus elliottii, Pinus palustris*, and *Pinus taeda*. Canadian Journal of Forest Research. 22(5): 683-689.

Wagner, J.E.; Holmes, T.P. 1999. Estimating economic gains for landowners due to time-dependent changes in biotechnology. Forest Science. 45(2): 163-170.

Walkinshaw, C.H. 1987. Field and greenhouse fusiform rust symptoms predict mortality in progeny field tests. In: Proceedings of the Southern Forest Tree Improvement Conference. 41: 292-299.

Walkinshaw, C.H. 1999. Promising resistance to fusiform rust from southeastern slash pines. Res. Pap. SRS-RP-16. Asheville, NC: U.S. Department of Agriculture, Forest Service, Southern Research Station. 6p.

Walkinshaw, C.H.; Bey, C.F. 1981. Reaction of field-resistant slash pines to selected isolates of *Cronartium quercuum* f. sp. *fusiforme*. Phytopathology. 71(10): 1090-1092.

Walkinshaw, C.H.; Roland, T.A. 1990. Incidence and histology of stem-girdling galls caused by fusiform rust. Phytopathology. 80(3): 251-255.

Wan, X.C.; Shen, B.K. 1998. Studies on new control measures for pine dieback and their mechanisms. Journal of Nanjing Forestry University. 22(1): 13-16.

Wang, A.L.; Gao, Q.A.; Chen, Q.J. 1995. The physiological effects of brassinolide (BR) in *Pinus elliottii* seedlings. Journal of Nanjing Forestry University. 19(4): 1-6.

Wang, Q.M.; Wang, W.; Chen, Z.Y. [and others]. 1998. Selecting provenances and individuals for resistance to die-back and brown-spot needle blight diseases and growth in loblolly and slash pine in Nanjing, Jiangsu. Journal of Jiangsu Forestry Science and Technology. 25(4): 1-7.

Wang, Y.Y.; Shu, C.R.; Li, H.Y.; Guo, Z.H. 2000. A study of the techniques of the rapid quarantine detection for diseased wood caused by the pine wood nematode. Scientia Silvae Sinicae. 36(5): 59-62.

Wang, Z.X.; Liu, D.C.; Han, L.S. [and others]. 1983. Studies on the selection of high gum yielding trees and forest types and the oleoresin composition of *Pinus elliottii* Engelm. Chemistry and Industry of Forest Products. 3(3): 3-10.

Ware, K.D.; Bailey, R.L.; Feduccia, D.P. 1983. Growth and yield predictions for slash pine: what information is available? In: The Managed Slash Pine Ecosystem. Proceedings of a symposium held at the University of Florida. June 9-11, 1981. 327-348.

Ware, K.D.; Borders, B.E.; Bailey, R.L. 1988. Estimating growth and yield of thinned slash pine plantations on old fields. Gen. Tech. Rep. NC-GTR-120. St. Paul, MN: U.S. Department of Agriculture, Forest Service, North Central Research Station. 33-46.

Watson, W.F.; Stokes, B.J.; Savelle, I.W. 1986. Comparisons of two methods of harvesting biomass for energy. Forest Products Journal. 36(4): 63-68.

Webb, R.S. 1990. Cross-sectional life table analysis of fusiform rust incidence and severity among slash pine plantations in north Florida. Applied Agricultural Research. 5(4): 302-308.

Webb, R.S.; Anderson, R.L.; Portier, K.M. 1984. Comparative seedling resistance of *Pinus elliottii* var. *elliottii* and *P. elliottii* var. *densa* to *Cronartium quercuum* f.sp. *fusiforme*. Plant Disease. 68(2): 145-148.

Webb, R.S.; Hollis, C.A.; Swindel, B.F. 1982. Incidence of *Heterobasidion annosum* basidiocarps on two low-hazard Florida soils after clearfelling. Southern Journal of Applied Forestry. 6(1): 39-41.

Webb, R.S.; Patterson, H.D. 1984. Effect of stem location of fusiform rust symptoms on volume yields of loblolly and slash pine sawtimber. Phytopathology. 74(8): 980-983.

Webb, R.S.; Reich, R.M.; Arvanitis, L.G. [and others]. 1986. Spatial patterns of incidence of *Cronatrium quercuum* f. sp. *fusiforme* in young plantations of *Pinus elliottii* var. *elliottii*. Applied Agricultural Research. 1(1): 45-49.

Wei, C.J. 1998. A study on the influence of pine shoot dieback disease on growth of *Pinus elliottii* and *P. taeda*. Journal of Nanjing Forestry University. 22(4): 31-34.

Weise, D.R.; Johansen, R.W.; Wade, D.D. 1987. Effects of spring defoliation on first-year growth of young loblolly and slash pines. Res. Note. SE-RN-347. Asheville, NC: U.S. Department of Agriculture, Forest Service, Southeaster Forest Experiment Station. 4p.

Weise, D.R.; Wade, D.D.; Johansen, R.W. 1989. Survival and growth of young southern pine after simulated crown scorch. In: Proceedings of the 10th Conference on Fire and Forest. Pp. 161-168.

Weng, C.; Kubisiak, T.L.; Nelson, C.D.; Stine, M. 2002. Mapping quantitative trait loci controlling early growth in a (longleaf pine x slash pine) x slash pine BC $_1$ family. Theoretical and Applied Genetics. 104(5): 852-859.

Weng, Y.F.; Qian, X.B.; Ye, Z.J. 2001. Inquiry into nursery soil fertility. Journal of Zhejiang Foresty Science and Technology. 21(6): 14-19.

White, T.; Powell, G.; Rockwood, D.; Parker, S. 1996. Thirty-eighth progress report. Cooperative Forest Genetics Research Program. 40p.

White, T.L.; Hodge, G.R. 1987. Practical uses of breeding values in tree improvement programs and their prediction from progeny test data. In: Proceedings of the Southern Forest Tree Improvement Conference. 41: 276-283.

White, T.L.; Hodge, G.R. 1988. Best linear prediction of breeding values in a forest tree improvement program. Theoretical and Applied Genetics. 76(5): 719-727.

White, T.L.; Hodge, G.R. 1992. Test designs and optimum age for parental selection in advanced-generation progeny tests of slash pine. Silvae Genetica. 41(4): 293-302.

White, T.L.; Hodge, G.R.; Powell, G.L. 1993. An advanced-generation tree improvement plan for slash pine in the Southeastern United States. Silvae Genetica. 42(6): 359-371.

Whitmore, F.W. 1982. Lignin-protein complex in cell walls of (a callus culture of) *Pinus elliottii*: amino acids constituents. Phytochemistry. 21(3): 315-318.

Wienand, K.T.; Stock, W.D. 1995. Long-term phosphorus fertilization effects on the litter dynamics of an age sequence of *Pinus elliottii* plantations in the southern Cape of South Africa. Forest Ecology and Management. 75(1): 135-146.

Wilhite, L.P.; Jones, E.P., Jr. 1981. Bedding effects in maturing slash pine stands. Southern Journal of Applied Forestry. 5(1): 24-27.

Wilkinson, R.C.; Chappelka, A.H., III; Kraemer, M.E. [and others]. 1982. Field responses of redheaded pine sawfly males to a synthetic pheromone and virgin females in Florida. Journal of Chemical Ecology. 8(2): 471-475.

Wilkinson, R.C.; Chappelka, A.H., III; Kraemer, M.E. [and others]. 1987. Effects of height on responses of redheaded pine sawfly (hymenoptera: Diprionidae) males to synthetic pheromone and virgin females. Environmental Entomology. 16(5): 1152-1156.

Wilkinson, R.C.; Popp, M.P. 1989. Oviposition behavior of *Neodiprion merkeli* (Hymenoptera: Diprionidae) in two-needle and three-needle fascicles of slash pine. Environmental Entomology. 18(4): 678-682.

Wilkinson, R.C.; Popp, M.P. 1989. Reduced fecundity in *Neodiprion merkeli* (Hymenoptera: Diprionidae) associated with feeding on juvenile slash pine foliage. The Florida Entomologist. 72(4): 700-702.

Will, R.E.; Barron, G.A.; Burkes, E.C. [and others]. 2001. Relationship between intercepted radiation, net photosynthesis, respiration, and rate of stem volume growth of *Pinus taeda* and *Pinus elliottii* stands of different densities. Forest Ecology and Management. 154(1): 155-163.

Williams, K.L.; Mullin, K. 1987. Amphibians and reptiles of longleaf-slash pine stands in central Louisiana. Gen. Tech. Rep. SO-GTR-68. New Orleans, LA: U.S. Department of Agriculture, Forest Service, Southern Forest Experiment Station. 116-120.

Wiswell, T.J.; Bailey, R.L. 1986. Yield prediction for unthinned natural slash pine stands. Forest Science. 32(2): 347-348.

Wolfe, J.L.; Lohoefener, R. 1987. The small mammal fauna of a longleaf-slash pine forest in southern Mississippi. Gen. Tech. Rep. SO-GTR-68. New Orleans, LA: U.S. Department of Agriculture, Forest Service, Southern Forest Experiment Station. 171-177.

Wolters, G.L. 1982. Longleaf and slash pine decreases herbage production and alters herbage composition. Journal of Range Management. 35(6): 761-763.

Wood, J.C.; Blackburn, W.H.; Pearson, H.A. [and others]. 1987. Assessment of silvicultural and grazing treatment impacts of infiltration and runoff water quality of longleaf-slash pine forest, Kisatchie National Forest, Louisiana. Gen. Tech. Rep. SO-GTR-68. New Orleans, LA: U.S. Department of Agriculture, Forest Service, Southern Forest Experiment Station. 245-249.

Wood, J.M.; Tanner, G.W. 1985. Browse quality response to forest fertilization and soils in Florida. Journal of Range Management. 38(5): 432-435.

Wu, J.Y.; Long, Y.Z.; Hu, D.M. [and others]. 2000. An approach to inheritance and variation of the main economic characters and comprehensive selection of half-sib families of slash pine. Scientia Silvae Sinicae. 36(4): 106-109.

Wu, J.Y.; Long, Y.Z.; Hu, D.M. [and others]. 2000. Genetic analysis and combined selection of main economic characters of half-sib families for slash pine. Scientia Silvae Sinicae. 36(1): 56-61.

Xiang, B.Q.; Yu, G.X.; Tang, X.H. 1998. Raising *Pinus elliottii* seedlings in containers. Journal of Zhejiang Forestry Science and Technology. 18(2): 55-58.

Xu, Y.M.; Gao, F.B.; Cai, S.Y. [and others]. 1998. Silvicultural techniques for slash pine pulpwood plantation under short rotation. Journal of Zhejiang Forestry College. 15(2): 116-121.

Xu, Z.H.; Saffigna, P.G.; Farquhar, G.D. [and others]. 2000. Carbon isotope discrimination and oxygen isotope composition in clones of the F_1 hybrid between slash pine and Caribbean pine in relation to tree growth, water-use efficiency and foliar nutrient concentration. Tree Physiology. 20(18): 1209-1217.

Xu, Z.H.; Simpson, J.A.; Osborne, D.O. 1995. Mineral nutrition of slash pine in subtropical Australia. I. Stand response to fertilization. Fertilizer Research. 41(2): 93-100.

Xu, Z.H.; Simpson, J.A.; Osborne, D.O. 1995. Mineral nutrition of slash pine in subtropical Australia. II. Foliar nutrient response to fertilization. Fertilizer Research. 41(2): 101-107.

Xu, Z.H.; Simpson, J.A.; Osborne, D.O. 1995. Mineral nutrition of slash pine in subtropical Australia. III. Relationships between foliar P concentration and stand growth. Fertilizer Research. 41(2): 109-155.

Xydias, G.K.; Sage, R.D.; Hodges, J.D.; Moehring, D.M. 1983. Establishment, survival, and tending of slash pine. In: The Managed Slash Pine Ecosystem. Proceedings of a symposium held at the University of Florida. June 9-11, 1981. 165-182.

Yang, B.J.; Wang, L.F.; Zhao, W.X. [and others]. 2002. The latent infection of *Bursaphelenchus xylophilus* and a new transmission way of PWN by *Monochamus alternatus*. Forest Research, Beijing. 15(3): 251-255.

Yang, C.D.; Jiao, R.Z.; Sheng, W.T. [and others]. 1999. Change of soil properties under slash pine in Dagangshan, Jiangzi Province. Forest Research, Beijing. 12(4): 392-397.

Ye, J.R.; Han, Z.M.; Li, C.D.; Gao, S.Z. 1986. Resistance to brown spot disease (*Mycosphaerella deamessii*) of geographic seed sources of slash pine and loblolly pine (*Pinus elliottii, P. taeda*) and selection of resistant phenotypes of slash pine individual trees. Journal of Nanjing Institute of Forestry. 2: 27-36.

Ye, J.R.; Li, C.D. 1987. Study on seed transmission of brown soft fungus (*Scirrhia acicola*). Journal of Nanjing Forestry University. 4: 21-25.

Ye, J.R.; Li, C.D. 1996. State and advances in studies on the resistance of slash pine to brown spot needle blight in China. Forest Research. 9(2): 189-195.

Ye, J.R.; Qui, G.F. 1999. Studies on the biological specialization of the toxin producing by brown spot needle blight fungus. Journal of Nanjing Forestry University. 23(6): 1-4.

Yin, R.; Pienaar, L.V.; Aronow, M.E. 1998. The productivity and profitability of fiber farming. Journal of Forestry. 96(11): 13-18.

Yoshida, M.; Tsuzuki, K.; Satake, K. 1981. On the growing process of loblolly pine and slash pine planted in the Shikoku region, part 1. Height growth and preparation of the volume tables for standing trees. Bulletin, Forestry and Forest Products Research Institute, Japan. 313: 1-35.

Young, C. 1983. The open-rooted nursery and establishment system for pines. Mededeling, Fakulteit Bosbou, Universiteit Stellenbosch. 98(1): 233-245.

Young, C.J. 1981. Production of oleoresin from *Pinus elliottii* var. *elliottii* stands on Tibury Estate in the Melsletter District of Zimbabwe. South African Forestry Journal. 118: 86-89.

Yue, C.L.; Gao, Z.H.; Chen, S.W. 2002. Photosynthetic characteristics of *Pinus elliottii*, *Elaeocarpus sylvestris*, and *Myrica rubra* and their relationship with ecological factors. Journal of Zhejiang Forestry College. 19(3): 247-250.

Zaman, A.A.; Deery, J.S.; McNally, T.W.; Frickle, A.L. 1997. Effects of pulping variables on density of slash pine kraft black liquors. Tappi Journal. 80(9): 199-207.

Zarnoch, S.J.; Feduccia, D.P. 1984. Slash pine plantation site index curves for the west gulf. Southern Journal of Applied Forestry. 8(4): 223-225.

Zarnoch, S.J.; Feduccia, D.P.; Baldwin, V.C., Jr.; Dell, T.R. 1991. Growth and yield predictions for thinned and unthinned slash pine plantations on cutover sites in the west gulf region. Res. Pap. SO-RP-264. New Orleans, LA: U.S. Department of Agriculture, Forest Service, Southern Forest Experiment Station. 32p.

Zeng, Z.P.; Zhao, P.; Peng, S.L. [and others]. 1999. Physio-ecological characteristics of three species of pine. Chinese Journal of Applied Ecology. 10(3): 275-278.

Zhai, Y.C.; Li, X.Z. 1983. Early determination of drought resistance and waterlogging tolerance of *Pinus elliottii* families in seed orchards. Forest Science and Technology. 12: 1-4.

Zhang, J.F.; Wu, Z.L.; Wang, Y.J. [and others]. 1996. Occurrence and control of nematode disease in pine forest of Zhejiang. Journal of Zhejiang Foresty Science and Technology. 16(1): 63-69.

Zhang, S.Y.; Lai, Y.X.; Zhou, C.M. [and others]. 1998. Study on replenishing feeding of *Monochamus alternatus* adult. Journal of Zhejiang Forestry Science and Technology. 18(2): 44-48.

Zhen, Y.S.; Dong, J.W.; Chen, L.U. 1999. A study on establishment of optimized stand trees volume table of *Pinus elliottii*. Acta Agriculturae Universitatis Jiangxiensis. 21(4): 586-591.

Zheng, Y.G.; Xu, Y.B. 1996. Study on the main regions for introduction of slash pine based on climatic factors in China. Journal of South China Agricultural University. 17(1): 41-46.

Zhou, X.D.; Burgess, T.; DeBeer, Z.W.; Wingfield, B.D. 2002. Development of polymorphic microsatellite markers for the tree pathogen and sapstain agent, *Ophiostoma ips*. Molecular Ecology Notes. 2(3) 309-312.

Zhu, S.K. 1988. Control of witches' broom in slash pine and loblolly pine through borax application. Journal of Zhejiang Forestry Science and Technology. 8(2): 38-39.

Ziehm, R.W.; Pearson, H.A.; Thurow, T.L.; Baldwin, V.C. 1992. Pine growth response to management of the subterranean clover understory. Agroforestry Systems. 20(3): 267-274.

Zutter, B.R. 1999. Response of a midrotation slash pine stand to hexazinone. Gen. Tech. Rep. SRS-GTR-30. Asheville, NC: U.S. Department of Agriculture, Forest Service, Southern Research Station. 446-448.

Zwolinski, J.B.; Hensley, M.; Monnik, K.A. 1998. Site conditions and growth of pines at the north east cape forests. Southern African Forestry Journal. 183: 1-16.

Zwolinski, J.B.; South, D.B.; Droomer, E.A.P. 1998. Pine mortality after planting on post-agricultural lands in South Africa. Silva Fennica. 32(3): 271-280.

Index of Authors

www.ingramcontent.com/pod-product-compliance
Lightning Source LLC
Chambersburg PA
CBHW080252290526
45790CB00005B/1786